EARLY GENESIS

The Revealed Cosmology

Seventh Edition

_____

Mark M. Moore

Copyright 2023, First Ed. 2017

ISBN: 978-1-7332778-2-2

The Ridge Enterprise Group, PLLC

****

Table of Contents

Introduction

And beginning at Moses and all the prophets, he expounded unto them in all the scriptures the things concerning himself. – Luke 24:27

--»-→»-❈-«←-«--

Several people who love me suggested that I give the reader an introduction revealing some things which I propose to prove from the scriptures regarding early Genesis. I was hesitant to do so. I feared that if I started with these claims then many people would refuse to even give the book a chance. How many would dismiss it without consideration because it was so different from what they have heard that it could not possibly be true? I thought the same myself when I started this journey. I came here by degrees and if someone had told me the end of it from the start, I don't know that I could have believed it.

But those who love me said that I should not wait so long for the "reveals". Rather, that I should come right out and say from the start what I meant to prove from the scriptures, and then lay out the evidence to support it. They said that the goal should be known in advance, before one wades through the evidence. So, I put aside my own opinions on this matter, and start out with what some may regard as wild claims. I beg the reader not to judge them as such without at least considering the exposition which I have so labored to provide.

Firstly, even the church does not understand early Genesis correctly, and this is because they have adopted the traditional Jewish view of what it was saying. That view of the text does not point to Christ, and therefore is a misunderstanding of its true meaning. The apostles did not take a Jewish view of the text, but rather a Christian one. If one looks at the text from a Christian view, that it is all pointing to Christ, what made no sense before becomes clear. Astoundingly, early Genesis makes a lot more sense if one assumes that God knew from the beginning that He was going to have to become man in Christ and redeem us. Perhaps the only way to really make sense of it is that Christianity is not some afterthought cobbled onto the text, but the point of it all along.

For example, I am prepared to show from the scriptures that the seventh day of Genesis, the true Sabbath, was not a 24-hour day in the life of Adam. God did not even end His work on the seventh day until after Christ was put on the cross. The day of rest which began when Christ rested in the earth will continue to the end of this age. I will show from the scripture that this is what the writer of Hebrews believed, and what Moses saw coming.

Obviously, I am not one who holds to the view that the creation week was six literal 24-hour days. I once hoped to write this book in such a way as to be open to both sides of the issue, but eventually I understood that it would be doing a disservice to the scriptures. You can't understand what they are really saying by forcing a literal six-day meaning onto the text. Indeed, I will show that in Genesis chapter one the speaker is creation itself- the heavens and the earth are giving an account of themselves.

Both the Heavens and the earth are being fashioned by God. What is called High Heaven responded to God's word immediately and perfectly. Earth and the natural universe took eons of time and worked out His commands haltingly and with many missteps. A close look at the text shows that this is the idea being conveyed. How long it took to complete His commands depends upon where you are asking from!

Some of you may think that you know scriptures which contradict what I have written above, and what I write next. I once thought that I did too, but I was wrong about what I thought they meant. I speak to them all in the pages of this book. Rather than disproving what I write, when rightly understood most of those scriptures instead affirm my thesis.

The church has Adam wrong too. I am prepared to show that the Bible does not really teach that he was the first man on earth, as in the sole progenitor of humanity. Rather, he was a shadow of Christ- he was the first man in the sense that Christ is the last man. He was the first would-be representative of humanity – made to act on behalf of the Heavenly King. He was humanity's best effort by natural means to attain right-standing with a Holy God. He was formed to rescue a human race that had already long gone astray, though in innocence. He failed, as flesh must fail in holiness, but where the shadow failed the Type succeeded.

Adam was a real person who lived in a real place and time in history. Though he failed, the results of his life had real impact. Signs of this are detectable in human history, in human civilization, and even in the natural world. He was a living man. He was not the original man, but he was the original man who was meant to reconcile us to God- and that he did through the Seed of Eve. I intend to show that this view of early Genesis does not do harm to any essential orthodox Christian doctrine.

As the creeds tell us, Christ is both fully man and fully God. I intend to show that this fusion of God and man was not something which began in Judea around twenty centuries ago. It was not God the Father's back up plan that He had to come up with once things failed to go as He anticipated. Rather, it was reality in heaven before the foundation of the world was completed. The second person of the Godhead, the Logos, stepped down from equality with God before the end of the first chapter of Genesis, and this event is spoken to in Genesis and the rest of scripture.

Can you see now why I did not want to start with a "reveal"? It would have all sounded preposterous to me not so long ago. And who am I? In terms of the world, especially the world of religious institutions, I confess that I am nobody. Yet we know from scripture that God sometimes hides things from the prudent and intelligent and reveals them unto babes (Luke 10:21, Mat. 11:25). I also know that God is apt to choose the foolish and weak things of this world to confound the wise and the mighty (First Corinthians 1:27), and I do take comfort in that. That I am not a "big name" in the world of theology or endorsed by a religious institution is no obstacle at all for Him, nor is He limited in His ability to reveal truth outside of some special caste of persons, but rather all who seek the truth with a sincere heart may, by His grace, find it.

I can only hope that my view of this matter of waiting for the "reveals" is incorrect and the admonitions of those who love me are proven right. That is, that readers will go on to examine the evidence before dismissing the claims; that readers would prefer this to going through large amounts of evidence without knowing where it leads until much later.

Once you start reading these accounts from a Christ-centered view of things it really changes what you see in them. For example, once you understand who Adam is, and who "the LORD" part of "the LORD God" is, you understand that the second chapter of Genesis is not simply a repeat of chapter one from a different perspective, rather it is a separate but related story. One is like "the rise of the Roman empire" and the other is like "the life of Julius Caesar".

This changes the way you look at the subsequent chapters, including the flood account. A careful reading of the text shows that the flood is both local and global in extent. In terms of what will be immediately wiped out in a flood, it is a local flood with a limited set of creatures. In terms of what will be ruined, corrupted and condemned to eternal destruction, it is global in extent. The Old Testament is very Trinitarian when rightly understood.

The account of the Tower of Babel and the genealogies in the Table of Nations all look different in a Christ-centered view of early Genesis. And not just a different view, but different in a way which makes them far less contentious regarding evidence from the natural world. Not that this is paramount, but those who refuse to consider the truth of Scripture and the Lordship of Christ on the basis that Genesis chapter one is a myth about a 6,000-year-old earth will have to find another excuse.

What I find most astounding in all of this is that some of what I will describe in these pages was beyond our natural understanding at the time that it was written. The words have been considered an enigma for generations. But now that we have more knowledge, words which were once obscure become crystal clear for those who dare to look. Christ is the key to understanding words which were written thousands of years before the Incarnation. Until He came, the real meaning of early Genesis could not be unlocked.

"For if you believed Moses, you would believe Me; for he wrote about Me" - Jesus in the Gospel of John, 5:46

The Nature of Truth vs. The Desire of Man

The Bible is a Divine Book, full of grace and truth. But just because the Bible contains truth does not mean that the understanding of truth is commonplace. The understanding of truth in any culture is proportional to that culture's love for truth. Jesus said, and I am paraphrasing here, that He spoke to people in parables precisely so that the casual masses would *not* possess truth which they had no real desire to understand.

Truth is meant to be desired. It is not found promiscuously displaying itself for those who have no serious interest in knowing it. Rather, we are told by Him who is Truth Personified that it is the one who seeks the truth who shall find it. This world is meant to be a test of character, and one of those tests is whether or not we care to prioritize truth. We must decide whether we will pursue it over other things, and for its own sake, rather than as a means to some other end.

Even the Disciples tended to reach for the plainest answers about what Christ was trying to say rather than meditate on His words long enough to find the deeper answers He was really pointing towards. In Mathew 16, for example, they decided that His admonition to *"beware the leaven of the Pharisees"* was a statement about their own failure to bring bread along for the journey. How often it is that we miss what God is really trying to say because we grasp for easy answers and we try to make it about ourselves and our own performance! Let's not pretend that the church today is above the same habit.

The nature of man, of all but the noblest of men at least, is to grab for the closest and easiest answer available which will suit our purposes and then let us get about our own business. Proverbs 25:2 speaks to God's ways in the matter of the presentation of truth, and man's role in the discovery of such truth. It reads *"It is the glory of God to conceal a thing, but the honor of kings is to search out a matter."* Again, the pattern reveals itself. Truth does not offer itself lightly to those who have little interest in receiving it. For some any plausible tale will do. Those of royal disposition press on.

In other places in scripture Divine revelation is given, and the recipient is told to seal it up or in some other way hide the true meaning until the proper time to understand it comes about. This surely glorifies God for any who care to consider the matter. How can it be, except by Divine arrangement, that mysterious words given in a former age suddenly make perfect sense once we get to the place that there is a need to understand them? Perhaps we are just now coming to such a condition regarding the first chapters of Genesis. In the interlude, we can only grope about darkly.

What I am arguing against here is this idea floating around in some Christian circles that scripture is supposed to be taken strictly at face value. I don't agree that the truths of scripture are necessarily simple. Some things are simple. The gospel is simple, but not everything in the scriptures is simple. In Second Peter 3:16 the Apostle writes of the epistles of Paul. Of them he says, "in which are some things hard to be understood, which they that are unlearned and unstable wrest, as they do also the other scriptures, unto their own destruction..."

Do you see? Some things are difficult to understand. That is what Peter, writing under inspiration, says of the writings of Paul under inspiration. They contain things which are hard to understand. He further warns that ignorant people and crazy people twist those writings. They assign them false meanings. And they do this to their own destruction. Despite this clear warning, there is a very large segment of the church today which wants to insist that the truths of scripture are all on the surface.

An attempt to force the meaning of scripture into the simplest and plainest meaning of the words is one of the ways it can become "wrested" away from the deeper truths which hold its real meaning. Some things are hard to understand by design, and if someone attempts to impose an understanding of it which is simple, then they misunderstand. Indeed, the "plain reading" doctrine leaves us with no need for the Holy Spirit to illuminate our understanding.

In Hebrews chapter five, verses 11-14 the writer admonishes his readers that they are continuing in the milk of the word when they ought to be able to move on to the meat of the word. I think that is where a lot of the church still is today. They count superficiality in the contemplation of God's word as a virtue, and a search for deeper meaning within it as some kind of vice! Verse fourteen tells us that it is the ones who take on the meat of the word who have their senses sharpened so as to discern between good and evil.

Not that the Divine Book isn't filled with clear principles and plain lessons. It is. For example, Jesus explained some of His parables to His disciples privately, and we have the benefit of that in the pages of The Book. But it is also shrouded in mystery. Much of the mystery at the ends is resolved by the middle, that is, it points to Christ. The first part points forward to Him, and the last part points backward to Him. Still, this clarity in the middle is juxtaposed against its mystery on both ends. Both early Genesis and the latter part of Revelation are full of things difficult for us to grasp.

I don't mean to say that there are not churches and people offering answers on what these books on first and last things mean. Many have given their best interpretations, while others have embraced the mystery over passages which seem contradictory both with internal evidence from the Holy Writ itself and with evidence from the natural world.

There is a temptation in both cases. In the former case, the quest for certainty can come into conflict with God's chosen method of progressive revelation of truth. We understand that God's revelation to mankind has been progressive. There is a pattern in the scriptures of giving a revelation and then sealing up its true meaning until the time is right for it to become known.

Too great a desire for certainty can lead believers, like the disciples in the sixteenth chapter of Matthew, to seek early and easy answers even if they are not sensible answers. We become like Sarah and Abraham, so anxious for the manifestation of some good thing God has revealed that we take matters into our own hands and supply our own answers in His name. Without faith we cannot please God, and sometimes faith means knowing that He has the right answer, even if we don't understand it.

The right reason to want answers is love of Truth itself, love of God Himself. The wrong reason to want them is to feel superior to those who do not have them, or to quell some inner insecurity we might have about the Father. These are things which can tempt us to grasp for pat answers which are not His answers.

The other route, embracing the mystery of God's revelations, leads to its own set of temptations. Among these is that we might lose our passion to discover God's truth. We might become satisfied with our unknowingness. But God does not hide truth because He wants us to remain ignorant. He hides truth because we are not ready for it or because He does not want us to take it for granted. He wants us to value it, and to pursue it.

Just by making the choice to do so we have already become more of the person He desires us to be, even in the case where we do not find what we are seeking. Yes, there are things which God has left a mystery and there is a time for us to accept that, but there is also a time when His mysteries are revealed to man and that is something those who love Him should urgently desire.

For years I searched for a satisfactory understanding of the words of the first part of Genesis. For years I found all answers wanting. What sorts of apparent inconsistencies in the text were troubling me? Consider these discrepancies between the accounts in chapters one and two:

The title given the Creator/Maker is somewhat different. Genesis chapter one says that "God created man". Genesis chapter two specifies that "the LORD God" formed man. No mention of a garden is given in chapter one. Chapter two goes to great lengths to describe the garden. Whereas the account in chapter two emphasizes that man was agrarian, no mention of agriculture is made in the account of man in the first chapter, other than to say that plants were provided as food.

In chapter one God immediately directs mankind to be fruitful and multiply and fill the earth. This is a great contrast from the account which begins in chapter two. In that account God not only waits a while to create Eve, but there is no mention of reproduction, or even of children, until after the forbidden fruit is eaten. In the chapter two account God seemed to have a lot of business with Adam and Eve before they get around to reproducing. In chapter one, "be fruitful and multiply" is the first command God gives newly created mankind- and thereafter there is very little information about any personal interaction with God.

When God busts Cain for murdering Abel, Cain immediately objects by telling God that "whoever finds me will kill me." Not, "his family" would kill him, but "whoever." He was already around his family. His objection was being forced to leave them. He was worried about what would happen after he was driven off from where the LORD, and his family, were. He talked as if the world was already full of people who would not hesitate to waylay a lone outcast from his family group. Cain spoke as if he knew that he was not the first murderer on earth. Furthermore, God takes his complaint seriously. He puts a mark on Cain that somehow offered protection from these mysterious others.

That does not even mention the famous question of where Cain got his wife. The standard answer has been that "Cain married one of his sisters". I can't help but notice though, that Cain is run off to the "land of Nod" and finds a wife apparently even before the birth of Seth (Genesis 4:25). Seth is said to be "a seed in place of Abel" so it is not likely Eve had any children, surely not any males, between the death of Abel and the birth of Seth. And not only does he find a wife, Cain winds up founding a city (Genesis 4:17), which he names after his own son. A city? Where are all these people coming from?

Not only are there people, but these people catch on fast. There was no hunter-gatherer phase for this bunch. Abel was a pastoral farmer. Cain was an agriculturalist. In verses 20-22 of chapter four we learn that the sons of Lamech, a near descendant of Cain, learn to herd cattle and live in tents, learn to play organs and harps, and even become skilled in metallurgy.

Lamech himself said (Genesis 4:23) that he took the life of "a young man". If everyone is related just five generations back it seems quite odd that he would refer to the deceased as simply "a young man". Why not instead describe him by his relationship to Lamech? If you killed your cousin, would you describe it as killing "a man" without any reference to how you are related?

These are the sorts of questions for which I had never gotten satisfactory answers. On the one side I found those who consider themselves the "literalists" pressing answers that seemed to torture the text and failed to account for not only our discoveries about the natural world, but also our knowledge of the languages in which the scriptures were originally penned. Those who work in languages know that sometimes translations can give a misleading idea of what the text is getting at. Just because something does not make sense in the English translation does not mean that the underlying material does not make sense.

On the other side I found that some had given up trying to make sense of the text, instead relegating it to the category of myth or parable. That can't be right. Though there is little doubt early Genesis contains allegory- the serpent is revealed by Jesus and in Revelation to be the Devil for example- reducing the account to just an allegory has serious theological implications for the rest of the text of the Scriptures.

There is something to the claims of "literalists" that undermining the historicity of Genesis undermines some fundamental Christian doctrines. If the beginning of the book is not historically true, then why trust the rest of it? This has led to a category of believer so focused on certain ideas about when and how the events described in Genesis happened that they miss out on the most important point of the accounts- that is not "when" or "how" but rather "what". What is God trying to say in those accounts? If we get the "what" right, then I believe you will find that getting the "when" and "how" right follows naturally.

After many years of listening, I just decided to just put the question away for a while. After all, I did not need a sensible reconciliation of the text in order to bolster my faith. God has blessed me with faith which has only gotten stronger as I see His hand in my life, and as my understanding of His Word deepened. Someday an explanation would come that made sense of it all. Someday it would come, either in this world or in the next. Of that I was confident.

Such a mode of thinking stayed with me over the course of many years, even as I continued to study the account of "first things". Then one day recently, at what I suppose is the proper time, I looked upon the familiar words and found meaning as if I were reading them for the very first time. I initially thought that what I seeing must be wrong. So, I searched all the scriptures for versus to refute these ideas. But careful study only confirmed the truth of what I'd been shown. This understanding slipped into place with such an elegant precision that at times it shocked me. And this new understanding points to Christ much more than any other view of these passages that I have found.

When I looked at the scriptures in early Genesis from that point on, something was different. I had what I would describe as a "phase change" in how I saw the scriptures. One moment it wasn't there, and the next it had been sitting in front of me the whole time. One moment I saw Genesis one and two as telling the same story from different perspectives and the next they were telling two connected but different stories.

The closest thing I can find to what happened to me is in Luke 24:45. There a resurrected Jesus "opened their understanding, that they might understand the scriptures." They did not get any new words, but they were able to understand the words which were already given. I didn't get it like they got it- but just a taste of it concerning the subject of this work. Even that is too wonderful for me. For decades I struggled with matters too great for me, and it was only after a Divine nudge that was I able to prevail.

In the verses in Luke just before that event, Christ explained to them how all the previous scriptures given were really pointing to Him. That is what I found too. Early Genesis cannot be correctly understood outside the context of pointing to Christ. The Church erred when we adopted the traditional Jewish version of things pretty much without changes. Their Divine mission was to carry and preserve the Word of God, but He has left it to the grafted-in branches to complete the understanding of what they preserved. It is fitting that each needed the other.

As a bonus, in the Christ-centered view of early Genesis evidence from the natural universe, far from undermining the veracity of scripture, is well-harmonized with it. Though it can be and usually has been done poorly, there is something to Concordism when and where it applies. The testimony of scripture and the testimony of the natural universe, when both are rightly understood, agree. This is to be expected from two works which have the same Author.

First, *What* is Early Genesis?

There are three schools of thought regarding the way in which the book of Genesis came to be. There is the fundamentalist or traditional school, which says that Genesis was directly revealed to Moses and that Moses is the divinely inspired author of Genesis, along with the rest of the Pentateuch. In this view, early Genesis was essentially dictation from God to Moses. Only a very few notes were added in later by others to clarify times, names, or locations.

An example of such a scribal clarification would be the aside in chapter thirty-six which says that certain kings were in Edom before Israel had any king. This time-clarifying note appears to be from a period in which Israel did have a king and therefore would have been added after the time of Moses. This position also allows for the possibility that place names might have been updated to reflect their current usage.

For example, if there were a "scribe" in the modern day who was making a "copy" of some work, they might substitute the word "Iran" in places where the original document said "Persia" since that is the modern name for that nation. Place names change a lot over time. We will see as we go on to some passages with place names just how much confusion this can bring.

Other than those insignificant changes, the traditional view is that Moses was the author of Genesis. In short, this school of thought says that Moses received Genesis by direct divine revelation which has been preserved for us with its original meaning intact.

Opposed to this view is the "Documentary Hypothesis" of the deconstructionist school. It is highly secular in outlook and points to differences in vocabulary and writing style in the various chapters of Genesis to make the case that the book was written much later in history than the time of Moses by several writers unknown. This school of thought basically discounts claims of Mosaic authorship, arguing instead that it was an amalgamation of sources- none older than the time of Solomon. It also posits that Genesis was subject to serious redaction over the centuries, particularly after the exile. This hypothesis was first popularized by those from the German schools of "Higher Criticism".

The differences in the text they point out are present, but nothing else about the theory fits the way the Jews looked at the text. They believed it was history and executed people for breaking its commands! They copied it precisely, with an unmatched reverence. None of that fits with some priests merrily redacting it for centuries. Nor does it square with the associated idea that early Genesis was merely conjured up as a "polemic" against the Egyptian or Babylonian origin stories. The idea that the Babylonian accounts must have come first is incorrect. It is based on an erroneous idea as to what early Genesis is. It is a misconception that I hope to clear up in this chapter.

I view each of these schools of thought as an expression of one of the two mentalities which I described at the start of this work. It is the quest for certainty over truth, certainty in their favored position, which leads people into error. We ignore the evidence which raises questions about our view and over-sell that which supports it.

I am guilty too. It is human nature. All the while what God is looking for is an honest heart. That is to say, a heart of faith willing to accept answers or willing to accept that we do not need to know all the answers. Each side in this case, as in so many, reaches for the quick conclusion that most confirms their existing prejudices regarding the nature of the text.

There is a third school of thought, much smaller and less well-known than the other two. Part of its obscurity, I suspect, is due to its advocates' narrow use of the principles behind it. This can include forcing the narrowest form of the approach on sections of the text where it does not apply. I think this third theory is true, but only where and how it applies.

I also suspect part of its obscurity is because it serves neither those who grab onto the simplest possible answers in matters of faith, nor those radical naturalists who dismiss any possibility of the supernatural, mysticism, or wonder from the pages of scripture. Neither extreme wins outright in this third school, though this view of the evidence is so marvelous as to lead all but the most cynical of hearts to see a Divine Hand at work. This middle path is known as the Wiseman-Harrison Hypothesis on Genesis, or sometimes just the "Wiseman Hypothesis". It is also called "The Tablet Theory".

I count this view as the one which rings most true. Though it is the least known of the three, I find that it, with some caveats and updates, fits best with both scholarly evidence and the testimony of the human heart which is designed to long for God.

P.J. Wiseman was a military attaché in Mesopotamia who supported many archeological digs. Wiseman noticed that many of the tablets recovered had phraseology much like some curious words in Genesis. The artifacts they discovered, in terms of both time and place, were rather close to that ascribed to the patriarch Abraham. We might expect literary devices used in his day to be found in the discoveries which Wiseman was encountering. Indeed, subsequent discoveries showed that the same literary practices were in use for over two thousand years.

Wiseman's son Donald became an accomplished archeologist at Oxford. He was so convinced that his father had hit upon something that he re-published his father's work with basically no changes. Now one might at first count this as simply bias due to family ties, but he in fact waited to publish until someone else supported the idea. His re-publishing of his father's work came more than a decade after another scholar, Dr. R.K. Harrison, gave new credence to the hypothesis (*Introduction to the Old Testament*, Eerdmans 1969). It also popped up here and there in other publications, an article called *The Generations of Genesis* by Dale S. Dewitt (*The Evangelical Quarterly, Vol. XLVIII, No. 4, Oct.-Dec., 1976*) being an example.

What did Wiseman find? The medium for writing in those days was clay tablets or cylinders. In many cases the writing on them would end with what amounted to what we would call a "colophon". Today the colophon is that early page in the book which gives information about the title, the identification number, who owns or publishes a written work, and normally with some time reference. Up until recent times though, the colophon was typically printed at the end of a book.

Wiseman noticed in the book of Genesis that up until chapter thirty-seven the phrase "these are the generations of X" cropped up repeatedly. The same phrase kept appearing in the tablets that the archaeologists around him were unearthing in Mesopotamia, birthplace of the patriarch Abraham.

Because that phrase often, but not always, appears right before a genealogical table in scripture most modern readers conclude that the word translated "generations" means a list of descendants. But Wiseman found that was not always what similar words meant in the tablets his associates unearthed. Wiseman found the phrase in the tablets his associates were discovering was used to mean "this is the account of" X or Y, where X or Y stood for the name of the owner and/or writer of that account.

It was not necessarily connected to a genealogical table. It (the word here was *towledah* or *toledoth*) served as the anchor for what we would today consider a colophon. If the toledoth phrase said "these are the generations of Isaac" it meant that it was the story of Isaac. The person who "owned" the account usually told the story of his immediate ancestors. In Isaac's case for example, that would be Abraham.

In early Genesis it looks like each generation was responsible for recording the story of the previous one. The life story of the father was usually told by a son or sons, so that subsequent generations called it by their name. The story of the previous generations was told (owned) by some member of the current one. The word toledoth does have a literal meaning more akin to giving birth, but as an author I can tell you that the metaphor fits. If you write a book you feel like "it's your baby".

The phrase identified whose work it was, either by ownership, authorship, or both. Often it would list the immediate descendants of the owner as an aide to identification, and to keep things in order when tracking family histories or property through time. It might also have a tag line, or it might repeat the first few words of the document in the towledah, much like we would use a title.

Wiseman found that the phrase was used at the end of the tablets, not the beginning. Later it was discovered, especially if the tablet was intended to be stored on shelves, that the toledoth would be found on the edge of the tablet so that a person looking through the shelves could easily find the right tablet. An example might be "this is the account of Omar, Omar had two sons, Ahu and Shedbab." Then it might have a few words describing the tablet or repeat a few words from the start of the tablet. Again, this would be at the end of the tablet, or on the edge of it.

This idea differed from the predominant understanding of Genesis that the phrase "these are the generations of" referred only to the material following the phrase. Wiseman said that they should instead be viewed as referring to the material *preceding* them. Sometimes the story of one patriarch would be written by that person himself, and at other times by one who came soon after him. Like you telling your dad's story.

Wiseman concluded that the phrase meant the same thing in Genesis as it did on the tablets he was finding. The phrase occurs eleven times in Genesis, or perhaps twelve depending on how narrowly you evaluate format. This implies that the writer of Genesis had in their possession clay tablets which they then compiled into the first thirty-six chapters of the book of Genesis.

According to tradition, Moses wrote the first Torah on leather, and they are still written on leather to this day. In Second Timothy chapter four the Apostle Paul asks Timothy to bring some written materials with him. In this request he says, "especially the parchments". A parchment as used here was writing on the hide of an animal, showing that this medium continued to be used and valued in New Testament times.

Though far more durable than our paper, leather does not last nearly so long as the clay tablets from which we might suppose the author/editor of Genesis drew his material. Still, clay tablets can only be so large before they become difficult to hold or transport, and the weight of large tablets makes them more breakable. The contents of many, many clay tablets could be fit onto one leather scroll. A scroll was a superior medium for recording large amounts of information and there is every indication that Moses was familiar with that superior medium.

Even though Moses was familiar with paper and leather scrolls, the concept of divine information being communicated in the form of tablets is well established in the Torah. Notice that in Exodus chapter twenty-four Moses receives God's law in the form of stone tablets. These tablets were inscribed by God Himself. Moses broke the original tablets in careless anger when he came down from Mount Sinai and observed Israel worshipping the golden calf. God commanded Moses to cut out slabs of stone like those he had broken, and God once again wrote His law on those tablets. Later they were put into the Ark of the Covenant.

Now I want to emphasize that Moses was raised as an Egyptian Prince, and the people of Israel had been in Egypt for hundreds of years. Papyrus was the medium of choice for writing in the society which they had just left. Indeed, using leather to form a scroll, which by tradition was how Moses wrote the first Torah, was far more like the Egyptian way of recording things as compared to the tablets of their Mesopotamian ancestors.

Yet despite all that, the commandments came in tablet form. And the tablet medium was not merely chosen because it was what was handy at the time God first delivered them. When they were broken God specifically commanded Moses (Exodus 34) to go back and prepare two more blank tablets (translated "tables" in some versions).

Why the insistence on going back to tablets in a culture which had advanced and was now used to writing on flexible and compact mediums like papyrus or leather? One explanation would be that Moses and the Israelites had the prior expectation that sacred writings would be received in tablet form. The commandments were to be considered the most sacred of writings- not just written by someone with a special relationship with the Almighty, but rather by His own hand.

This does add some weight to the idea that Moses had in his possession ancient tablets inherited from the Israelite's ancestors, and that these tablets were treasured as sacred records. It is recorded in Exodus 13:19 that when Moses left Egypt, he took with him the bones of Joseph who had died hundreds of years beforehand. This shows that Moses had possession of what might be termed heirlooms of his people.

Not only that, the reason given for taking the bones for re-interment in the Promised Land was the knowledge that Joseph had commanded that this be done some hundreds of years before, as recorded in the final two verses of Genesis. Therefore, I conclude that Moses not only had the bones, but he had the written accounts which told him what to do with the bones!

Earlier in the fiftieth chapter of Genesis the burial of the patriarch Jacob is recorded. Jacob is buried in a field bought by his grandfather, Abraham, and the account even lists from whom the purchase was made. This was even though the clan of Jacob had vanished from the land of Canaan for years before they decided to come back and bury him in a plot of land purchased by his grandfather Abraham.

Apparently, there was a sophisticated record of land ownership in Canaan so that even an absentee landowner could come back and be buried in a cemetery purchased by their ancestors. The evidence suggests that when the Israelites returned to the Promised Land, they possessed written records which they had retained for generations.

The traditional view that Moses received the whole of the Torah by dictation is contradicted by the Torah itself. Scripture explicitly states that at least part of the text was received by Moses from God personally writing on tablets. I suggest that this was not the only portion of Torah which was received in the form of tablets. Rather it may be that much of Genesis was transmitted in tablet form through the less dramatic but still awe-inspiring procedure of inheritance of records that even in that day were of great antiquity.

Moses was therefore familiar with sacred records in that form. In such a case the tablets directly inscribed by God represented the most miraculous example of a class of tablet records from which much of the earliest sections of the book of Genesis was compiled. I mostly agree with Wiseman and Harrison that the first thirty-six chapters of Genesis appear to have been sourced from tablets handed down through the generations.

Where I disagree, and I think this has also hampered acceptance of their theory, is that they appear to have assumed that all the tablets used to create most of the book of Genesis had the very same format. The tablets discovered in Wiseman's day typically had writing on one side only. The toledoth phrase was written at the end of the tablet or the edge of it. Therefore, when Wiseman saw a "these are the generations of" in Genesis he assumed that it was, in every case, only referring to what was written before the toledoth. Sometimes his way of looking at it made sense, but other times it did not.

We now have the benefit of decades of new discoveries since Wiseman's day. Now we know that the tablets do not have to be one-sided. We have even found a couple where one side has a genealogy on it, with the toledoth phrase at the bottom or on the edge, and the other side has a narrative-type story of some individual in the genealogy. If some of the Genesis tablets had a format like this, it would make a lot more sense of the text.

When one considers that these would be tablets from accounts separated in some cases by many centuries it just makes sense that not all the tablets would follow the exact same format. There was a general style that was used, but we should not expect the format for all of them to be rigidly uniform.

Once you allow for the idea that the toledoth phrase could be in the middle or edge of tablets which had a narrative account on the front and a genealogy on the back, most of the critiques of the Tablet Theory melt away- and I will deal with the rest in the next chapter. The material in Genesis both before and after the phrase could be, in some cases, from the same tablet. Basically, if we look for some of the same types of literary devices found in past, and even present, we can better understand the material.

But perhaps you are still unconvinced by these data points supporting a modified version of the tablet theory. That is fine, because there are more. And they are to be found in, among other places, addressing the mystery of "gopher wood" and the mystery of the unusual number pattern in the genealogy in chapter five. I will in due course connect each of these to this issue, but for now I ask you to entertain this idea even if you are not yet convinced.

Now here is a part of the wonder I spoke of earlier. According to early Genesis, the owners of the tablets are some of the most familiar ancient names in the Bible. The words of early Genesis are their own accounts. They include Jacob, Esau, Isaac, Terah, Shem, Ham, Japheth, and even Noah. There is even included in Genesis "the account of Adam".

Please put aside for the moment any doubts or questions you might have about how old an account from Adam himself would have to be. The answer to that question (the age of the account) is tied into the question of who Adam really is in scripture. I will go into the depth of time aspect in more detail later, but only after the question of his role in scripture is thoroughly addressed. For now, just share with me the awe that men should feel at the thought that when we read passages of scripture from early Genesis, we are reading the words of the early patriarchs in Genesis.

In the same vein, some of you may have doubts that an account from Adam could be preserved for so long. Written language capable of relating a complex narrative (as opposed to something more straightforward such as a genealogy) doesn't seem to show up in the historical record until around 3200 B.C. I ask you to also put these misgivings on the shelf for now. While I recognize the difficulty of long periods of oral transmission, once the order of world as laid out in early Genesis becomes clear, it will be seen that there is a very logical explanation for how the accounts could be preserved with precise accuracy until the time we know writing was in use.

The tablet theory answers the accusations that Genesis was based on earlier Ancient Near East (ANE) stories. Even if Genesis itself was written later than some of these stories, it was compiled from tablets written earlier! If someone today wrote an anthology of tales from ancient Greece, we wouldn't claim that the Greek tales were no older than the anthology. At any rate there would be no necessity to "borrow" or adapt accounts from the Sumerians or Babylonians because the ancestors of the children of Israel came from that same region. It was family history to them, and they had independent accounts of those same events.

We live in a post-truth age of skepticism. Most of the unbelieving world has long ago dismissed even the possibility that the accounts of early Genesis are anything but myth. The mostly secular scholars of the church have claimed that they are worse than myth. They propose that Genesis is the secret work of unknown priests late in Israel's history. These priests would have ascribed it to Moses so that the people would consider it sacred. Bluntly put, these scholars assert that the accounts are forgeries.

Even the moderate mass of the church has largely reconciled to the idea that these are only allegorical stories for some spiritual truth. That they are meant to teach us some nice lessons but in no way are they an account of things which actually happened. Then there are the fundamentalists. I do consider myself a fundamentalist in the sense that I believe the Bible is the inspired word of God. I believe that it is historically true and not a collection of myths. What I do not believe is that my own understanding of it is necessarily true and certainly not complete.

I fear what most fundamentalists of today have been tricked into defending is not the idea that the scripture is God-breathed and true, but that the understanding of it promulgated by certain Bible teachers is true. It is a matter of what one's mind is open about. My mind is not open on the question of whether scripture is God-breathed. That is for me a settled question. My mind is always open to the possibility that I have misunderstood it in some way.

To believe otherwise subtly shifts the object of our faith from God's word to our own wisdom, or that of the man whose doctrine we enshrine. To believe that the teachings of some pastor or scholar are so complete and correct that no other view of scripture need ever be contemplated is to place them on a pedestal of infallibility which rightfully belongs only to God and His Word.

I fear that this work will not be welcome among many of those whom I have described, even if it is intended to increase their faith. The unbelieving may resent that there is an understanding of Genesis which fits so well with the rest of reality. They thought that they had God dead and buried, but these pages testify that what was in the grave was just a straw man with His name on it. The truth of His Word lives on with Him.

The learned but faithless scholars will be loath to think that what they imagined were their neat theories on how Genesis was concocted in fraud are not nearly so neat, nor so plausible, as they seemed. What they claim as the truth about Genesis can be found to fail on every level, including a failure to inspire the heart of man with wonder, as truth about life's larger questions should and so often does.

The post-modern Christian who has made peace in themselves with relegating the words of Genesis to curious metaphors for some vague spiritual principles might also view this work with distaste. Perhaps some will be annoyed at having to reconsider the question of whether Genesis might be true, in every sense of the word. They might be tempted to think "How embarrassing it will be if the sophisticates at the Club lump us together with those crass fundamentalists from whom we have worked so hard to distance ourselves!"

Some of those fundamentalists might fight it hardest of all. Not from certainty that their ideas are right, but from fear they might not be. If one's faith is in a doctrine alone, and not the truth of the holy text which the doctrine purports to describe, then questioning the doctrine is questioning the faith- even if the answers to those questions do not conflict with any essential orthodox doctrine and support the authenticity of the text in a most spectacular fashion.

Part of early Genesis is an account of things from Shem, and another is an account of things from Noah. And yes, some of it is an account of things even from Adam. The tablet theory suggests that these characters were not myths, but men. They were actual historical figures who once walked the earth. But more than that, it postulates that we still have their words. Their words, and not the words of any of their contemporaries anywhere in the world, but only their words, are preserved for us from their own day to the present time. They are preserved in the pages of the Holy Bible which sit upon your bookshelf!

Matching Toledoths with Passages

⤙⤚⟫◉⟪⤚⤙

L et us go through the places in Genesis where these toledoth phrases are used and see if the text makes more sense when looked at as a series of accounts formed around these phrases. Bear in mind that the breaks I am proposing are just that, proposals. I leave it to others more scholarly than I to find better reasons for changing this one or that. My goal here is to give the reader a grasp of how early Genesis can be divided by these toledoths in a sensible manner. I will refer to them as colophons because that is close to the modern equivalent of what they are function-ally. I start at the beginning even though it is perhaps the most enigmatic. Because it is, I will take more space explaining it as compared to the others.

The **first colophon** begins in Genesis 2:4. We might expect the first and earliest account to be the one least likely to conform to the systems devel-oped later. And that is how it seems to be. It says, "these are the genera-tions of the heavens and the earth......" and according to the tablet theory it is the start of the colophon for every verse before it from Genesis 1:1 until then. It is not the history or account of a person, but of creation itself.

Adherents of the Documentary Hypothesis have objected to connecting this colophon together with the prior account. They argue that verse 2:4 is from a different writer than the previous verses and should be grouped with the passages which follow rather than those before it, or at the least claim that it was penned much later and inserted into the account. In sup-port of this view, they point to the fact that 2:4 refers to the Supreme Deity

~ 21 ~

as "The LORD God", instead of God. That is, it specifies "*Yahweh Elohim*", while the first chapter just says "*Elohim*".

While I agree that verses four through six of chapter two were written from a different perspective than the preceding verses, that does not mean they shouldn't be grouped together. These verses function as the colophon for the preceding account. There is no reason why the publisher of a book who writes the description of that book for his catalogues has to use the exact same terminology as the author of the book might use within it.

A reporter who listens to the story of a witness can faithfully record the testimony of the witness and later use different language in summarizing the testimony. This is especially true if either the witness or the reporter knows the person whose actions are being discussed in a different degree or way than the other.

If the account were in a form like an investigative report, then it also makes sense that the name for God would be different in the summary than it is in the account. If someone interviewed you about the work of the carpenter who built your house, you might use the phrase "the carpenter" to describe that person.

The person compiling the report may take down your quotes as you said them, but if they knew the carpenter personally then they might well identify the carpenter by name in their summary. Thus, the account would use the less specific label "the carpenter", but the summary of the account would have the proper name "Master Carpenter John Franks". The difference in labels does not at all demand that the accounts are unconnected.

By the end of this book, we will delve a lot more as to why *Elohim* is used in some places, and *Yahweh-Elohim* in others, while it is just *Yahweh* in yet other places. I trust that by the end of this volume, once the full picture is laid out, that the fair-minded reader will have no bother at all about the disparity in names.

I am not always a fan, but I was pleased to see that my wife's Scofield Reference Bible had a commentary note which lumped verses 2:4-6 together as "Summary of the creative work of Chapter 1". It seems on that at least Cyrus Scofield and I agree. Verses 2:5-6 served a function a bit like what we see today on the inside jacket cover of a hard-cover book.

These verses are not trying, as some allege, to make a statement that there was no such thing as rain until Noah's flood. Rather, they are recapping the conditions of the early earth before God's completed interventions brought order and illumination to the creation. The recap adds just a bit of editorial detail about surface conditions on the early earth and bridges to the creation of Adam the agricultural man. Genesis 2:5-6 is describing the early earth as it was in Genesis chapter one before God's interventions were complete. More detail on that will be forthcoming later.

Some versions of the Bible, like the ESV, lump these verses together on the page in a manner which makes it more visually difficult to see this break. Others, like the Scofield, make it plain that verses 4-6 are associated with the prior verses- as the Tablet Theory prescribes. Verse five sounds like it is speaking of a time before plants were present, but in verse eight it says that the LORD-God planted a garden, implying plants were already in existence. It just seems like a lot happened between verse six and verse seven, which would be the case if verses five and six were a summation of conditions at the start of the prior account rather than solely referring to the second account.

Though I lean to the Scofield presentation on this particular issue, I also think it likely that the work defined in the first two colophons go together as literature in what verse 5:1 calls the "book of Adam." That is, they run together in the text because what they are supposed to represent is an Account of the Heavens and the Earth, as relayed by Adam, with verses 2:5-6 being his editorial summation. The account which follows is Adam's story as told by Adam to his near descendants, with the second colophon written by him or his immediate descendants who recorded his story. As literature, that is what the text is representing.

The **second colophon** is that of **Adam** and is found in Genesis 5:1-2. Here the purpose of the colophon is in part to show where it fits into the creation account. Verse 5:2 is very much like, but not identical to, verse 1:27.

This shows where in the first account (the account of heaven and earth) that the account of Adam begins. The account of Adam begins on the sixth creation "day" of the account of the heavens and the earth. It is where Adam comes into the story. This is all the more reason to see the two as a "set" with Adam being the editor/publisher of the first account and the owner/subject of the second account.

Therefore, the material from Genesis 2:7 to Genesis 5:2 is the account of Adam, and it and the first account (1:1 to 2:6) appear to be connected to form the "book" of Adam mentioned in 5:1. The word "book" in that verse is the word *sepher* which is word number 5612 in Strong's online concordance. It is not used in association with the other colophons, which is more textual evidence that the first two accounts belong together. The account (generations) of the Heavens and the Earth and the account (generations) of Adam go together to form the "book" of Adam. This word *sepher* was used to indicate multiple accounts which were connected.

A new account begins in Genesis 5:3 and ends at the next colophon in Genesis 6:9-11. This **third colophon** is the account of **Noah**. Noah started his account by tracing the line of his family all the way from Adam to his own sons in a way which very naturally fit and followed the material in the "book" of Adam.

I find it probable that the "book of Adam" had the early part of this lineage as an addendum, which Noah completed up to his generation. Either he or his sons added a narrative to the genealogy as if to fold the Account of Noah into "the book of Adam" with the other accounts. The first part of his account was his genealogy showing how he was a descendant of Adam. The next part of his account is a narrative which describes (unfavorably) conditions in the world when he was alive.

Please notice verses eleven and twelve of chapter six and how they are practically a repetition of one another. This is an indication that this place was a bridge between two tablets. That is, the last sentence in Noah's tablet was paraphrased with the first sentence in the next tablet. That way people reading the accounts one tablet after the other could check to make sure that they had the right tablet in the series. R.K. Harrison reported

(*Introduction to the Old Testament*, Eerdmans 1969) that this technique was also found on tablets in Mesopotamia. So then, verse eleven is where the tablet of Noah ended. Verse twelve is where the account owned by his sons begins. They fit together so well it is possible that Noah wrote the genealogy, but his sons wrote the narrative part of their father's life, in addition to the account named for them.

Genesis 5:3 through 6:11 is therefore the account of Noah, but it is written in a form so that it could be an addition to the "book of Adam".

The **fourth colophon**, found in Genesis 10:1, is the account of **Shem, Ham, and Japheth**. The account begins in Genesis 6:12 and tells the story of their father and the ark- a story in which they played major roles. Wiseman would likely say that this colophon marks the end of the tablet of Shem, Ham, and Japheth. This is where I have to part ways with that great man. The colophon in 10:1 is not just describing the preceding material but is connected to both preceding and following material.

It is reasonable to believe that the remainder of chapter ten, the table of nations, is a part of the same meta-account to which the names of Noah's sons are attached, though it was compiled by others much later. The account of the Tower of Babel in the first part of chapter eleven also goes most naturally with the Table of Nations. The Babel account describes what divided many of them, and the Table describes where they went.

A close inspection shows that there is what could be a **fifth colophon** in non-standard format in verse 10:32. Non-standard because it does not ascribe ownership or authorship to an individual or few individuals but says these are "*The families of the sons of Noah, after their generations*" (accounts). They all owned the "Table of Nations". It was family history.

So we would have a tablet whose longest side contained the story of Noah as told by his sons, and whose shortest side had the material from 10:2 to 10:32 or even 11:9. Moses put the longest side in Genesis first and the shortest side, which was added to the account of Shem, Ham and Japheth much later by their descendants, after it. The colophon in 10:1 was at the bottom of the flood account, or on the tablet edge as the title of the whole account, and the colophon of sorts at 10:32 was at the bottom of the table of nations.

Genesis 6:12 through Genesis 10:1 is the account of Shem, Ham, and Japheth and what follows is the account of their families as they spread through the lands. Their colophon in verse 10:1 is between the narrative of the flood and the Table of Nations, which I believe served as an epilogue which was fleshed out by descendants as time went on, perhaps at the end by Moses himself.

The **sixth colophon** is that of **Shem** but here this is misleading. The **seventh colophon** is that of **Terah**. With this tablet perhaps the great Lawgiver found the exact opposite situation that he encountered with colophons four and five. The account of the flood was longer than the genealogical material. But the account of Terah was shorter than the genealogy of Shem's line. He could be consistent and put the longer side of the tablet first, or he could be consistent and put the side of the tablet which was not a genealogy first. He chose the consistency of putting the longer side first, which also had the advantage of keeping the genealogy information closer together in the text. In both cases, with Noah and with Terah, the genealogy leading to the person whose account it was preceded their narrative.

So then on one side of the tablet was written the genealogy of the line of Shem leading to Terah. I think in this case verse 11:10 is misleading in that it does not refer to the material before it, but it uses the "generations of Shem" in the sense that it was the account of the line of Shem *leading to Terah*. There was no narrative from Shem to preface the genealogy of chapter eleven. This is an exception to Wiseman's rule which turns out to be a rule with many exceptions. Noah added a genealogy after Adam's *toledoth* at the end of the Book of Adam. Someone added the Table of Nations after Shem, Ham and Japheth's *toledoth* at the end of the flood account. By the time Terah came along it seemed natural to start a genealogy with a *toledoth* as well as end a narrative with one.

We can imagine that the tablet was titled, perhaps on the edge, "the generations of Terah". On one side it had a genealogy called the "generations of Shem". It is not really the entire generations of Shem though, except as it leads to Terah. It is Shem's account within the account of Terah.

The other side of the tablet was the sad story of Terah's life. I believe it was written sometime after Abram (later Abraham) left Ur but before Sarah gave birth to Isaac. It was written from the perspective of someone who lived after Terah and was telling his story, but unlike some of the other accounts, a son did not choose to put their name on it.

Notice that there is no "these are the generations of Abraham" in Genesis. This alone undermines the idea that this book is the result of forgeries done centuries later by deceitful priests. If they had written a forged account, then they almost certainly would have put an account alleged to be from father Abraham in the text.

If Abraham wrote the "obituary" for his father, then why didn't he call it "the account of Abraham" as was done with Shem, Ham, and Japheth? Put yourself in Abraham's shoes. The only notable thing your father did was compile the generations of his line of Shem. There was little to say about his life, and all that could be said was tragic. Most importantly though, at this point it seemed as though Abraham would have no son, so putting it in his name would be tantamount to ending the line of ongoing accounts. So he left it all in his father's name. Maybe he hoped that Lot, a direct descendant of Terah, would be more likely to pick up the torch that way.

While Abraham may not have had much to say about Terah, his sons had much to say about him. The **eighth and ninth colophons** are those of **Ishmael and Isaac** respectively. These begin in verses 25:12 and 25:19.

Here again the Wiseman hypothesis falls into difficulty. If one is to rigidly adhere to the theory, Ishmael must tell the story of Abraham and Isaac that of Ishmael. But I don't think that's what is happening here. These two colophons are so close together that it would be reasonable to take them as one. I think Ishmael and Isaac *together* shared the honor of owning the account of their great father Abraham. It is the story of them both. So just like Noah's sons, they shared in owning the account. This is one account with a double colophon. It is split, one for each of the owners, just as Abraham's line is split by the descendants of these two men.

Now it does appear that this account was recorded after the death of Ishmael, but I can see the wisdom of Isaac taking pains to share credit to avoid causing offense to Ishmael's numerous and warlike descendants. If it is viewed as one shared account with two colophons, then we must notice that the description of Ishmael is lengthy and elaborate. It takes great pains to identify him and connect him to his many sons.

By contrast, the part mentioning Isaac is a single terse verse which does not name his offspring. This has every mark of a young son who inherited the bulk of his rich father's wealth taking great pains not to give his pillaging half-nephews a reason to take offense. That was precisely the situation in which Isaac found himself! Conclusion- these two colophons are really one double colophon because the account had two formal "owners". I suspect that Isaac wrote most or all of the account, but shared the credit for the ownership.

There is a similar situation with the last three occasions in which Genesis uses the colophon catch-phrase *"these are the generations of"*. This is Genesis 36:1 where the **tenth colophon** (if one counts the prior two separately) is that of **Esau**, as is the **eleventh** in verse 36:9. The last colophon, **fittingly the twelfth** ...is that of **Jacob**, in Genesis 37:2a.

It is not credible to maintain that it is Esau who tells the story of Jacob's life and Jacob who tells the story of Esau's. It is not credible to say that Esau owned the account from the second part of chapter 25 all the way through chapter 36. Yet this is what one must do if one rigidly applies the Wiseman formula.

Notice though that Jacob found himself in a situation much like that of his father Isaac. His powerful neighboring sibling, with whom he had had mixed relations at best, was the eldest son and possibly expected the right to own the account of the family history. Like his father, he and his brother buried their father together just before the colophons start.

If I am right about the Isaac and Ishmael colophons being one account with two owners, maybe Jacob decided to handle the problem the same way his father did. That is, the two would "share" credit in the text, and the one who did not actually write it would not only be treated fairly in the text, but their accomplishments would be elaborated on at length within the colophon.

What I am suggesting is that it started out with verse 36:1 and verses 37:1-2a listing them as the co-owners of the long account which begins in chapter twenty-five. Then, just as Isaac is careful to list all of Ishmael's family, so Jacob goes overboard and inserts everything he can find on Esau's family into the text of the colophon. Traditionally, a few immediate descendants of the owner might be listed to help nail down the identity of the owner, but in this case the practice was taken to extravagant lengths to make sure that none of his powerful kin took offense.

So then at its simplest the colophon would look like this:

"Now these are the generations of Esau, who is Edom. These are the generations of Jacob."

That is 36:1 and 37:2a put together. A shared colophon just like Isaac and Ismael did before. But Jacob then inserted the long account about Esau in between those two sentences. That is represented by the Esau colophon in verse 36:9. This 2nd Esau colophon could be from a tablet which had a narrative on one side (verses 2-8) and a long list of prominent offspring and allies on the back (verses 10-43 of chapter 36) with the colophon on the edge. It would be sort of like the main author of a book giving a minor co-author a big plug at the end.

Jacob wanted to emphasize that his brother was a great man with many prominent offspring. It was the least he could do considering how things went between them. Even though Esau sold Jacob his birthright it may not have been clear that writing and co-owning the family history was part of the deal. If Jacob wrote basically everything from the back half of chapter 25 up to the end of chapter 35 as I suspect, he would want to try and make up for it by playing up the greatness of the "co-owner" who got iced out of the deal. That is consistent with Jacob's character I am afraid.

After emphasizing that Esau was Edom so much, Jacob probably thought he should at least mention what his land was, thus he put in verse 37:1 before claiming ownership of the account.

After Genesis 37:2 we no longer find the phrase "these are the generations of" in Genesis. That is not a coincidence. From here, the story of the Hebrew race passes to Joseph. Joseph will be trained in the Egyptian way of documenting things. He will be influenced by that culture, as will his brothers once they are brought into the land. One can easily see at this point how Moses with his heirloom of clay tablets written in cuneiform or something like it might be comparable to our getting some eight-millimeter film of our famous great-great grandparents. We would treasure the information while understanding that it was time to transcribe it onto a newer medium.

The Account of the Heavens and the Earth

‑⁌⮞⊚⮜⁌‑

I wish to return to something I mentioned briefly in the preceding chapter. The first account, the very beginning of Genesis, is described in verse 2:4 as "*the generations of the heavens and the earth*". That is, this is the account of the Heavens and the Earth. No human owner is given, because no man was around until near the very end of the account. The story of creation does not belong to any man, because no man witnessed it. It was the story of no man's life, and it was therefore no man's tale.

How then was it obtained? Here is where the modern mind runs up against the biases and limitations of its own worldview. The temptation is to immediately assume that the account was devised by some human author who, as a literary device, attributed ownership of the account to "the heavens and the earth." The idea that the LORD God, or even creation itself, somehow communicated an account to someone who passed down the information they received is not even considered by the modern mind. If the thought occurs to one, it is at once dismissed out of hand.

I believe that such haste, such impatience, and such lack of meditation, is a mistake which hinders us from discovering truth. It is a mistake to indulge in the hubris of deciding to judge events outside of our normal experience by "what we know." This is so whether the subject is truth found in scripture or anywhere else.

Even the mind which is open enough to accept the mystical, if there is good reason to believe it applies, may have trouble grasping what the text is claiming. I fear that even though Christians should by default be persons able to accept the mystical, that instead they have been bound by their mental training to reject the claims of the actual text in favor of whatever they have been taught to think about it.

For example, if they first opened this book believing that God revealed the text to Moses directly, rather than Moses having already inherited inspired text from his ancestors, then that mysticism might derail any consideration of any other sort. Many of us are just not used to the idea that creation itself, with the help of its Creator, somehow transmitted this account to (for example) Adam, and he preserved it for us. We have trouble with this even though this is what the text says about the ownership of the account. We have trouble with this even though in the other part of our brain we understand that God can do anything!

I would like to explore the scriptural case that the account of the heavens and the earth is just what that implies. Perhaps when Adam was in the garden, in fellowship with the LORD God Himself, he had access to the natural universe in a way that we do not. Perhaps before Adam fell, he was so in tune with the natural world that he could receive visions or information from creation itself in a way that we cannot.

There is an exceedingly large amount of scripture which describes creation as having a voice which it is to use. Creation is described as able to communicate. Perhaps not communicating as a living thing in the modern scientific sense of the word, but able to convey information nevertheless. We obtain information from non-living things such as computer programs or automated phone systems every day. They provide us information when we give the proper prompts.

We are the first generation to experience this, so perhaps we are the first generation for whom this revelation makes sense. For us it is therefore not so incredible to believe that creation itself can be made to provide an account of God's activities within it- for a man with the right access.

Here are just a few examples of scriptures where creation itself is described as having a voice:

Isaiah 44:3 *Sing, O ye heavens; for the LORD hath done it: shout, ye lower parts of the earth: break forth into singing, ye mountains, O forest, and every tree therein: for the LORD hath redeemed Jacob, and glorified himself in Israel.*

Psalm 69:34: *Let the heaven and earth praise him, the seas, and every thing that moveth therein.*

Jeremiah 51:48 *Then heaven and earth and all that is in them Will shout for joy over Babylon, For the destroyers will come to her from the north," Declares the LORD.*

Luke 19:39-40 *And some of the Pharisees from among the multitude said unto being done him, Master, rebuke thy disciples. And he answered and said unto them, I tell you that, if these should hold their peace, the stones would immediately cry out.*

We also know from the book of Romans that creation "groans" and is in "travail" until the children of God are manifested. The Old Testament cites instances where the land "vomits out" its inhabitants due to their great wickedness. It seems as if the natural order is not neutral in the struggle between God's will and the chaos of the Dragon. Creation has a preference for the Creator.

You can probably think of many other passages. Notice in some of these passages that the verses make a distinction between heaven and earth and all the things that move within them. In other words, it is not using "heaven" in the sense of the angels nor is it using "earth" in the sense of mankind. Rather it is saying both creation itself and the inhabitants moving within it should all communicate what God wants said.

Of course, the modern mind is quick to dismiss passages like this as merely literary devices. I do not deny that these are literary devices, and to the great mass of humanity this is all they are. But the Account of the Heavens and the Earth hints to us they can also be something more for beings in a spiritual state to hear.

Perhaps the very reason such a literary device was so often used in scripture, and why it "works" as such, harkens back to this account. I'm going to make the case that all the days of creation are describing things happening in two realms – high heaven and the natural universe. What is a mere literary device to those of us "down here" may be something literally true in the spiritual realm. I am going to show how Genesis chapter one is a window into both places.

We also see that the form of communication most often attributed to creation is that of singing. I note that some scholars have said that Genesis chapter one through verse three of the second chapter reads like a song or poem in the Hebrew. The passage has what is called a "Chiastic Structure" typical of that found in songs and poems. Regardless of how the information was communicated, the owner of the account is said to be the heavens and the earth.

For most of human history, people were mystical enough in their thinking to accept that idea, but they had no practical experience with receiving communications from inanimate matter. For the last century and a half until recently, not only have we had no practical experience with which to understand that concept, but modernist thinking blocked us from seriously considering it. Now not only are the limitations of such thinking becoming apparent, but many of us in the western world receive communications from inanimate objects on a regular basis. We are the first generation in a while to be in position to receive the truth of what I am writing about the account of the heavens and the earth- if we are willing.

I believe you will find as we go on that the contents of the first chapter make more sense if it is understood that it is from the perspective of creation itself speaking. This is an account of the heavens and the earth describing God's work within it. Whatever your own view of the matter, I beg of you not to take the attitude that it is ridiculous to believe that any human being could have received a useful narrative via communications with inanimate objects- and then head for a new adventure with your vehicle's GPS talking you through every step of the way.

Before the First Day

It is a very humbling thought to consider that after two thousand years of Christian theology we do not even properly understand the first verse of the first book of the Bible. Still, humility isn't evil, pride is evil. Let's take comfort in that as we deepen our understanding of His Word.

Some readers might be surprised to learn that "day" one in Genesis does not begin in verse one. A careful reading of the text shows that it does not begin until verse three. God does not create the heavens and the land on "day one". Rather, on day one He separates darkness from light in a universe which had previously been created, as is stated in verse one. Therefore, the universe had existed for an unstated amount of time prior to what is called "day one" in Genesis chapter one.

Notice that in verse one the Hebrew word translated "created" (*bara*) is in the "Qal perfect" form. That form is used to indicate completed action. That means that it is talking about something which had already happened. In the beginning, God created the heavens and the earth. The text moves on from there to say that the earth was formless and void "*and the Spirit of God was moving over the surface of the waters*".

Verses one and two are like a "set up" of the account of God's intervention on the earth, which starts off "formless and void". These two verses are not a part of the first "day". Instead, they are setting the scene for the account of the days which follows. Each day is an intervention of God in some area.

Just look at the structure of the other days. Each one starts with the phrase "And God said". The pattern is thus: God makes a statement, creation responds, the text describes God doing something related to His statement. Then the text says (in all but the seventh day) that "there was evening and there was morning, day "X"". Here is the pattern:

1. God speaks...
2. Creation responds (sometimes recorded only as "and it was so")
3. God acts (sometimes only "seeing" and sometimes more direct action)
4. Day is summed up: There was evening and there was morning, day X.

Each of Creation's days starts off with "And God said". Including the first day. The first "And God said" is found in verse three. Therefore, verse three is the beginning of "day one". The first two verses then can only be referring to things which occurred before this "day" began.

I also want to confess that I entitled the chapter "Before the First Day" for dramatic effect. I do not even think the text is claiming it was the "first" day. Many translations including the NASB and Christian Standard Bible render the Hebrew at the end of verse five as "one day". Not the "first day" but as "one day". The text is starting a list of days in order without necessarily saying it is the "first" day in creation. Either way, verse five defines *the light* as day, and there was no light in this world before God spoke it into existence in verse three.

That leaves us with "in the beginning" as something before that. "The beginning" started before the "first" day of creation started. How long before that? One might be tempted to ask, "how long does the beginning take?" However, I think that is asking the wrong question here.

"Young Earth" creationists often point to Mathew 19:4 and Mark 10:6 to claim that Jesus considered the creation of mankind to have occurred "in the beginning of creation". Their thinking is that since the creation of the cosmos was also "in the beginning" then the heavens and the earth could not have been created billions of years before people. So even if heaven and earth were created "before the first day" they assume they were made in a very brief period.

I will have more to say about these passages later but let us start with the reasoning. This argument does not make sense logically. Jesus said male and female were made "at the beginning of the creation" when the text shows they were made at the *end* of the creation "week." So, either Jesus is referring to the beginning of the creation of men and women, or of the creation of the institution of marriage, or He considers the "beginning of creation" to be when the ordering of creation is *finished* on the end of the sixth day. None of these make a statement about how long it took to create the heavens and the earth or how long the earth stayed formless.

Sure enough, when you look at the Greek for both verses, the usual word for the physical universe, or even the world of men, *kosmos*, is not found. Both verses say, "the beginning" but neither says that this is the beginning of the universe, or even men. Rather, Christ is referring back to the beginning of male and female in the institution of marriage. The word translated "the creation" in the KJV is a form of *ktisis*. That doesn't mean (unless modified) "universe", it just means "the created thing". It is often used of the founding of a city or ordinance. If you are in a passage talking about the universe or "all things" it can mean universe. But in a verse talking about marriage, the "created thing" is marriage.

After all He is addressing the subject of divorce in these passages, not the creation of the universe or even humanity itself for that matter. He is telling the pharisees that God not only created them male and female but connected that creation to His declaration that the man and his wife were to be one flesh. God's original intent for all humanity was reflected in this special example.

The idea that "the beginning" can take immense amounts of time while the middle and end of the story are wrapped up in a comparatively brief time seems wrong. To us, it should not take vastly more time to create a world than that world is scheduled to last. But that is us. The whole objection is based on the idea that God views time the same way we do, but that idea is explicitly rejected in scripture. Second Peter 3:8 says:

But, beloved, be not ignorant of this one thing, that one day is with the Lord as a thousand years, and a thousand years as one day.

Peter asks believers not to be ignorant about just one thing, but apparently that's too much for us! We are so wrapped up in ourselves that we just can't get out of our own time-bound skin to appreciate things the way that God sees them. God is not bound by time. He has no problem taking fifteen billion years to set up a story that plays itself out in thousands of years. Nor to Him does the set up necessarily take any longer than the playing out. That we have trouble grasping this is no limitation on Him, it's our limitation.

Haven't you seen elaborate patterns of dominoes which have been set up just to watch them fall in a particular way? It may have taken hours for the creator to set up a series of dominoes which fall in a matter of seconds. The first few dominoes to fall may be the "beginning" of the story playing out- but it took a lot of time to even prepare that beginning. So even we humans, made in His likeness, sometimes have a penchant for similar things. The joy comes from setting up the event as much as the event itself. The beginning of the event comes long after the set-up for the event. The life of the event takes much less time than the set-up.

Further, we do not even know if God considered the set up as "taking more time". The amount of time one perceives passing depends on the position of the observer- and remember no humans were around to observe the events of Genesis chapter one until the very end of it. From our view setting up the dominoes was a lengthy process. To Him, the falling of the dominoes may be the lengthy process.

In the next three chapters I am going to communicate some pretty heady stuff about time and perspective. If you are not convinced now, I hope by that point you will see that the argument being used from Mark 10:6 is based on a flawed assumption about God and time, and faulty logic.

To be clear, I am not advocating for the old Scofield "Gap Theory" which postulated a long gap in time between Genesis 1:1 and Genesis 1:2 during which a prior creation populated the earth and was destroyed. I am just saying that the text allows that there was a large interval of time between the creation of the heavens and the earth and the start of the first "day" in verse three. I am not claiming there is a missing story there.

My point is simply that the text shows that Creation's first day does not begin until verse three. So regardless of how long the "days" of chapter one may have been, verses one and two happened an undetermined amount of time beforehand.

I also want to point out that the heavens are something which God creates, not something He is contained within or bounded by. 1 Kings 8:27 *et al* point out that *"the highest heaven cannot contain Him."* God is not constrained to exist "in" Heaven. He is beyond the heavens. He may be "in" heaven in the way that I sit "in" a chair. I am not within the chair. As it is written (Isaiah 66:1) *"Heaven is My throne and the Earth is My footstool"*. Later, a person of the Trinity does enter heaven, but I get ahead of myself.

Another thing I want to point out is the condition of creation prior to God filling it with Light. It was not a good place to be. The initial conditions are not good, in any realm of creation. They are dark and foreboding. When it says "the deep" in this passage, the Hebrew word "tehom" is used. This term also means "abyss" and can refer to subterranean waters. It is thus comparable to the Greek term used to describe the place where the spirits who left their proper abode are kept in chains (Jude 1:6), or the place in Revelation from which such creatures emerge (Rev. 9:11). In Luke 8:31 the demons who possessed a miserable wretch begged Christ not to send them to "the deep." The word here again refers to an abyss.

The initial conditions of creation were like the realms where the very worst spirit offenders are kept in custody, like some sort of other-worldly super-max facility. Perhaps the "abyss" spoken of in later scripture is a realm or void where things have been left exactly as creation was at this point. It is a space utterly lacking in the light of God's wisdom, judgement, personality, or word.

Even vice enjoys the fruits produced by virtue, and even evil spirits dread to be confined to a place where the light of God has in no way entered. They don't want too much of it to shine, they wish to lurk about in the evening shadows. Despite this, they dread the deep and utter darkness.

Did God create the universe as a place of evil? Consider what evil is. He created it as a place of darkness- a place which lacked His Divine light. This is not because He made creation evil, but because He had not at this point illuminated it with His own Word. Evil is not a thing in itself- it's the absence of good. It's the absence of God, or more precisely (since God is omnipresent) an absence of His Word. When He made something outside of Himself, it was dark until His Word was injected into it.

I know that a lot of people are convinced that God created an unfallen universe which was in a state of perfection comparable to that of heaven at its holiest, but that is not what the text says. The text says that when God creates something outside of Himself it is an undesirable place to be- until He begins to put His Word and His actions into it. As we proceed, I will show how the other scriptures used to support a doctrine of a perfect initial creation are wrong. The universe was created a dark and chaotic place which was made better as God worked on it, ending with God giving Man dominion to continue the process of taming it as His representatives.

I should also mention something about Exodus 20:11 while I am on this subject, and I will have more to say on it later. It says that *"For six days the Lord made the heavens and the earth"* as well as what is in them. Though the King James Version says, "For in six days...." we find that the word "in" is not actually in the text. Plus, the word translated "made" here is a different Hebrew verb than the one translated "created" in Genesis 1:1.

My point is that you cannot equate Exodus 20:11 with Genesis 1:1. This is because 1) Genesis 1:1 speaks of the creation of the earth and the universe before God spoke the first day into existence in Genesis 1:3 while Exodus 20:11 speaks of God's work *on* the heavens and the earth during the six days of Genesis chapter one. And 2) the word "in" is not in the Hebrew text. It isn't saying that God created the world *in* six days. Rather He worked *on* His previously existing creation for six days. He made it into something suitable by working on it for six days. He created it "in the beginning".

This fits a lot better with the context of the verse where it is arguing that man should rest from his own labors on the land for one day out of seven because the Lord Himself did the same. He worked for six "days" and on the seventh He rested. Farmers do not "create" the earth they farm, but they do *make* it into something productive. That is mostly what the Lord did during the so-called "Creation Days."

That is why I object to even the term "Creation Days." (I prefer *Creation's days*.) God worked on His creation, and on some days the creation helped. The "days" are being described in the account from Creation's perspective. The Hebrew word translated "created" is not even used regarding God's activities on days one through four. He did most of His "creating" *prior* to day one. Except for the creation of living things in the waters, and then of Man, the rest of His work was ordering the heavens and the earth which He had previously created. During the six "days" He worked on them, but they were created "in the beginning."

But the Young Earth Creationists are not the only ones getting Genesis 1:1-2 wrong. Many of skeptical scholars have somehow managed to err worse. For the last two thousand years, Christians have held that scripture teaches that God created the universe out of nothing, or at the least "*things which are seen are made from that which is not seen*" (Heb. 11:3). The great majority of rabbis have agreed with this view. One of the main verses used to support this position is the first verse in the Bible. It is almost universally translated as "*In the beginning, God created the heavens and the earth.*"

During the centuries that men thought that the cosmos was eternal, Christians were jeered by the faux intellectuals for believing that it had a beginning. But in the last one hundred years science has found that our universe is not eternal after all. It had a beginning. Rather than rejoice that scripture alone, of all the ancient creation accounts of antiquity, had gotten this one right, some wish us to believe that we have had Genesis 1:1-2 mistranslated these past twenty centuries.

They now claim that the text allows for a translation which leaves the door open to make it more like the pagan creation accounts of the ancient near east. That is, instead of God creating the universe from that which is not, they suggest a translation which allows that He might have stumbled upon a universe which was already here, but in a disordered state. I've seen this suggested: "*In the beginning of God's creating of the heavens and the earth- when the earth was..*", or something close to this.

To accomplish this textual butchery all they had to do was delete the accent marks, delete and alter the vowel marks, and delete and alter the punctuation marks- enabling them to re-write the verses. And I do mean "verses" since to make it work, they have to turn verses one through three into one rambling sentence. They argue that most of these marks were added later to the Hebrew text and this is true. But the Septuagint is translated from a much older Hebrew text and it agrees with the traditional translation.

They justify all this by saying that the first word in scripture, *be-re-sit*, is part of a "construct phrase" in every other place it is used in scripture. Thus, they add by construction the "of" and "when", and change vowels to make "created" into "creating" etc. But *be-reisheet* is only used four other places, all in Jeremiah, and all in the same context. They say "In the beginning of the reign of ____". Genesis 1:1 is in a different and unique context-. In most situations, the same people would say that isn't enough data to build a rule, or justify such large changes to the text.

Professor Shlomo Karni has pointed out that a basic rule of Hebrew is that the prefix *be-* in front of an abstract noun converts it into an adverb. So "respect" becomes "respectfully", "joy" becomes "joyfully" and so on. Thus, he suggests the translation "Originally, God created the heavens and the earth." – a restatement of the traditional translation.

Intriguingly, translating it "in *a* beginning" works in Hebrew without making it into a construct. Even if it is a construct, we can leave "created" as is if we just see that the Hebrews had no word to describe the all-beginning. The noun was left blank after "of" because it was inexpressible (2nd Cor. 12:4, 1st Cor. 2:9). So "In the beginning of ____, God created the heavens and the earth" would be correct. They could not name the totality of it!

Refuting the Three Main Arguments for Literal Days

—⊱⟩◉⟨⊰—

"Young Earth" creationists (YEC) maintain that "*yom*", the Hebrew word translated "day" in Genesis chapter one, refers to a literal 24-hour day. One of the most common arguments they use to support their position is the presence of the terms translated "evening" and "morning" in those verses. They claim that the use of these terms with "*yom*" proves that the "days" are regular 24-hour days.

I am not insisting that they are completely wrong. I only maintain that the "days" are an extended period in this realm. Genesis chapter one describes creation occurring in two realms, the realm above and the realm below. The realm above exists in His will and responds to God's commands quickly, perfectly and without the need for further intervention. In the realm below conforming to God's commands is a long-drawn-out process with lots of errors and missteps. In fact, it is not even possible without His further intervention. In other words, it's a suitable place for flawed and sinful human beings like us.

For all I know, the events of Genesis chapter one all happened in what an observer up there would experience as six 'literal' days. But that was there, and no human observers were around anyway. We are here, and here it took ages. But I get ahead of myself. Let me start by showing that their claims about the significance of these terms being used together are erroneous.

No one disputes that the word "*yom*" in the Old Testament can mean either a literal day, the hours of daylight only, or a long and indefinite length of time. The argument from the Young Earth camp is based on how the Hebrew word translated "day" is used elsewhere in scripture when paired with the Hebrew terms translated "evening" and "morning". Various YEC sources have made various claims about this relationship, some factual and some not.

One of the largest YEC outfits for example, Answers in Genesis, makes the claim that "in over 100 instances where the phrase "evening and morning" accompany the word "*yom*" in the Old Testament (as it does in the days of Creation in Genesis), it always refers to an ordinary 24-hour day."[1]

This is not true because there are not even close to one hundred instances of the phrase "evening and morning" being paired with the word "*yom*" in scripture. Nor are both terms in the same verse of scripture with "*yom*" in some other phrase one hundred times. We don't even have to quibble about whether the instances refer to a 24-hour day because the instances don't even exist! The phrase is found with "*yom*" in early Genesis, and the other claimed ninety-four instances are not to be found.

Even in the handful of cases where "*yom*" exists with just one of the terms the structure is different. In the first five days of Genesis chapter one there are no articles or prepositions associated with the terms for "evening" and "morning" or the word "*yom*". It just says "(There was) Evening, and (There was) Morning, Day X".

For example, if I say, "on the day we got married" then I have referred to a specific day by the word "the". It is a definite article which specifies a definite day. There is no definite article like that in Genesis chapter one, at least until the work wraps up on the sixth "day." Thus, you can't validly argue that the usage is the same when the sentence structure associated with the term is different. It would be like claiming that I meant a "literal 24-hour day" when I said, "in my grandpa's day" because that is what I meant when I said in another conversation "on *the* day my grandpa was born".

Likewise, "evening" in Genesis chapter one is not associated with a specific evening. It does not say "the evening" (or "the morning") on any of the six days. Nor does it have other qualifiers or prepositions to modify what is meant by "evening" as almost all those passages outside of Genesis do.

Here's another example, the phrase "Twilight for the Gods", the title of a movie made in the nineteen-fifties, does not refer to a specific evening but rather a condition of fading of power and respect that the 'gods' in question are experiencing over what could be a long time. The campaign slogan "It's Morning in America" does not refer to a specific morning, but rather represents a change in condition in which things are improving, and people are more optimistic.

In the same way, the use of evening and morning in Genesis chapter one doesn't refer to a specific literal day or dusk. The use of these terms in Genesis chapter one without the modifiers which tie them to a specific literal day should not be assumed to be literal. As with the movie title, "evening" can just as well be describing a condition which occurs over time rather than a literal twilight. In this case it refers to a worsening condition that some aspect of creation is subject to prior to God's Word intervening.

Like the campaign slogan, "morning" in Genesis chapter one could be referring to an improving condition rather than a specific literal morning- the result after God's Word orders some aspect of creation to His will.

Lest someone claim that these views are mere contrivances that modern people use to "try and force the clear meaning of God's word to conform to scientific theory" I offer you the work of a medieval Rabbi named Moses ben Nahman, more commonly known as "Nachmanides". He noted that the root of the Hebrew word for "evening", *erev*, meant "chaos". Like me, he connected "evening" to a condition of disorder and an inability to perceive rather than a literal evening. The word picture of an "evening" is used to represent the condition of some aspect of creation until God illuminated it with the light of His Word.

In a like manner, Nachmanides did not consider the Hebrew word used for "morning" in Genesis chapter one, *boqer*, as a literal morning. Rather it represented the light of God's word illuminating the earth and bringing some aspect of it to a condition of *bikoret*, or orderliness. Obviously, this thirteenth century rabbi did not come to these conclusions because of pressure from modern science.

You will see in the next chapter that there is a very strong case that "darkness" and "light" are used in Genesis chapter one in a deeper sense than mere physical light and darkness. Indeed, these terms are often used in the deeper sense. For example, in Ecclesiastes 11:8 and Isaiah 60:2 the same term (*ha-ho-sek*) for darkness used in Gen. 1:4 clearly refers to something more than physical nighttime. Here the most natural meaning of the evenings and mornings should be viewed in the same manner. It isn't that they aren't being used "literally" so much as the spiritual realm is seen as "reality." The darkness and light of our temporal realm are mere figures of more real and permanent spiritual conditions.

Returning to the claims of those arguing for literal twenty-four-hour days, let's look at an article by Eric Hovind in "Creation Today". In the article Hovind claims this: "The words "morning" and "evening" occur together, without "day" 38 times outside Genesis 1. Each of these occurrences refers to a literal 24-hour day."[2]

Well, he is a lot closer to right than the "Answers in Genesis" claim cited above, but I want to show you some of the "38 times" and you can see that just because a verse of scripture has the words for "evening" and "morning" in it does not mean that it is referring only to a literal twenty-four-hour day. In some places it means that, but in other places it means less than twenty-four hours. In yet other places it means more time than 24 hours.

In very few of those thirty-eight cases is the phrase "evening and morning" even used together in that order, and that is on top of the differences in definite articles, prepositions, and modifiers I mentioned previously. For example, the word for morning, *boqer*, is used outside of Genesis chapter one without prefixes less than forty times. In the first chapter of Genesis all such instances of the word lack a mark called a dagesh. Outside of that chapter it is only found without a dagesh three times!

Those verses are Job 38:7, Psalm 65:8, and Isaiah 21:12- and it is far from clear that any of them are referring to a specific literal morning. For some reason, those who developed the Masoretic text gave the days of Genesis chapter one a rare pronunciation. I don't put too much stock in that, but if you are going to use this method of scholarship then the forms of the word most like those in the passages in question should carry more weight than different forms of the word.

I consider it an abuse of language to claim that the different use of a variable form of a word in one place dictates the same meaning in another. But even if it did, Hovind is simply incorrect in his claim that "each of these occurrences refers to a literal 24-hour day".

Here is an example. In Exodus chapter eighteen the words are used together twice as shown:

And so it was, on the next day, that Moses sat to judge the people; and the people stood before Moses from morning until evening.

So when Moses' father-in-law saw all that he did for the people, he said, "What is this thing that you are doing for the people? Why do you alone sit, and all the people stand before you from morning until evening.

In Exodus 18 the phrase "morning until evening" refers to less than a twenty-four-hour day- it is "from sunup to sundown". This is important to our discussion because Genesis chapter one uses the phrase "evening and morning". If YEC reasoning applies (it doesn't) then this phrase is literally describing a night rather than a "literal 24-hour day", just as the terms in reverse order in these two verses are describing daytime and not a whole 24-hour day. Thus, the most "literal" view of the terms in Genesis chapter one doesn't make sense if one insists that the usage in one place dictates meaning in another.

Another example used the words "evening" and "morning" in the right order- Exodus 27:21:

In the tabernacle of meeting, outside the veil which is before the Testimony, Aaron and his sons shall tend it from evening until morning before the LORD. It shall be a statute forever to their generations on behalf of the children of Israel"

Here the phrase means "perpetually" or "continually". It is not a 24-hour day- it is for all generations so as long there is a flame to keep burning. It's an indefinite period. The following verse in Leviticus 24:3 is very similar:

Outside the veil of the Testimony, in the tabernacle of meeting, Aaron shall be in charge of it from evening until morning before the LORD continually; it shall be a statute forever in your generations.

In Job the brief life of a man is compared to the time from morning to evening- so the words are used to describe a period of time that, though brief in the grand scheme of things, is far longer than a literal twenty-four-hour day:

Job 4:20 ~ *They are broken in pieces from morning till evening; They perish forever, with no one regarding.*

Psalm 90:6 uses similar language to describe the brevity of the life of a plant. Daniel 8:26 is more controversial, but it does have the terms for "evening" and "morning" in it and it does refer to a period of more than one literal day.

I think you can see that among these thirty-something instances there are many places where the terms are used to mean something other than a "literal 24-hour day". The "young earth" Creationists are trying to determine "usage" in a flawed manner. They are taking a tally for where the same word is used in different contexts, regardless of whether it is connected to the other parts of the passage in the same way. They are using a "majority rules" mentality. That is, "however the word is used most often in other situations is the way it should be used in this situation".

Look, that is a valid scholarship tool when used properly, but here it is not being used properly. Part of the reason is that they are ignoring the other language elements of how the terms are used as I have shown. But it is also because this situation in Genesis chapter one- the foundation of creation-is a unique situation. It is not like those other situations, so any allowable use of the words must be considered to discern context. Sticking with what the word means in most instances is a poor guide for determining its meaning in unusual situations.

Imagine you had a document with many accounts in it. Some are from office settings where the phrase "just a second" comes up. Another set of stories is about a track coach. The last story is about a duel. You cannot determine how the word "second" is used in the last account by how it is used in the other accounts. You must consider every allowable meaning and see what fits the rest of the circumstances- especially if somewhere else in the document there is a reference to the account of the duel.

The principle I am claiming here is that the context of words in a passage is better determined by what the rest of scripture says about *that* passage rather than how the same words are used in *different* passages on other subjects.

Take for example the account of Abraham and Sarah and Hagar. The way that words used in that account are used in passages about other subjects may offer us some value, but whatever value we get from this tool must be superseded by what Galatians chapter four says about the passage. That is, we can't continue to insist that it is simply a story about a guy, his wife, and a concubine, when Galatians tells us that its real meaning is much more than that.

What the rest of scripture tells us about the account means more than how the same words used in the account are used elsewhere. What the rest of scripture tells us about the days in Genesis chapter one must be considered more authoritative than a word count of how similar words are used in different passages which describe different situations using different sentence structure.

Now a Young Earth Creationist might be tempted to say, "OK then, look at Exodus 20:11 and see what other passages say about Genesis chapter one." Exodus 20:11? Well, they have that one wrong too. I already mentioned this verse in a previous chapter, but now let me add that according to other passages of scripture, the seventh day in Genesis chapter one (and thus in Exodus 20:11) is not a literal 24-hour day in the life of Adam.

If I can demonstrate this to you, and I mean to a few chapters hence, then I hope that you will see two things. One is that Exodus 20:11 can't be rightly used to support the idea that Genesis chapter one is strictly referring to literal 24-hour days. The other is that this undermines their claims that "in all the places in Scripture where the word *yom* is preceded by a number (as it is in the days of Creation), it always means a 24-hour day"[1].

It is not true. They use circular reasoning and *assume* what they are trying to prove- that the numbered days in Exodus 20:11 refer to literal 24-hour days. That the days of our week are compared to the days of creation might imply that these are the same kind of days, but it doesn't require it. We must see if there are other passages which speak to the issue of whether God experiences time the way we do. And of course, other verses of scripture tell us that God sees time differently, and in a way that suggests that his "days" take vast amounts of time. Psalm 90:4 (NIV) says "A *thousand years in your sight are like a day that has just gone by, or like a watch in the night.*"

But I should not stop with saying what the context of "day" in chapter one *isn't*. Let's go on and look at what the context of day *is*. It turns out that the creation account itself defines what a "day" is in that passage!

⁓ ⧐◉⧏ ⁓

References: as of May, 2019 my citations are accurate representations of what is on these links...

1.   https://answersingenesis.org/age-of-the-earth/what-a-difference-a-day-makes/

2.   http://creationtoday.org/the-hebrew-yom-taking-one-day-at-a-time/

The Light He Called Day

***

God called the light "day," and the darkness he called "night." And there was evening, and there was morning–the first day. – Genesis 1:5 (NIV)

❦

The Hebrew word "*yom*" can mean "day" in a lot of different contexts, but the creation account specifies what is meant by "day". It gives the context. The *light* is what God is calling "day" in this account. "Day" in the creation account is explicitly defined. The meaning for "evening" and "morning" must be connected to the meaning of the term in the account which is explicitly defined. They should not be used to define what "day" is, because the account itself defines what "day" is.

It's not a 24-hour day because, for one reason, the evening is not a part of the day. It is just the condition which precedes it - things are marked by an increasing condition of darkness. Some English translations obscure this because they add words onto verse five which are not in the Hebrew. There is no definite article ("the" or "a") in the Hebrew here in front of either the word "evening" or the word "morning". It just says:.

"There was evening and there was morning - first day." (Or better, "day one")

The Holman Christian Standard Bible puts it, *"Evening came and then morning: the first day."*

When written like this it shows more clearly that the evening is not considered to be a part of the day. The light is the day. The morning is the breaking forth of the light. The evening was not a part of the day, just the condition which preceded it. This naturally fits and builds with the immediately previous text- as the world in verse three is said to be in darkness to begin with. This condition was then altered by God uttering His first command into creation "Let there be Light".

How did this light come to enter creation? Not by any of the means mentioned in the following days. Rather the very act of God speaking into His creation produced the light without any other action necessary. This is a clue, later affirmed in scripture (see below), that God's Word itself is the Light. If I say "I want to speak to you now" then I have accomplished my desire in the very act of saying it. In the same way, God calls light into existence merely by speaking, for His Word is light.

In the context of the creation account, a "day" is the light. And the light is a consequence of God's word being spoken into creation. The word for "light" used in Gen. 1:4 is that same root word used in Psalm 27:1 when David said, "*Yahweh* is my light." As mentioned in the previous chapter, the word for "darkness" in Gen. 1:4 is the exact same form of the same word used in Isaiah 60:2, where it is speaking of spiritual darkness and moral confusion in contrast with the light which is *Yahweh*. See also Isaiah 10:17, 60:1, and Micah 7:8.

The first ten verses of the Gospel of John strongly point to the idea that the Word and the Light are connected, just as they are connected in Genesis chapter one:

In the beginning was the Word, and the Word was with God, and the Word was God. The same was in the beginning with God.
All things were made by him; and without him was not any thing made that was made. In him was life; and the life was the light of men.
And the light shineth in darkness; and the darkness comprehended it not.
There was a man sent from God, whose name was John.
The same came for a witness, to bear witness of the Light, that all men through him might believe. He was not that Light, but was sent to bear witness of that Light. That was the true Light, which lighteth every man that cometh into the

world. He was in the world, and the world was made by him, and the world knew him not.

Each of these "days" in Genesis are initiated by God speaking His Word into the cosmos. The light is the day and this light is an aspect of God's Word entering the World- presaging the Incarnation. The Greek term translated "word" in John chapter one is *Logos*. Logos does not just mean a spoken word. It also signifies reason and rational communications. An example would be the communication necessary to turn a formless world of darkness and emptiness into one of light and life.

This meshes well with Colossians chapter one, where it is made clear that the Son, the second person of the Trinity, made everything. The light, the illumination which is a consequence of the Logos of God entering the universe, is another way of describing this process. God the Son instructed the universe. Genesis chapter one is a record of the Son, He who would incarnate as Christ, entering in and ordering creation on behalf of the Godhead.

This has immense theological implications. For one thing, it argues against the idea that initial conditions in creation were perfect until the fall of Adam. Creation may not have started sinful, but it started as a place of increasing darkness and emptiness (evening), only becoming illuminated and orderly once God spoke His Word into it (morning). This is just a small part of why I call this view of the text the "Christ-Centered Model" for early Genesis. As the verses above indicate, the apostles made the same connection between Christ as being both the Word of God and the Light of the World.

This is what really happened on each of the "days" of the creation account. It has nothing to do with literal 24-hour days, except as metaphor. The sun was not even authorized for the tracking of time until the fourth day! Instead, God speaks His word into some aspect of creation and His word transforms some area of creation from increasing darkness, emptiness, and disorder into increasing illumination, fruitfulness, and order. Without

God's word this world is in a condition of evening. That is, decaying, and getting darker and darker.

Once His word comes forth this condition is reversed for whatever part of creation God addresses. This includes our individual lives! No wonder that on the first day God saw only that *the light* was good. He said nothing about the darkness or evening being "good". This is in contrast with other days where the works of the days are called "good". This is a huge textual clue that God is not speaking about mere literal evenings and mornings here.

Backing up a bit, the most accurate term to describe the days of Genesis Chapter One is not "Creation days" but "Creation's days". When determining the context, the starting point must be the question of who is telling the story. Whose perspective are we hearing?

The account we read about in Genesis chapter one and early chapter two is, according to verse 2:4, the account ('generations' equals account) of "the heavens and the earth." This is the account of Creation itself and it is told from Creation's perspective. Its "days" are not our days.

So how does Creation track time? If you are "the heavens and the earth" what is your reference point for the passage of time? Not the earth, because if you are the earth then it is always evening somewhere, and it is always morning somewhere. Further, this was not just the story of earth, but it was the account of the heavens as well. It was the account of all of creation, even high heaven!

Creation doesn't count time as man measures time, by tracking the movements of objects within the creation relative to his own position. I suggest to you that the way creation tracks time is in terms of the words and actions of its Creator. When God speaks a new word, it begins a new day, a new *yom*. When the creation has fulfilled that Word, and God Himself has acted on that word or approved what creation has done with it, then that day, that *yom*, is in some sense completed. The text shows the days as starting when God speaks and I do wonder if these days even end with God's approval, or if creation simply "keeps up the good work" once it is approved?

Creation tracked time by the Word of its Creator. The Creator spoke a command and His Word illuminated whatever part of creation He addressed. In the last four days creation acted on that command until God's word was accomplished. Our expression "all in a day's work" would apply here. A "day's work" can be how creation is describing its own "days" both observing and carrying out God's expressed will.

You will soon see that even this term is inadequate to describe the true complexity of the situation, because when you measure time in such a way you must consider that not all realms of creation respond to God's command the same way or in what we would think of as the same time. That is why Christ asked us to pray that the Father's will be done "on earth as it is in heaven." There it is done immediately and perfectly. Here, it's a process.

That being so, you might expect to find in the text a disagreement or variance between heaven and earth as to when the day's work was done. Spoiler alert: we will find such a divergence in the text once we study the six days of creation.

This account is supposed to be the Heavens and the Earth communicating to man. They are communicating an account of God's intervention in the natural universe. To whom was this communication made? The obvious choice is The Man, Adam: the one who had fellowship with the LORD God in the Garden, and as such could have had access to the creation in ways that we cannot even now fully conceive. Later we will see how the "generation", or account, of Adam fits into this account. That is, Adam fitted his story into this one.

The account itself was from creation's point of view, but the colophon was written from the point of view of the one who recorded the account, presumably Adam. This suggests an explanation as to why "the LORD God" (*Yahweh Elohim*) is used in the colophon for the account (2:4-6) whereas the account itself uses only "God" (*Elohim*) to describe the Almighty. Adam, child though he was, just an insignificant speck against the vastness of the Cosmos, still knew the Creator in a way that Creation did not: as a person. There is more theology in that one thought alone than I can even speak of here.

The first line of the Nicene Creed says that God the Father is the "Maker of all things" yet in the third line it says that the Lord, the Son of God, is the one "by whom all things were made." Is that a contradiction, or a matter of perspective? From creation's perspective, all members of the Godhead were involved in the work of bringing the earth to its present condition. From Adam's perspective, he knew God as "The LORD God" because it was by Him that God made the world. Did the architect build the house or did the contractor, or did both do it together? There is more than one right way to look at it.

I would suggest, and please file it away until more has been explained, that "The LORD God" does not appear in creation's account because God had not manifested Himself as such at the start of the account. Nor would that occur until the sixth day, even though as God He had been involved in every aspect of creation. Creation did not use the term "The LORD God" because 1) it used another name for the same being and 2) that being did not make His appearance as such until late in the account. This paragraph will not make sense to most readers until we are much further along.

The Heavens and the Earth would look upon Adam, at best, as you might look upon a child. Just as we speak to children in terms that they can relate to and understand, so I should think would creation in telling its story. Especially when telling that account to Adam- a young being, fashioned in the image of The Creator yet so limited in experience and understanding.

When the Genesis chapter one account uses terms like "day", "evening" and "morning" it is not using those words to describe what we would call an "evening" or a "day". Creation is using words which are familiar even to an innocent young child to describe events and actions beyond the comprehension of most men even today.

To wrap it up, the words in the text do not describe a solar day. People who read it casually may think that it is describing a solar day, but if one looks closely the reverse is true. If we are being literal, the literal translation of the phrase "there was evening and there was morning, a X day" does not describe a day at all, but literally describes a night. It says there was an evening, followed by a morning. It is the hours between and inclusive of twilight and a new dawn. That is not a day, it is a night. The "literal" meaning does not make literal sense as a 24-hour day. It only makes sense the way I am putting it- evening is not a part of the day, only what precedes it.

The text defines for us what a day is- *the light* is the day, and the morning is the breaking forth of that light. That is, the light which is produced from God's word entering creation (as in the Incarnation). This isn't "figurative" light. Rather, the sun is the mere figure of this, the true light of the world. God intervenes in His creation with His Word and His deeds. Creation responds. The effect of His interventions is to take some part of His creation that was sinking into gloom, formlessness, and darkness and transform it into illumination, order, and light. This is the effect of God's Word on the physical creation, and on our lives, and in our very souls.

The "evening" then represents the condition of the natural universe (and everything in it including ourselves) without God's intervention. It unwinds. It deteriorates. From whatever position He started this world, separate from Him it descends into a condition of increasing darkness and emptiness. Even though He created what was before, without His Word to further shape and sustain it neither the creation nor those who live in it get better on their own. Rather, things get worse until His Word brings light, truth and order to some aspect of creation.

After His Word goes forth, whatever part of creation is being addressed has a breaking forth of dawn- an increase of order and illumination. This is a foreshadowing of the role that the Word, the Logos, God the Son, the Light of the World according to the first chapter of the Gospel of John, plays in the life of everyone whose faith is in Him. As we discover Him and trust Him, one by one the areas in our life that were dark and getting darker become redeemed.

I am not saying that Genesis One is just a metaphor. I am saying it is describing things that God really did using language that seems to us metaphorical. If I said "Joe became Sheriff and he cleaned that office up" I may not be saying that Joe scrubbed the floors and dusted. But that does not mean that there was no Joe, or that if there was that he did not really do anything. There was a Joe, and he did act, and I am using a metaphor which describes those real actions. I am describing real things that happened in the real world, but I am using metaphorical language to describe those real events.

It would diminish the real accomplishments of Sheriff Joe to say what was meant was that he scrubbed the floors. In the same way, God brought forth days and it diminishes what God did to make them about mere solar days.

Using a man-centered definition of "literal", I am not a "literalist" regarding early Genesis. I am taking a God-centered view of what is real and what isn't. The eternal is real, the temporal a mere figure. But either way, I am an "Actualist". The text is describing things which really happened, either in this realm, the next, or both. Whatever Ancient Near East practices which later arose in mimicry of the forms presented in this text, the account was not *just* describing ethereal spiritual patterns.

The bottom line is that Genesis chapter one is not describing Deism, or a God who simply wound up the clock of the universe and watched it wind down. It wound down from the moment He created it until His intervention reversed the deterioration. He continued intervening after the initial creation. That is one takeaway from the account in Genesis chapter one. But that is not all, or even the most important thing that Genesis chapter one is trying to say, and the single-minded obsession with when all this happened diminishes the mystery of Christ in the text.

The Meaninglessness of Time in Creation's Account

I have made the earth, and created man upon it: I, even my hands, have stretched out the heavens, and all their host have I commanded. – Isaiah 45:12

***

Remember the former things of old: for I am God, and there is none else; I am God, and there is none like me, 10 Declaring the end from the beginning, and from ancient times the things that are not yet done, saying, My counsel shall stand, and I will do all my pleasure: – Isaiah 46:9-10

L et me start off by saying this chapter will not be easy reading for some. If one does not have a science background it may be a little harder sledding than the rest of the book. If your interest is more the theology than the science, I ask you to slog on through anyway. They will be connected shortly.

Albert Einstein demonstrated that even time was relative to distance and velocity. That is, if two observers were far enough apart, and/or moving in different directions fast enough, then what they observed would be affected by this distance/velocity difference. For example, if a star 10,000 light years away had been snuffed out when Christ walked the earth, we would not know it for another 8,000 years. This is because light does not move at infinite speed. The light we see from that star tonight would not be from the photons emitted by the star recently, but rather the ones emitted by it roughly 10,000 years previously. The photons of light took that long to reach us and register on our eyes.

Further, Einstein demonstrated that if someone sped past earth at near the speed of light, time would slow down for them relative to us. The earth might age millions of years, but the traveler would age, and experience, only a few years of time. I shall not take the space to demonstrate the details here, but it is common knowledge among those who understand relativity.

We may say from these observations that when reference points are far enough apart, and they are not moving in the same direction but there is very great relative speed between them, that questions of how much time an event took, (or in some cases even the order in which some events occurred) do not have simple answers. One must account for the effects which distance and motion have on time as measured by observers in different places.

If the measurement of time between two distant points within our natural universe is complicated, how much more so is a comparison of time on earth with the realm above? Once the two realms are separated, their timelines may mirror one another, but they are not the same.

Measuring time in this universe can show us this problem in some degree. We know that space-time itself is expanding. Light waves are passing through space that has been and is being stretched. On that secular scientists and Isaiah 45:12 agree. Were space not constantly being stretched, light would fill the universe and the sky at night would not be dark. As we go on, we shall see that God made this realm a place of evenings and mornings- not total darkness but not total light either.

So not only was the light which we see from a distant galaxy originally emitted long ago, it is also light which has been "stretched" as it goes through space. This phenomenon is referred to by astrophysicists as the "redshift" of light waves. It is so called because light that was originally in a higher frequency (more wavelengths per segment) such as blue light is transformed as it passes through stretching space into lower frequency (fewer wavelengths per segment) light- such as red light.

The shift from blue visible light to red visible light is very subtle. The frequency of the former is not even twice that of the latter. But if one continues this process across the entire electromagnetic spectrum, we can see that some types of electromagnetic energy are very much greater or lower in frequency.

Visible light is toward the middle of the spectrum and it has a frequency which is roughly 100,000 times higher than the Cosmic Microwave Background Radiation (CMBR) which permeates space in all directions. If the CMBR was originally emitted in the form of gamma radiation rather than visible light, the difference in frequency swells by many orders of magnitude. Additionally, most evidence indicates the universe was already somewhat stretched by the time the CMBR was released.

To give you some idea of how meaningless a statement about time can be when one is describing two very different reference points, see my crudely drawn diagram (Fig. 1) below. Imagine the light wave moving from the event on the right side of the figure to the eyes of the observers on the left side. We see the diagram just as the wave with information containing the start of the event reaches the eyes of the two observers, one near heaven and the other on Earth.

Consider "A" to be the view from near High Heaven, and "B" to be the view from earth. In "A" space-time is not stretched. In "B" it is. Imagine the distance from X to Y equals one minute of time to observer "A". An observer at point "A" sees ten wavelengths of light pass across their eyes from time "X" to time "Y".

(See figure 1 on next page)

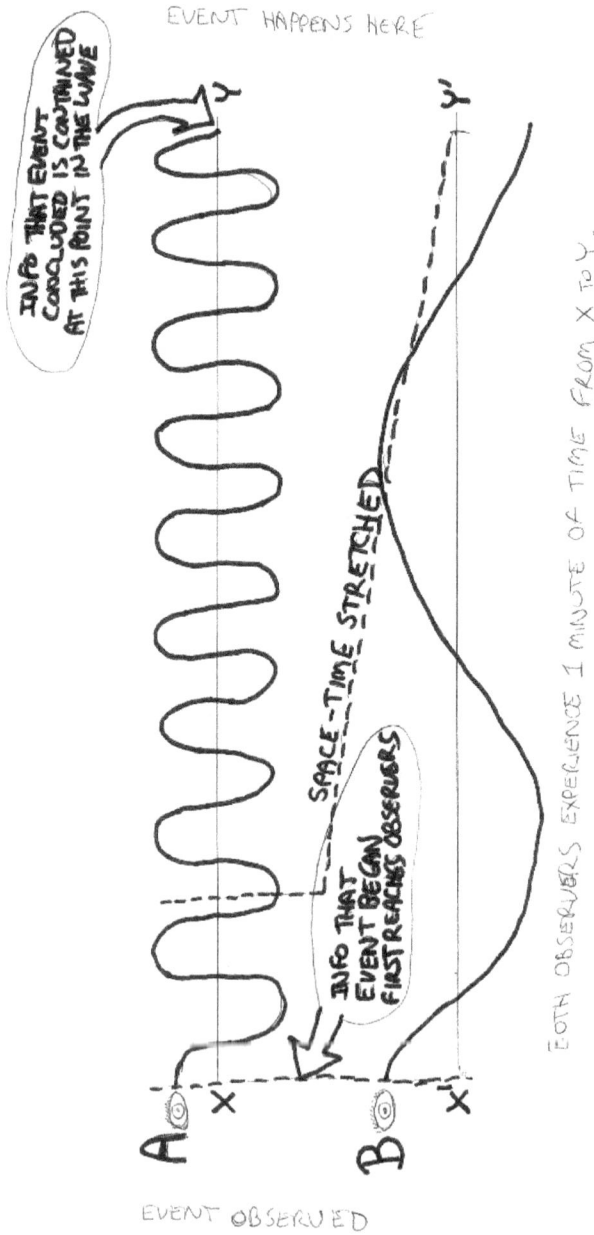

Now consider what an observer at point "B" sees. "B" is fully within the natural universe a great distance away from the near-Heaven observer. Space-time has been stretched. Not just space, but the information about what has occurred in time has also been stretched. To "A" the event concludes when the tenth wave reaches them. This is at the end of the minute, which is the distance from Y to X. To "B" it is only 2/10ths complete after a minute (the distance from Y' to X'). The truth of the event's conclusion has not yet reached the second observer.

In this case both observers experience a minute of time, but what they observe happening in that time is different. Near Heaven "it was so". The job was done. But to an observer on earth looking into the distance, the job takes much longer than one minute to complete.

If an observer on earth were attempting to copy step-by-step a pattern of events (or carry out instructions) that they saw in heaven, they would use much more time in doing so. In fact, for each event there would be an amount of time when heaven sees the event as completed, while on earth it appears that it is not completed. The event was completed, but the electromagnetic waves (such as light) that contain the information that it was completed had not reached observer "B".

Figure two below shows this in a different way. In this diagram time is broken into "days" which represent the same amount of perceived time passing on heaven or earth. In this case, the dashed line from the eyes of the angel and the dashed line coming from earth indicate that both perspectives are experiencing "Day 2".

Each length of wave carries information about something that happened (or instructions about what should happen), which are labeled with letters on the crest of each wavelength. Notice that in heaven, the angel observes event "F" occurring early on day 2. On earth, event "A" has not even concluded at that point on day two.

Carrying this process out further, by the end of day four Heaven has experienced events (or received instructions) labeled A-N. On earth, observers on day four only experience the beginning of event "B". The information has entered the universe, but the expanding nature of space-time means that the information packets are a bit like someone at an airport walking the wrong way down a conveyor belt. Even walking quickly, they make only slow progress.

Some Young Earth Creationists have proposed that this strange property of time means that, despite all appearances to the contrary, the physical universe was created in only six twenty-four-hour days. But they have it backwards. This is not the realm where things happen quickly, heaven is the realm where things happen quickly. Down here there is resistance to God's word being fulfilled. It will be, but it takes what to us is a long time, with many missteps. Just like us! It is the kind of creation fitting for us now, but when we become what we were meant to be creation will be renewed accordingly. And this is what Romans refers to when it says the creation groans and suffers waiting for the children of God to be manifested.

(See Figure 2 on next page)

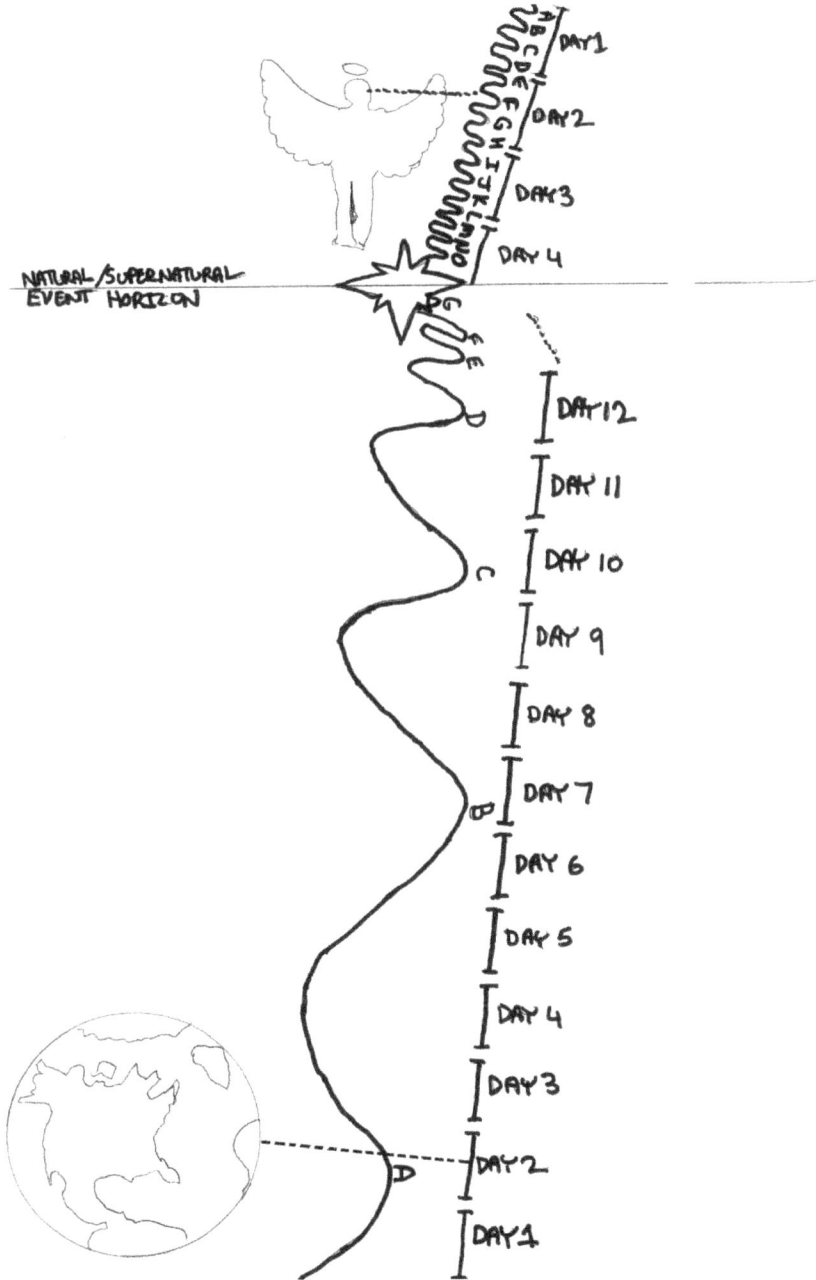

NATURAL/SUPERNATURAL
EVENT HORIZON

DAY 1
DAY 2
DAY 3
DAY 4

DAY 12
DAY 11
DAY 10
DAY 9
DAY 8
DAY 7
DAY 6
DAY 5
DAY 4
DAY 3
DAY 2
DAY 1

Defining a "day" in terms of one rotation of the earth about its axis does not fit in this diagram though, because we are not just tracking time on earth, but in heaven. Additionally, the events that happened during Day One on earth do not match up with what happened on Day One in heaven. Which "Day" do we use?

Heaven's "day" in this diagram has four wavelength events passing (A-D for Day 1, E-H for Day 2, *etc.*). In four of those "days" events A-N have occurred. In four of earth's days (the same length of light wave passing) event "A" has barely concluded. It would take many days on earth to complete instructions or events of the first "day" in heaven.

When we study the text describing days one through six it will become apparent that creation is happening in two different realms. The earth below somewhat mirrors what happens in the land above. There is similar activity going on in two realms, but the two realms are not equal in terms of how readily and completely they respond to God's commands, or how much help they need in executing them. This is a bold claim, but when we study days three, four, six, and seven it will become clearer.

As odd as the claim seems, effects on time due to deformations in space are well known in science. For example, you may have heard the claim that the most distant galaxy in the universe that we can observe is 13.2 billion light years away. But the galaxy is very likely much further out than that by now. It is not "where it appears to be" because the light we see from it left a long time ago. We see where it was, and a lot has happened since then. We just have not gotten that information yet and may never!

The stretching out of the heavens even within the natural universe means there is a difference in "conformal time" and "proper time" of distantly observed events. A ray of light emitted by that galaxy in the distant past travelled through 13.2 billion light years of space to reach us but the space through which it was passing kept expanding on the journey. During the process, those light rays were stretched (redshifted) many times their original wavelength, making even blue light appear red. Both the energy and any information contained in such a wave would be reduced per unit of time.

Again, this is like travelling on a conveyor belt in the wrong direction. You walk one-hundred and thirty-two steps in your frame of reference, but you travel only forty steps relative to the airport. Imagine you were dragging a long scroll behind you on the belt. Someone not travelling on the belt read it aloud as each line passed their position. Because your travel is slower than if you were not on the belt, the reader gets the information slower than they would if you were dragging the scroll past them walking off the belt.

Lastly, I call your attention to figure three. Secular scientists have debated, and are still debating, whether the expansion of space-time has been at a constant rate or if it accelerated greatly in some epochs while slowing its acceleration in others. This could mean that events which happened in a consecutive manner in one place appear to be overlapping in another. The top half of the figure shows that a distant observer sees events in order if space time does not stretch, or does so at a constant rate. The bottom half shows what is more likely in our universe. Spacetime stretches at different rates in different epochs, thus the information could reach the observer in an overlapping manner even if it was given sequentially.

Fig. 3

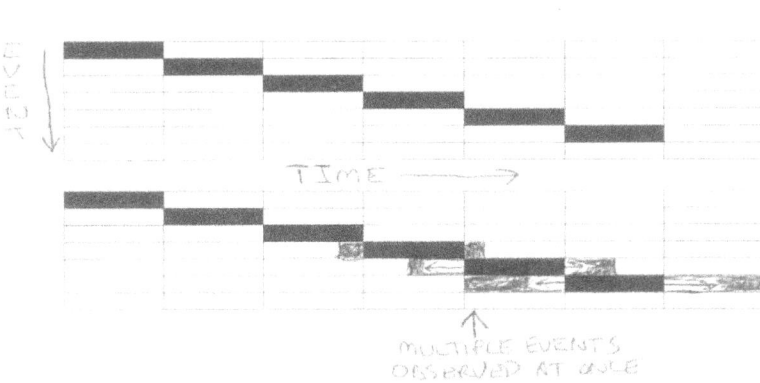

This is part of why whether the days of creation were literal 24-hour solar days or not isn't worth fighting over. Maybe in heaven they were. Maybe they were less. God spoke, and heaven immediately conformed to His word. Heaven is the Type, Earth the Shadow. That process of conformity in this realm could have taken eons. It could have taken that long for the reality in heaven to be copied, manifested, or accomplished here.

This issue of time being stretched so that beginnings and endings can contain mystery applies to the first Sabbath. Therefore, I wish to start our talk of days with the seventh day.

The Seventh Day

The seventh day is probably the best example to demonstrate the effects of differences in time between the natural and supernatural realms. This is in part because there is so much more scripture on the seventh day than on the others. Once you see how scripture speaks of the seventh day it becomes easier to understand how the time issue applies to all of creation's days.

The other reason that the seventh day is a good choice to demonstrate this difference is that the different realms- High Heaven, the Cosmos, and the earth and sky- did not start off as separated as they are now. We will see that much of the first three days of creation was the process of separating High Heaven from the rest. So, let's look at the seventh day, in part to see what it can tell us about time, but even more importantly, for what it says about the Messiah.

After the sixth day of Creation God completed His work and rested. This is described as the seventh day, or the Sabbath. "Sabbath" means "rest". When God took a rest from His works, He was taking the first Sabbath.

This Sabbath rest, or completion of His work, continues to this day. We do not see the sort of wholesale changes to the surface and atmosphere of the planet described in the creation account. We don't see whole new categories of living things spring up. We will never see another Cambrian Explosion for example, because we are in the "seventh day", God's Sabbath rest, even still. He has ceased ordering the physical features of the planet so as to make it sustain advanced life. He has ceased the creation of

The Seventh Day

new phyla of living things. That work is completed. But this sense of the passage is only the most superficial one. The more wonderous meaning is to follow.

Genesis never does end the seventh day, as it ended the previous six, by saying "the evening and the morning were the seventh day." The Sabbath rest that God entered into on the seventh "day" is ongoing. I have heard it said that His finished work of creation is a shadow pointing to His finished work in Christ, who (in Matthew 12:8 *et al*) called Himself "Lord of the Sabbath." As you read on to the end of this chapter, I think that you will see that the full truth is even more glorious than that!

Hebrews chapter four teaches us that God's Sabbath rest is available to believers today, one which paradoxically we must labor to enter into (because we keep trying to substitute our own efforts for faith?). We can rest from our own efforts to attain right standing with God through works and instead enter into the rest of His already completed work.

Indeed, the Apostle Paul writes in Colossians 2: 16-17:

Let no man therefore judge you in meat, or in drink, or in respect of an holyday, or of the new moon, or of the sabbath days: Which are a shadow of things to come; but the body is of Christ.

The Sabbath for man (the seventh day of rest) is just a shadow of the real Sabbath- whose substance, or body, is Christ. The Sabbath for the Land (the seventh year of rest from Leviticus 25:4) is merely a shadow of the real Sabbath- whose substance, or body, is Christ. The original Sabbath of the Creation is Christ Himself. The substance, the body, the intent, of these Sabbath rests is found in Christ. He also "finished" His work to redeem Mankind. He completed the work of obtaining right standing before His Father by living the sinless life that we could not.

That is the substance of the Sabbath rest for which both Man's Sabbath and the Land's Sabbath are figures. Unlike the type Sabbaths, which last only for the length of time assigned to each of them, the archetype Sabbath of Christ's finished work on the cross is eternal.

This is the real Sabbath rest. It is a Sabbath which, according to Hebrews chapter four, believers can enter into. We do that when we repent of our own ways and further when we accept by faith that God's ways are just. We do that by, rather than trying to earn our way to right standing with Him, loving and trusting Him and the Righteousness which He has provided in Christ.

The way to enter into His rest is to rest from our own efforts to attain our own right standing before God and instead learn to love and trust Him more. Every Sabbath mentioned in the Law should be seen in this light, whether it is the twenty-four-hour Sabbath of man, the one year out of seven Sabbath for the land (Lev. 25:4), or Creation's Sabbath where God rested from His Creative works and ceased issuing "work orders" to the natural universe. It all points to Christ, the Word.

The Sabbath days are but shadows pointing to Him. We see that the Word of God was actively working in Genesis chapter one. Christ, the Logos, or Word according to the first chapter of John's Gospel, created the material universe. This is confirmed in the first chapter of Colossians (and elsewhere):

For by him were all things created, that are in heaven, and that are in earth, visible and invisible, whether they be thrones, or dominions, or principalities, or powers: all things were created by him, and for him:

The surrounding verses make it clear that the "him" is Christ, God the Son. When Genesis chapter one shows God creating the universe and the world, it is God the Son doing the work - just as He also did the work of attaining right standing with God the Father. And just as the seventh "day" never ended in Genesis, so the rest that Christ obtained for us through His atonement for our sins will never end.

It's not a twenty-four-hour period. It is not something that we have to repeat week by week, it's an eternal rest made possible by the finished work of Christ. Trying to force the text into being about literal 24-hour days doesn't point to Christ, it diminishes Him. It actually blurs the picture concerning what God is saying about Christ and the Sabbath. I will further demonstrate this when discussing when the morning of the Sabbath Day in the creation account began.

This understanding adds new depth to the teachings of Jesus on the Sabbath. He said, "The Sabbath was made for Man, not Man for the Sabbath." It becomes a statement on law and gospel. Man was not made to earn his way to salvation by works such as keeping the Sabbath. Rather the substance of the Sabbath is a rest from our own works because The Word of God has finished the work for us. Truly the Sabbath is for Man- for his salvation!

The book of Hebrews in chapters three and four has a long argument which touches on the Sabbath, and also on the contents of the previous chapter concerning the variation in observed time. It is a difficult passage to understand outside of the context of what we discussed earlier regarding what perceived time would look like in a place where space was unchanging as compared to what we see in the natural universe.

These are things about the nature of time and space that humanity did not understand before the middle of the 20th century. Despite this, several paradoxes in scripture are cleanly resolved once this understanding of space-time is applied to the passages! Generations of Christians had to accept on faith that they were true, even if they could not give a good explanation of how they were true. Today, we can explain.

Chapter three of Hebrews says: *And Moses verily was faithful in all his house, as a servant, for a testimony of those things which were to be spoken after; 6 But Christ as a son over his own house; whose house are we...*

Moses was, in his life, in his acts, in his acquisition of the Law and composition of the Torah, testifying "of those things which were to be spoken after". That is, he testified about things which were yet to be plainly revealed to humanity. What he was saying in his own day was really meant to point to things in the future which would be spoken about long after the Torah was composed. The things in the Torah were mere shadows of the reality which came to pass in our realm much later- in Christ.

Though Moses and Joshua came well after Adam and the events of early Genesis, Hebrews 3:5 says that when Moses recorded them, he was testifying of things which were to be spoken of later. This is much like the diagram in the previous chapter. In Heaven, the Sabbath day had started at the last of the foundation of the world. On earth, the true meaning of that Sabbath had not yet reached earth. This is what is alluded to in the mysterious words of the following chapter (4) in Hebrews:

For unto us was the gospel preached, **as well as unto them** (emphasis mine) *but the word preached did not profit them, not being mixed with faith in them that heard it.*

For we which have believed do enter into rest, as he said, As I have sworn in my wrath, if they shall enter into my rest: although the works were finished from the foundation of the world.

For he spake in a certain place of the seventh day on this wise, And God did rest the seventh day from all his works.

And in this place again, If they shall enter into my rest

So even though the "rest" was supposed to be on the seventh "day" in Genesis chapter two, God spoke thousands of years later of men entering that rest as a future event. In one place in scripture the Sabbath rest of God began long ago, but in another place, we see it is thousands of years later and it is still questionable whether or not they are able to enter into it. Further, the writer of Hebrews seems to tie the words of Genesis to the gospel being preached. What gives?

Those who believe that the first six days were literal 24-hour days must explain the strong evidence that the seventh day is not. It is a rest that men had still not entered into (because of unbelief) all those generations later. It happened in Heaven long ago ("although the works were finished from the foundation of the world"), but on earth men had not entered in ("if they shall enter into my rest").

As I showed in the diagrams in the previous chapter, time here is stretched, and we see only the foreshadowing of things which have long since transpired in the eternal sphere. Moses lived in the foreshadow of what was to come, and when he wrote he testified to the coming reality which cast the shadow.

In verse nine the passage points out that other scripture still speaks of yet another day to enter into that rest. It was not a day in the life of Adam, and not a day in the life of Moses. Let's read further, starting in verse eight of Hebrews chapter four:

For if Jesus (editor's note: many modern versions read "Joshua") *had given them rest, then would he not afterward have spoken of another day.*

There remaineth therefore a rest to the people of God.

His rest is not limited to one of our days. We can celebrate one day out of seven to rest, but those days are not the true Sabbath. They are only shadows of it. The true original Sabbath rest is not a particular solar day that happened on earth long ago. It is a spiritual condition we can enter today. That the Sabbath Day is a condition as well as an event strengthens the claims of this book about days one through six.

The true Sabbath Day of rest had not begun here on earth in the time of Adam. It had not even begun at the time of Moses and Joshua, for the writer of Hebrews points out that it said in another Old Testament passage that there "remaineth" yet another "day", another Sabbath rest for the people of God:

For he that is entered into his rest, he also hath ceased from his own works, as God did from his.

Let us labour therefore to enter into that rest, lest any man fall after the same example of unbelief.

If we believe in Him, then the rest which He entered into becomes our rest. And what is the "labor" which we must do to enter in? Jesus said (John 6:29) "This is the work of God: to believe on the One whom He has sent." We must work to have faith, rather than fall back on faith in our own works. That is unbelief, which prevents us from entering in. How then might we strengthen our belief? Well, "Faith comes by hearing, and hearing by the word of God. (Romans 10:17)." If you truly hear what His word says, then you will believe. You will not have to psych yourself up to believe. You just will.

Since hearing His word is the key, hear then what His word says about the Sabbath in Genesis chapter two, and what it does *not* say:

Thus the heavens and the earth were finished, and all the host of them.

And on the seventh day God ended his work which he had made; and he rested on the seventh day from all his work which he had made.

And God blessed the seventh day, and sanctified it: because that in it he had rested from all his work which God created and made.

Notice that though the creation was finished at the end of the sixth day in verse one, God did not end His work at the end of the sixth day. He ended it *on* the seventh day. The heavens and the earth were completed at the end of day six, but God did not end his work then. They were finished, but God's work was not finished. He had yet one more work to perform, which is mentioned here only obliquely.

I have noticed that some translations try to make verse two say "And *by* the seventh day God ended his work". It seems they noticed the paradox of the narrative showing the work of creation being finished on day six while this verse says God ceased from His work *on* day seven. The phrase "by the seventh day" is a terrible translation of "bay-yowm". I think this was an ad hoc translation to force a false resolution to this paradox. The same term is translated "on" a given day or "that day" in the rest of scripture, including in the second part of that very verse- "he rested on the seventh day." I have another resolution to this paradox in the text: one which points to Christ.

I guess you might call this a "gap theory" in Genesis that I do accept. There is a gap between verse one and two, not in the first chapter of Genesis, but in the second. Things were finished and complete on the sixth day, but God's work was not ended then, but on the seventh day. I shall endeavor to show that what happened between verses one and two was the fall of Adam. These days have evenings which precede them. The evening which preceded the seventh day was the fall of Adam. Because of that God would have one more work to do. That work, which ended *on* the seventh day, the morning of it, was redeeming what He had created in the first six days.

The text in Genesis chapter two never says concerning the first Sabbath "there was evening and there was morning, day seven." Now we see that the book of Hebrews says that, as far as we on earth could tell, the Sabbath rest never even began in early Genesis. In heaven it did, but on earth it did not happen in the time of Adam, or even that of Moses. On earth it was still the "evening" before the seventh day- an increase of gloom due to Adam's fall. When then did the morning of this seventh day, the start of the true and eternal Sabbath rest, begin here on earth?

In the gospel of John chapter five (v16-17) Christ says something quite remarkable when the Pharisees complained that He was working on the Sabbath:

And therefore did the Jews persecute Jesus, and sought to slay him, because he had done these things on the sabbath day. But Jesus answered them, My Father worketh hitherto, and I work.

Jesus said that the Father was working right up until then, so He was going to work too! Jesus was telling them that the Father had never stopped working. He did not stop working on the seventh solar 24-hour day- either the original one or the one the Pharisees were complaining about. The Greek here reads that the Father was working *continually* up to that point.

Wait, didn't God take the seventh day off? How then could He be working right up until that point? The resolution to this mystery is that the rest which came from finishing the work on that first Sabbath had already occurred in heaven, but the manifestation of that event had not quite reached earth. Much like a radio broadcast of a live event in a distant galaxy would not reach the earth for eons of time, we understand that what was accomplished in heaven at the beginning was now about to be received on earth.

We know that God's Sabbath rest had not yet begun on earth because of what is said in Hebrews three and four about the order of things in the time of Moses and Joshua. Moses was testifying of things in the future, and they were looking to a future day. It had still not occurred when Jesus told the Pharisees that His Father was working right up to that moment.

Sure, God had finished making heaven and earth, and the host of them, but He had other work to do, and would not rest until all was accomplished. God finished His creation, but not His work. Or more precisely, His work was finished long ago in heaven but the manifestation of it had not yet reached the earth below.

Then when did it reach this earth? When did God take His rest? When did God's Sabbath rest from the first account of Genesis finally begin on this earth?

The answer to all those questions is the same. The work ended when Christ announced on the cross "It is finished". His rest began on that Sabbath day. He "ceased from His labors" by resting in the ground until the resurrection! Since that time Christ and the Father have been at rest. The Holy Spirit works still, but Christ sat down at the right hand of God, as is written in Hebrews 10 (12-14):

But this man, after he had offered one sacrifice for sins for ever, sat down on the right hand of God; From henceforth expecting till his enemies be made his footstool. For by one offering he hath perfected for ever them that are sanctified."

God was not finished with His creation until the cross. Up until then the Father had been working, and so the Son would work as well. Jesus was serving notice that as God He was not on an earthly seven-day schedule. He was on the Father's seven-day schedule. He would continue His work of "making Man in our image" right up until He proclaimed, "it is finished!" on the cross. Then the Sabbath rest of that seventh day could begin, and that day continues up until the present time.

Revelation 13:8 is properly translated, "And all that dwell upon the earth shall worship him, whose names are not written in the book of life of the

Lamb slain from the foundation of the world." Some versions translate this verse so as to make it about the names being written in the Lamb's book of life from the foundation of the world. That is true too according to Rev. 17:8. But if the Lamb had such a book since the foundation, then there was also a Lamb back then - that is, from the foundation events in the seven days of early Genesis. Hence passages like Isaiah 53 were written before Christ but still read as past tense:

Surely he hath borne our griefs, and carried our sorrows: yet we did esteem him stricken, smitten of God, and afflicted.

But he was wounded for our transgressions, he was bruised for our iniquities: the chastisement of our peace was upon him; and with his stripes we are healed.

God's rest spoken of in Genesis chapter one was completed in heaven long ago but was not revealed here on earth until the resurrection. First Peter chapter one (v 18-20) shows that Christ was chosen before the world began, but only revealed in these times:

For you know that it was not with perishable things such as silver or gold that you were redeemed from the empty way of life handed down to you from your ancestors, but with the precious blood of Christ, a lamb without blemish or defect. He was chosen before the creation of the world but was revealed in these last times for your sake.

The work was determined in the heavenly realm in the beginning, testified to by Moses in the law, but revealed on earth in Christ 2,000 years ago. Why is the seventh day so special? Was God in need of rest? Was He really looking forward to His day off so that He could finally do all the things that He wanted to do? That is seeing God as man, but He's not.

He did not bless the seventh day because He could finally get a rest, but because we could finally share in His rest. He blessed the day because His efforts to deliver the things He had created and made were fulfilled on the Sabbath. This is "testifying of things not yet spoken of." This was Moses speaking of a day which he had not yet lived through.

God did additional work beyond making and creating everything. There was also His work of redeeming the race which He created and made. He built creation with the freedom to choose other than Him, but also made a way for its errant inhabitants to be delivered from the consequences of that choice- if they repent. This work He completed on "the seventh day", and therein He rested.

While the debate rages on whether early Genesis is reliable history, and many even dare to claim that the debate is over and that it isn't, the truth is now being revealed to you with each page of this book that you turn over: Not only is early Genesis reliable history, it is also reliable prophecy! As it is written, He has "declared the end from the beginning". Because the history is reliable you may know that the prophecy is also reliable. And as some of this prophecy has come to pass you may know by the prophecy being reliable that the history is also reliable.

After all these accusations hurled against the reliability of early Genesis by the uninformed, we at last come to understand the truth of the matter. The only thing which was unreliable was our ability to understand it! The reliability issue lay not in the veracity of the word, but rather in the understanding of the readers.

The Structure of Creation's Days

⇢⇾❈⇽⇠

O ne of the main themes I will advance is that the language of chapter one is using the same words to describe what is happening in both the natural and the supernatural realms on each of the "days". It is referencing the land above and the land below with the same language. The words have a double meaning and if one thinks that they only refer to the physical realm then they will not make sense. If one considers they have only a spiritual meaning, then one will likewise miss the mark.

This is not to say that what goes on above is an exact duplication of what occurs below, only that they operate in parallel and that things in the natural universe are representations of things beyond it.

There is also the issue of time. The structure of the text screams out that the responsiveness to God's Word is not equal in the two realms. Above "it is so" as soon as He speaks. In the realm below nature struggles to fulfill its parallel course of action. This will be shown in some detail as we proceed. For now, please notice the structure of the days of creation. Hopefully, referring to this structure will help us to understand what follows.

Day One:

God said: (Let Light)

> God **saw** THE LIGHT **was good.**

> God DIVIDED and CALLED

> ~There was Evening & There was Morning~

Day Two:

<u>God said</u> (Divide Waters)

> God MADE

>> *And it was so*

> God CALLED

> ~There was Evening & There was Morning~

> - no mention of God seeing anything was good

Day Three:

<u>God Said</u> (Let Gather Seas and Appear LAND)

>> *And it was so*

> God CALLED

> **And God saw that it was good.**

<u>God Said</u> (Let Earth Bring Vegetation)

>> *And it was so*

> The earth brought forth vegetation (why after "it was so"?)

> **And God saw that it was good.**

> ~There was Evening & There was Morning~

Day Four:

<u>God Said</u> (let lights appear in the heavens)

>> *And it was so*

> God MADE and SET (if "it was so" already, why MAKE?)

> **And God saw that it was good.**

> ~There was Evening & There was Morning~

Day Five:

<u>God said</u> (Let Waters and Sky fill with Living Things)

    God CREATED (the "it was so" is missing on this day)

    And God saw that it was good.

<u>God said</u> (blessing- be fruitful and multiply)

    ~There was Evening & There was Morning~

THE Sixth Day:

<u>God said</u> (Let the Land bring forth living creatures)

    And it was so

    God MADE (if "it was so" why must He then make?)

    And God saw that it was good.

<u>God said</u> (Let us make Man in Our Image)

    God CREATED and MADE

<u>God said</u> (Blessing; Have Dominion and Eat Vegetation)

    And it was so (here it only becomes so after God acts)

    And God saw that it was VERY good.

        (only time these two phrases are adjacent)

~There was Evening & There was Morning~

"It Was So" - the Dual Nature of the Creation Week

❦

What you are about to read may be different than how many of you have understood the first chapter of Genesis. The problem is that there is so much richness and depth in every verse of it that my powers of explanation are grossly inadequate to contain it all. I cannot explain the glory of a single verse and the perfection with which it all fits together with the rest of scripture even if I take a whole chapter to do so. What I must do instead is offer up an explanation without adequate proof. I ask you to stay with me as I go fill in the proof for the explanation I provide.

Genesis chapter one (and the first part of chapter two) is the account of the heavens and the earth. Notice that there is more than one heaven. The first heaven I presume to be the air or atmosphere before which the birds fly. The second heaven is presumed to be the Cosmos, outer space where the stars and planets run their course. The third heaven is the abode of the angels. In Second Corinthians chapter twelve the Apostle Paul writes of a man, commonly understood to be Paul himself, who was taken up to "the third heaven" and described it as beyond human words.

Genesis chapter one and the start of two is an account of creation describing to Adam God's word at work for two realms, the natural and the supernatural. To complicate matters His word works differently in each. Because it works differently in each, Jesus instructs us to pray "Thy Kingdom come. Thy will be done, on earth as it is in Heaven."

In Heaven God speaks, and His Word instantly and without resistance comes to pass. This is not so on the earth. There is resistance to His will being done "on earth as it is in Heaven." Christ instructed us to pray that this variance in responsiveness to God's Word ends- by unifying the two realms in favor of heavenly conditions.

What we will see as we progress through the creation week is that the separation of the realms leads to an oddity. Once the two realms are fully separated scripture will record God speaking a word and then the Higher Realm of Creation declares "And it was so", only to then have God and/or creation subsequently work to fulfill that word. If "it was so" then why does the earth subsequently have to bring forth something, or God have to make, or set, or create something? Shouldn't the "and it was so" come at the end? Why does the declaration that something is "so" repeatedly come prior to its making?

To see the answer, you must again understand that this is coming from creation's point of view. It is a song, or poem. Look at it as a quartet singing. Each of the three heavens and the earth are telling the story, and each has a voice, but they don't all agree on the details.

The third heaven's part is "and it was so." There, when God speaks a word, that word is quickly accomplished. It becomes reality right away. Perhaps a day up there was even less than twenty-four of our hours. But this immediate response to God's word is not so in the other three realms, the Cosmos, the Clouds, or the Earth. In those other realms there is a process initiated, which God finds suitable. It doesn't even necessarily mean the job is finished or complete, just that things are on the right track. When He finds it suitable, they report "and God saw that it was good."

The word used for goodness here (towb) does not mean moral perfection. Indeed, even the fruit of the tree of knowledge of Good and Evil is described as appearing "good for food" with the same word. I will later show how it is used in other places in ways which rule out the idea that it is describing moral perfection or a state of deathlessness.

It is impossible to speak of a single timeline when saying how long Genesis chapter one took. The answer depends on which of them you are asking. In the third heaven, it is finished. It was finished in six of Creation's "days". The other realms are supposed to respond to God's word as the third heaven has. Darkness, futility, and rebellion have slowed things down in this realm, but we are going to get there. Some will welcome that, and others will dread it.

As you read on you will discover that no "it was so" was needed on day one, because the speaking of the word was its own accomplishment. On day two the subject is having separate standards for the accomplishment of God's judgments. Therefore, on that day the "it was so" happened at the same time for all realms- right after God established the separation.

On day three the phrase "it was so" appears twice. It appears once at the final separation, and once after the command for the earth to bring forth vegetation. In that second case we see for the first time a difference in how quickly the two realms respond to God's word. The scripture says, "it was so", but the land acts subsequent to that declaration. It was only *after* "it was so" that the earth brought forth vegetation. Only after the Earth caught up to what "was so" in heaven does God see that "it was good."

Once the three separations (light/dark, waters above/waters below, water/land) were complete, the realms were fully separated. After that each began to respond to God's commands in its own way and time. The Highest Heaven instantly responds with an ideal version of what God intended. In this realm however, it is not instantly so. A process must occur, and what is made here is an imperfect image of the reality which is up there.

The same thing happens on day four. God speaks, and the third heaven says "it is so" but then the verses say that God had to make things and set things in place. Only after doing so does He see that "it was good". Please refer to the previous chapter to confirm the pattern. In the third heaven, His word is accomplished at once. In this temporal world, additional work or intervention is required.

High Heaven is the well-behaved child, who does what their father says right away. The natural realms are like the disobedient child, the parent sometimes must get involved to make sure the intent of the parent's words becomes reality. Not even the natural universe can do God's will on its own merits without His intervention. After all it can't be any better than the humans who are in it!

On day five the phrase "and it was so" does not appear, indicating that this was not something which also happened in the third heaven, but only in the waters and the lower heavens. If we consult the last two chapters of the book of Revelation, we notice that there "is no longer any sea" in the New Earth to come. I will show you that in scripture "the sea" represents God's negative judgment. As such it does not apply to the third heaven. Nor does it apply to the abode of the fowls of the air which are to fly about in the space between the land and heaven. Since nothing on this day applies to the third heaven, the phrase "and it was so" does not appear.

In day six, the pattern returns. Twice it says, "and it was so" and yet it then records that God did something else after that in order to make what was "so" happen. The reason is the same. It is "so" in the third heaven because in that place as soon as the Word leaves His mouth, His creation accomplishes it. It is done, and it is done completely and perfectly. On earth, it is not yet "so" as it ought to be. It takes time, and it takes intervention. Rather, the state of things is pronounced "good", i.e., "suitable" for that day's jurisdiction. They are where they need to be for His purposes to be accomplished. At the end of day six, heaven and earth at last align, for it was so and God saw that it was very good right on top of each other!

Concordism, the attempt to correlate the scriptures to modern scientific discoveries about our natural universe, is all well and good- but every attempt I have seen so far has a major problem. They act as if Genesis chapter one is speaking only of our natural universe. It isn't. It is describing both the natural and the supernatural realm being formed together. Doesn't the rest of scripture tell us that heaven is our home, and that the things of this world are passing? Why then would we assume that the Creation account would only speak of the natural realm? Failure to see the true cosmology is a big part of why a lot of concordism seems awkward and forced.

The Creation Week Part One: Days of Separation

—◦⊱⊰◦—

In the first account of Genesis creation is explaining, or more likely po- etically singing, to Adam about how the world he lives in came to be. It sets the stage by describing in verses 1-2 what the scene was like before God began His interventions. The universe was not a comforting place. The earth was formless. Darkness and emptiness reigned. Nothing was sure. And then God spoke.

The first thing God did to give order to creation was to inject light. He did that simply as a consequence of speaking, for His Word is the Light of the World (John 1:9), and of all creation. Order and illumination spring from His Word. That is why all He had to say was "Let there be light" and there was light. He did not have to perform any other action to make or create it, as He had to do for example, to help the seas bring forth life.

Nor did creation have to perform any other action in response to His Word, as was the case on those later days. In this case, His Word was its own fulfillment. If a man says to you "I should speak to you" he has ac- complished his word in the very act of saying it. So it is here. Spiritually and morally, God put illumination into the universe by the very act of speaking into it.

John 1:9 describes the Logos, the Word of God who came as Christ, as the true Light which enlightens every man who comes into the world. In Gen- esis 1:3 the Word entered the universe. The Creator entered Creation.

"Day" is that part of creation illuminated by the Light. Night is that part of creation which is not.

Evil is not a thing in itself. It is an absence of the Divine Light of the Word of God. This is not a philosophical evasion though, because in making a creation of darkness God did create a Cosmos whose randomness and disorder was a cause for adversity. Bad things can and did happen. Things not of His will (hence Christ asked us to pray "Thy Will be done"). Things not desired by Himself or His people. God made that kind of calamitous evil, though not moral evil. See Isaiah 45:7: *"I form the light, and create darkness: I make peace, and create evil: I the LORD do all these things."*

God is doing on the first day what Christ will do on the last, dividing creation into those illuminated by the Light and those who are not- the sheep from the goats. The scripture is about Christ from the first day to the last.

God not only divided the light from the darkness, but the Hebrew says that He put a space between the light and the darkness. The word is *bayin*, word number 996 in the online *Strong's Hebrew Concordance*. This has led many people to conclude that the "space" God placed between darkness and light is only the literal evening and morning. Physically yes, that is the result, and I will get into that directly. But it was mostly something else.

If you look up *bayin* you will find that its primary usage is to separate out that which is holy from that which is unholy. The main place in the Bible where we view it differently is right here in Genesis chapter one. That is justified regarding physical outcomes, but something else is also happening here. This word is used in the rest of scripture to indicate people, places, or things being sanctified, or set apart either because they were too good or too evil. It describes the separation between the holy and the profane. Here we have the Word of God entering His own creation for the first time, and for the first time, Creation can operate according to its rightful moral reference point. Creation can be guided by the light of its Creator.

This is what is happening in what we would call the "supernatural" realm. Both realms are being formed at once. Creation described what was happening both in the heavenly realm and the natural realm with the same words. They had a double meaning. The primary meaning was that God determined what the relationship between good and evil, truth and lie, darkness and light, was going to be in this natural universe. It is speaking of good and evil, not just physical light and darkness. That is why unlike on days three through six where God proclaims it *all* "good", on this day He only says that *the light* is good. He will not call darkness good, even if He can turn it to good purpose.

Consider His options for constructing how truth and morality would be contained in this Creation. He could have left it all dark – as dark as the Abyss which makes even the demons tremble. Or He could have illuminated each corner of it and made it shine as bright as highest heaven after the last trumpet sounds. Or He could have left it all a gray area where light and darkness both existed, but the difference was unknowable. Or He could have had both in the universe present and sharply divided. That would have been a binary universe with a Heaven and Hell switch.

God did not select any of those options. Instead, scripture tells us that He put a space between darkness and light. Here is how He made this world: Good and evil would both exist, but in this realm neither would be perfectly pure all the time. Our days would consist mostly of evenings and mornings. Either we are twisting away from the light, or we are experiencing the increasing illumination of the morning. One day we will pass beyond the other side of the veil, either into the eternal light of Day, or the unending darkness of the Night.

If one wishes to tie this into mere physical events then I would say that early in our planet's history there was a time when the Sun was just being birthed as a star, and the earth had barely coalesced as a planet. At that time, the sun would have been shrouded in a stellar nebula of the sort we can still detect astronomically around young stars today. Planets orbiting such stars are themselves still forming (hence, formless and void). It would have taken some time for the newly ignited sun to generate enough energy to begin giving off light. Look at a picture of the Orion Nebula, or any similar nebula which was left over from recent star formation, to get a feel for what I mean.

Imagine the sun and the earth inside a similar glowing nebula. From a position on the earth's surface at such a point in time, light would come into existence, without being divided into periods of light and darkness.

As time went on solar radiation would shake off the enshrouding nebula. At this point day and night would be distinct from one another. Earth would have "evenings and mornings", both days and nights. They would be separated by spaces we call "evening" and "morning". That is not to say the skies would have been clear as they are today. The early atmosphere of earth was still quite different from our present version. The sun and moon and stars would not necessarily be visible as distinct objects until more had been accomplished in the skies of our world.

The atmosphere of earth would have been thick, more like that of Neptune today. Astrophysicists believe that all the inner planets of our solar system once had thick atmospheres like those of the outer planets. We lost our thick atmospheres due to a combination of factors, not the least of which is our closeness to the sun's rays. The lightest gases were driven away by the strength of solar radiation.

Like many clever lyricists, creation is using a double meaning and a play on words. Both the natural and supernatural meanings are true. The end of the physical process on the earth mirrored what was happening spiritually in the universe due to the interjection of God's Word: a space or separation was being made in the physical universe between darkness and light. The end result of the first day of creation was this separation.

It's not saying that it happened in a literal twenty-four-hour day, nor is it ruling that out. It is making no statement at all about the human time it took. It is saying that the material outcome of the first Day of Creation mirrored the spiritual outcome. In the physical earth, evenings and mornings came to be. In the moral universe, our days on earth are composed of evenings and mornings. We have not fully come into the perfect light of

Day in heaven nor entered the eternal darkness of Night in Hell. Our days are evenings and mornings. We are either increasingly headed for the light, or increasingly descending into darkness.

The second Day of Creation is also a day of separation. In this case God separated the waters by making a firmament. This put a space between the waters which were above from those which were below the firmament, thus separating the two bodies of water.

This passage has led to a lot of misunderstandings. One reason for this is that the ancient Hebrews, like the Greeks, viewed the top of the expanse of the firmament as being a solid dome, perhaps of clear metal or crystal, with more waters on the top side of the barrier. This has led critics to dismiss the text as the myths of an ignorant group of ancient tribes.

Their confusion comes in part from a failure to understand that in the first three days of separation creation is primarily speaking about what happened in moral and spiritual reality and is describing events in the physical side of things only secondarily. What is happening in the physical universe during the whole creation week is merely a shadow or a reflection of what is happening in that deeper part of nature which in our present primitive state of understanding we refer to as "the supernatural realm."

We think of this world as what is "real" and the spiritual realm as insubstantial. The prophets saw it as the opposite- In Second Kings 6:13-17 Elisha prayed that God would "open the eyes" of his servant that he might see the forces of the spiritual realm. He spoke as if those who only saw things in this realm could not see what was most real.

As we proceed, I am going to build the case that what is in high heaven is the archetype, and what is on earth (or the physical cosmos) is the type. A shadow, reflection, or hologram of a solid barrier is not solid. We exist in the hologram or shadow, but the reality which cast the shadow is of substance even if the shadow itself is not. Indeed, the clearest place this "firmament" is described in scripture is not in Genesis at all, but rather in a vision of the heavenly realm as recorded in Ezekiel chapter one and again in 10:2. *There* the firmament is explicitly described as a solid, with the Throne of the LORD atop it.

I will go in reverse order here as compared to day one and describe what I think happened in the visible world. To put it simply, God was establishing what we know today as the "water cycle." Prior to this point we had much water, no cycle. The early earth was a hotter and wetter place than the one we know today. Scientists have told us that Mars had significant amounts of water in its distant past and have speculated the same for Venus. Today both are dry. If they had abundant water in the past, it evaporated and was lost into space. On earth, the process of water escaping into space was arrested. A functioning and stable water cycle was established.

I am going through a lot of science fast here but imagine early earth just as you might see it portrayed on a nature channel broadcast. It's the standard picture of a planet shrouded in clouds, with steam rising everywhere from a hot surface. In many spots, lava flows as vents spew out molten rock and ever more water vapor. Crust sinks and rises with no build-up, and therefore no mountain ranges. If there was any rain, the heat emanating from the surface would evaporate it before it ever got near the ground. Isn't that about right?

Now consider Genesis 2:4-6, which is the *towledah* for the chapter one material:

These are the generations of the heavens and of the earth when they were created, in the day that the LORD God made the earth and the heavens, And every plant of the field before it was in the earth, and every herb of the field before it grew: for the LORD God had not caused it to rain upon the earth, and there was not a man to till the ground. But there went up a mist from the earth, and watered the whole face of the ground.

I have already said that this *toledoth* includes a summary of the previous chapter, with perhaps a bit of editorializing and a bridge to the material which follows. This summary is describing things on earth as they were before verse ten of chapter one, before a true water cycle is established and before dry land emerges. There were not even any plants or herbs in the ground (the vague wording does allow for them in the seas). There was no rain, but the whole ground was covered with water anyway. No dry land yet. All of this is a description of how things were before God started his interventions on the earth. Naturally, there were no people then either.

Those conditions described in 2:4-6 change in the latter part of chapter one. A true water cycle is established. Dry land emerges, and the earth brings forth vegetation. Then animals and people are made, but Adam doesn't repeat all that in his summary because it is supposed to be about what it was like *before* God started shaping and filling the land: like a teaser on the back of a novel. Then in verse seven he jumps back up to his worms-eye view of day six. He goes right to *his place* in the story of how people are made on day six. Some people look at verses five and six and go "Oh, it says there was no man so there must not have been anyone before Adam." Well, it says there were no plants in the earth at that point either, but we know from chapter one that they came along before people were created. The verses are just a recap of initial conditions before His interventions.

So, verses five and six of chapter two are not saying that there was no rain before the flood of Noah, or that there were no people before Adam. They are saying there was no rain, plants or people before God started his interventions on the earth in the account in chapter one.

Before He did, water went up but did not much come down. Earth was very wet, but it was drying out just as scientists think Mars and Venus dried out. If the process had not been arrested, it stands to reason that in time our world would have been as barren as those places are now. But what should impress the reader is how very similar this description is to what one might see watching a nature channel program on the same subject of conditions on the early earth.

Now one might quibble at the idea of the division of the waters above and those below because clouds today are such a very small proportion of the earth's water compared to her oceans. That is true today, but I don't think it reasonable to suppose this was the case at the time described in Genesis 1:6-8. I should think that cloud cover would be much greater. Not only would the early earth still have a much thicker atmosphere, but until plants became common that atmosphere would contain more CO2 than now.

This abundance would have caused earth to retain much more heat, and thus evaporate much more water into the air. In addition, the oceans would be much shallower because the crust of the earth would be "spread out" and not piled up into continents. The water would be distributed more evenly across this ground, and at this point a lot more of it was still trapped in the crust and had not yet been released via volcanism.

Perhaps you have seen how much faster the water in a puddle evaporates when the water in it is spread out? Between the increased greenhouse gases and all the factors listed above one could expect evaporation of water to have occurred at a very much higher rate. So much higher that an observer at the time could very well speak of the establishment of a functioning water cycle as "the separation of the waters that were below from those that were above."

Present day mockers might look at the sky and ask where the "waters above" are considering that the water in today's clouds is only a tiny fraction of those in the oceans. Those waters were thinned out by the work which occurred in the days which followed. Here the mocker's error is in presuming that today's skies represent the condition of earth's skies throughout her history. There is abundant scientific evidence that this has not been the case.

As God continued to make changes which affected the atmosphere, one might expect the proportion of waters "above" to decrease and those below to increase, but regardless of how the proportions changed later, the basics of what is being done- a separation of waters, remains the same.

Let us move onto the aspect of God's work in the unseen (by us) world on the second day. I have said that His work in the realm beyond is the type and what is happening in what we call the 'natural world' is a mere shadow of that. On the first day, He determined what the relationship between good and evil would be within this universe. It would be a mixture of Day and Night. Having made and executed that decision, God next dealt with the issue of how justice and judgement would be applied in the two realms. Very much related to this is what degree of connectedness there would be between them.

Water is a fundamental. It is one of the four classical elements. It flows. It connects. It sustains. And in scripture, it judges. It acts either to give life and make clean or to destroy and bring death. Water represents judgement. If you have one realm, heaven, where there is no darkness at all, and another realm, the natural universe, where there is both darkness and light, how does one mete out judgement in each realm?

The best of men might be worse than the worst of unfallen angels. Indeed, like the Pharisees, in terms of outward conduct even a fallen spirit might be better able to temporarily restrain their outward actions compared to humans burdened by the weakness of our flesh. Yet it would not be just to judge us, in this life at least, by the standards of those who live in the light of heaven. Nor would it be fair to judge them by our standards. They ought to do better than the best of us.

For minds restricted by modernist thinking, the issue of what degree of connection there will be in the natural world and the supernatural one is never considered because they have mental chains which restrict their thinking. They can only think in terms of "what is seen is all that there is." Broader minds consider the possibility that there could be more out there than what they can perceive with their own senses.

Indeed 2nd Corinthians 4:18 instructs us to focus on what is unseen rather than that which is seen, because what is seen is temporal, but the unseen is eternal. Hebrews 11:3 expresses the thought that what is seen is made from that which is invisible to us. The Hebrew belief was that many things on this earth were simply flawed copies of that which existed perfectly in the heavenly realm.

If there is a spiritual realm, a world normally unseen to those of us trapped in time, one of the first questions a Creator might consider is "what shall be the degree of connection or flow between the two realms?" What happened with earth's water parallels what the Creator did regarding this question of connectedness. And by "connectedness" I don't just mean physical access, but by being connected in terms of standards for justice and judgment. The two factors are strongly correlated. Heaven and the Lake of Fire for example, are most separate.

As with the question of the connectedness of darkness and light on the first day, the question of the connectedness of the heavenly realm and the earthly one had several possible answers. God could have decided that there would be no access between the two ever, or that there would be access always. The Creator could have decided that there would be no space between them and therefore no separation or barrier to access. That would have been unfortunate for us, because if there is no barrier to access then there is no room for a separate standard for justice or judgement.

This decision of access or connectedness must be made for every realm which is created. For example, in Luke 16:26, the story of Lazarus and the rich man, we see very similar language to that in Genesis chapter one in the sense of a space being placed between two things to keep them separate. In that passage the separation is between the abode of the unrighteous dead and that of the righteous dead. In the abode of the unrighteous dead, there is no water. I have a lot I could say about that regarding the nature of Hell but let me move on. Here is the verse:

"And beside all this, between us and you there is a great gulf fixed: so that they which would pass from hence to you cannot; neither can they pass to us, that would come from thence."

The wording about the "great gulf" cannot help but remind one of *bayin*, the space put between the darkness and the light on the first day, and the space placed between the upper and the lower waters described on the second day. On the second day God was establishing what sort of access/standard for judgement there would be between heaven and earth.

Regarding those two realms in Luke 16:26, God made a separation, and it was an impassable one. What He decided in the case of heaven and earth was that there would be a separation, but not an unpassable one. Not an impermeable one. Moving between them would be easy for those above but difficult for those from below.

This separation in geography and space was a secondary effect of what was really happening here- a separation in standards for judgement. **In scripture, water is connected to judgement.** This is shown in the flood of Noah's day, where Adam's seed was judged. It is true in the crossing of the Red Sea, whereby Pharaoh's army was judged. The prophet Jonah was cast into the sea to calm the waters troubled by his disobedience. If you are found innocent, the water represents a cleansing judgement. This is true for each of us, where the water of baptism represents God's judgements purifying our souls in repentance. For churches which practice full immersion the entry of the body under the water represents death and burial.

The emergence from the water in baptism represents new life. It is identifying with the death, burial, and resurrection of Christ. Either way, whether water is washing away what is dirty, or representing the death of those who were disobedient, water represents judgement whether for good or ill. Much like water in the physical world, His judgements are wonderful if you are His, and terrible if they are against you. The Holy Spirit was called "Living Water" in the seventh chapter of John and is another form of judgement for the world (John 16:8-11), an internal one.

That the waters above were separated from the ones below is a description of how God's standards for judgement were going to be, for a time, different on earth than in the heavens. He does not tolerate up there what He allows down here. For a time, until the end of the age, He has established a lower standard for judgement than that which prevails above.

It is well for us that He did so, lest all of us share the fate of the Devil and his angels. In the age to come this separation between the waters will be abolished. By His Mercy we have a temporary ability to remain unjudged according to His Perfect will until such time as we may ourselves come to embrace it. Don't worry. His Perfect Will is not to do a bunch of religious acts. It is to believe on The One whom He has sent!

This condition will persist until the last trumpet blows. Revelation 21:1 says that "there was no longer any sea" on the new earth. Instead, according to Revelation 22, a crystal-clear river shall flow from the Throne of God to water the Tree of Life. The clarity of the waters indicates that we shall understand His judgements whereas here they are beyond our understanding. Instead of being deep seas which can rage and bring death, His judgements are as a river which provides sustenance to the Tree of Life-that Tree through which the nations are healed.

In the new heaven and the new earth there is no more separation between the two realms, physically or in terms of cleansing. It is written (Rev. 21:3) "the abode of God is with men." After the Great White Throne of Judgement in the New Jerusalem His judgements are no longer harmful for God's children, and thus at last "there was no longer any sea".

The separation of judgements is necessary to display God's mercy, of which even the best of us are in dire need. But His first choice would be to not have to display mercy because we do not sin against Him, each other, or ourselves. His division of the waters represents a temporary necessity, not a desired outcome. This produces an enigma in the text.

The second day is the only day of creation in which it is not said that God found something to be good. On the first day He at least saw that the light was good. On days three through six He found all that was done to be good. But on this day alone, nothing is said to be good. Men have argued for centuries as to why. Now you know. Here He subjected creation to futility, in the hope that He can uplift it later (Romans 8:20). Here He divides only in the hope that the division will one day be removed. This is the day of necessary evil. This is the burial before the resurrection.

Notice that the first three days are days of separation. God makes light, then divides day from night. God makes a firmament which divides the waters below from those above. On the third day land is separated from the waters and becomes dry. These are the three days of separations.

The Third Day

⟶⟶⟶⟶◉⟵⟵⟵

On the third day, the seas are separated from the land. I am using "land" instead of earth here, because the Hebrew term used, "erets", refers to land and not necessarily the whole earth. God is making *erets*, or the land, in the supernatural realm and the natural realm at the same time. He is making the Promised Land in heaven and the Promised Land on earth at the same time. The Promised Land of Israel is a foreshadowing of the true Promised Land above.

Just as the waters are connected to judgement in scripture, so dry land is connected to deliverance from judgement. Noah finally found deliverance from the flood waters when dry land appeared. The children of Israel found deliverance from the Egyptian army when they walked across dry land on the bottom of the Red Sea. But the land did not remain dry for that army, for they were judged by the waters rather than delivered by the dry ground. The prophet Jonah cried for deliverance from the belly of the whale and was coughed up on dry land. The very term "Promised Land" connects the land to deliverance from our alien condition. The dry land is associated with deliverance.

The analogies and parallels line right up. But the greatest of them is this: Adam was formed from the *dust* of the earth (Hebrew word *aphar*). That is, The Man was made from the dry ground. Therefore, the Son of Man is also of the dry ground (as well as of heaven). Christ is the Dry Land rising up from the waters of God's judgement. Even as Christ descended into Hades and suffered judgement on our behalf, and was raised again on the third day, so it was that on Creation's third day the dry land was raised up from the depths of the seas. And it was God's doing. Out of the midst of God's judgement, comes deliverance. And God Himself is that deliverance!

The picture of the land rising up out of the waters on Creation's third day is a picture of Christ's resurrection from the dead on the third day. The dry land is associated with deliverance. The events of the third day are the foreshadowing of the reality found in the work of Christ. The first day of creation is a picture of Christ as the Word. The third day of creation is a picture of Christ as resurrected savior.

Of course the third day of creation is a picture of His resurrection on the third day. *Of course* it is about the resurrection. How can "the third day" not be about Christ and His resurrection? Is God so poor an artist as to miss a chance to connect that? All the scripture, from start to end, is about Christ and His finished work.

I don't know whether creation "knew" about God's plan for the redemption of mankind. I believe that what creation was doing in this song, or poem, was just what it did in the first two days. It was tying what was happening in the natural realm with what God was doing in what we presently consider the "supernatural realm." Yet you will see as we read on that this account is both history and prophecy.

In this case, God was establishing what the relationship would be within creation between judgement (waters) and deliverance (land). Without His intervention, there would be neither judgment nor deliverance- neither deep seas nor dry land. Moral outcomes would instead exist in a grey area. The design question was whether creation would be a realm that, for as long as it existed, had no special Divine deliverances, nor specific Divine judgements? Or would it be a place where God would, in ways and at times known to Him, intervene in the natural order of things to deliver one and to judge another? Here creation tells us that God chose the latter.

Though the world we have seems wicked enough, and chaotic enough, had God not chosen to do so then the world would have been much more chaotic than it is. Everything regarding deliverance and judgement would be more muddled than we now see it. The most important thing about this decision though, is what follows: He built the natural universe so that Divine Deliverance and Judgement could operate within it, not sealed off from that which exists in the higher realms. It is this design which allowed His Son to bear the Judgement in this realm which permitted our deliverance in the next.

The realms are separate on the third day, so once God calls for Deliverance (the dry land) to come out of Judgment (the waters) we begin to have a natural creation which helps God fulfill His Word. Until then, God did all the heavy lifting. On days one and two it was God who divided and made the firmament. God worked on Creation in days one and two, but Creation is not helping. On day two it does not say "and it was so" until after God did the work. Starting on day three, creation helps fulfill God's commands- *the earth* brings forth vegetation. The Land Above does so instantly and perfectly and says, "and it was so", the Land Below does so slowly and imperfectly but at least can report "*God saw that it was good*".

I know that there is a doctrine in many circles which says that since God "saw that X was good" then this creation must have been in an unfallen state. A closer examination of the actual Hebrew word used for "good" in these verses shows that this doctrine is untrue. The same word is used in Genesis 6:2 when it says that the sons of *Elohim* saw that the daughters of men were "fair". I think a lot of the women in my family. I think they are "fair" and "good" too, but I do not think that they are in a state of sinless perfection. Nor is God saying so in Genesis chapter one when creation says, "God saw that it was good."

The word is better translated "suitable" or "attractive." Sinless perfection is better represented by another Hebrew word. I will get into this in more detail when I address the subject of the initial state of creation before the fall of Adam.

The bottom line is that it is the supernatural realm which responds to God's command by saying "and it was so". The natural realm responds by saying "and God saw that it was good." In the one realm, reality conforms to His command instantly and completely. Exactly what He says happens. In our realm nature responds, but it's a process, and this nature does not claim that the process produces exact compliance with God's word, but rather a suitable copy of it. Super-Nature up there says "it was so". Nature down here says "God saw that it was good." It was a suitable and attractive copy of what is up there, or at least the process of becoming so is on the right track.

In the natural realm His word of light meets resistance from the darkness of that which is not filled with His word. That is why we are to pray "Thy will be done, on earth as it is in heaven." That is, completely and at once. After this separation of the two realms, The Land in heaven above and The Land on earth below, things no longer occur in a synchronous fashion.

When God commands that the land bring forth vegetation verse eleven immediately afterward says "it was so", but then verse twelve subsequently describes the land bringing forth plants by a process. One can tell by the Hebrew grammar that this process is subsequent to the events of verse eleven. This resetting of the time frame is often indicated by starting a sentence off with "And", as in "And the earth brought forth...."

What is going on here? The answer is that now that a time divergence has begun creation is telling the story from two temporal perspectives. Now that the supernatural realm (the third heaven or High Heaven) has been separated from the natural world things happen at different rates. In High Heaven God's word to "The Land" is fulfilled completely and at once. That is why High Heaven says "it was so" as soon as the command from God goes out.

The Land in the natural realm gives a different answer. It responds with a more drawn-out process. Then, instead of "it was so" which the higher creation can report, the lower creation says of the process that "God saw that it was good." If you go back to the chapter showing the structure of Genesis, you will see the same pattern shows up on day four and day six.

After the emergence of the dry land on the third day, Creation begins helping execute God's plan. Notice in the last part of day three that God does not bring forth the plants. He says let *the Earth* do so, and it does so. Until God completed the work of deliverance by bringing forth the dry from the waters, creation could not respond to His Word as it ought. Once He did the three days of work which culminated in the emergence of the land from the sea, then creation could begin to help Him in His work effectively. In the same way, the religious acts which we do before we have been delivered by Christ are not helping God. The rising of the dry land from the waters parallels what happened with Christ- deliverance came out of judgment.

Christ is our Promised Land who rose on the third day. Our fruitfulness and good works are in Him, just as that of those plants is in the earth. So, the earth did bring forth fruit "on its own" but only after the raising of the land permitted it, just as His raising permitted ours. Our fruitfulness is "in Him."

This leaves me with nothing else to say about this day except tying the words of Creation concerning the third day to events in the mere physical universe. They fit quite well with much of what modern science tells us. First, let us consider the construction of the world as it now is: The current configuration of the surface of our planet is a relatively thin layer of solid crust over its inner more viscous layers.

The crust itself is divided into two basic forms. There is a layer of denser rock, primarily basalts, over the entire globe. This is often called "oceanic crust" because we find it at the bottom of the sea floor, but we believe it is beneath continents as well. Piled up in a few locations on top of this are "bumps" of the less dense rock granite. These chips or lumps of granite which are "floating" over the denser oceanic crust form the cores of the seven continents. Hence, they are sometimes called "continental crust".

Genesis chapter one, Genesis 2:6, and modern science all inform us that the earth did not begin in this condition. They all speak to a time when there were neither continents nor great oceans. As I mentioned concerning the previous creation day, the land was more spread out. The vast stores of granite and basalt were melting and re-solidifying and had not yet separated out. Nor had the vast stores of water in the earth separated out from the rocks and the interior to the extent they have today (there is still a lot of water under the subduction zones of the earth's crust). The earth was much hotter in its interior as compared to today. The heat led to a much higher rate of volcanism than we see today. Water vapor was constantly outgassed by this process.

Genesis 2:6 describes this time before God established a water cycle (day two) and before God established definite seas and dry land (day three) by saying "there went up a mist from the earth and watered the whole face of the ground." This then was the condition of the early earth before God's intervention. After the third day, this was no longer the condition of the earth. Scientists refer to the emergence of the dry land as the building up of earth's continental crust. Either way you describe it, it's the same event.

A Problem with the Order in Which Living Things Appear.

Creation describes seed plants, and even fruiting seed plants, as coming before the day in which God makes ocean creatures and winged creatures. They come on day three and the others come on day five. For those who hold to 24-hour solar days, this poses no problem. If one thinks there are ages of time in each of the days, then it appears that we have fruit trees around for a long time with nothing around to eat the fruit!

The fossil record indicates that flowering seed plants, such as fruit trees, appeared in the middle of the Mesozoic Era and did not really dominate until the Cretaceous, long after both land and sea were filled with creatures. On the other hand, lichens were present, maybe even dominant, long before the Cambrian Explosion (which has been connected to the fifth day by Old Earth Creationists). Further, a 2009 study from L. Paul Knauth and Martin J. Kennedy entitled "The late Precambrian greening of the Earth" concludes land plants were around 850 million years ago.

It looks like the emergence of vegetation is in "slow motion" compared to life on the seas and land. It started before those other events, but didn't really unfold until after them. The command given the third day is not fully executed on earth until much later. This is in spite of the fact that Whole Genome Duplication, a powerful driver of evolution, works far better in plants. Is there any textual explanation for this incongruity?

There is. On the succeeding days God Himself *helps* His creation accomplish His commands. On day three, He simply commands and *the earth* does the work. The less God helps, the slower and more convoluted the work goes. This fits what I have said about this natural universe.

Imagine you are in creation's position. The angels themselves are but children next to you. For vast ages creatures of every sort have lived on the earth. They have come, and they have gone. Then you are presented with The Man, created in the image of your Creator. And The Man asks you a question.

If the question is "Can you tell me all of the things that God has done in you and with you?" then Adam may have gotten quite a long answer. If that is the question perhaps you should spend some time mentioning the trilobites and the ammonites and the cynodonts and all the living creatures which came and went before The Man was ever formed. The first chapter of Genesis would surely be much longer were that the question.

But if The Man asked Creation "How did all this I see come to be?" then this different question is most suitably addressed by a different answer. With respect to the order of things, in heaven it is clear, for when God spoke heaven responded immediately. Down here everything is more muddled, including the order of things.

If Adam only asks about creation from the perspective of his present time it simplifies the problem. When it comes to living things, you can leave out the losers. You can simply state in what order the living things The Man sees around him came to be, without getting bogged down in telling the story of the vast myriad of living creatures which are no longer around and not relevant to the question being asked.

So yes, if the question is "How did all this I see come to be?", then the plants came first. We don't know exactly when they first came forth. But we do know that with rare and minor exceptions, plants with seeds and trees which bore fruit were around at least before the animal life that we know today, or that Adam would have known in His time.

In the same way, birds are ancient. Many feel that they are the only surviving group of dinosaurs. Researcher Gregory S. Paul, who has named or helped name eight dinosaur species, has even proposed that certain theropod dinosaurs evolved from birds rather than the other way around. They started as winging creatures, but later lost the power of flight. Let's say that's true, and that dinosaurs, as wondrous as they were, were but a dead end. The real 'point' of this category was birds. Then wouldn't it be fitting to mention birds after sea creatures but before the land animals Adam sees about him, which were predominantly placental mammals?

This is besides the neat literary symmetry noted by others that the separation of the waters into those above and those below on the second day compliments the filling of the seas and sky on the fifth day.

You may think I am cheating by saying that creation was speaking of plants by categories, but animals by those specific creatures alive at the time of Adam. To assuage those concerns let's skip ahead a bit and notice that in verse twenty-one it says that on the fifth day God created "every living creature that *moveth*" in the waters.

Hebrew does not have tenses the way English does, but to the degree it does it is referring to living things which are moving at the time the account is being told. Not "every living creature that move**d**" in the seas, but "every living creature that **moves**" in the seas. Regarding animals, Creation was not making a statement about what was created before and had perished, but rather what was extant in the age in which Adam lived.

Without being "anti-evolution", I am pro-creation. Genesis One speaks of a God who intervenes in His creation. He did not just make it and watch it unwind. It describes how at key points He stepped in to direct and reverse the unwinding. Therefore, the more Deistic forms of what some call

"Theistic Evolution" cannot be the explanation for the world's life. That is, the idea that God just made the universe to unfold the way it did, and that once He set initial conditions things would unfold in a way which culminated in the life we now see even without His further direction.

I don't doubt that there is some genetic adaptability built into living creatures as part of the genius of their design. *The earth* after all is tasked with bringing forth living creatures. But Genesis tells us that this cannot be the whole story. Indeed, the recurring theme of the account is that this universe cannot and was not even designed to work "right" without God's continued intervention and care. We may or may not be able to detect His intervention in Nature, but at some points at least, He did so.

That being said, if ever there was a day and an area of creation in which earth responded without His further intervention it was within this third day. God commanded *the land* to bring forth vegetation (the "grass" in the King James is misleading) and seed plants and plants which bear fruit. The earth then did so without it being recorded that God did anything to help the earth do it.

What I am getting at is that plants seem to be more likely candidates for the more naturalistic versions of "Theistic Evolution" than creatures of the sea or land, or certainly Mankind itself. God simply produced the initial conditions in which plants could thrive and then commanded that the earth produce plants. Then they did so without further intervention from Him. That sounds a lot like God simply got things set up right and let the creation itself handle things.

Not only that, the Earth could have continued this process and be continuing it today. God did not need to directly do anything else in order for the Earth to bring forth such plants. He never told the earth to stop bringing forth plants. So, it is reasonable to suppose that the earth continued to bring forth different seed plants and fruit plants on days four, five, and six- and that it is still doing so today.

When did this first happen? In the higher realm it happened as soon as God spoke the words. In this realm it was a process. The first plants are extremely ancient. The first seed plants originate from what is called the Cambrian-Triassic boundary. Conifers, Gingkoes, and Cycads were among the earliest fruit bearing plants, and they are still with us today. They are called "false fruit", but it is still fruit, it just doesn't swell from the base of a flower as most common fruit does today. They were all well established by the Jurassic. Later, but still many millions of years ago, the plants we know today appeared and soon dominated the landscape.

That was the physical manifestation and conclusion of the three days of separation, but the spiritual manifestations are the archetypes of those things. In summary, they are as follows: On day one, God determined what the relationship between Good (light) and Evil (darkness) would be in His creation. That condition is one of light in the High Heaven, but for the rest of creation a division of light and darkness, but with both light and darkness leaking into that separation.

On the second day He determined that there would be a separation between the judgements that were above, and the judgements that were below. Heaven and earth would not be held to the same standard in this age. On the third day, He began executing His judgements (seas of water). But in the midst of His judgements, He also revealed His deliverance (dry land). His judgements and His deliverance were just what the natural realm needed to be brought to the place where it could "be fruitful" and assist Him in His work. From that point on, it does so.

The days of separation were also days of "calling". On the first three days of creation, it is written that God "called" things by various names. The meaning of the word for "called" has connotations of making a proclamation or reading from an official document. The term is not used again after the third day.

This implies that God had written words- words which were inscribed somewhere before God spoke them. Perhaps they were inscribed on creation itself, perhaps as some of the Jews say, there is the true Torah in heaven and the ones we have on earth are just shadows of it. Regardless, the letters were dead before God spoke them and became living reality once He did. As He uttered a proclamation, it became so.

The Fourth Day and Time

We begin the three days of "fillings" with day four. But prior to my writing about what that day means for creation, I should write about what it means regarding the subject of the length of "days" in Genesis chapter one. Though I have previously written about it, this has been a matter of some controversy within the church. Therefore, I feel I must discuss it thoroughly.

By now I hope you can see that the answer involves a matter of perspective. The days are workdays, and the amount of time involved with getting the job done depends on where one is standing. In the High Heaven, the work of each day was over shortly after it began. In the natural realm, we lollygag in our mixture of darkness and light.

Some might question the appearance of darkness before the fall of Adam as having any spiritual dimension. This pertains to the issue of whether sin and death existed before the fall of Adam. I ask that you remain patient on that score, and I will address the matter at length. For now, let's delve into what the fourth day can tell us about the length of days on earth during the Creation week. Then we will finish out the week, and then at last come to the problem of sin and death before the fall of Adam.

Some Christians think that God does not begin to use figurative language in Genesis until chapter two. For example, in verse seventeen He tells Adam not to eat of the fruit of the tree of the knowledge of good and evil "for in the *day* that you eat of it you shall surely *die*." The word for "day" in this verse is the same as that for "day" in chapter one, yet after Adam ate the fruit of the tree, he lived physically for over 800 more years. There-fore at least one of the two words I italicized in the quote of scripture above must be in some manner figurative language.

One may argue that Adam died *spiritually* that same 24-hour day, and that when early Genesis speaks of "death" it means separation from God. I agree, but in such a case instead of "day" being used in a sense outside of how we literally use the word, it must be that "die" is used outside the sense in which we literally use the word. Either way "non-literal" language, at least outside our normal use of words, was used.

My own view is that both words were used literally, and both words were used figuratively. Adam figuratively died (was separated from God) the same literal day He took the fruit. Adam literally died in the same figura-tive day he took the fruit.

Notice that the "literal" meaning of words is not necessarily the deepest or truest sense of the word. For example, what we normally consider literal death is not as real as the "figurative" death of separation from God. The one who dies a "literal" death, yet is connected to God, lives even though they die. The one disconnected from God is dead even while they live. Because this natural universe is not all that there is, words which describe things in it can have a deeper and truer meaning when used figuratively to describe spiritual events and principles which are beyond it. We need to change our perspective of what is most real!

I would also add that in chapter three where scripture speaks of the "ser-pent" in the Garden it is commonly understood to be the Devil. The Devil is identified with the serpent in Revelation. It is commonly accepted by Christians that God used figurative language in Genesis, at least by chapter three. Other Christians think that figurative language (to describe real events, and not just as allegory) was also used in Genesis chapter one. I am of this latter view, except of course I think what is "figurative" to us can be more real than mere physical reality. As we shall see, when the word of God defines "light" as something that is a consequence of God speaking, that light is more real than the light of the sun. The sun is a figure of it!

The rest of scripture basically mandates this approach as it applies to the seventh day. Please go back and read the chapter on that subject if you do not recall what I mean.

But even within the text of Genesis chapter one there is contextual proof that these "days" are not solar human days. Consider what is said about the fourth day. There we see that God did not even establish 24-hour solar days for the purpose of tracking time until then. We note from verse fourteen of chapter one that God does not declare the sun, moon, and stars to be given for times, days, and seasons until then. Here is the verse:

And God said, Let there be lights in the firmament of the heaven to divide the day from the night; and let them be for signs, and for seasons, and for days, and years:

Since God does not give the Sun and the moon and stars for the purposes of keeping days until the fourth "day", who are we as mere men to declare Him in error and say that these "days" are the same as solar days from "day" one? "Young Earth" creationists are trying to use solar days to track time before God even established solar days to track time! It would be like interpreting a contract that said "You own land equal to ten units of measure square" by assuming that the "measure" was a meter even if the contract was written before the metric system was established!

If we are looking for more "context" to determine whether to interpret the language ("day", "evening", "morning") as earth days or as something else, then if verse five wasn't enough verse fourteen ought to be. The Logos is the true light and the sun but a mere figure of this Light. We ought not expect Creation's days to be bound by the length of solar days any more than we would expect our solar days to be bound by the rotation of a model of the Sun-Moon-earth system that sits in some junior high classroom.

Creation-Evolution Wars

─⊰✦⊱─

When people read the title "Creation-Evolution Wars", most of them will recognize at once just what I mean. At the same time, almost all Christians, creationist or not, accept that some evolution has occurred and is occurring. Even many "young earth" creationists think that the creatures on the ark rapidly diversified into a variety of forms after the flood. "Evolution" is not the opposite of Creationism. *Naturalism,* the idea that nature alone (without any help from God) can pull itself up by its own bootstraps, is the opposite of Creationism.

Naturalism is the belief or philosophy that nature is all that there is and all that there needs to be to explain what we see. Creationism is a subset of Theism as it applies to creation. It is the belief that the universe and everything in it is the product of a Creator who intervenes to work on His creation even after the initial creation event. Another position, I'll call it Deistic Evolution, is the belief that God created the universe to wind up a certain way and did not intervene after the initial creation of the cosmos.

I think naturalists have very cleverly shifted the argument from an indefensible position- the assertion that the natural universe is all that there is – to one which gives them some wiggle room. The argument that the Cosmos and the richness of life on earth came to be without help from a creator is an extreme position that we almost certainly don't have the means to really test, especially scientifically. To the extent we do I find it grossly implausible. But they have interposed "evolution" in front of their real position so thoroughly that most of us believe that the conflict is between creation and evolution. That's mostly not true.

The conflict really ought to be called the "Creationism-Naturalism Wars" – ism vs. ism. It is a battle of one philosophy against another. Evolution is just the battleground on which much of the war is being fought. The Naturalists are adamantly insisting that natural forces alone can produce all the diversity of life we see, and Creationists are saying that Creation must have had help. It couldn't do all this on its own. Naturalists cling to evolution not because it is the philosophical opposite of creationism, but because it's the only answer they have to their actual opponent- Creationism.

Some skeptics may cry "God of the Gaps" when I mention nature having had help. This is another rhetorical trick. Christians aren't saying that God found a ready-made universe complete with natural laws and decided to intervene in it from time to time. Our position is that He is God of *both* the laws and the gaps. "God of the gaps" is an argument for God's existence which says that gaps in scientific knowledge can be evidence of supernatural action as an explanation for events in the natural world. Should an argument for God's existence be dismissed because it is a "God of the gaps" argument? No. There are good and bad arguments in this category. Each case should be evaluated on its own merits.

Consider what would happen if Jesus appeared at a wedding feast today and repeated the miracle of making water into wine under similar conditions. I propose to you that Jesus turned the water into wine by using supernatural power and this is evidence for the existence of God. This would be a "God of the gaps" claim. That is, there is no reasonable natural explanation for how the water became wine, and I am using the absence of such an explanation to support my argument that it is a supernatural act, indicating that God exists. There is no doubt that I am making a "God of the Gaps" argument, but I hope you would agree that in this instance my argument is sound whether it is a "God of the gaps" argument or not.

Science operates using methodological naturalism. That is, it is a search for natural causes only. It can never prove an action had a supernatural cause. It isn't even designed to do so. In that sense, science couldn't detect God if God were standing right in front of it! It assumes all causes are natural in an effort to find natural causes. So even here, when Jesus performs a genuine miracle right in front of you and others, there is no scientific way to prove it was a result of supernatural action. The very best science can do is say "we currently have no natural explanation, but we will keep looking." In other words, it becomes a "gap in scientific knowledge".

I hope the reader will see that if "god of the gaps" arguments were *always* invalid, then no evidence for miracles from the natural universe, even overwhelming and direct evidence, can ever be considered valid. It is a backdoor way of imposing not just methodological naturalism but philosophical naturalism (an *a priori* assumption that nature is all that there is).

This argument in effect imposes philosophical naturalism on all evidence from nature, since any appeals to "gaps" in science's knowledge is a "god of the gaps" argument and is dismissed. This is begging the question in the extreme. If you will only accept scientific evidence for supernatural actions, and science can't by definition show that any act has a supernatural cause, that's checkmate. The reasoning is circular. The only honest way to consider the subject is to admit that there is more than one possible reason for a "gap in scientific knowledge" to exist. One possibility is that there is a natural cause and we just haven't found it yet. This will ordinarily be the case. Another possible reason is that there *is no* natural cause. It was the result of a supernatural act.

If you assume all actions have natural causes period, then you are a philosophical naturalist. You can't consider the evidence of supernatural action fairly because your assumptions about reality don't permit you to. You can't prove the assumption but you are imposing it on the evidence.

What about the fact that history shows natural causes displaced proposed supernatural ones with clock-like regularity as our knowledge grew? It is true that at the beginning of the age of science there was a series of phenomena that were often attributed to supernatural acts that were later shown by experiment to simply be nature operating according to regular laws. This is a strong argument against divine action as a cause- but only regarding questions where our scientific knowledge is scant. At the beginning of the age of science, that was almost everything. That's why the history is so one-sided. At the start of the age of science, very little was attributed to natural law and much to direct divine action. We are now reaching the point where the pendulum begins to swing the other direction. That is, there are some subjects where our knowledge is increasing, but the proposed natural explanations grow less likely with our increase in knowledge, not more likely.

The more we know about something, the more likely a natural explanation for it should become. At some point, when reasonable natural explanations are lacking even though we have accumulated great knowledge of the thing in question, the "God of the Gaps" argument becomes reasonable. So, it is a poor argument in an area where we know little but can be a sound one with reference to certain scientific anomalies. Especially if the findings which defy natural explanation line up with the character of God and scripture.

That understood, let's discuss the "wars". There is a great deal of overlap between creationism and some versions of evolution. Despite all the shouting, there are gray areas between creationism, "Intelligent Design" and Evolution. One could in fact be an "Evolutionary Creationist" of some sort. If such a position involved God intervening to guide evolution, then naturalists would oppose this position just as much as they oppose the idea that all species on earth were produced by God fashioning them out of clay. There are no gray areas between naturalism and creationism, but there are between creationism and evolution.

In the chapters to come I am going to make the case that Genesis chapter two is describing a very important smaller and more limited work of God within the much larger work of creation described in chapter one. That is, chapter two "zooms in" and describes in detail a special event which is necessarily only very briefly touched on in chapter one.

Chapter one is the story of the whole of creation from the beginning of time until the end of the age. Chapter two is telling the story of what happened in the Garden of Eden not too many thousands of years ago in a brief period. It is the story of a new work within creation which God intended to use to redeem and reconcile creation to Himself. Creation began as a place where the Word of God wasn't, even if framed by His Word.

That the account of Adam and the animals fashioned for him is a discrete event within the larger story of creation raises some interesting possibilities. One of them is regarding the extent that what we might think of as "evolution" is responsible for life on earth.

This is a very touchy subject for a lot of people on both sides of the issue, and I understand that what I have to say about the text in this chapter and those beyond it will probably make both sides unhappy at first. "Compromise" is seen as evil and anathema to both sides. I think compromise *can be* evil- when the truth is what is being compromised. I reject compromise at the expense of truth as much as anyone. But I also reject rigidity at the expense of truth. In this case, the truth is that the text of early Genesis takes a much more complicated and nuanced position than either of the extremes in this discussion advocate.

For example, the account in chapter two is clearly describing a situation where both Adam and the animals of the garden are specially formed. This is what we would consider the most direct form of "special creation". But in the Christ-Centered model, this isn't the whole creation. It's a new work within a small portion of it. It is that mustard seed destined to grow and provide a home for many. It is a shadow of the remaking of the world which comes after we are born again through the sacrifice of Christ.

The text gives us much less detail as to how the original creation was fashioned. And what little information it does give could best be described as a synthesis of creation and evolution, as well as a spectrum of Divine intervention. Regarding vegetation, God just holds back the futility and chaos of creation to let the land to bring forth plants. The land then does so without any further action by God. At that point it almost sounds like deistic evolution. Regarding animals, the waters and the land obey God's command to bring forth living creatures but only with God's help. He must also create and make them. Regarding humanity, God may have *used* earth, but He did the creative work Himself.

Earlier I talked about gray areas between evolution, creationism, and intelligent design. "Descent with modification" is a standard accepted definition of evolution. But it could also be a form of creationism or at least intelligent design, depending on how the "modifications" occur. For example, farmers breed animals for certain traits and get them through descent with modification. They select far more powerfully for desired traits than nature does. So that fits this definition of evolution, *and* intelligent design.

Let's have a thought experiment: Suppose instead of farmers who went around selecting for traits, God Himself did so. If a certain group of animals had a rare mutation that could produce a benefit if paired with another rare mutation which existed only in a second isolated group, then He would know it. He would be able to put those two populations together so that they would have the suite of mutations that, when combined with yet another rare mutation that He knew would occur four generations later, would result in a new function.

In this scenario the Intelligent Designer is using Divine knowledge to leverage natural processes to produce something new. I would say that is evolution (descent through modification), intelligent design (intent drives the changes not natural selection) and "soft" creationism. By that last term I mean that God intervened in the natural world to produce outcomes even if He never touched the genomes directly. He merely guided natural events to produce outcomes that nature herself would not have, either at all or at anything like the same rate.

Now suppose that instead of taking the role of a selective breeder (with perfect knowledge) only, He also assumed the role of Genetic Engineer. Instead of just waiting for Nature to come up with mutations which could be combined to create new function, He did just what our genetic engineers do, though far more elegantly. He made changes in genetic code.

Maybe nature alone would never have gotten a certain protein to fold just right by waiting for chance to make the proper mutation. Maybe the species would have died out before the right changes happened along to allow them to become something else. If our scientists can do such things now, couldn't God Himself have fashioned the right genes at the right time, to help the earth along as it tried to obey God's command?

Scientists have made mice which glow because jellyfish genes have been inserted in them. When this population breeds is this "descent with modification"? It is, and thus meets a generally accepted definition of "evolution". But the modification did not come wholly by "natural" descent. It is doubtless also intelligent design and special creation- as well as, by this definition, "evolution".

That said, such a situation could still *involve* natural descent, but that would not be where the key modification would come from. Take the gap between a fish and an amphibian. What if over the course of thirty or forty generations, God acted to put just enough changes in each generation so that they would still be able to be birthed and bred by natural means, but each generation would also be further toward the amphibian? This so that even though no amphibian was created out of thin air, one still had a very different creature though only forty generations removed from the fish.

That result would be due to "genetic engineering" moving things a bit further along each generation. That is "descent with modification" but the modification that matters was via genetic engineering. Is that evolution, special creation and intelligent design all rolled up into one? So long as you are not a naturalist, it is all three rolled up into one. Naturalism can't accept the idea that the changes came from anything but chance and the natural environment.

Now I have used the analogy of God acting as a "Genetic Engineer", but it is not necessary to assume that He required any lab coats or test tubes to pull this off. He can turn stones into children of Abraham (Luke 3:8)! Ultimately, we know that at the quantum level the universe does not behave mechanistically. Things can happen without apparent causes. Information coming from the realm beyond need not be blaring on AM radio waves. If one has sufficient knowledge and ability, they could send information into this world which would seem to us to be a "lucky break". A molecule could bend this way instead of that, resulting in an improbable change which would otherwise take ages. Information could in principle seep into our world at a quantum level and we could not distinguish it from chance- at least not with our current state of technology.

There is biblical precedent for this line of thought in the nineteenth chapter of First Kings:

11 "Then the LORD said, "Go out and stand on the mountain before the LORD. Behold, the LORD is about to pass by." And a great and mighty wind tore into the mountains and shattered the rocks before the LORD, but the LORD was not in the wind. After the wind there was an earthquake, but the LORD was not in the earthquake. 12After the earthquake there was a fire, but the LORD was not in the fire. And after the fire came a still, small voice."

And of course, Proverbs 16:33: *"The lot is cast into the lap; but the whole disposing thereof is of the LORD."* That is, even events which seem like chance are really determined by Him.

Science might be able to come along later and detect the past presence of the wind which shattered the rocks, the earthquake which shook the earth, and the fire which burned it, but science would have no way of gleaning the information from the "still, small voice" by which God spoke. Science can only say it was an unlikely coincidence that high winds, an earthquake, and a fire struck the same locality contiguously, but there was doubtless a natural cause for all three.

Is there really any scientific evidence that known evolutionary processes can operate at the rate and scale necessary to explain all the "modification" of life on earth through its history? Another way to ask it would be like this, suppose there were a billion earth-like planets and a single celled organism was placed on each. How many of them, using only known biological processes without any intelligent intervention, would have a biotic phase which looks anything like the history of life on earth?

I think the number would be "zero". Someone else might think the answer would be in the thousands or even millions, but none of us have done the experiment or anything like it to say for sure. Therefore, neither side has a *scientific* basis for saying either way, though one might have naturalistic assumptions on the question. It is a pity so few people can even recognize there is a difference between the philosophy of naturalism and the process of the scientific method.

I don't think "natural selection" or any of the natural means we have discovered thus far could have, on its own, produced the vast diversity we see today or in the fossil record. I think nature had help. I think some of this arguing is because we are talking past one another on terms.

If we get better at figuring out how fast these processes can really work to produce great change and what if any limits there might be, I can see a situation in biology arising which is very similar to that which has already occurred in the realm of Astrophysics. Many years ago, scientists thought that the universe was eternal. Then they discovered that it is likely that it started with a hyperinflationary "big bang" (it had a beginning rather than "just always being here"). Then it was determined that the fundamental forces which control the structure of this universe had to fall within very, very, very narrow parameters for the universe to be able to support life as we know it and perhaps even life as we can conceive it. If any of those parameters varied for a whole host of fundamental measures, then life could not exist. It was like the universe was *designed* to be able to host life.

This was called the "Anthropic Principle" and it drove "naturalists" to distraction. How could they avoid the conclusion that the universe had a Designer when its fundamental forces had to be so precisely balanced for us to be here? It was like we were *meant* to be here. Chance failed as an explanation because we aren't that lucky. It would be like winning a billion lotteries and for the last thousand wins you didn't even buy a ticket! Ironically, some Christians are still opposed to the idea of a "big bang" because they don't see how it is really an overwhelming problem for the naturalist viewpoint. The universe had a beginning, just like it says in The Book.

The top escape hatch for the naturalists has been the "multiverse" hypothesis. This idea says that this universe is only one of an infinite or near-infinite number of universes which have all come about by chance. We were not lucky, rather if there is a vast number of universes then by chance one of them could turn out to be able to support life, and eventually, again by chance, evolve beings able to ask questions about where we come from. Of course, a multiverse by itself does not rescue the naturalist thinker. Even if trillions of other universes exist, God could have created them all.

They need an infinite number of randomly ruled, uncreated universes to avoid what this universe is telling them. I'm not even sure we can test for that. Does this even sound like "science"?

I call it what it is, a desperate escape hatch for those who want to deny the existence of a Creator. It's an act of rebellious faith that there is no one to whom they are accountable. Assuming we have an infinite number of universes when our known set is "one" is surely a gross abuse of probability theory. And I repeat, even if there are vast numbers of universes, it still is not proof that there is no God since He could have created them all and maybe all of them support intelligent life within them.

The same thing that happened at the cosmic level can be said about the universe at the smallest scale. We once thought that Newtonian Physics could explain all motion mechanistically and therefore naturalistically. But when we looked closer, we discovered quantum mechanics which aren't mechanical at all. There are natural effects that don't have natural causes. At the edge of what we know things can filter into nature from "somewhere else" and shape things.

I mention all that about astrophysics and quantum "mechanics" because it is possible that we are at the same place with "evolutionary science" that we were in with those fields some decades ago. Biology may be the last big holdout to what we have found at the largest and smallest of scales with inanimate matter: With a small amount of knowledge, it looks like laws and chance could explain all we see. But as we learn more, we may discover that like the cosmos itself, earth's biota will appear to have gotten very, very, very, very "lucky" to ever wind up with creatures like us or many other of the living things in the vast array of life on this planet.

That won't prove that God guided nature, but I predict that if we ever get that far, naturalists will have to resort to the same types of evasions that we see with astrophysics to deny the implications that biological nature would be screaming at us- without Him nothing that is would be.

The Creation Week Part II: Three Days of Filling

It was therefore necessary that the patterns of things in the heavens should be purified with these; but the heavenly things themselves with better sacrifices than these.

For Christ is not entered into the holy places made with hands, which are the figures of the true; but into heaven itself... -Hebrews 9:23-24.

* * * * * * *

By faith we understand that the world was framed by the word of God; that from invisible things visible things might be made. Hebrews 11:2-4 - Douay-Rheims 1899 American Edition

—⊹→❖←⊹—

On the fourth day of creation, God ceases separating and begins filling. First, He fills the heavens. Notice it does not say that He "created" the sun, moon, or stars on the fourth day. Rather it says that He "made" and "set" them. It is my guess that the Sun, what later became the Moon, and the stars, were all created in verse one with the creation of the Heavens and the Earth. While verse one says that God "created" the heavens and the earth (using a verb "bara" which can indicate a fiat miracle), in describing day four a different Hebrew word is used. That word is *asah*. Instead of being translated as "created", this different word is (in the King James Version) translated as "made."

Like the Hebrew word for "created", *asah* also has a wide variety of meanings. But it has more of a sense of "doing" or "bringing forth" something from a pre-existing material or state than does the Hebrew word *bara*. *Bara* is the word which is translated as "created" in Genesis chapter one, verse one. *Asah* can even mean "appoint" and that is a meaning which fits well here. The Sun, Moon, and stars were created in the beginning, but made or brought forth into their present position, condition and visibility on "day" four.

Secular scientists think that the Moon was a latecomer and that early in the planet's history we did not have our moon. Some great mass that would later form the heart of it may have been floating around the solar system somewhere, but it was not in its present course around the earth. The moon has a stabilizing effect on the axial tilt of the earth. It greatly tamps down on our planet's 'wobble' about its axis of rotation.

This stability means that we can count on the sun and the stars to keep close to their relative positions in the sky year after year. It is what allows them to be used to accurately track time. In addition, Dr. Hugh Ross and others have speculated that changes in the earth's early atmosphere allowed the position of heavenly bodies which were previously obscured to become visible. That is, the sky became clearer. Was this due in part to the emergence of land plants on day three? Plants convert CO_2 into oxygen, helping cool things down so that there is even less evaporation and cloud cover.

But so much information is packed into so few words that there is at least a double meaning in these verses. Let me leave behind the superficial discussion of what these words might mean regarding the natural universe only and talk about the deeper subject of what these things are referring to in the supernatural one.

In Hebrews chapter eight we are told that those who served in the temple or the tabernacle were serving in an earthly shadow of a heavenly thing. That is, they were mere copies of the real ones which existed in heaven. Heaven had the original, earth had a copy. Moses had to be careful to build the copy on the pattern of the original. Moses did not "create" the tabernacle as in, he did not form a new thing from nothing. He "made" it on a pattern of the original one which is above.

So it is with many things on earth, not just the temple. Indeed, we are told the whole city of Jerusalem is going to be replaced with a new one from heaven. There are many earthly things which are not their own thing, but rather a shadow of the original which is in heaven. This is another reason that the proper word in these verses is "made" rather than "created". If what is being brought into existence in this realm is a copy of that which is above, then during the days of filling it is said to be "made". If something new is being brought forth, of which there is no pattern in heaven, it is said to be "created."

The sun is said to be "made". It is a pattern or copy of the true light, God's Word, which God spoke into the creation on the first day. Its role is to give light on the earth. The physical illumination that the sun provides is a copy of the true illumination which God's Word provides in the realm above. The sun is made (not created) to "rule the day". That is, wherever the light is, wherever the good is, in that place the Word of God rules. And I mean the "Word" in the living sense. Just as the sun is the ultimate power source of life on earth, so the Logos of God, the second Person of the Trinity, is the power source of life eternal.

The Son of God is made (not created but appointed) to rule the eternal day of heaven. You may recall in Revelation 22:5 that in the world to come there is no more need for the light of the sun, and there is no more night. The Lord God Himself provides the light. So gloriously bright is the illumination of Christ that the light of the sun itself is but a pale shadow of it. The "greater light to rule the day" is in reality but a shadow of which "the Light of the World" is the substance. It is easy to see that the sun in the sky is a foreshadowing of the living Word of God, the light of the world (John 8:12). Once again creation uses double meanings.

Compare that to the moon. The moon represents the written law of God, the Torah- and by extension the rest of the scriptures. It is recorded in the scriptures (Psalm 119:105) *"Thy word is a lamp unto my feet, and a light unto my path."* That is, the written revelation from God through scripture guides us in the night of "this present darkness" (Ephesians 6:12). So long as we

walk in its light, we are not deceived by the powers and rulers and author-
ities of this present darkness who attempt to usurp the rule of God.

The woman in Revelation chapter twelve, often associated with Israel and
the Church, is connected to both the sun and the moon. She is "clothed
with the sun". That is, her shame is covered by the Living Word of God.
The Moon is beneath her feet. That is, God's written revelation to man
guides her steps.

Just as scripture teaches that the tabernacle on earth was a mere copy of
the one in heaven, some Jewish traditions teach that the original Torah is
in heaven. Those on earth are supposed to be copies of the one in heaven.
There has been much dispute about how this can be. Much of the dispute
on this question concerns how a Torah could exist prior to creation.

I think that is the wrong question. The Torah did not exist before creation,
but it was made from a pattern which did exist (the Logos of God). Just as
the moon is a reflector of the sun's light, so the Torah is a reflection of the
Logos of God. This reflector was set in place on the fourth day. Until the
Torah was given to man we had to make do with the moon, placed in the
second heaven, to represent that heavenly Torah.

The moon was "made" as a functional type of it. That is, the moon does
in nature what the Torah is to do in our spiritual walk- directs our steps
until the light of day comes at last. Ultimately God revealed His written
word to Mankind. Once it was given, we had written words that are mere
copies of those above, and a reflection of the true light which emanates
from the Living Word.

This view of the text is in sharp contrast to the speculations of some wayward scholars who claim that the text was written much later as a "polemic" against pagan mythology. They latch onto the detail that the sun
and moon are not called by name and propose that this was because the
writers did not want to even dignify them with a moniker which may also
have been used in pagan worship. They left them as created objects appointed to their position by God. If that view of it were true, then the text
would not say that one was appointed to rule the day and the other the

night. I believe I have shown that the lights were not given a name because the text is referring to more than just the physical sun and moon. As the rest of the scriptures confirm, they are a shadow of the Living and written Word of God respectively.

In the chapter one account, evenings come first and then comes the mornings. While this does not describe a literal solar day very well, it precisely describes the spiritual condition of creation. We have only the moon to give light to guide us. But the day will come, and all will be illuminated. Creation is in an evening of sorts now, but morning will come and then the sun shall rule the day. God will abide with His people.

God also "made" the stars on the fourth day. In scripture, stars are correlated to angels. This is so in Revelation (1:20 and 12:4) and Daniel (8:9). It is implied in other places as well, such as Genesis 2:1, where it says, "the heavens and the earth were finished, and all the host of them". See also Nehemiah 9:6, where the "heaven of heavens" is described as filled with "hosts" who worship the Lord. The phrase "heaven of heavens" connotes a realm even beyond the stars of the sky. The word for "host" used in all these verses refers in the literal sense to an army or a group of warriors. The third heaven (heaven of heavens) was therefore either filled with inhabitants and/or they were set in their positions on the fourth day of creation. It is from their ranks that God's messengers, the angels, are drawn.

Here again there is a reference to a "firmament" and again this is a reference to a solid barrier in the *spiritual* realm, the eternal reality of which this realm is only a shadow. The angels were ordered and set in their positions in the third heaven. The ancients considered the course of the stars in the night sky to be a shadow or reflection of the order and majesty of God's host marching about. The prophets at least seem to have understood that the solidity of the firmament was in the spiritual realm, judging by the enhanced detail of this firmament in Ezekiel 10:2, and chapter one. This is during a vision in which he is caught up to High Heaven, the world unseen by men.

The Fifth Day: Filling Realms with No Counterpart Above

I have already mentioned that in the age to come it is recorded that "there was no longer any sea." There being no oceans in the third heaven, there is no pattern or original in heaven to be used as a template for the inhabitants of the oceans. Seeing as how His judgments are not punitive in heaven, there is no raging sea there. Hence, there is no analog in heaven for creatures of the deep.

It is the same thing with the fowls of the air which fly in the space between the heavens and the earth. The winged creatures, made on the fifth day to fly in the space between the heaven and earth, were not copies of the things in heaven. Like the deep-sea creatures, they are a feature of this realm that is not a copy of what is above.

Birds move about in the space between earth and the lowest heaven. What analog can there be in the third heaven for that? There is no realm above the third heaven. There is no higher realm, so the winged creatures here are not made from a heavenly template. The fifth day is the creation of living animals which have no analog in the heavenly realm, neither in the seas beneath the land, nor the space between the land below and heaven above.

That is why there is no point on the fifth day in which the words "and it was so" appear. Remember from the previous days the words are uttered by high heaven which responded immediately to God's word. He spoke, and in heaven "it was so". But it was not yet so on earth. Other things had to happen before "God saw that it was good" on those other days. On the fifth day, the words "and it was so" never appear. That is because God is not working on both Heaven and Earth on the fifth day, but only on the earth. God was not speaking something into existence in heaven and then making shadows of them on the earth using the heavenly version as templates. He just went straight to the natural world.

Because there is no template in Heaven for them, these creatures are not said to be "made" as were the Sun, the Moon, and the Stars. Those lights were patterned on heavenly things- God's spoken word, the record of the

Proclamations of God (of which the Torah is a shadow) and angels who carry His word respectively. By contrast, there was no heavenly pattern for the creatures spoken of on the fifth day. Because of that, they are said to be "created", not "made". They are new things.

Because they were living things with the breath of life which only God can give, the waters could not do as the dry land did with regards to plant life-fill itself up with plant life without God's additional intervention. On day three God ordered the earth to bring forth vegetation and it did so without God making the patterns. Not so here. In Heaven they have life itself, and that eternal. On earth we have the "breath of life" and that from God alone. God had to make the patterns. That is, He "created" these things by "kinds". He started things off, and the waters then brought forth abundantly according to the patterns which He created.

With regards to aquatic life, this is not really describing "deistic evolution". In deistic evolution God designed the universe to unfold in such a manner that advanced life would be the result even if He never intervened in the natural universe after He created it. That is not what the text in Genesis one describes.

Rather, God somehow intervenes repeatedly after the creation of the universe. He created the templates or first examples. Only then did nature fill the seas with creatures of that type in accordance with His directive. To obey God's command and fill every niche of the seas, nature may produce variations within a kind, but they are variations on a theme designed by God. Maybe there is more evolution going on than a strict creationist would be comfortable with, but there is surely more Divine Creation going on than secular evolutionists would be comfortable with.

There is a caveat to the above, and that is the mysterious Ediacaran forms which appeared well before the Cambrian Explosion. Whatever they were, they never evolved much over their one-hundred-million-year existence. According to the 2007 paper "Autecology and the Filling of Ecospace: Key Metazoan Radiations" by Bambach, Bush, and Erwin, they only filled a dozen possible "life modes" from start to finish. The first four stages of the

Cambrian, lasting about one-third as long, nearly tripled this number. And life went on diversifying from there.

Most scientists agree that Ediacaran forms we know of were not the ancestors of life as we know it today. It seems as though nature's first attempt to fill the seas with living creatures was a failure. Naturalists might ask me how this bizarre episode fits into my belief system. I would ask the same of them. Despite the assurances of the scientists in those "Jurassic Park" movies, which only echoed what real-life fans of naturalism think, life *didn't* "find a way". Instead, it came up short, failed to adapt, and died out quickly when a new ecosystem very suddenly arrived. Why didn't evolution do all the wonderous things we are constantly told it can do in the case of the Ediacaran biota?

How does it fit into my view of things? Any answer I could give would be speculative, since the text itself doesn't mention the forms that came and went. That said, it fits well with what I've said here. My guess is that the Ediacaran represents nature trying to fulfill God's command for the seas to "bring forth living creatures" on its own. It may be an example of the limits of nature's unaided creative power. On the third day, nature was told to produce vegetation and it seems to have done that on its own just fine. Maybe it tried to do the same with living creatures from the seas in whom was the breath of life. It just couldn't pull it off.

This occurs to me because of my own walk with God. Not just me, but even Moses had such a journey. We think God wants us to do something, so we jump right into it with our own strength and our own wisdom- and no good comes of it. Later, when *He* opens the doors, we succeed. God wants us to do good works *in* Him and *with* Him, not just for Him.

In the previous chapter I wrote about the "Creation-Evolution Wars" and how a close reading of the text shows that neither side is completely right or completely wrong. That will probably make adherents for both sides unhappy instead of making both sides happy, that's just the way human nature works. But for the rest of us I think there is some comfort in knowing that this view of the text can bring peace on a contentious issue. At least for those inclined to peace.

I also think this matches the fossil record much better than either narrow creationism or narrow evolution (of any kind, including "deistic"). Any "deistic evolution" here occurs only after Divine intervention shows nature how. In the fossil record we do see that new types appear rather suddenly, and from there radiate out into an array of related types.

God creates the great sea monsters, and everything which moves about in swarms in the ocean (i.e., modern fish). The "sea monster" is sometimes translated "whales" and perhaps that is what is meant. It is worth mentioning however that the word used in Hebrew has connotations of a dragon or great serpent. Does this have connections to Babylonian traditions of a primordial sea monster with which the creator had to struggle? An embellishment perhaps added for dramatic effect?

These verses reveal the truth of things. Though both ancient and modern seas held terrifying and powerful creatures, they are not rivals to God. God has no rival. Even the strongest of them is instead His handiwork on which He pronounced a blessing. And His blessing was needful. The hosts of heaven lived before His presence, the greatest blessing possible. His blessing to these creatures was a lesser blessing, for their temporal prosperity only. The Leviathan is a different subject, beyond our scope here.

Now for much of my life I wondered about the order of things on day five. Sure, creatures in the ocean came along before creatures on the land. Science agreed with that part. It was the oddity of including the fowls of the air with this group which had perplexed me. Surely winged creatures were not the first of the land-animals worth mentioning.

Now I understand that placing them together makes perfect sense, for the same reasons I gave regarding the plants. The account creation is giving Adam is not an account of everything that ever happened. It is an account of what Adam sees in creation around him. That is, it is an account of creation as it is in Adam's "now." Yes, there were ages of animal life which came and went. Some may have even helped bring the earth to its current state in some way- but it's the ones alive at the time that creation is giving an account of.

Therefore, it makes sense to say that the animals Adam might find in the sea and in the air were created before the beasts which Adam might find on the land were made. Dinosaurs are not even mentioned, nor all the beasts which came before the dinosaurs, nor all those which came after the dinosaurs but before the ice ages. All of those were long gone. One group survived along with the water dwellers in anything like their present form from the days of the dinosaurs to the time of Adam- the birds. Thus, it makes sense to group them together with the sea creatures, not only because they were not based on a heavenly pattern either, but also because they fit well temporally with that group. Both categories were ancient survivors present since the days of the dinosaurs.

Scientists have named the first dinosaur, Eoraptor, "dawn bird" for a reason. Fossilized feathers have been found which have been dated to two hundred million years ago. Even without the text of Genesis, it is enough to make persons of some imagination wonder if dinosaurs weren't meant to be birds all along. Perhaps Nature just needed time, and help, to get there. It was a marvelous winding course with lots of interesting detours, wild experiments, and playful dead ends. But at the last when the harsh sifting of nature was done only the most extreme examples of the type remained- birds.

The Sixth Day: Filling the Land

By now you see the pattern. In verse twenty-four God initiates the sixth day by commanding the land, in whatever realm it may be natural or supernatural, to bring forth living creatures after their kind. The land in the supernatural realm, the third heaven, does so immediately and exactly as God says. High Heaven then reports "And it was so."

But while the land above performs His word completely, we learn in verse twenty-five that in our world God Himself must act to fulfill His word. Our natural world can't seem to get started until God makes "kinds" of land animals. Unlike in the heavenly realm, the earth only brings them forth after God has made- in some way - the kind, or category, for the earth to work with.

Were the chapter two account a record of all types of animals on the earth, we would have more information about what happened this day. Chapter two is describing special creation. But as I will show, that is a separate event, and that special and relatively small set of animals was not formed until after Adam was. We have much less information about how God "made" the animals described here in chapter one. We know that nature had help, but perhaps it was by means of the subtle-yet-powerful mechanisms proposed in the previous chapter. We just don't know.

Notice that the word "made" is used here, not "created" as was used on day five. Again, this indicates that God was basing something in this realm off something which already existed in the realm above. He was working from a heavenly pattern- like the tabernacle on earth was built on a heavenly pattern. When the work was done the natural realm reported that God "saw that it was good." Maybe not perfect, as in the world above, but suitable and attractive, nevertheless.

Ironically, what occurs in the land above sounds a lot like "deistic evolution". God commands the land to bring forth the living creatures by kinds and the land does so. But it is not our land. It's the land those who love God will enjoy in the life to come. Down here on earth, creation can't pull this process off without God's continued direct intervention. God "made" the land animals kind by kind. He gives to the earth patterns of what is in heaven and the earth takes it from there.

In this view of things, the many disputes between those who think life diversified via deistic evolution versus those who believe God used direct creation seem almost irrelevant. Which view is correct? Well, both are correct in their respective realm. On the one hand, in the realm we live in God had to in some fashion make prototypes of the animals by kinds. So that's divine creation of some kind. On the other hand, it's only divine creation because this realm doesn't have it together yet- what happened in the land above looked more like theistic or deistic evolution.

According to this passage that is not what happened down here though. God directly intervened and got things going for "the land." In the record of nature that might still look a lot like evolution, because nature (the land) was working off a pattern which looked very much like superfast theistic, or even deistic, evolution in the heavenly realm. In this mixed realm of darkness and light, the land could not pull it off alone. God had to step in and by some means fashion examples for the land to work with. We don't know the means. It could be as subtle as filtering information into our world at the quantum level or as direct as that described in chapter two of Genesis. So, both sides are right and both are wrong. Can't we all just get along here? Probably not, sinful humans being what we are.

Imagine a color printer that an adult can use to print off a color picture from an electronic file at the touch of a button. The adult does not have to paint the picture. The printer does that for them on command, and then "reports" when the job is done. Then the adult hands that picture to a small child with a paint set, and the adult asks the child to paint a copy of that picture. The child needs a lot of help from the adult to get started, but once the adult gets them started, they continue from there. It is a very imperfect copy of the original, but the adult compliments them on it just the same. The child then reports that the adult "saw that it was good". It was not a perfect copy of what was above, but it can be used to accomplish whatever purpose the adult had in mind.

In this analogy, the printer is the land above and the child with the paint set is the land in our realm. The result would also look like the original, yet not prepared in quite the same way. In the same way, our record in nature may look similar to what it would if deistic evolution produced the results we see, even though it was not strictly produced by that method.

Confusion on the Creation of Man

The word translated "Man" (*a'dam*) in early Genesis is an unusual word. It is like our English word "Deer" in that it is the same word whether singular or plural. To add to the complexity, it is also a proper noun. Add to it that the singular for man, whether in Hebrew or English, can also mean "Man" as a species or even a concept. So, it can refer to all men (and women) or even just the idea of humankind. The Hebrew even carries connotations of the color red, as in the red earth.

Put that together with a document inspired thousands of years ago in a foreign language that uses very few words to both say and mean a lot of different things, and you have a recipe for confusion. And there has been confusion about early Genesis, but it goes beyond obscurity concerning the term for "man." As I read the text of Genesis chapters one and two, it seemed like it was talking about two different creation accounts.

In chapter one, men and women were created together, after the animals were created. In the account in chapter two the most straightforward translations (I will show why I think so later) say that the animals were made between the creation of the man and the creation of the woman. Plus, God brought the animals to Adam to see what they would be named before Eve was made.

The list of animal types in the chapter two account is smaller and less complete than that in chapter one. For example, no mention is made of anything that lives in the waters in the second account. The beasts formed in the second account were "of the field" (*has-sa-deh*), not "of the land" (*eretz*) as in chapter one. "The land" is general. "The field" implies cultivated ground or pasture, or land suitable for such. When I describe the categories of animals taken onto the ark, I will show this in some detail. The second account is talking about a more restricted set of creatures. When were the marine animals and the beasts of the forests, mountains, deserts and so forth made in chapter two?

Even the verb used to describe the creation of man is different. In Genesis 1:26 the intent is to "make" man in God's image. "Make" in that verse is from the Hebrew word *asah*. In the next verse (Genesis 1:27) it uses a different Hebrew word (*bara'*) three times to describe the creation of man.

You may recall from my earlier point about the "Heavens and the Earth" being created in Genesis 1:1 and the Sun, Moon and Stars being made on "day" four that the different English words "created" and "made" represent two different Hebrew words. "Bara'" is the word translated "created" and can include connotations of a fiat miracle: A production of something new from nothing in this realm.

Adam was created (*bara*) in 1:27. By contrast, in chapter two Adam was not "created". Verse seven of chapter two says the LORD God "formed" Adam. The word translated "formed" is the Hebrew word, *yatsar*, which means to fashion or squeeze into shape. The image is one of a potter molding clay. It has if anything even stronger connotations of working from a pre-existing material than the more general word translated "made". This implies there is a part of man which God created - something new, and a part of man which God made that came from something pre-existing, dust in the case of Adam. Man is thus both a new creation and the shaping of that which previously existed into a new form- shades of the Incarnation.

Even the title given the Creator/Maker is somewhat different in the two accounts. Genesis chapter one says, "God created man". Genesis chapter two specifies that "the LORD God" formed man. The extra English word is because there is an extra Hebrew word in the manuscripts. Why? I don't think it was because God was being careless when He inspired the account. Nor is it, as many of the highly educated and utterly unseeing proponents of the documentary hypotheses claim, because there were two different traditions with two different gods cobbled together in these accounts.

Instead, there is a message there which will be missed if the reader of the accounts is careless.

No mention of a garden is given in chapter one. Whereas the account in chapter two emphasizes that man was agrarian, no mention of agriculture is made in the account of man in the first chapter. In chapter one God immediately directs them to be fruitful and multiply and fill the earth.

This is a great contrast from the account which begins in chapter two. In that account not only does God wait a while to create Eve, but there is also no mention of any children until Adam and Eve are expelled from the garden. In the chapter two account God seemed to have a lot of business with Adam and Eve before they get around to reproducing. In chapter one, "be fruitful and multiply" is the first command God gives newly created mankind- and thereafter there is very little information about any personal interaction with God.

The first creation account of man seems to end at the start of chapter two (dividing the text into numbered chapters was added much later, they are not a part of the original text) with God taking the first Sabbath. Then early in chapter two it is like the story starts over again.

As I mentioned before, when God confronts Cain for murdering Abel, Cain raises an interesting objection to his punishment. He tells God that "whoever finds me will kill me." Who on earth was Cain so worried about? Not his family, he was already with them. His fear was leaving the place where they were. He talked as if the world was already full of people. People who he believed would not hesitate to waylay a lone outcast from his family group. Cain speaks as if he was not the first murderer. Furthermore, God takes his complaint seriously. He puts a mark on Cain that somehow offered protection from these mysterious others and vows that if they kill Cain, He will take sevenfold vengeance. Who are these people that need a threat of losing seven of their own number to deter them from murdering the outcast Cain?

And again, all that does not even mention the famous question of where Cain's wife came from. The standard answer has been that "Cain married one of his sisters". I can't help but notice though, that Cain departs to the "land of Nod" and finds a wife, apparently before the birth of Seth (Genesis 4:25). Seth is said to be "a seed in place of Abel" so it is not likely Eve had any children, at least not any males, between the death of Abel and the birth of Seth. And not only does he find a wife, but Cain also founds a city (Genesis 4:17), which he names after his own son. A city? Where are all these people coming from?

As I have mentioned, not only are there people, but these people catch on fast. The stone age? Forget it! There was no hunter-gatherer phase for this bunch. Abel was a pastoral farmer. Cain was an agriculturalist. In verses 20-22 of chapter four we learn that the sons of Lamech, near descendant of Cain, learn to herd cattle and live in tents, invent playing certain musical instruments, and even become skilled in metallurgy.

Lamech himself in verse twenty-three said he took the life of "a young man". If everyone is related just five generations back it seems quite odd that he would refer to the deceased as simply "a young man". Why not instead describe him by his relationship to Lamech? If you killed your cousin, would you describe it as killing "a man" without any reference to how you are related?

People have noticed these sorts of paradoxes before, and the reaction has typically gone one of two directions. Those who are anxious to dismiss the authority of scripture use these difficulties to dismiss it all as myth. There is a class of people who are quick to judge both the scriptures and the God of whom those scriptures speak as unworthy of serious consideration as a place to find truth. I have observed that such people virtually never turn that same critical eye upon themselves. They do not question their own motives for challenging the authority of scripture.

People such as that will never discover the truth about eternal things because they refuse to first consider the truth about themselves- a necessary precondition. If they look too closely, they might discover that in Him they would find a reference point for transcendent truth- truth to which they would then rightfully be accountable. There is a class of people who take comfort from clinging to the idea that there is no such truth accessible to man. Such souls would prefer uncertainty to the knowledge of the truth.

On the other extreme are those who prefer certainty to truth. They want answers, and they want them now. Like the first group, which prefers un-certainty to truth, this sort of person will also miss truth. The reason they miss it is because they want something else more. With the first group what they want more than truth is autonomy, the false freedom which comes from the belief that there are no real answers.

With the latter bunch it is security which they want more than truth- the false comfort which comes from believing we possess the real answers so that we never have to consider any other answers. We never have to admit that we don't know. We never even have to hope or trust that God will show us someday, basing our hope on all the things that He has shown us. We can seek comfort in our set of answers rather than go back to Him as The Answer.

This group will also miss the truth. Indeed, anyone who has any priority which is higher than finding the truth will very likely fail to find the truth. That is just how precious truth is to God. He designed the universe so that only those who seek it earnestly will find it.

The critics point to Genesis chapter one and two and say "See, this is a collection of creation myths, and they don't even tell the same story, there-fore at least one of them must be untrue." If one of them is in fact untrue then the Bible would contain untruth- which would serve to undermine the claim of Christians that it is the product of Divine Inspiration. One typical response of the Christian church to claims of this nature is some-thing akin to "The accounts are not conflicting. They are just telling the same story from a different perspective" and gloss over the contradictions.

I for one am a Christian who has never found those claims of mere per-spective shifting to be reasonable. The textual differences previously men-tioned are real and not insubstantial. Trying to make those two accounts different views of the very same story seemed clunky, forced, and inelegant.

Because of that, this answer never really fit in with the pattern of previous truth which I had discovered in scripture.

What pattern is that? I am talking about seamless unity of ideas from different books written in different ages by different people in different languages that make me set my Bible down on the table with mouth agape at how wonderfully it all dovetails together. I refer to those rare occasions where all the paradoxes resolve elegantly into a doctrine of understanding which uplifts as well as enlightens.

Indeed, the previous truth I had discovered in scripture, contrary to all expectations of our sick postmodern age, is what gave me the confidence to face the fact that the two accounts of the creation of man have real conflicts. I faced the textual problems with the assurance that even if I never resolved these paradoxes, the scripture was still true. Based on the truths I had discovered before it was reasonable to suppose that all of it was true- even if the details of how and why they were true in this instance eluded my grasp until the day I passed on.

I accepted by faith that there was a resolution, even if I could not see it. What I accepted by faith beforehand has become a reality in my understanding today. Indeed, it was only faith, a gift of God, that there was an answer which permitted me to honestly pursue my doubts about the pat answers. And it was only by that willingness to doubt the pat answers that I could ever dare to take the fresh look needed to discover the real answer. There is a simple reason the two accounts seem to tell related but not quite the same stories- they are telling related but not quite the same stories. And they both really happened.

As I begin to "tip my hand" some of you who have studied the Bible for many years may start off thinking "that can't be right. I know of too many scriptures which contradict it." That is just what I thought when my "phase shift" in understanding first struck me. I ask you to hold on as I take you through the journey I took when I first came to see it. One of the first things that I did was to try to locate the scriptures which I thought would disprove it. I think that, like me, you will be surprised at what we will find.

Verse Twenty-Six: A Plan to Make Man in Image and in Likeness

-→- -≫-◈-≪- -⊷-

In this case we must start before the beginning if the beginning is to make any sense to us. Let's establish more precisely what God did to fulfill His plan to make Man in His own image, and according to His own likeness. To understand that plan we must first thoroughly understand the words that Genesis uses in describing what God intended to do.

I have already spoken of the difficulties of the Hebrew word for man, *a'dam*. I am going to delve a bit more into the Hebrew here. I feel compelled to preface this by saying that I am not a Hebrew scholar. I am not claiming that I have discovered something about the Hebrew which no one else has found. Rather, there has always been ambiguity in some of these passages in Genesis.

Even those who are Hebrew scholars have difficulty deciding, for example, when to use the name of "Adam" rather than translating the Hebrew into "the man." The Hebrew here has always been enigmatic. This should have been a hint to us that the passages contained further illumination. The uncertainty pointed to mystery, not a passage to be understood superficially. With this disclaimer done, let us dive in.

The word for "man" used in early Genesis is the word *a'dam*. It is from a root which means "ruddiness" or "redness" and may be a reference to the color of the earth- the earth from which, according to Genesis, Adam was made. The parent root, the last two of the three Hebrew letters which make up the name, means "blood".

Interestingly, "adam" is not the most common word for "man" in the Old Testament. Another term, *iysh*, is used far more often once one gets past early Genesis but is a masculine form which could best be considered "man" as in a male human being. There is yet a third term for "man" which emphasizes that he is a mortal, which we will discuss more later. "Adam" would then be more like "the human race or some member or members of that race."

Its first use in reference to humanity is in Genesis 1:26 where God said, "let us make man in our own image, according to our likeness". Here the form for *a'dam* is the simplest, אָדָם. It means "mankind" or "human race". So, in verse 1:26 God is saying "Let's make humans to be like us".

We can speculate about what it means to be "like us". And who is the "us" anyway? Is this a reference to the Trinity, or some sort of Heavenly Council or the royal "we"? The short answer, especially if one considers the next verse where a plural noun for God is used in a singular context, is "yes" to the Trinity and perhaps "yes" to the Royal We. It isn't a Divine Council and by the end of this book I hope you will see why. It has to do with the nature of God's image. For now, let's look at God's intent in creating man in verse twenty-six:

And God said, Let us make man in our image, after our likeness: and let them have dominion over the fish of the sea, and over the fowl of the air, and over the cattle, and over all the earth, and over every creeping thing that creepeth upon the earth.

The trend of late is for contemporary theologians to lump the ideas of "image" and "likeness" together and assume that God was repeating Himself and that He is unnecessarily verbose. I don't buy that- when the Bible is quoting men they may be so, but not Him. This view was also not the practice of the ancients. The Orthodox Church and the Latin Church both thought there was a difference between being made in the "image" of God and being made in the "likeness" of God. They did not agree with each other on what those differences meant, but they agreed that there was a distinction, as did the famous Jewish sage, Maimonides.

I agree with the ancients who looked for meaning in every shade of difference between terms in scripture and take umbrage at the trend of recent scholarship when it attempts to lump different Greek and Hebrew words carelessly together with a single meaning. Christ Himself told us not to be like the heathen who "suppose that they will be heard for their many words". Christ silenced the Sadducees with an argument which hinged upon the tense of a single word (Matt. 22:32) in a statement from God. When God is speaking, every iota of every word has meaning. This being the attitude of God, it does not seem reasonable to suppose that He repeats Himself without purpose.

I am with the ancients on this subject, though in this instance the Hebrew meanings of the words do appear to be so close that they could be considered synonyms. In determining what scripture is telling us about the difference in word choice let us start out with what is clear. The Hebrew preposition attached to "image" in this verse is a more specific term than that which is attached to "likeness". Man is to be made "in" the image of God, but only "after" or "according to" His likeness. The former then may be viewed not as a synonym of the latter, but as describing a more precise condition of it. In English we might say "He looks like you" to describe one level of similarity but say "He is the spitting image of you" to express a higher and more exact level of similarity.

The Hebrew term for image is used to describe graven images- idols of gods (Num. 33:52, Second Kings 11:18 *et al*). It is used where it was thought in the pagan context that the block of metal, wood, or stone was not merely a figure of the god but the actual representation of the god. If you were looking at the idol you were looking at the god. An analogy might be that you cannot see my spirit, but if you are looking at my body then you are looking at the closest thing to an image of my spirit.

In the Septuagint, the Greek version of the Old Testament, the word used for "image" is *eikón* from which we get the English word "icon". The word picture for this term is the image from a reflective surface, such as a mirror or in molten silver when it reaches a high level of purity in refinement.

Thus, the resemblance referred to is not just because of similarity in some form, capacity, or property, but a high-fidelity representation of an original. For example, someone who is not closely related to you may look "like" you. But they are not made in your image. You share a similar form, but it is not because of you coming out in them. You just share a similar appearance. But when your child looks like you it is because it is you coming out in them. A mirror image suggests there is an original being reflected. It is a reflection based on an original. A likeness does not imply that.

It also had other meanings, for example it could be used for things that were stand-ins for the original, such as when the Philistines sent a sacrifice to God consisting of golden images of the tumors and mice which plagued them. The term came to mean "vanity" or a "shadow" because the children of Israel were later taught that the idols were merely blocks of wood and stone, and not the visible representation of an actual divine being. In this very early document though, the word can reasonably be supposed to be connected to the former meaning.

The New Testament resolves the mystery about what is meant in scripture by "the image of God." Colossians 1:15 says that Christ is the image of God, and further that as far as we are concerned God has no other image than Christ. It says of Him, "*Who is the image of the invisible God, the firstborn of all creation.*" The phrase "firstborn of all creation" is interesting too, and I will come back to it when I discuss the next verse. That Christ is God's image is confirmed in Second Corinthians 4:4 which says of Christ "*Who is the image of God.*" Hebrews 1:3 says that Christ is the "exact representation" of God's being or nature- in other words, an image.

Christ is the image of God, and God has no other image that is accessible to anyone but Himself. That is why when Thomas asked to see the Father, Jesus said "if you have seen Me, you have seen the Father." That is why First Timothy 6:16 describes Christ in the full glory of God with these words: "*Who only hath immortality, dwelling in the light which no man can approach unto; whom no man hath seen, nor can see*". It is why the first chapter of the Gospel of John says: "*18 No man hath seen God at any time; the only begotten Son, which is in the bosom of the Father, he hath declared him.*" Some translations say "He has explained Him" for that last phrase. Further, in chapter six that gospel declares "*46 Not that any man hath seen the Father, save he which is of God, he hath seen the Father.*"

To be clear, this word suggests a closer connection between the image and the source than even our English word 'image' suggests. The image is the *visible part* of the original. As with an idol which was thought to be the physical manifestation of the heavenly god on earth, so Christ as the Image of God is not just a picture of God. He is *of* God. He *is* God manifesting in physical form and acting on earth.

Michael Heiser in his introduction of a 2002 re-print of Alan F. Segal's *The Two Powers of Heaven* describes Hebrew Two Powers theology like this: "The ancient Israelite knew two *Yahwehs*—one invisible, a spirit, the other visible, often in human form. The two *Yahwehs* at times appear together in the text, at times being distinguished, at other times not." After the rise of Christianity, the Rabbis declared this view to be a heresy. But it's not a heresy. As we shall see in the course of this book, it is something in the text from the beginning. God as more than one person (as in the Trinity) sharing the same perfect nature has been a part of the text from the beginning.

When God says, "let us make Man in our own image" He is saying that the goal is to make man to be in Christ. The ultimate goal of God is not to have a bunch of independent little figures of God-like beings running around creation separate and unconnected to Him. Man can do that, it is what we are born into, but that is the path of disobedience. It is the choice that the Devil wants for Man. It is a choice which promises freedom but ends in the slavery of delusion. God wants His children to choose Him as He has chosen them. He made us to become little god figures. But what sort of god-figures shall we be? His plan was for us to become the Christ kind. Christ, the Logos made flesh, is His image.

Past generations of Christians knew that Christ is the image of God, and that we were not automatically born in God's image. This isn't some new teaching. I did some research on the classic Christmas hymn "Hark, the Herald Angels Sing". It turns out it was written back in 1739. And it had fourth and fifth verses- since cast aside. The last verse was:

> *Adam's Likeness, LORD, efface,*
> *Stamp thy Image in its Place,*
> *Second Adam from above,*
> *Reinstate us in thy Love.*
> *Let us Thee, tho' lost, regain,*
> *Thee, the Life, the Inner Man:*
> *O! to All Thyself impart,*
> *Form'd in each Believing Heart.*

Believers three hundred years ago understood that Adam was not in the image of God outside of a relationship with God. Humans are not in the image of God until God stamps us with the image of His Son and we are conformed to that Image more and more via sanctification.

In 1758 George Whitefield edited a more enduring version of the song. The last verse was shortened to say:

> *Adam's Likeness now efface,*
> *Stamp thy Image in its Place;*
> *Second Adam from above,*
> *Work it in us by thy Love.*

Again, they understood what scripture said about our being born in the image of Adam, our federal head in the natural, and that upon salvation and rebirth we received a new image from our new federal head. He is the One called Jesus Christ and the scripture (1 Cor. 15) refers to Him as the "second Adam".

The version of the song we most often sing today was not even composed until 1961. It was a greatly shortened version, with the last two verses removed. A lot of theology has been taken out of Christian hymns. In this chapter I am not teaching a new theology. A lot of it is independently discovered old theology which has been massaged out of the church over the decades as part of an effort to remake the Church of God in some other image.

It was always God's intent to both create Man in His own image in the eternal realm and to make man in His own image through a process in the temporal realm. The fall of Adam interrupted that process, but the death and resurrection of Christ re-established in the temporal realm what God declared done in the eternal realm.

One must take the scripture (Genesis 9:6) which says that "God made man in His own image" in light of this larger picture. He did originally. That is where Adam started, and it was God's original intent. But that does not mean that men currently born into the world are in the image of God. It is what is in heaven where His will is done and what can happen on earth when God's intent is fulfilled in our lives. Indeed, this verse really says "ha-Adam". That is, He made *the* man in His own image. More on that later.

When we are born in this world, we are not born in the "image" of God. All men are born in the likeness of God, but not the image. We have an earthly image. This is why it is written (John 3:7) "you must be born again." If you were born in the image of God the first time, you would not need to be born again a second time. When we are born again, we have a heavenly image, and through faith and the renewal of our minds by the Holy Spirit we become conformed to that new image which we have. Here are some scriptures which support this declaration, starting in Romans chapter eight verse 29:

For whom he did foreknow, he also did predestinate to be conformed to the image of his Son, that he might be the firstborn among many brethren.

And further in Colossians the third chapter, verses 9&10:

Lie not one to another, seeing that ye have put off the old man with his deeds;

And have put on the new man, which is renewed in knowledge after the image of him that created him

And then from First Corinthians the fifteenth chapter, verses 47-49:

The first man is of the earth, earthy: the second man is the Lord from heaven.

As is the earthy, such as they also that are earthy: and as is the heavenly, such as they also that are heavenly

And as we have borne the image of the earthy, we shall also bear the image of the heavenly.

And in 2nd Corinthians the third chapter, verse 18:

But we all, with open face beholding as in a glass the glory of the Lord, are changed into the same image from glory to glory, even as by the Spirit of the Lord.

From these four passages, and from others besides, it should be clear that man is not automatically born "in the image of God". All men are made "according to the likeness" of God, but this is not the same thing as being created "in the image" of God. Only those in relationship with Him are in His image. Hitler was not created "in His image", nor was Jack the Ripper, or any other number of notorious monsters in human form. They were according to the likeness of God in the sense that they had the potential for connectedness and moral awareness. They used that god-like capacity to ungodly ends.

We are not made in His image when we are born. An image is an exact representation. We are according to His likeness, but our natural image is more similar to that of Adam, after the fall. We who believe are born again with a new image are being conformed to God's image by the renewal of the Holy Spirit. This is what the scripture teaches.

To that you may say "Aha, but Adam was created in the image of God." Well, he started that way. Then the fall happened. By the end of things not even Adam considered himself to be in the image of God, only the likeness. See Genesis 5:1 which is the *towledah* for "the generations" or account of Adam. He says that God made man "after the likeness" of God, but never mentions "image". We will explore that passage in more detail later.

When we are born again, and Christ said we must be born again, we are reborn in His image. As we walk with Him in faith, we are conformed to that new image which He has given us. This is a view consistent with Romans 8:29 and the rest of these verses.

Now let's consider the term "likeness." The term used for "likeness" is a variation on the Hebrew term *demut*. It is often translated as "resembling". The word is used twice in Ezekiel 1:5 when the four living creatures who had the "likeness" of a man appeared in a firestorm. Although those creatures looked like a man, it was not because they were copying man or inspired by man. It was just what they looked like. In Psalm 58:4 the lies of the wicked are "like" the venom of a poisonous snake. *Demut* is used to mean that two things or people are alike in some way, and not because they have the same nature in all aspects.

From the way the word is used, and the weaker preposition with which it is paired, it is clear that "according to the likeness" of God is a less exact representation of God than being "in the image" of God. "According to the likeness" of God is a state which applies to all humans. This is confirmed in Genesis 5:1. Being "in the image of God" is a closer state of connectedness which all humans may have the ability to attain but is only manifested in those who have a relationship with the Divine.

So, what does it mean to be "according to the likeness" of God? What makes man like God in a way which does not apply to anything else He created or made? I mean what makes us different in kind, not just in degree. For example, you might say that we are more intelligent than animals. OK, but animals can still be intelligent, and we are dim bulbs indeed compared to God. If our degree of intelligence makes us different from beasts, it still does not make us "like God." Our differences in intelligence with the animals are differences in degree, not in kind. The same is true with our use of language, and our use of tools.

No, what separates us from the beasts of the earth in kind is our ability to unite in Spirit with the Divine. The doorway to this unity is embedded in another feature which we possess- an ability to make moral judgements. We have a spiritual aspect or dimension which other living things lack.

We can cooperate with one another based not on mere instinct or just mutual advantage for some material need, but because we judge some common cause to be in the right.

Where we are different in kind from the beasts is that humans have the potential to be of one nature with God. Sinful man can only access this potential through membership in the body of Christ, and we sense only the barest glimmer of it in this world, but when we finally become one with Him, we will understand how He is one with the Father- one in nature. Beasts completely lack this capacity.

I know there has been a debate over to what degree higher animals possess "self-awareness." Mankind though, goes beyond self-awareness and seeks out true connectedness. We are self-aware, but at our best we are also aware that there is something beyond ourselves, and bigger than ourselves. We can connect and serve not out of mere instinct, but by our conscious choice.

We are "religious" by nature. Properly connected, we are capable of accessing a reference point for right and wrong which is beyond ourselves and our interests. This is what truly sets us apart from the higher animals in that here our differences are of kind, not just degree. That man rarely uses this potential does not mean that it is absent.

This is why I am unthreatened by the idea that there may have been hominids, two-legged beings, with relatively large brains walking around making some sort of tools back in the dawn of time. I never considered that being "according to the likeness of God" (much less being "in the image of God") meant having two legs, or a large brain, or even being able to make a flint scraper. When we say that someone is inhuman, we don't mean that they can't make a flint scraper! That is not what makes us human. If we give up our humanity, I suppose that is what we can degenerate to- trousered apes as C.S. Lewis once put it, but that is not how we were made.

We have a spiritual dimension which permits us to relate to one another and to God in a deeper way than that available to the beasts. If these other creatures did not have that, then they were not made in His image or after His likeness. In Genesis 1:26 God proposed creating something new. That was Man.

In combining this verse with the next one we see that it goes from plural ("let them have dominion") in verse twenty-six to singular in the first two parts of verse twenty-seven (more on that in the next chapter), and then back to plural again in the last segment of that verse. This is a chiastic structure where parts one and four are connected and between them parts two and three are connected as shown below...

26 "let them", Point "A" is **plural**

27a "the Man" (see next chapter), Point "B" is **singular**

27b "created He him", Point "B prime" is **singular**

27c "created He them", Point "A prime" is **plural**

Thus, it can be concluded that the three parts of verse twenty-seven are not the same thing repeated three times from different angles to fulfill God's announced intent. Rather, they are a *list* of three things God did to fulfill his announced intent in verse twenty-six. Further, points "A" and "A prime", verse twenty-six and part "c" of verse twenty-seven, are connected. Point "B" and "B Prime" (segments "b" and "c" of verse twenty-seven) are also connected.

I am going to present the case that verse twenty-six (Point "A") is God's goal. It is more than a single event. It is a process for humanity. Point "A prime" is among other things, referring to the beings He intends to move to that goal, and "B" and "B prime" are the means by which this goal will be accomplished.

Verse Twenty-Seven: The Execution of the Plan to Make Man in His Image

Let's look at verse twenty-seven where God executes the plan by which He intends to "make" man in His Own Image:

So God created man in his own image, in the image of God created he him; male and female created he them.

The King James is pretty accurate in translation here, but there is one thing that I want you to be aware of. In verse 1:27 when man is "created" (*bara*) the Hebrew form of "adam" is אֶת־הָאָדָם. That last letter (pronounced He or Ha) tacked on to the right side of the word "adam", which looks a lot like the English letter "n", is a definite article. It is often translated "the". So, in this form "adam" means "the man". "Ha-a-dam" not just "a-dam". I find it odd that so many translations just say "man" here while translating it "the man", or sometimes "of man", throughout the rest of the scriptures.

I have admitted that I am not a Hebrew Scholar, but regarding Genesis 1:27 and the propriety of translating the first part "So God created *the* Man in His own image", I have been tested by one. I had an extensive dialogue with a professor of Hebrew who started out convinced that I was wrong. By the end of the dialogue his tone had changed. He only said that there "could be" a good reason for the traditional English translation of verse 1:27. Not that he had one. If you've any doubt, confirm it yourself.

I am going to argue that this verse, far from repeating the same thing three times in an overly verbose manner, is instead one of the most content-packed verses in all of scripture. It is not just saying the same thing in a slightly different manner three times. It is **both** 1) a list of three things done to set in motion God's intent stated in the prior verse **and** 2) it has a triple meaning within its three parts. It is speaking about Christ and the Church, Adam and Eve, and Men and Women generally. All these things are spoken of with the same words.

There are three layers, or a sort of "triplet" of creations, in this verse. The Hebrew grammar has the first expressed part by itself, and the last two parts linked together. With this understanding, the triplet phrase split in half is:

God created (The) Man in His own image.

In the image of God He created him. Male and Female He created them...

Some translations say, "God created *them*" in the second part of the verse rather than "God created *him*". Perhaps the translators assumed that the verse is speaking only of Adam and Eve throughout. Therefore, they translated the pronouns as a plural form throughout. The King James Version does not make that assumption and in this case appears to be truer to the original language. In the middle part of the verse the Hebrew word used is *o-tow* which is normally a singular pronoun form (him). In the last part of the verse the word is *o-tam*, which is a plural pronoun form (them).

The casual reader might think that creation is merely repeating itself for poetic effect. That is one possibility. Maybe it's saying three times that God created man with the last time adding the detail that He created man in both male and female form in the person of Adam and Eve. If that is *all* that it means, then this interpretation does not address any of the difficulties in the text of early Genesis which we talked about earlier. Nor does it fit in with the pattern which has occurred in previous days. In most previous days there was something occurring in heaven, and also on earth. In previous days heaven gave a report, and so did earth. Days three, four, and this day had two reports which were characterized by a certain phrase, one of high heaven and one of the natural world.

You may recall my earlier point about the phrase "and it was so" occurring when God's intent was completed in the higher realm of heaven, the true Promised Land above. The phrase "and God saw that it was good" applied to things being made into a suitable condition for His purposes in the earthly realm. In days three and four the phrases were separated because of what had to occur in the two realms. The events of day five were not applicable to the realm above, and so only the latter phrase was delivered.

The first part of day six repeats the pattern of days three and four- there is a space of time during which something happens between the two phrases. But day six is the only day where the phrases are used twice. Further, the second part of the sixth day is the only place in which the two phrases occur right beside one another. Once God blessed man, nothing else happens between "it was so" in heaven and "God saw that it was very good" on earth.

Heaven and earth were at last moving in accord. This is also the only one of the six creation days in which a definitive is used to describe a particular day. As I have mentioned, days one through five don't have a definitive article, indicating that the word "day" was used to describe a condition, not a specific earthly day. Not so on the sixth day. I think there was a specific literal morning on earth where things were according to plan in both realms and God said, "It was very good".

I would like for you to put aside for a moment who you think Adam is in the Bible. In the next chapter I will answer the question of what Adam's role is in scripture. Please suspend any preconceptions you may have and look at what verse twenty-seven says in the context of the verses around it, and in the context of what we have learned about the image of God.

Every other place the two phrases "and it was so" and "God saw that it was good" are used it is because something is happening in two different realms. It is no different in this verse. If there is a difference in the pattern it is this: in the previous instances God gave a command and creation itself did the work in heaven, and earth helped Him do the work once He got things started below. In this instance God never commanded creation to do anything. Instead, He decided to do something Himself.

He did something Himself in heaven, and just like in many of the previous days something was also done by Him on earth. Creation reported what was done on every level in this verse. High Heaven reported that in heaven "God created (The) Man in His own image". Earth reported that on earth "In the image of God created He him" and "male and female created He them."

As with each of the previous days, something happened in heaven, and on earth. Applying the pattern found in the other days we can then see that there was a Man created in heaven in His image, and there was a man created on earth in His image. The land also reports that male and female were created, but the text does not claim they were made "in His image."

Notice that though God said in verse twenty-six that He wanted to "make" man in His image, verse twenty-seven says that the Man was "created", not made. Those two English words, created vs. made, represent two different Hebrew words. The "creating" of the Man in His own image in verse twenty-seven is not the same thing as God's stated intent of "making" Man (not *the* man but man, as in the human race) in His Own image. Rather, the creation of *the* Man in verse twenty-seven represents the first heavenly step in God's plan (stated in verse twenty-six) to make humanity in His own image. He starts by creating a template, a pattern Son as it were.

In the last third of the verse, it says He "created" man male and female, but it does not say that He created them in His image. It does say that of *The* Man; both of "the Man" in heaven, and "him", the copy of The Man on Earth. But it does not say that humanity male and female were in His image. It says He created them, but it does not say there that they were "in His image" as it did of The Man in the previous two phrases.

The reason for this is that one intended meaning of this verse is that God created the human race separately from Adam and Eve. This section of the verse is not just referring to Christ and the Church, and not just referring to Adam and Eve, but also to the creation of men and women generally that were not yet in His image, but who were after His likeness and had the potential to be made in His image. That was the stated intent all along- to make man in His image. God created the pattern in heaven, the pattern on earth, and the people on earth whom He desired (and still desires) to conform to that pattern.

God wants to "make" (that is a process of formation) those who He created in His own image. It is His desire and intent to "make" human beings in His image, even those who do not start off that way. We will see that the end point is to make the men created on earth like The Man created in heaven. The process of sanctification is *making* "man in Our own image."

I want to be clear here that the text is not making a statement about women somehow not being in God's image while men are. Being in the image is the result of relationship with God, not gender. It is just that Adam started with it and the rest, even Eve, did not (1ˢᵗ Cor. 11:7). The use of "man" in 1:26 is the same version of "Adam" used to mean the human race, both sexes, elsewhere in scripture. Galatians 3:28 says that in Christ "neither is there male nor female." Further Genesis 5:2 says that God "called their name Adam" when they were created. That is, male and female were both called "Adam", which is "man." This is not about a struggle between the sexes. It is about a struggle to bring mankind upward to their Maker.

Even more critically, and I want to be very clear here, the second Person of the Trinity is *not* created. Just like it says in the first chapter of the Gospel of John, He was with God and is God. He was present originally with God. The Logos never came into existence. He was always in existence. But Christ is not just fully God - He is fully man as well. The Man side of Him did come into being. On this earth this happened in the incarnation. The God side met the man side in the womb of the woman Mary. This is orthodox Christian doctrine.

Just as Christ is both uncreated God and created Man, so The Man in heaven is a unity of uncreated God and created Man. This is Christ and the predestined Church joined in one body, with the two becoming One Flesh. Think about what I said concerning the Sabbath in the previous chapter. Like the verses on the seventh day, this verse is both history and prophecy. If you read it from heaven down it is prophecy to us on earth, if you read it from the earth up, it is history. And both are reliable.

From the perspective of heaven, the first thing is that "The Man" is created in heaven. The Logos becomes the The Man. The Logos is not created, but He takes a different form. The Man, the corporate body of Christ and His Church, is created. It is created by fusing created humanity with Uncreated God.

In the view from heaven down, first God created The Man in heaven. This Heavenly Man is Christ glorified and united with His Predestined Church as one body, with Christ as the head. The reality of that has not fully manifested itself on earth yet, but it's coming. When God decided to make The Man in His Own image that is the goal of the plan He had in mind. Through Christ we have access to the Father by the same Holy Spirit (Ephesians 3:8) and we are members of the corporate body of Christ (Romans 12:5) of which He is the Head (Col. 1:18).

This is elaborated on in Ephesians the fifth chapter, shortly after Paul encourages them to put away filthy conduct and live like they are who God says that they are:

So ought men to love their wives as their own bodies. He that loveth his wife loveth himself. For no man ever yet hated his own flesh; but nourisheth and cherisheth it, even as the Lord the church: For we are members of his body, of his flesh, and of his bones. For this cause shall a man leave his father and mother, and shall be joined unto his wife, and they two shall be one flesh. This is a great mystery: but I speak concerning Christ and the church.

The "great mystery" Paul spoke of two thousand years ago is now resolved in the pages of this book while you are present and reading. The Man created in heaven is in the future to those of us on earth but is present reality to God in heaven. The male and the female become one flesh, the uncreated and the created join in one body- God the Son and the Church.

In verse twenty-seven when God creates man, He starts by creating Someone. He created Someone who we still do not fully see from this side of the veil but are promised in scripture that the day will come when we "*shall be like Him, for we shall see Him as He truly is* (1 John 3:2)." God the Father created The Man in heaven and those of us yet to be born were "of His flesh, and of his bones".

We think that this is to happen in the future because to us on earth the unity of Christ and the Church is in the future, but to God it happened before the conclusion of the creation week (the "Foundation of the World"). As it is written in the first chapter of Ephesians (v3-4):

Blessed be the God and Father of our Lord Jesus Christ, who hath blessed us with all spiritual blessings in heavenly places in Christ:
According as he hath chosen us in him before the foundation of the world, that we should be holy and without blame before him in love

"*He hath chosen us in Him before the foundation of the world*". Before the Foundation was completed, some at least were chosen. The God part was present, and the man part was made present by creation. We think of the Marriage Supper of the Lamb as the end of the story, but God established the end from the beginning. From heaven, the end was done first in the mind of God, and then the story was rolled out. We are progressing our way through the story, so we see the end as something that is ahead and has not yet occurred.

When it says "God created (The) Man in His own image" we see that first God created "The Man" in heaven as a fusion of the uncreated Son (the Logos, the second Person of the Trinity) with the created Church, which is His Bride and Body, to form a corporate Man ("*ye are the body of Christ and members in particular*" First Cor. 12:27). Some at least were chosen in Him before the foundation of the world. The first of the three segments of Genesis 1:27 is the record of that event.

In Him we have access to the Father through the Spirit (Eph. 3:8). The Spirit is interested in connection. The Spirit convicts us of sin and comforts us and does everything related to renewing our minds so that we can operate as who we are in Christ. Not wretched sinners full of unbelief, but members of the Church, the Body of Christ with Christ as the Head. The Holy Spirit helps the two to become "one flesh".

I do not wish to enter into the debate of predestination vs. free will here, but in respect to sanctification, it is the will of our new life in Christ to choose God. If Man is to follow God's will to be "in the image of God" it is first necessary for one to have an image visible to man. Scripture tells us that seeing Him as He really is, will cause us to be like Him. As we have shown, God had no image accessible to anyone other than Himself. By becoming The Man, God assumes a form accessible to men. We have an image to go by- The Man in heaven, the visible image of the invisible God.

This also resolves the mystery in Colossians 1:15: "*Who is the image of the invisible God, the firstborn of every creature*". Cults have misinterpreted this verse to take God the Son, the Logos of God, out of the Trinity. It is true that the Greek for "first" can refer to place or position and not order. But it still says "born". It still says "creature". So the cults say "aha, it says He is born. It says he is a creation." They are wrong. The Logos is not the "creation." Rather "The Man" in heaven is the creation, and even that from a fusing of God and Man in the heavens. I could go on about this, but as it pertains more to the Trinity than to early Genesis, it will have to wait for another book.

Let us next consider the second of the three parts of this verse. When scripture repeats "*In the image of God created He him*", this is the creation of The Man on earth. It is an echo of the first part of the verse, an echo on the earth of what had already happened in heaven. Here God the Son formed The Man (Adam) on earth. More details concerning that are to be found in Genesis chapter two, after we discuss who Scripture says Adam really was.

The third and last phrase also has more than one meaning: one for Adam, one for mankind, and one for Christ. In the context of Adam, it refers to Eve. In the context of Christ, It refers to the Bride without spot or wrinkle. Regarding mankind it refers to the creation of the human race generally. We see that the human race was created "male and female". They are not necessarily "one flesh" but they have the potential to be when paired as man and wife. Nor does it say that they are created "in the image of God." They have the potential to be when they move from unbelief to faith.

God is timeless. He sees the end from the beginning. He starts at the goal and then the elements to reach the goal. The view from heaven down is:

First: In heaven - God created The Man in His image. Christ and the Church, united as one flesh, **is God's goal**. It is reality in heaven but that reality must work itself out here until the temporal meets the eternal.

Second: On earth- He created the shadow of that Man, the man Adam, on earth in His image. From him springs the line of Messiah: This is to be the means by which men and women are transformed into Christ and the Church.

Third: And He created male and female humans- *a'dam* the race. These are the ones whom He desires to conform to that image. His intent stated in verse twenty-six to "make" (a process) mankind in His own image starts with creating a human race which isn't in His image yet. He wants to get this race from its starting position to Christ and the Church. Adam is formed to begin that process.

All these things have occurred from creation's perspective, from Heaven down. In all the preceding verses where something is happening in both heaven and earth what happens in heaven comes first, then what happens on earth follows. So it is here. Even more so since with the creation of man God Himself is doing all the work. He is not just commanding creation to do it but then helping in the Land Below. He works from heaven down, but we see it from earth up.

When viewed from the earth, The Man in heaven is not yet manifested – that is for the future. The Man on earth, Adam, was manifested long ago, in the distant past. Even further in the past was the initial creation of Man, male and female. He sees "the end from the beginning" but we see it the other way. From earth it looks like this:

The human race (*a'dam*) is created male and female.

The man Adam (*ha'adam*) is formed...leading to the Incarnation.

> Yet to come: The Man in heaven appears – He is a unity of Christ....and the Church. He is the second Adam.

If we are starting from heaven and reading down The Man came first, but the view from earth shows the creation of the human race, male and female, coming first. After that comes the creation of Adam (and from that later Christ) in the middle. The Man in heaven (as the union of God and Man via Christ and the church) has yet to appear to us.

In First Corinthians chapter fifteen, verses 44b-49 the Apostle Paul was describing the view from our earthly perspective when he wrote:

... If there is a natural body, there is also a spiritual body.
So it is written: The first man Adam became a living being; the last Adam became a life-giving Spirit.
However, the spiritual is not first, but the natural, then the spiritual.
The first man was from the earth and made of dust; the second man is from heaven.
Like the man made of dust, so are those who are made of dust; like the heavenly man, so are those who are heavenly.
And just as we have borne the image of the man made of dust, we will also bear the image of the heavenly man. (HCSB)

From a heaven-down perspective, the Heavenly Man was first. From an earthly perspective though, he was after Adam. He was the second Adam. If we are to view these things in reverse order of the heavenly perspective, then the "male and female created He them" comes first. We see the shadow before the archetype, the raw material before the finished product. Before the appearance of the second Adam, before the appearance of the first Adam, the view from earth is "male and female created He them". Last for us is when the veil is lifted, and we see The Man in heaven as He truly is.

Now I write that, but we have seen him manifested, though not in His full glory because at the end of that story we who believe are a part of that glory. Still, once we understand that there was first a man made in heaven then many mysteries of scripture are solved. One of these is the identity of the figure Melchizedek. The office of King and Priest were united in the person of Melchizedek. Of him I will have more to say later, but Hebrews 7:3 says of him:" *Without father, without mother, without descent, having neither beginning of days, nor end of life; but made like unto the Son of God; abideth a priest continually."*

He was "made" the way that the Son of God was made. Not precisely, because one was translated and born of a woman in corruptible flesh, while as Melchizedek His translation from Heaven to Earth was not so radical. Still both times translation was involved. This is none other than the Heavenly Man making an appearance on earth. This is (one form of) how He was before becoming corruptible flesh born of a woman for our sakes. Or perhaps someone has a better explanation of who might fit the description laid out in Hebrews chapter seven!

Some might object because under the view of scripture I present here, Adam and Eve are not the first humans on earth. The first humans were created when He 'created them male and female', before Adam was formed. The common view is that Adam was the first male human to walk on the earth and Eve the first human female. I beg you to bear with me for two more chapters and it will be laid out what the scriptures say about who Adam really was, and who he wasn't. There is much theology about Adam which is not in the Bible.

That many men and women were created on the sixth day is indicated by the very first verse of chapter two: "Thus the heavens and the earth were finished, and all the host of *them*." Other versions translate this verse "with all *their* hosts." The Hebrew word for "host" means "army" or ranks of troops. When referring to things on earth, it is not used of inanimate objects or animals. It is used of sentient beings. The ancients regarded stars as physical representations of spiritual beings so that even when it refers to stars, it was considered to be referring to sentient beings like angels. And the verse said "the host of *them*"- Heaven has their host, the angels, and earth has its host, people. Adam and Eve alone would not constitute a "host." Ergo, there were more than two people on earth by verse 2:1.

God's blessing to man at the end of Genesis chapter one (vv. 28-30) is very unlike His later interactions with Adam. Perhaps it sounds like a different conversation because it *was* a different conversation, with people who lived long before Adam was formed. Indeed, it would have taken a "host" to "subdue" and "have dominion" over the earth and all that moves on it as God commanded in these verses. It is a job for an army. It would have been a tall order for a single couple.

Prior to developing advanced technology, our main advantages over the beasts were our powers of cooperation and communication. This is an advantage which is useless outside of groups. It is true that the first part of the blessing in verse 28 is to be fruitful and multiply, but that is the same blessing given to the creatures in the ocean and the fowls (verse 22), and no one considered that this meant that only one male and one female of each of them were made.

Besides, in chapter two and three God seemed very unconcerned with Adam and Eve multiplying until after the fall. It is the first order of business to whoever He is speaking to here. It seems reasonable to believe that God was speaking not to a couple here, but to a host as it says in 2:1.

Because God's blessing at the end of the sixth day has application to a common erroneous doctrine concerning the existence of physical death and the potential for sin before the fall of Adam, I will not discuss that blessing further here, but go through it in detail three chapters hence where I will at last present the scriptural evidence that this doctrine is erroneous.

Comparing Genesis 1:27 with Genesis 5:1

~❦~

God had a plan to make humanity in His image, and His image is Christ who is the Heavenly Man. Christ is fully God and fully man. As God the Son, He *is* the Image. As "son of man", He is *in* the Image, the "first-born of many brethren" (Romans 8:29). As believers, we too are to be conformed to this Image. Even as He is the Image of the Father, so we are to be the image of Him.

Remember that to "make" is not the same thing as to "create". When He created them male and female, humanity generally, it is not said that they were in His image. Only *the* man and His copy on earth is said to be so. But God had a plan to get us from where we were created to where He wanted us to be- Christ and the Church. God created eternally in heaven what He wanted mankind to be "made" into as we proceed temporally - "The Man" in heaven. He then created The Man on earth (Adam) in His image. He was meant to be a template, a pattern for the rest of us to conform to in order to make what was declared so in Heaven a reality here: A man living in perfect fellowship with God. Adam was to have a role reconciling mankind with their Maker. Just not the role he thought.

In Adam's fall the Devil opened what it thought was a schism between heaven and earth. Earth and heaven were meant to be connected, where what happened in heaven was eventually mirrored by what happened on earth, albeit more slowly and imperfectly- a suitable world for us who do His will in a like manner.

When the Devil enticed Adam to fall it thought that it had wrecked this process by which earth reflects and follows what has already occurred in heaven. Perhaps the Devil imagined that it could reverse the process and make heaven more like earth, or at the least that the two realms would then be forever separate. The Devil did not realize that God's true fulfillment of the plan was not to be found in the shadow of The Man, but in The Archetype of The Man. Not in Adam, but in Christ.

From a human perspective Adam came first and Christ came after. But in Heaven, The Man came first and Adam after. The Man is the substance, and Adam is only the type. In this fallen world of darkness, we see the shadow first and only later the archetype which cast the shadow. But from the point of view of the light, the archetype comes first and the shadow after.

Here the reader may compare Genesis 1:27 with Genesis 5:1:

So God created man in his own image, in the image of God created he him; male and female created he them.

As I mentioned earlier, the word for "man" here should be translated "the Man" - "*ha-adam*". The same term is so translated elsewhere in scripture. It should be translated "the man" and points to a pre-incarnate Christ taking a human form and becoming God's visible image. In the "two powers theology" popular in first-century Judaism this would be the "visible *Yahweh.*" Adam, the copy on earth of this heavenly event, was the "created He him" echo. But compare that to Adam's view of the same events after his fall as shown in Genesis 5:1-2, the *toledoth* for this section. He mimics the style but leaves off two elements- "the" man and any reference to image. In addition, instead of a series of three creations, Adam uses only two and slips in a "made" in place of the third:

This is the book of the generations of Adam. In the day that God created man, in the likeness of God made he him; Male and female created he them; and blessed them, and called their name Adam, in the day when they were created.

In chapter five the form for "Adam" is the more basic version, "Adam" not "ha-Adam" as in 1:27. Not the word which is normally translated as "The Man", but just "Adam". He is not "The Man" anymore, either in heaven or on earth. He is just "man", with all the weakness and frailty which that implies.

He too is both "created" and "made" but verse 5:1 makes no mention of the state in which he was created, only the state in which he was made- a fallen one. It is a diplomatic way to put it. He was created in innocence, in the image of God. After the fall he was only in the likeness of God. He was "made", but his making was an unmaking. He started life in a higher condition than he finished it and the phrasing here obliquely reflects that.

That the second (Gen. 5:1) attempts to stick to the form of the first (Gen. 1:27) is more evidence that Adam was the recorder of the account of the heavens and the earth. When he gave his own account, he used a similar line. A similar one, but they are not the same. In Genesis 5:1 Adam attempts to repeat the triplicate pattern of 1:27, but to do so he must slip in a "made" between the two "creates". He is created, then he is (un)made, and male and female are also created.

In 1:27 there are three creations. One in heaven (The Man); (2) the echo on earth (Adam); and (3) the creation of male and female (humanity). Adam mimics the same format, but he was not privy to three creations, but only two- his own and his wife. He was not around for the creation which was a fusion of uncreated God and Created Man in heaven in the form of the Son. Thus, he says he was created, then he says he was made (unmade as described above), and then that man was created male and female.

In the first passage two of the three "creates" are said to have been made in the image of God. In the second none are said to be made in the image of God. It merely says that Adam was made in the likeness of God. In comparing the two passages we see that at the end of his life, after his expulsion from the Garden, not even Adam is talking about his being created "in the image of God". He mentions only that he was created "in the likeness of God".

This supports my point that humans are not, in themselves, intrinsically in the image of God. Christ is the image of God, and we only share that image when in harmonious fellowship with Him and so conformed to His image. Once his fellowship was corrupted, Adam was no longer in God's image, just His likeness, as are all men.

Adam's version in Genesis 5:1 is a more limited perspective than that of creation in 1:27. In this verse there are hints that the "male and female" are indeed Adam and his wife Eve. It says that God "called their name Adam", perhaps a nod to God's proclamation earlier that "the two shall be one flesh" or an indication that the male and female in this case were indeed man and wife. Or, conversely, it could simply be a play on words because "Adam" can also mean "man", as in Mankind.

A similar style is used, but not an exact match. Adam is a part of what is happening in 1:27, but just one part and not the whole thing. The mimicry is a literary device which connects Adam to that story, but it does not mean that he is the whole story in verse twenty-seven of chapter one.

If you were the captain of a team that won the Superbowl then there could be a story about the whole team, and then your story as captain of the team. And you might use some of the same catchphrases used in the first account when describing your role in it. It does not mean you were the whole team. It means you were a big part of that story.

Adam was not trying to say in chapter five that he and Eve were all of humanity. He was trying to make a connection to 1:27 but that is not the connection he was trying to make; else he could have repeated the wording exactly instead of just mimicking the general style but with differences, or just let 1:27 stand. He was saying they were a *part* of the larger story of 1:27. They were a smaller creation within that creation, formed to advance God's plan to redeem all of Man. They were a new chance for humanity. They were given more personal attention and protection rather than just being set loose in the world with minimal guidance. Yet they fell.

On a sidenote: When people use Matthew 19:4-5 or Mark 10:6-7 to argue that Genesis 1:27 is *only* talking about Adam and Eve, they seem to forget about Genesis 5:2. Both places say God made them male and female. We can't even say for sure that Christ was connecting Genesis 2:24 to the "male and female" in chapter one. In context, it fits better with the same phrase in chapter five, where it says God "called *their name* Adam", emphasizing that the two are one flesh. When Adam says they were created "male and female" in 5:2 he is saying that what is true for the whole race is true of himself and his wife. So, the phrase in 1:27 could be talking about all of humanity, including Adam and Eve, while 5:2 is talking only about Adam and Eve. Either way, connecting the "male and female" phrase to Gen. 2:24 is not proof that Adam and Eve were the first or only humans created. Just that they are the pattern for humanity.

A second sidenote: Something similar could be said for a passage in First Corinthians chapter eleven. If you consider verses 7-9 to be referring to the current status of all men and women, then it looks extremely misogynistic and seems to say that men are in the image of God, but women are not.

For a man indeed ought not to cover his head, forasmuch as he is the image and glory of God: but the woman is the glory of the man.
For the man is not of the woman: but the woman of the man.
Neither was the man created for the woman; but the woman for the man.

I believe this passage refers to the created order in early Genesis- "the man" here is Adam. It is referring to *that* couple and what happened with them. It is not a statement about the general condition of humanity as regards the image. The reason given as to why, within marriage, the husband represents God and the wife represents the church goes all the way back to the example God gave as a pattern of Christ and the Church- Adam and Eve.

Paul is saying that Adam was originally in the image of God, but Eve was not. This was not because women cannot be in the image of God. It was because of exactly what I have been saying for the last several chapters: neither men nor women are intrinsically in the image of God absent a pure relationship with Him. Adam had it, and Eve, and whoever else was running around at the time, did not. The only way we can get in the image today is through repentance and faith in Christ. Without that, we may be in the likeness of God, as Adam reports He is at the end, but not the image-for Christ is the Image and we must be in Him.

All born-again believers today have a new image to correspond with their new birth, His image, to which they are being conformed. This is whether they are male or female, as the verses following allude. But Paul writes these things because he wants believers to accept, model, and live according to the created order established by God.

To do that we must understand that Adam and Eve are a shadow of Christ and the church. The heavenly man, the God Man, who later incarnated as Christ, is both God and Man. As God He *is* the Image, and as man He is *in* the Image. The church gets there through relationship to the Head. This fits well with what Paul wrote about these relationships in Ephesians 5:21-32. Not that I either I or my lovely wife are close to living that passage out, but we at least acknowledge that is the goal. That is the model, and it is based on the example of Adam and Eve at the start, but Christ and the Church was what they were really pointing to.

Thus, in my journey I came to a place where it appeared to me that Genesis was really saying these things about humans outside the garden, about Adam, and about Christ and the Image of God. Almost as soon as I realized that this view of things might be consistent with the rest of the Holy Writ, the thought came that this must be contradicted by other scripture. What I found was that it contradicted only assumptions about scripture, not scripture itself.

Could it be that God set mankind loose in His creation, and let them go their own way for ages before He chose to progressively reveal Himself to a wayward Mankind starting with the human we know as Adam? A proper scriptural understanding of who God intended Adam to be is essential to answering this question. There is a lot of theology about Adam that is not actually in the Bible. That will be the subject of the next chapter

Who Was Adam?

-:-➣-➤◉◄-≪-:-

Before we talk about the "creation" account in Genesis chapter two, I think it is important to look at what scripture says about Adam. When I started this line of study, I thought that the scripture said that Adam was the first human being in the sense that he was the sole male founder of the human race. I thought that we were born sinners because he sinned, and we inherited our sin nature from him.

I thought that because I had been taught that. Eastern Orthodox Christians don't believe that. It is an Augustinian notion. I thought that because I had read scripture but I had not much meditated on scripture.

I started looking at what the scripture really said about who Adam was as a part of my effort to show myself that I must be wrong about these new insights into Genesis. But instead, I started seeing more and more evidence that they were true!

Once I started looking hard at what the Bible explicitly says about him, I realized that scripture does not tell the same story about Adam that many of us learned in Sunday School. I discovered that the function of Adam is not to be the first human being. The primary function of Adam was to be a figure of Christ. He was also to begin the line, through Eve, that was to lead to Christ. Christ would then succeed in the task at which Adam failed- an intermediary who reconciles God and Man.

Whatever one's view of Adam is, it must be built on a thin supply of scripture references. There are surprisingly few passages about Adam in the Bible once one leaves Genesis. One of the two most informative passages is in First Corinthians chapter fifteen (44-47) when Paul speaks of the resurrection:

It is sown a natural body; it is raised a spiritual body. There is a natural body, and there is a spiritual body.
And so it is written, The first man Adam was made a living soul; the last Adam was made a quickening spirit.
Howbeit that was not first which is spiritual, but that which is natural; and afterward that which is spiritual.
The first man is of the earth, earthy: the second man is the Lord from heaven.

The only passage of scripture which says that "Adam was the first man" also gives a context in which he was "the first man". He was the *first* man in the same manner that Christ was the *second* man. He was the first man in the same context in which Christ was the last. Christ was not the second male human on Earth. Nor was Christ the last male human on Earth, but He was the last Adam.

In context, the passage is not saying that Adam was the first male human being ever created. He was the "first man" compared to Christ, who is the second man, and this is because on earth the natural comes before the spiritual. Adam was the first man of the two men being compared; it isn't a statement that he was the first man to walk the earth. Adam was the first man God used in His plan to bring humanity into fellowship and right standing with Himself. That is, to "make man in Our Own image." Christ is the last man in this same sense.

Once I really thought about it, I realized that rather than making a statement about who the male founder of the human race was, Paul is addressing (in the whole passage, verses 37-58) those who question the truth of the resurrection and how we would get new bodies. He is using a comparison of Adam to Christ to show how the bodies we will receive in the resurrection are superior to the ones which we have in this life. The natural comes first, and those bodies are after Adam, our first stand-in. He's not saying that Adam was the first male human being on earth, but that he represents the natural which must come first. The last is the spiritual Man-

Christ. We will get better bodies because Christ is a superior stand-in. It isn't about who the physical progenitor of humanity was.

Adam was the first man, and Christ is the second man. That is, they are the first and second men in the comparison in chapter fifteen, and in God's plan to redeem and reconcile the human race. It started with Adam, and it is finished in Christ.

In Genesis Chapter two Adam was "formed". That Hebrew word is *yatsar* and the image is one of a potter forming clay into a vessel. Therefore, it describes something pre-existing taking a new form. When the passage in First Corinthians says that Christ is the last Adam it is saying something about who and what the first Adam was.

Isaiah chapter forty-three, verses six and seven, speaks of a future gathering of the sons of Jacob specifically and all of God's children generally. This passage uses all three of the terms associated with producing human beings found in Genesis chapters one and two- the term for fiat miracle, *bara*, which is translated as "created"; the more intimate *yatsar* which refers to forming or fashioning from a material already in existence and is translated as "formed"; and the vague *asah* (accomplish) which is translated "make" or "made" in a wide variety of applications.

I will say to the north, Give up; and to the south, Keep not back: bring my sons from far, and my daughters from the ends of the earth;
even every one that is called by my name: for I have created him for my glory, I have formed him; yea, I have made him.

He is the potter, and those of us who belong to God are His clay. He forms us and fashions us into who He wants us to become- made in His Own image. All three terms apply to those people who are His. The first of those terms can be applied even to those who are not His. All of mankind is a product of God's creation of the human race- even those who don't believe. But some people are also formed by God. What they become is shaped and fashioned by Him. His intervention is real and present in their lives, not simply an ancient First Cause of which they are the result. The goal of His forming is that we become made in His image.

The Prophet Jeremiah spoke of God forming him in the fifth verse of chapter one of the book named for him. He records God saying, "before I formed you in the womb, I knew you." God formed Jeremiah. This was not something that took place in the beginning of the world. This was God intervening in His physical creation in historical times to fashion Jeremiah as He desired. God created man, but after that He commenced some other action which formed Jeremiah to be specifically who he was.

In Genesis chapter one only two of those three terms are used in reference to man: created and made. In Genesis chapter two only two of those terms are used in reference to Adam: formed and made. That the word "formed" is left off in Genesis chapter one but used in chapter two is meaningful. That the word "created" is left off in chapter two is also meaningful.

In the first case, it implies that God left off His personal fashioning and shaping of mankind for a time. He let mankind go our own way. Of course, humanity went astray. We know that God sent Christ into the world to reconcile a world gone astray back unto Him, but Christ was The Archetype. He was preceded by His shadow, Adam, who was meant to do the same.

In chapter two God makes the man as a figure of Christ. His personal intervention, His shaping and fashioning of Adam into a form of His choosing, is emphasized. So it is with all of us who are called by His name. He forms us. This is true of Christ most of all. Nevertheless, because the man is a figure of Christ in chapter two it cannot be said there that he was created by God. That aspect must be left out of the account so long as Adam serves in this role, for the Logos who is Christ is not a created being, but with God and is God.

The Logos as God pre-existed creation. Logos is the Greek term translated "The Word" in the Gospel of John chapter one. The Word was not created. He already existed as God the Son, or the Logos. He was not a new thing. With the Advent, He became flesh and dwelt among us. He did not come into existence with Jesus Christ, rather He changed form. He was translated, not created.

This is verified in places such as Galatians 4:4, where it says that Christ was "born from a woman, born under the law." The word for "born" in this passage is the Greek word *ginomai* which means "to become". It too speaks of something pre-existing going from one state to another. It is not the normal word for born. There is another Greek word for "procreate", but it is not applicable to Christ because He was not procreated in any normal sense of the word. Rather He "became" flesh such as we are.

How wonderful that scripture takes such care to separate out the formation of Adam from the creation of humanity generally, so that Paul's connection of the two events thousands of years later points to Christ as both created man and pre-existent God. In Genesis one Adam is created and as a man Christ was created. In Genesis two Adam is not said to be created but formed from pre-existing material, and as God Christ was not created but only changed form.

It may even be that Adam received the first taste of the Holy Spirit that any human had ever enjoyed, for Paul's quote about man becoming "a living soul" is referring to Genesis chapter two where God breathed on Adam. Breath, or wind, is often used in scripture to refer to the Holy Spirit. In John 20:22 it is recorded that Jesus breathed on the disciples and said "receive ye the Holy Spirit."

In the twenty-sixth and twenty seventh chapters of Job the word used for "breath" in Genesis 2:7 is identified with, and connected to, God's spirit. See also Job 33:4. Life is defined, in this passage in early Genesis and throughout scripture, as "connection to God". Those who are not connected to God are dead, even while they live. Therefore, The Man became a living soul in the true sense of the word when God breathed on him and he received the Holy Spirit joined to his own spirit, which then came to life. Man became connected to God.

Proverbs 20:27 uses the same word for "breath" used in Genesis 2:7 to refer to our human spirit, as enlivened by God:

The spirit of man is the candle of the LORD, searching all the inward parts of the belly.

The word translated "spirit" in the verse above is that which is used for "breath" in Genesis 2:7. The "belly" is a metaphor for "inward being". When things are working right, our spirit serves as illumination for us. When we are doing the wrong thing, our conscience bothers us. This is because when we are connected to God, we have a reference point outside of ourselves to determine what is right and what is wrong.

In this view, Adam was a natural man who had received the Holy Spirit, but Christ is Spirit who became Man. Christ is the Spirit who received a natural body, which is superior to a natural body which receives the Spirit. The body in its own strength cannot keep the connection to the divine and thus in time it dies. The Spirit though, can give life to the body. That was what Paul meant when he wrote that the first Adam "became a living soul" but the last Adam is "a life-giving Spirit."

Adam was given ideal circumstances. He was placed in a paradise. He had daily fellowship with the LORD God. He had a strong marriage. His health was obviously near the peak of what is possible for the natural human form, for scripture records that he lived for over eight hundred years, almost all of it after the fall. He had no worries, and only one law. He was not to eat of the forbidden fruit- he was not to desire being his own determiner of what was good or evil. All he had to do was to continue to trust that God was right in determining what was good and what was evil. In other words, all Adam had to do was have faith in God. Faith was his law.

For us the natural man had to come first, before the spiritual man. Before we could accept righteousness God's way, we had to have a turn at it our way. Even in early Genesis, we see God giving man an opportunity to be in right standing with God through his own works, by his own will, and in his own natural strength and wisdom. And even in early Genesis, we see the fulfillment of the law is to have faith in God. Salvation by faith is not some new thing invented by the Church. It was and is God's intent from The Beginning.

Despite all those advantages, Adam was at best just a natural man who had received the Holy Spirit. Christ was one with the Holy Spirit, also being God. That was the superiority of the second Adam to the first. That will be the superiority of our resurrection bodies to our natural bodies, and that is the superiority of the Gospel, of embracing the salvation God has provided, over our efforts to attain our own righteousness by good works.

I came to see that in context First Corinthians chapter fifteen is a comparison of the superiority of the spiritual over the natural in terms of bodies, and by extension shows the superiority of salvation by God's provision versus attempts by Man to attain righteousness in our own natural strength. The passage begins by discussing the gospel. It goes back to the gospel in comparing the first Man to the second Man. Right understanding of scripture will consistently point to the gospel.

The Epistle to the Romans, 5:14, confirms the view that the Bible does not teach that the role of Adam was to be the genetic progenitor of our race. That idea is just an inference we have made from the scriptures in which Adam was the first human to be named – yet even his name is the same as "Man." What the Bible actually teaches is that Adam was the first *stand-in* for Man. He was a "federal head"- one to represent the group. Adam's role "is the figure of him that was to come", or Christ. His role as "the first human male ever created" is inferred by theologians from scripture, but this not what is really said by scripture. Scripture says Adam is a figure, or foreshadow, of Christ. The other role theologians have assigned him is based on supposition.

It just made so much sense. If Adam was the figure of Christ rather than the first man, that would make humanity's relationship with Adam (except for that portion who are his direct descendants) brothers rather than our father. Another reason this passage supports the idea that the creation of mankind was a separate event from the creation of Adam is the comparability of our relationship to Christ. We are "brethren."

Hebrews 2:17 says *"Wherefore in all things it behooved him to be made like unto his brethren, that he might be a merciful and faithful high priest in things pertaining to God, to make reconciliation for the sins of the people."* Verse eleven says *"He is not ashamed to call them brethren."* Romans 8:29 reads *"For those who He foreknew He also predestined to become conformed to the image of His Son, in order that He might be the first-born among many brethren."*

Christ was not "first-born" in the sense of being the "father" of all believers in the natural, but in being the first human with a special unity with the Godhead. This is a unity which we can access through Him. His family relationship to us is brother, not father.

Though He is King of Kings, and Lord of Lords, the rightful ruler of the human race, He is also a brother, and Christians are to be as brothers and sisters to one another. To fit the comparison with Christ, Adam too was first- in the sense of the first human on earth to have a special relationship with the Godhead. That did not make him the father of all humans though. He was a shadow who fits the Substance better as a brother, not a father, to the rest of mankind.

Adam was a son of the one true God, as is Christ. Adam is so named in the genealogy of Jesus in Luke 3:38. Adam is not a son begotten of God, as is Jesus, for Adam did not come from God, but rather was fashioned by Him. This is yet another way that the spiritual is superior to the natural. Still, He is a son of God.

Adam is named as a son of God, and therefore brother to us. Though he is father of the line of humanity from which Christ sprang, and therefore ultimately did help fulfill God's original plan to reconcile with mankind, Adam is a brother rather than a father to mankind as a whole. This also makes him a better shadow of Christ, who is the substance of that shadow.

The people of Christ's day kept calling Him "Son of David", but He kept calling Himself, over and over again, "Son of Man." In the Greek, the word for "Man" is "*anthropos*" but Jesus was speaking in Aramaic. If we go back to Aramaic, there are two candidates for the word which Christ actually used. He could have said "*bar e'nash*" ("*Ben enosh*" in Hebrew) which would have been "Son of a mortal man", or He could have said "*Ben Adam*". That is, "Son of Adam" (or "man"), a phrase used in the Torah many times. He could have used both at different times. The former for example, would fit with the figure in Daniel chapter seven. I have no doubt that passage applied to Him, but it says there was one *like* a son of man. And this figure is revealed to be "the holy people of the Most High" later in the chapter. Since "*enosh*" emphasizes man's mortality, I don't think that is the word Christ used. He was not the son of a mortal man. I believe He was saying "*Adam*" in this title. But what exactly was the title?

Again, the translators may have let us down. What Jesus literally says in these eighty places is "the Son of *the* man." It is true that Greek uses "extra" definite articles that can be properly dropped in English, but the text says what it says. And in the context of the Christ-centered model it makes perfect sense to read the ambiguous text as it is written.

If we don't delete the "extra" definitive article as the translators have done, Christ called Himself the Son of "the man", even as Adam is referred to as "the Man" in chapter two. Even as, if I am right, the Son himself was "the Man" in Genesis 1:27. How strange that "*the* Man" has been hidden in plain sight in both Genesis 1:27 and in the gospels. In these times of unbelief, hidden truth pours fourth from the scriptures glorifying Christ.

The Jews who supported Him wanted to proclaim Him "Son of David", the rightful king of their race. But I think He referred to Himself as the "Son of *the* Man", and as such was the rightful representative of the whole human race. He came here to do that which His ancestor in the flesh failed to do. The mantle of the first Adam was on the shoulders of the Second. The Man above and the one below united in Him.

I have not yet exhausted all the parallels I discovered (in my attempts to prove this all wrong) showing Adam is intended to be a foreshadowing of Christ. He best fulfills that role not as the father of all mankind, but as the father of that portion of mankind through whom God reveals Himself and brings about His plan to redeem all who believe.

There is one scripture in the New Testament which has been mistranslated in some versions of the Bible so as to seemingly contradict my position that Adam is not the father of every member of the human race. That is Acts 17:26 which reads:

And hath made of one blood all nations of men for to dwell on all the face of the earth, and hath determined the times before appointed, and the bounds of their habitation

Many versions read "has made of one man" all nations of men. If indeed the actual Greek text said that, then the view of Adam I am expounding would be wrong. But there is a reason that the King James version says "of one blood" while other versions say "of one man" or even something else altogether. The reason is that in most manuscripts the Greek does not specify in that place what "the one" might be. The *Textus Receptus* says "one blood", but most manuscripts just say "of one" and the translator must fill in the blank. The other texts just say, "Of one, God has made every ethnos", which is where we get our word "ethnicity".

Of one what? If the Holy Spirit had wanted us to believe that one man was the sole founder of humanity, this would be the perfect place to say so. It could have said "one *anthropous*". They don't. If the manuscripts say anything at all there they say "one blood", and we know that God can make children of Abraham even from stones (Matt. 3:9).

It is much like the national slogan of the United States in reverse. That slogan is "E Pluribus Unum", or "Out of Many, One." What Paul is saying here is "Out of One, Many". But the one is a nation or ethnicity, not necessarily an individual, unless that One is God Himself.

Now it must occur to a large proportion of readers that such a view of Adam is contradicted by other scriptures. That is what I thought too. I intend to take you on the surprising journey I took once I saw the creation accounts in Genesis in a new light. Even as I was examining Genesis Chapter two I was thinking, "this cannot be right, there must be scriptures which contradict this view". Indeed, one place in the scriptures that I thought would contradict it was the passage in First Corinthians which I just expounded on. As you can see, when properly examined not only does this passage **not** contradict this view of Adam, but in fact *confirms* it. That happened more than once on my journey.

Now there is another verse in First Corinthians which is sometimes used to make the argument that Adam and Eve were the progenitors of the whole human race, rather than an example for it destined to produce the Messiah who would redeem it. First Corinthians 11:8-9 reads:

"For the man is not of the woman: but the woman of the man.
Neither was the man created for the woman; but the woman for the man."

Some translations use "man" rather than "the man" and "the woman" but the King James Version looks truer to the Greek here. The words used for "man" and "woman" are not those which refer to all men or women, but rather it is talking about a *particular* man and woman.

I think the particular man and woman are Adam and Eve. Paul is applying their example to all mankind with respect to marriage. He is saying that particular woman came from and for that particular man, not that all women came from and for the same man. The wife was formed for the husband and from him in our pattern example. But saying that they are an example for the whole human race is not saying that they were the sole progenitors of it. There is what the text really says and then there are ideas which we infer about the text because we have heard them from elsewhere.

I agree that God made Adam and Eve in part to model how the relationship of married people should be. This in no way demands that they be the very first humans. Many things in the Old Testament were given to us for an example. For the Jews they were both examples and forefathers. If we are Gentiles, then they are not our forefathers nor is it essential for them to be in order to serve as an example.

The same applies to Mark 10:6-7 and Matthew 19:4-5. Christ showed how God set up the relationship of man and wife "in the beginning." As I will have explained earlier, the "beginning" there is not the beginning of the cosmos, or even necessarily men and women, except that they are a prerequisite for marriage. In Mark 10:6 it says "the beginning of creation" but the word translated "creation" isn't *cosmos* but *kitisis*. It means the created thing you are talking about. It often was used to denote the founding of a city. If you are talking about the universe, it can mean universe, but the conversation in both passages is about the institution of marriage.

He created them "male and female" (Gen. 1:27 **or** 5:2) and declared: *Therefore shall a man leave his father and his mother, and shall cleave unto his wife: and they shall be one flesh* (Gen. 2:24). That statement alone suggests that there were mothers and fathers around at the time to profit from the example.

Christ connects the creation of male and female in Genesis one (or five) with the declaration that man and wife are to be one flesh in chapter two. In other words, the example (Adam and Eve) came in chapter two after the creation of humanity in chapter one. But Christ's connection of the two only establishes that God meant Adam and Eve to be the example. It does not answer the question of whether there were already people on this earth to whom this example was given, or if the example was given only for those who would come later.

I propose that for the children of Israel the answer was the latter, but for the gentiles the answer is the former. Our ancestors were already on the wrong track, though in innocence, when God made Adam and Eve as both an example to man and as the foundation of the plan to redeem man.

I confess that I cheated a bit in showing you at this point how First Corinthians chapter fifteen supports this view of Adam rather than contradicts it. I cheated a bit because I showed you in advance what I only discovered later when I was looking for scripture to contradict my newfound view of Adam and early Genesis. First, I received a new view of Genesis chapters one and two, then I went about looking for scriptures to show myself that what I thought I had been shown must be wrong. Instead of invalidating this new understanding I found those passages confirmed them and even added meaning.

Sin and Death Before the Fall of Adam

I have probably waited longer than I should have to take a time out in this story and visit upon a subject which will be of vital interest to some readers and of passing interest to others. Many readers may be dubious of everything I have said unless I give good account of another strain of theology which impacts our study of early Genesis. For their sakes it is high time I addressed what they might consider "the elephant in the room" over the question of Adam's identity, and indeed everything here discussed.

There is strain of theology which teaches that God made the initial creation perfect. That is, both morally perfect (without sin) and without physical death, even of animals. According to proponents of this idea, long associated with young earth theology, there was no death, no decay, and no sin on earth before the fall of Adam.

In this view, before the fall of Adam lions lay down with lambs. There was no predation. Even the laws of thermodynamics were different so that what we consider the "natural" process of decay was absent.

To support this idea, some believers cite the many instances in Genesis one in which God describes His work as "good." They combine that with questions like "is death something God would describe as 'good?'"

As we discussed in the section on the days of creation, the Hebrew word for "good" in Genesis chapter one is *towb*. It does not mean moral perfection. Indeed, it couldn't because the sixth day is described as "very good."

If "good" means "sinless perfection" then what does "very good" mean? How can one get better than sinless perfection? In addition, in chapter two God describes Adam being alone as "not good", so something can be "not good" even before the fall.

Clearly creation was not perfect in some moral or absolute sense. God made the world suitable and beautiful for His purposes and that is the sense of "good" conveyed by *towb*. This world was never meant to be perfect, or even permanent. It was meant to be a place between Heaven and Hell, a place of choice between two eternities. It is the spinning coin- a temporary state with the question being: on which side will it land? Not land for the earth as it is now, for this world is meant to pass away, but what side will the hearts of each of us in it choose?

The same word, *towb*, is translated as "fair" in Genesis 6:2 where it says that the sons of the *Elohim* saw that the daughters of Adam were "fair". Does that mean that the females from the line of Adam were in a state of sinless and deathless perfection?

If God had wanted to convey the idea of "perfect" to describe His creation He might have inspired Moses to use the word *tamiym* which is translated "perfect." It is used in places like Genesis 17:1 where God tells Abraham to walk before Him and be "perfect". Abraham was only able to do this by faith (just like us).

Others take God's statement in Genesis 1:29-30 as further evidence that there was no human or animal death before the fall since the text only mentions plants as being authorized for "meat" for man and beast. These are probably the strongest two verses of scripture they use to support their view of the original condition of creation, since the New Testament verses they use are wrenched badly out of context. Let's look at this passage. I am going to start with the previous and connected verse:

And God blessed them, and God said unto them, Be fruitful, and multiply, and replenish the earth, and subdue it: and have dominion over the fish of the sea, and over the fowl of the air, and over every living thing that moveth upon the earth.

And God said, Behold, I have given you every herb bearing seed, which is upon the face of all the earth, and every tree, in the which is the fruit of a tree yielding seed; to you it shall be for meat.

And to every beast of the earth, and to every fowl of the air, and to every thing that creepeth upon the earth, wherein there is life, I have given every green herb for meat: and it was so.

It is reasonable to believe from this verse that God wanted humanity and wild animals which live on the land to be vegetarian. I get that. It is fair to say that was God's intention. On the other hand, the text does not say that animals did not eat meat. It says that plants are what God wanted animals to eat- it announced God's intentions. It doesn't say that predation never happened, only that the provision of plants for food for land animals did happen. Every parent understands the difference between what you provide your children to eat, what you wish they ate, and what they actually eat. There is a difference between your stated goals for their diet and their actual diet.

If God telling us that He has given plants for animals to eat somehow means that every animal in fact ate only plants, then why isn't God telling us that He has provided a means of salvation to everyone evidence that all are saved? As we shall see with more detail and clarity in a bit, it is a mistake to confuse what God says He has provided as a statement about what His creation is doing.

Beyond all that, proponents of this view also use this passage to say that there was no physical death of any kind before the fall (some concede that plants might have died). The passage does not say that. It doesn't even really say that animals never ate meat before the fall of man, much less that they never died.

It is a huge leap from the idea that God's desire or goal for creation was for wild animals and humans to eat only plants to saying that there was no physical death before the fall. The passage does not even say that sharks, fish, whales and other animals which live in the water were given plants for food. It only says that about land animals and birds. I'm going to make the case that when God gave mankind dominion part of what he wanted man to do was elevate nature.

This idea that there was no predation on earth before the fall is more theology that is not actually in the Bible. It is only inferred from something that the Bible says viewed through the lens of misunderstandings about the initial conditions of creation. It is a misunderstanding founded on previous misunderstandings.

The root misunderstanding is about what this earth was supposed to be. Before the fall of man, there was the fall of Lucifer. Sin was in the universe prior to the fall of man. The Garden of Eden was a special place on the earth where God fellowshipped with Adam. It was not indicative of the condition of the world as a whole, though perhaps the world could have been lifted up to be like Eden had Adam not fallen.

Even in Eden the serpent was there, challenging God's integrity. The Devil dares not do that in Heaven; it is only recorded that he challenges our integrity, accusing the brethren night and day. There is no reason to believe that the rest of the world, outside of the Garden of Eden, was in any better shape and every reason to suppose that it was worse.

From this evidence it is clear that God did not create the world as a place of sinless perfection without physical death or decay. He did not create the world as a place where His will must be done at all times. That is, He did not initially create the earth as an extension of Heaven. Nor did He create it as a place where His will is excluded, as an extension of Hell. Rather, the world was created to be the battle ground between Heaven and Hell where an argument is being played out between God and the Devil. One question is whether faith in God or faith in self produces true freedom.

The answer to the question becomes ever clearer to the angels: Hell lost at the cross. Its defeat is made manifest through the body of Christ, which is the church. But in vengeful rage Hell will, just before History's end, form a compulsory collective of the great mass of mankind in mimicry and mockery of the body of Christ. But that my friends, is another book, for another time.

Earth was created as a place where His will can increasingly be done, not a place where it is *automatically* done each moment (though in the end it still will be). If those whose faith is in Him have their way, it will look more and more like Heaven. If those who disregard Him have their way, it will look more and more like Hell. Are we in "evening", an increase of darkness and gloom, or "morning", an increasing bursting forth of the light?

Creation (minus the fallen angels) was in a state of *innocence*, which is not the same thing as a state of obedience to God's will. My small children do things that would, for you or me, be sin, but they don't see the sin in it. They are selfish without the capacity to see their selfishness. They parade around naked without seeing the shame of their nakedness. They eat candy when I want them to eat vegetables.

When animals or toddlers take from others, we don't think of it as stealing. When a lion kills a zebra, we don't think that the lion is committing a sin. They are not morally accountable for those actions because of their state of innocence. Sin is not counted where there is no law (Rom 5:12).

The Bible defines sin in Romans 14:23. It says, "Whatever is not of faith is sin." When Adam and Eve took the forbidden fruit, it was an act of unbelief. They did not have faith in what God said. Not only in that instance of disobedience, but in the desire to be able to decide right and wrong for themselves, rather than trusting God to decide what is right and wrong.

The text implies that they had wandered around naked in front of God before the fall but had never considered that it might be something to be ashamed of. The action was there before the fall, but the awareness of right and wrong was not present. Man was in a state of innocence, not sinless perfection. They were "without sin" only because they had no knowledge of right and wrong, not because they were perfectly behaved.

Going back to the passage in Genesis, what it says in verse thirty should be taken in the context of what is said in verse twenty-eight. That is, the provision of plants as food for fowls, creeping things, and "beasts of the earth" is in the context of humanity being given a mandate to subdue the earth and exercise dominion over the animals.

The word translated "subdue" is *kabash*, and it means "to tread down" or "to conquer, subjugate, violate: —bring into bondage, force, keep under, subdue, bring into subjection." The word translated "dominion" is from the Hebrew *ra-dah* and it means "to tread down, i.e. subjugate; specifically, to crumble off: —(come to, make to) have dominion, prevail against, reign, (bear, make to) rule,(-r, over), take." In both cases these meanings are taken from "Strong's Concordance", online version.

I note here that some of those who hold to a young and perfect earth try to skirt around the harshness of these terms by saying that man was told to subdue only the earth, not the animals. They say man was told to "have dominion" over the animals. Then they give a very soft definition of "dominion" which does not convey the full meaning of the word in the original.

These are shady tactics. If humankind is to subdue the earth, surely the "beasts of the earth" are a part of it. Regardless, the proper definition of the word used for "dominion" also includes subjugation. They both confer a sense of "treading down". The meaning of both of those words is very evocative of Christ giving His disciples the power to tread on serpents and scorpions. I invite you to get to a concordance and read for yourself who is giving you the most accurate and complete meaning of these Hebrew words.

The use of both these words implies that the world was not in a state of sinless perfection, or even general obedience, to God. Rather, with the creation of humanity, things were finally in place where God could through humanity begin the process of making the earth – including and starting with the people in it- more like heaven rather than the middle ground it was created as.

God's plan was unfolding. Earth began formless and void, a place of darkness and confusion. That was the original state of creation. With each intervention of God's Word into the physical world, it became more illuminated and orderly. His crowning work was the introduction of man, made in His own likeness and with the potential to share His own image. Humanity was there to complete the task of subduing it, of subjecting it, and of exercising dominion over it.

Verse thirty of Genesis chapter one is not describing what wild beasts and fowls and creeping things ate prior to the fall of man, it is describing what God *intended* them to eat and established for them to eat when man finally exercises his authority according to the will of God. The provision is within the context of God's commission to man to have dominion. It is the desired outcome when mankind subdues the earth and assumes godly dominion over the creatures in it. It wasn't a statement of how things were at the time, but how He wanted us, as His newly appointed rulers, to make them!

This desire of God will come to be reality in the Messianic age, such as is foretold in Isaiah 11:17 and again in chapter 65 where it says that "the lion will eat straw like an ox." It will happen once man, in subjection to Christ, rules the earth according to the will of God instead of his own will.

As further evidence that this view of the matter is correct, compare the list of creatures created on the sixth day in verse twenty-five with the list that God said He provided vegetation for food in verse thirty. "Creeping things", such as lizards, snakes, and small animals which scurry about on the ground, are on both lists. "Beasts of the earth", wild animals like lions and bears, are on both lists. Fowls are only on the list of creatures for which plants have been given for food, because they were created on the fifth "day", not the sixth. Finally, cattle (the word is *behemah* and in the form used here means large domestic-type quadrupeds) in all its kinds are created on the sixth day, **but they are not on the list of animals to whom plants are given for food!**

That last should be a giant red flag that the no predation/no death view has it wrong. Many wild animals, lizards, and fowls are known to be predators, but they are on the list that God wants to be vegetarians. Cattle and animals of that class are known to be vegetarians, but they are the only category of land creature from verses 24-25 which is *not* on the list of things which God wants to be vegetarians in verse thirty.

A reasonable explanation is that cattle and such did not need to be on the list because they were *already* plant eaters. The other categories were rife with predators, rife with carnivores. That they were on the list of animals for which God had provided plants for food was not a statement of initial conditions. It was a statement of the desired goal for man, who had just been given dominion over these creatures! So "behema" were already plant-eaters, and once the three categories listed in verse thirty *also* became plant eaters then *all* creatures of the earth "in which there is the breath of life" would be living in God's provision for their diet.

Man was to set about making the earth into the kind of place God intends for the millennial kingdom to be. We are simply ridiculous failures at it in our own strength. On our own, we can't even fully understand the instructions, much less carry them out. We can't do God's will without a continuous vital connection with God.

First Corinthians and the Entry of Death into the World

There are also New Testament passages which are used by those who say that because there was no sin in the world there was no physical death even of animals before the fall of man. I had already determined that they were mostly wrong on this question from studying the issue of the age of the earth according to scripture. Those who claim that there was no physical death before the fall of man have it very wrong. Not totally wrong as it pertains to man, but almost totally wrong. Let's examine the passages used to support this theology and see what I mean.

One passage is in First Corinthians the fifteenth chapter. I would like for the reader to try and look at it for what it says and not through the lens of theology which teaches that the universe was without physical death before the fall of Adam. It is only fair to do that, because this is one of the most often cited passages used to support that theology. It would be circular reasoning to say, "if we interpret it like X is true then this passage proves X." The very question at issue is whether the passage really supports the doctrine that there was no physical death before the fall of Adam.

Our pre-existing ideas about what we read can blind us to what is actually written; i.e., if we think it is talking about a world where there is no physical death then we will assume it is referring to that, even if the text there and elsewhere indicates otherwise. I suggest instead that if you wish to read it into a larger picture, that you go back to what we have learned about Genesis and consider it in a framework in which this world is a copy and a shadow of the permanent one above.

Instead of quoting only the two oft-cited verses (21 and 22) I want to quote the verses around it in order to give real context.

We start with the previous verses:

And if Christ be not raised, your faith is vain; ye are yet in your sins.
Then they also which are fallen asleep in Christ are perished.
If in this life only we have hope in Christ, we are of all men most miserable.

The passage describes what our condition would be if our faith was in vain and Christ had not been resurrected, while at the same time recognizing that this is not our actual condition (because Christ has been resurrected). Notice it does not use the word "death" for those who have passed on in Christ. It describes them as "fallen asleep." Since our faith is not in vain, they are not dead. They are only waiting between this life and the next one.

Only if our faith were in vain would those in this condition have "perished." People who are not in sin when they "die" do not "perish". Paul is careful not to use the term "death" to describe those who have fallen asleep in Christ. Further, he points out that our hope is not "in this life only". Ergo, there is another life, after this one. If we do not die in our sins then this is the life we enter upon the resurrection (or our translation, which I will discuss later).

Add up what Paul is saying there and he is describing a universe in which physical death is not the end of human life- unless one dies "in your sins". Death in this world is only true death if you die in a state which precludes your gaining the next life. I suggest to you that this was the initial condition of creation.

The condition of the world before Adam's fall wasn't an absence of physical death, but rather it was an absence of permanent death. Men who "died" before the fall would not have died in their sins, and so could have "graduated" from the copy world below to the real world above. They are subject to resurrection and can then move from the shadow land on earth to the true land in heaven.

With that said, let's look at the key verses:

But now is Christ risen from the dead, and become the firstfruits of them that slept. For since by man came death, by man came also the resurrection of the dead. For as in Adam all die, even so in Christ shall all be made alive.

It was Adam who brought sin to life, and when sin came alive, mankind died. The next chapter will exposit Romans chapter five in detail. For now just see it like this: Christ put sin to death and gave us life. This passage is not talking about a past earth where bunnies do not get stepped on by elephants, or lions eat straw like lambs. It is not talking about animal life. It is talking about resurrection life.

The land above may be more like that, but this passage is not making any claims that the world down here was like that. Rather it is talking about Christ restoring the condition (for those who believe) whereby graduation unto the real world above is once again possible. For those whom Christ has restored to this condition, death is once again described as "sleep."

People who claim the Bible teaches that there was no physical death before Adam, even of animals, are necessarily teaching a very serious error- that the work of Christ did not completely undo the fall of Adam. Think about it. If there was a deathless world down here in the beginning, then the work of Christ has not restored all that Adam wrecked. But He has restored it. Thus, on the cross He declared "it is finished" and thus scripture calls Him "the Author and the Finisher" of our faith. He has once again made things so that death is not the end. It is an interlude until the true life, the eternal life, begins. The way to the Tree of Life is again open in Him. Conditions are therefore restored to how things were originally made to be for those who believe. Let us continue reading (v23-26):

But every man in his own order: Christ the firstfruits; afterward they that are Christ's at his coming.

Then cometh the end, when he shall have delivered up the kingdom to God, even the Father, when he shall have put down all rule and all authority and power.

For he must reign, till he hath put all enemies under his feet.

The last enemy that shall be destroyed is death.

In the context of the passage, "death" as described is something only applicable to humans, not animals. It is death with a physical and a spiritual component. It is the sort of death that God means to correct with resurrection or translation, not eternal existence on this plane. That is why mere physical death for believers is described as "sleep" in verses eighteen and twenty (and other places).

Once God has resurrected His own then the land above will merge with that below and will be stocked with inhabitants as it was always intended. The world below as a temporary abode will no longer be necessary. That is why it is written in Rev. 21:1, *And I saw a new heaven and a new earth, for the first heaven and the first earth were passed away...*

The scripture views death as separation from God, and physical death is only the end if one dies in their sins. Keep reading in this chapter and you will see the plan was always for man to be resurrected (or translated) with a heavenly body, and never to inhabit this lower world forever. The plan was for the earth to grow citizens for heaven and the world to come. But they don't start out that way. They are like grains of wheat which must "die" to their original form to become what they were meant to be. The following verses make that clear:

But some man will say, How are the dead raised up? and with what body do they come? Thou fool, that which thou sowest is not quickened, except it die: And that which thou sowest, thou sowest not that body that shall be, but bare grain, it may chance of wheat, or of some other grain: But God giveth it a body as it hath pleased him, and to every seed his own body. All flesh is not the same flesh: but there is one kind of flesh of men, another flesh of beasts, another of fishes, and another of birds. There are also celestial bodies, and bodies terrestrial: but the glory of the celestial is one, and the glory of the terrestrial is another. There is one glory of the sun, and another glory of the moon, and another glory of the stars: for one star differeth from another star in glory.

So also is the resurrection of the dead. It is sown in corruption; it is raised in incorruption: It is sown in dishonour; it is raised in glory: it is sown in weakness; it is raised in power: It is sown a natural body; it is raised a spiritual body. There is a natural body, and there is a spiritual body.

In explaining that our eternal bodies are not the same as our bodies in this lower realm, Paul refutes the idea that this world was originally created in a state in which our natural bodies were fit for deathless existence in this realm. Our existence down here is the grain of wheat. Up there, we are translated to become the whole of the wheat, producing much fruit. Our bodies here are sown in corruption. Our bodies there will be raised in incorruption.

Did Adam have a spiritual body on earth? Did all the animals? No. That would be more theology which is not in the Bible. The incorruptible is meant for the next realm. It was never intended for this one. We are to fade from this life unto the next- unless we are hindered by the sin of un- belief.

Adam was meant to be a shadow of Christ, an opportunity to bring mankind in closer fellowship to its Creator. Instead, Adam brought spiritual death, eternal death, because he failed the test. The shadow failed but the archetype passed. Christ trusted God the Father even unto death, and thereby obtained eternal life for all who believe. Adam did not believe, and his lack of trust took him from life (fellowship with God) unto death- separation from God because of sin.

This is the definition of death according to the Bible, and it's just not applicable to animals or to this creation. This world was never intended by God to be eternal. Animals were not designed to be in perfect fellowship with Him, and indeed they have no capacity to do so. Given scripture's view of what death really is, how then could they have been deathless? There is simply no reason to believe that the earth's animals were able to live forever before Adam sinned. Adam was sown in corruption, but only to be raised in incorruption. His sin interrupted God's process.

Let's keep reading in First Corinthians Chapter Fifteen (44-47):

It is sown a natural body; it is raised a spiritual body. There is a natural body, and there is a spiritual body.

And so it is written, The first man Adam was made a living soul; the last Adam was made a quickening spirit.

Howbeit that was not first which is spiritual, but that which is natural; and afterward that which is spiritual.

The first man is of the earth, earthy: the second man is the Lord from heaven.

These verses verify what I have been talking about and stands against the idea that things in this world were originally created in a state of physical deathlessness. Adam was created in a natural body. Christ was raised in an incorruptible body. Adam was not spiritual, he was earthy. Christ is spiritual, the eternal Lord from Heaven. The physical came first, just as our physical life in this world comes first, but it is not meant to last forever. It is meant to be preparation for the spiritual life in a spiritual body and it is the latter which does not decay.

Let us confirm this by reading that which follows:

As is the earthy, such are they also that are earthy: and as is the heavenly, such are they also that are heavenly.

And as we have borne the image of the earthy, we shall also bear the image of the heavenly.

Now this I say, brethren, that flesh and blood cannot inherit the kingdom of God; neither doth corruption inherit incorruption.

Can it be made any clearer that this flesh and blood creation was not meant to be deathless? Adam's fall did not bring that kind of "death" into the world. It was always the plan for us to bear the image of the earthly prior to our bearing the image of the heavenly. We can't inherit the kingdom of God in our present state, so why would God have made that state endless and undying prior to the fall of Adam?

God told Adam in the garden "in the day you eat of it, you shall surely die" yet in physical terms Adam lived on for centuries after he ate the forbidden fruit. That alone should be enough to get people to realize that God was speaking of death in terms of lack of access to the true life, not merely an end to existence in the lower land. People miss the point when they try to spin it into a yarn about there being no physical death in this world before the fall. That is not what God is talking about any more than Jesus was talking about loaves of bread when He warned His disciples to beware the leaven of the Pharisees.

To God death is separation from Him. Adam was a "dead man walking" from the moment fellowship with God was broken because he could not be resurrected unto the next life in that condition.

If you read the whole chapter of First Corinthians fifteen, what it is talking about is the resurrection, and the resurrection body. What Adam lost was resurrection power, not eternal life in the flesh and blood state in which he was formed. Adam was meant to be the first fruits of the resurrection power of God, which would fill the heavenly realm with people who would live with Him forever.

So, I say again, the definition of death according to the Bible is just not applicable to animals or to this creation. Given scripture's view of what death really is how then could they have been "deathless" in the sense of "living forever here and never passing from this life to the next"?

There is simply no reason to believe that the earth's animals were able to live forever before Adam sinned, and even less reason to think Adam was able to do so. Passing from here to eternity was the point. Adam was sown in corruption, but only to be raised in incorruption. His sin interrupted God's process.

Concerning His process; physical death is not the only way to enter into the life to come. We are given one example to show what God could have done, had things gone differently with the human race. Hebrews 11:5 says: *By faith Enoch was translated that he should not see death; and was not found, because God had translated him: for before his translation he had this testimony, that he pleased God.*

Enoch was said to have "walked with God for 300 years." I suspect that had Adam done well, the normal passage for human beings from this life to the next one would have been translation, not physical death. The Greek word for "translation" which is used in that verse means "to transpose, to exchange one thing for another." It is the best word to describe what Paul was writing about in First Corinthians chapter fifteen.

Enoch was changed out of his earthly body and into his heavenly one without experiencing death. He had nothing left to learn on this earth. He was fully ready for heaven before his body ran out of time. It is not that his earthly body was meant to last forever without dying. Rather, he was changed out of that body before the event occurred, rather than afterward.

Enoch is just a hint of what things could have been, and what things will be for the last generation. First Corinthians 15 (v51-54) goes on to say:

Behold, I shew you a mystery; We shall not all sleep, but we shall all be changed, in a moment, in the twinkling of an eye, at the last trump:

For the trumpet shall sound, and the dead shall be raised incorruptible, and we shall be changed.

For this corruptible must put on incorruption, and this mortal must put on immortality.

Perhaps there will be a generation, who stays faithful through the Great Tribulation, which does not see death. If so, they will be translated like Enoch. If Christ had continued to live a sinless life without having to die for us, I think He would not have passed through death to go back to the Father. He would have been translated, like Enoch.

Romans Five and the Entry of Sin and Death

⤙⤚⬥⤙⤚

The other passage most often cited in support of the view that there was no physical death, even of animals, before the fall of Adam is Romans 5:12. As before, I would like to quote several verses both before and after this verse to gain context:

For if, when we were enemies, we were reconciled to God by the death of his Son, much more, being reconciled, we shall be saved by his life.

And not only so, but we also joy in God through our Lord Jesus Christ, by whom we have now received the atonement.

Wherefore, as by one man sin entered into the world, and death by sin; and so death passed upon all men, for that all have sinned:

(For until the law sin was in the world: but sin is not imputed when there is no law.

Nevertheless death reigned from Adam to Moses, even over them that had not sinned after the similitude of Adam's transgression, who is the figure of him that was to come.

But not as the offence, so also is the free gift. For if through the offence of one many be dead, much more the grace of God, and the gift by grace, which is by one man, Jesus Christ, hath abounded unto many.

And not as it was by one that sinned, so is the gift: for the judgment was by one to condemnation, but the free gift is of many offences unto justification.

For if by one man's offence death reigned by one; much more they which receive abundance of grace and of the gift of righteousness shall reign in life by one, Jesus Christ.)

Therefore as by the offence of one judgment came upon all men to condemnation; even so by the righteousness of one the free gift came upon all men unto justification of life.

For as by one man's disobedience many were made sinners, so by the obedience of one shall many be made righteous.

Moreover the law entered, that the offence might abound. But where sin abounded, grace did much more abound:

That as sin hath reigned unto death, even so might grace reign through righteousness unto eternal life by Jesus Christ our Lord.

Romans 5:12 says that "*by one man sin entered into the world, and death by sin*". This is the basis of the claim that there was no sin in the earth before the fall of Adam, and therefore no death, not even animal death. The confusion comes from a misunderstanding, partly over what the word "world" means in this context, but mostly over what the word "entered" means here. The Greek word for "world" is the same as that used in the famous John 3:16 "for God so loved the world that He gave His only begotten Son, that whosoever believes in Him should not perish, but have everlasting life."

The Greek word translated "world" is *kosmos*, and it can mean the universe, or the physical planet, but it also frequently means the world of man. In both these verses it refers to the human inhabitants of the earth, and not the rocks, or trees, or fish or other animals. This is very clear from the context of John 3:16. God's love for "the world" is really love for the human inhabitants in it. It says that "whosoever believes" can be saved.

Rocks and trees and animals don't have the spiritual dimension necessary to access salvation. As magnificent as nature is, God does not care so much about the rocks and rivers and trees as He does for us. God does care about the animals, for He blessed them. But not so much as He cares about us, for we "are of more value than many sparrows" (Luke 12:7).

In Romans 5:12 he is also using the "world" as a term to describe the human inhabitants of the planet, not the whole planet and biosphere. This can be seen where it gives the result of Adam's fall; "sin passed upon all men, and by sin, death". It says nothing about death passing onto all animals, or the laws of nature being changed because death was on the rocks and rivers. That is more theology that is not in the Bible! What the passage says is that sin passed upon *men*, clearly indicating that the use of the word "world" is that which means the human inhabitants of the earth.

I suggest that the same thing is true of the word "death" as used in Romans 5:12. Taking the Bible "literally" should not be an excuse for a believer to interpret a passage the same way a secular atheist would. The "death" that Adam was subjected to was spiritual death. It later manifested in a physical death, but God told him that he would die in the day that he ate the forbidden fruit. His body lived on for centuries, but the death God was speaking of was separation from Him. Perfect fellowship was broken. That is the same meaning of death Paul speaks of here.

The death which passed to all men was a spiritual death. This was not about whether their physical bodies would be subject to decay, but about where their souls would spend eternity. In Adam, mankind moved from innocence to accountability, and in ourselves we failed at giving a good account.

Christ has died for our sins and removed the curse, but we still "die" a natural death which we understand as sleep until the resurrection. I repeat my assertion from the previous chapter. The idea that there was no physical death before the fall, even of beasts, is in error because it diminishes the work of Christ. It means that the work of Christ has not completely undone the sin of Adam, but it has. He has redeemed us from the curse. You need only keep reading past Romans chapter five into the sixth and seventh chapters to understand the context in which the Apostle Paul is using "death", and we will do that here soon.

Is our goal to get back to the Garden, or is it to get to Heaven? And if our goal is Heaven, is it not true that this world is only but a steppingstone, a test to bring glory to God? Don't the sages tell us that this world is not our home? It wasn't our home before the fall either. It's not that Christ's atonement somehow failed to fully redeem us from the curse of the fall. He has fully redeemed us. This world was never meant to be eternal. Nor were our bodies within it meant to be eternal.

Early Genesis says as much in chapter three verse six when Adam and Eve are about to eat the forbidden fruit. It says, "and she gave unto her husband with her, and he ate." The word translated "husband" there is *enosh*. Like *a'dam*, it is a word which means "human" or "humanity" but, according to Strong's Exhaustive Concordance, in a less dignified sense than *a'dam* because it emphasizes man's mortality. That this word was used to describe Adam just before he ate of the forbidden fruit indicates that he was a mortal. "Mortal" is a fair translation of the word *enosh*. Adam was a mortal man about to cut his own lifeline.

Before I go on, I want to make a point about the role of Adam and more evidence from scripture that Adam had a role as a federal head or representative of humanity, just as Christ did. Eve took the fruit first, but sin didn't enter "the world" through her. Romans 5:12 says that through one *man* sin entered the world. She wasn't the stand-in for humanity, but he was. Her decision applied to her, but Adam's decision applied to us all. If there were ten thousand humans and any of the others had broken the command, would sin and death have entered the whole world or just them? I suggest to you that it would have been the end of just them. They were not the privileged stand-in for humanity. Neither was Eve. Adam was.

That Adam had to eat of the Tree of Life to become immortal is another indication that He was not immortal prior to his fall. One might say "but maybe he did not need to eat of the tree of life before he fell because he already had eternal life on earth until his fall."

If that was true, then the existence of the Tree of Life becomes superfluous. If that view of physical death is true, then the Tree of Life is not needed to produce eternal existence unless Adam chooses to be his own god, at which point God makes it unavailable anyway. The Tree of Life is a type of the Kingdom of Heaven and it makes no sense at all for this tree to be an unnecessary element. This should be a clue to us that Adam did not have eternal physical existence without access to the Tree of Life, even prior to his fall.

The Tree of Life gives us our own choices eternally without decay- as an act of ultimate love. Had Adam chosen the Tree of Life in faith then the world would have become much more like what the no-death-before-the-fall folks think that it was. The existing earth would have become more and more like the New Earth; the earth to come; the eternal home without death or decay that we are promised.

After that age of peace, during which Man would have made souls to fill the earth to come, God's plan for a New Heaven and New Earth would have unfolded. Our planned age of peace was pushed back due to the fall, but the ultimate goal will still be accomplished. Despite this terrible de-tour, the ultimate destination has not changed. God's plans will still un-fold- for those who believe.

As it was, Adam chose to put his faith in his "self"- in his own discernment to judge what was good or evil. Had Adam then eaten of the Tree of Life in unbelief- the tree which gives man eternity in a permanent state- it would have eternally separated man and God. Hell is separated from God. Hell is permanent. In Hell there is no decay. It is written of those in Hell *"their worm does not die, and their fire is not quenched."* This is an eternal state, just like heaven. The Tree of Life gives eternal existence to all, but eternal life only to those whose faith is in God.

Had Adam chosen to eat of both trees, earth would have been just as sep-arate from God as Hell will be. Therefore, humanity would have been eter-nally cut off from the eventual reconciliation God had ordained. No won-der God thrust the man out of the Garden before Adam made the choice of separation and self-sufficiency permanent for the whole race of man by eating the fruit of the Tree of Life in a dead spiritual condition.

But ultimately, God will all allow each of us our choice. Scripture teaches that God will give believers a new earth like the one the confused think that Adam had. One that is eternal and unchanging in its blissful fellowship with God. Christ as judge will also give those who disbelieve an eternal and unchanging state commensurate with their own choices and desires. This granting us our own choice of faith in God or faith in self, of granting us our own choice permanently and irrevocably even if our choice breaks His heart, is the ultimate loving act of a loving God.

I support taking the Bible literally where the context supports taking it literally. But taking it "literally" should not be confused with taking it as a natural person would, for Christians are supposed to see things from a supernatural perspective by reason of their connection to the Holy Spirit. "Death" is not the end of our earthly life. For the believer death is separation from God. When Paul uses the term "death" he means what God says death is, not what a natural man thinks death is "literally".

Let us not be like Nicodemus, who when told that a man must be "born again" thought Christ was talking about a man entering his mother's womb for a second time. Nicodemus interpreted Christ literally, but not correctly, because he thought and spoke in natural terms whereas Christ spoke in supernatural ones.

This view also matches better with what we know about who Adam was. As verse 14 above says, Adam "is the figure of him that was to come." That is, Adam was a figure of Christ. So which scenario fits the template better, that Adam started with a world that was an eternal paradise and was there to keep us in that place, or Adam started with a creation that needed to be brought to eternity?

I submit to you the latter view of Adam makes him a better "figure of him that was to come" than the former. Both Christ and Adam had a mission to reconcile man to their Creator. In so elevating man, even the natural order would be elevated as much as is possible in a world that was never meant for eternity. That is, the world can be made to look like scripture tells us the millennial kingdom will look. In that age the wolves and sheep dine together, and the lion will eat straw like an ox. One who dies at a hundred will be mourned as one who dies in their youth.

It is written "They will not do harm on all My Holy Mountain". That Holy Mountain is Christ's kingdom. It is the stone made without hands in the second chapter of Daniel. This stone crushes the kingdoms of the world into dust and grows into a mountain which fills the whole earth. And when that is done, the material universe will have served its purpose. It will have demonstrated that faith in God produces freedom, and faith in self, or the collective man, or any other system or being whatsoever, produces ruin and death. Once this is done, it will then be the proper time to make our choices permanent, and we can look forward to a new heaven and a new earth.

What I Learned in Romans Chapter Five

Now when I said before I was taking a time out in sharing with you my journey of discovery, I do not want to give you the impression that I learned nothing from Romans chapter five. It is true that I already understood some of the basics, such as the real meaning of "death" as used in the passage. From this I knew that it had nothing to say about the spread of animal death.

But I also got my hat knocked off in Romans five. I realized something that seems so obvious now but remained hidden in plain sight until what I suppose was the proper time for it to be revealed. As if in answer to an age of doubt, truth shows itself to be true, even if our prior understanding of it was flawed.

When it first struck me that the formation of Adam in Genesis chapter two was at most a subset of the account of the creation of "man" in Genesis chapter one, I set off to find scriptures to invalidate the idea. After all, it seemed contrary to every version of the story in every Sunday school class I had ever heard. One of the places I felt confident that I would find scripture which refuted this rash notion was in Romans chapter five.

What I thought Romans chapter five said was that sin spread from Adam to all of mankind because we were his descendants. I thought that it said that we inherited his sin nature by virtue of our physical descent from Adam. If that were so, then the idea that not all men were physical descendants of Adam would be out the window. Adam's main biblical role would then be the physical father of the human race, rather than the figure of Christ, who is "the firstborn of many brethren" (Romans 8:29).

The truth is that the Augustinian notion of "Original Sin" inherited from Adam was a later Roman Catholic development. It wasn't from the apostles. It was from Augustine. The Eastern Orthodox churches don't teach or believe in our inherited guilt through Adam's "Original Sin". Nor do the Mennonites. The Jews don't either, though they do have a concept that man is by his nature prone to evil.

There are a lot of American Evangelical Christians who think the Augustinian doctrine of original sin was an essential part of the Christian faith from the start, but that's not so. Saint Augustine was quite a brilliant man, but this notion isn't a part of the Apostle's Creed, the Nicene Creed, or even the Athanasian Creed. These are the "big three" creeds by which the church has always measured who was an orthodox Christian and who was a heretic.

I've heard Dr. Michael Heiser claim that Augustine was using a flawed translation of Romans 5:12 when he developed the doctrine. One that said "in him all sinned" rather than "because all sinned." Augustine's doctrine sure isn't in the text as it stands, and it is alarming to me how most of the western church has passed the doctrine along without noticing.

Let's take another look at the relevant passage from Romans five. I think you will see that the doctrine of inherited original sin through descent from Adam is not there, and if it were in the Bible, that passage would be the most likely place to find it. Let's look at it again a few verses at a time:

Wherefore, as by one man sin entered into the world, and death by sin; and so death passed upon all men, for that all have sinned

(For until the law sin was in the world: but sin is not imputed when there is no law.)

Nevertheless death reigned from Adam to Moses, even over them that had not sinned after the similitude of Adam's transgression, who is the figure of him that was to come.

But not as the offence, so also is the free gift. For if through the offence of one many be dead, much more the grace of God, and the gift by grace, which is by one man, Jesus Christ, hath abounded unto many.

Verse twelve does not say that we inherited our sin nature from Adam because we are his physical descendants. It says that sin entered the world through Adam and death "passed" upon all men. Why? Was it because Adam was their ancestor? No, but rather "for that (because) all sinned."

"Entered" in this verse is the Greek word *eiserchomai* and it is used in the metaphorical sense of "arise, come into existence, begin to be". Another way to put it is to "come to life." Sin came to life and mankind died when Adam transgressed. Paul himself used very similar language nearby, in chapter seven of Romans when he describes the role of the law and sin. Here I quote chapter seven, verses eight and nine. This time from the New International Version:

For apart from the law, sin was dead. Once I was alive apart from the law; but when the commandment came, sin sprang to life and I died.

If you read the whole passage, you will see what I am suggesting about how sin "entered" the world. I say the same thing Paul says about the relationship between sin, death, and the law. Before he knew the law, he had life and sin was dead. But once the commandment came, sin came to life (it entered his world) and he died. What I am suggesting is that the condition Paul describes is just what it was like for those men who lived before Adam. They were alive apart from the law. They were acting out of God's will, but there was no law and hence no accountability.

Once Adam, as the stand-in for all mankind, broke the law then sin came to life and Adam died (as the Bible defines death). If any of them had been perfect, they would not have died, but none of them were. All of them needed the protection afforded by Adam as the stand-in for all of mankind, even as we need the protection afforded by Christ as our stand-in.

Sin sprang to life. What was once dead had existence in the world. That is what is meant by sin "entering" the world. There is no need for theologians to concoct another method of entry of sin into the world besides the one Paul describes two chapters later. Sin was dead before Adam's failure. After that, it was alive, and Adam was dead. Sin entered, became alive, in the world.

That word "passed" is from a Greek word *deirchomai*, which means just that- to pass through or spread through. It is used to describe events like going on a journey or the children of Israel "passing through" the Red Sea. It has nothing to do with inheritance. Paul could have used the word for inheritance, *kleronomeo*, if he had meant that.

Notice that Paul writes that sin entered the world, but death passed through the world. Sin did not have to pass through the world like (spiritual) death did. It was latent in the environment, but without law sin was dead. There was no way for it to bring any spiritual death. But it was only waiting for knowledge of the law to become alive. It was only waiting for the failure of Adam to become animated and thus make its entrance.

When Adam chose to be his own god, sin sprang to life. It entered the world by animation, as would some creature of stone that suddenly became viable. The stones were always there, all around, but until they had life, the creature did not exist. It did not enter the world until it came to life.

Death did pass to all men. Not that the evil deeds were greater, but our knowledge that they were evil was greater. The deeds were old. The guilt was new. The shame was new. The separation from God due to willful disobedience and a stained conscience was new.

Romans 5:12 is saying that spiritual death passed, or spread through, all of mankind when Adam sinned, not because of his sins, but because of theirs. Mankind was already doing things God disapproved of, but they were doing so in a state of innocence, like children. As it says in the next verse, *"where there is no law, the penalty for sin is not imputed."* That is, it is not charged to one's account. Therefore, any souls who died before Adam's sin are not damned to Hell.

God made the man Adam as the stand-in for all mankind; as the Second Adam Christ is also. When he was given a law, the state of innocence was over. When Adam broke the law his role as stand-in for man afforded no protection for the rest of our race.

If any of them had been perfect, it would not have mattered that the stand-in had failed. They would not have needed Adam's protection. But because they had their own sins, they did need it, just as we need the protection of the Last Adam. At that point, death reigned. They were condemned even before the law was given, because, as Paul points out earlier, they had a conscience, a sort of natural law put in their hearts, so they are without excuse.

Prior to the Garden no man was ever asked to live as a person who had faith in God rather than themselves. Adam was the "first man" who had that fateful choice. God decided to take man from a state of innocence to a state of responsibility. He did it with what is still the key question- do we have faith in God to determine what is good and evil, or do we wish to decide that for ourselves?

To give mankind the best possible odds, God did not start accountability with each person, from lowliest to most privileged. He started at the top. He started with the best man on earth, the one with the most ideal circumstances and possessing the greatest privilege: The one who had received the breath of God which is the Holy Spirit and the one who had daily fellowship with the LORD. The one with a spouse created of him and for him. That one would be the stand-in for mankind to see if man would, for an age, be liberated or mired.

That one would begin, with his wife, a Royal Priesthood, and a Holy Nation that would take His glory to the ends of the earth. Then a Millennium of peace would be ushered in, ending in a New Heaven and a New Earth. I say that this was what God wanted the First Adam to do, because it is what the Last Adam is doing and has done. I will offer more scriptural proofs as we go on.

I remember thinking in my prior misunderstanding how unfair it seemed that we would all be condemned to have a sin nature because of the choice of Adam and Eve. Even Exodus 20:5 only refers to punishment being visited to the third or fourth generation, and that only for those who hate God. Later even this threat seems mitigated by the beautiful words of Ezekiel chapter eighteen. Just read that chapter and you will see that the idea that we bear the guilt of Adam's sin is utterly against the scriptures.

Now I see that what we inherit is a lack of ideal connection to God. Our sins are our own, even as they spring from that disconnected nature. Only the absence of law kept sin out of the lives of our forebears. The way God chose to do it gave us the best possible odds, and humanity still blew it. This creation, which was never made to be eternal, came built-in with the capacity to trust ourselves more than God. Not that God is the author of sin, but He authored choice. It is the wrong choices, the choices outside of faith, which are sin.

Man was always in need of reconciliation. From the day the first man was made and from the moment we ourselves are born, we needed to be reconnected to our Creator to produce righteousness. We can't do it on our own. Man did not just get saddled with a sin nature when Adam came along. We had one, but we were not penalized for it. We did things which would have been sinful from the start, but since sin was dead in the absence of law (Rom 7:8), we were let off the hook. In the beginning the penalty for sin was not imputed because as it says, there was no law.

We were not held accountable until God gave the man, Adam, a law. This command not to eat of the tree of the Knowledge of Good and Evil embodied the very choice every man must make between faith in God or faith in self (or anyone or thing else) to determine right from wrong.

As Paul said of the idol worship of the pagans in Acts 17:30: God winked at wrongdoing in the times of ignorance, but now calls on us to repent. God's revelation to man is progressive, and the more we know about who

He is the more responsible we are to live in that knowledge. Israel was held to a higher standard than the heathen nations around her. Christians are expected to have a higher standard than the faithless. God had given man dominion over the earth. In Adam, God began the process of progressive revelation to man.

Mankind always needed reconciliation, and Adam was the figure of Him who was to reconcile us. Even as Christ was the royal representative on behalf of the whole human race, his foreshadow Adam was meant to be also. Adam was given every chance to make the right choice. God did not pick a stand-in for us who had poor circumstances. Rather, he had ideal circumstances. He had it "as good as it gets".

Even as Christ came from a special place of fellowship with God the Father, Adam had a special place of fellowship with God- the Garden of Eden planted by the LORD God Himself with every pleasant tree that gave good fruit. There would be no deflections about poor environment or a disadvantaged upbringing that some men still use to hide behind or obfuscate the truth. The truth is that man cannot be righteous in himself even in the best of circumstances. Adam and Eve did not make the choice of faith. They made the choice of self, and innocence was lost.

After the eyes of mankind were opened, we were self-condemned. We wanted the power to know for ourselves what was good and evil and as soon as we got that power it forced us to realize that we were evil! And so, as verse fourteen says "death reigned from Adam till Moses." Mankind went from a state of innocence to a state of sin, and our stand-in now afforded no protection. Until the Law of Moses came there was no other law to keep in order to obtain right-standing with God. Not that we could.

Man had still not, and most have still not even to this day, learned that it is faith God desires. Even the first law, the commandment to Adam, was about faith. If our faith is truly in Him, our obedience will in time follow. If it is not, then no matter how determined our efforts are to be righteous by following the law, we will fail.

While the mass of mankind sought a law, a list of rules to follow to earn right-standing on a basis of our own efforts, one man got it right. In Ur of the Chaldees, one descendant of Adam we now know as Abraham believed God, and it was counted to him as righteousness. That is not to say that he was righteous, but God counted it as righteousness. Abraham did what his ancestor Adam failed to do. He believed God. And from this descendant of Adam would come another- Moses the lawgiver.

Once Moses came, God gave man The Law. Man at last had his list of rules he so coveted. A way he might keep score or have some basis of negotiation with which he might bargain with his Maker. Death didn't have to reign. Righteousness could come through following the law, if anyone could.

But of course, man can't do that. Death reigned from Adam until Moses, and it reigned even afterward. That is because the law, meant to give a way back to life, instead produced more death. But the point of all that death, produced by more law springing more sin to life, was to make it clear to man how guilty we are. It was to show how hopeless it is to count on our own works to be righteous. It was for the purpose of driving us to God's real goal: Grace obtained by faith. Let's look at that bit of Romans chapter five:

For as by one man's disobedience many were made sinners, so by the obedience of one shall many be made righteous.

Moreover the law entered, that the offence might abound. But where sin abounded, grace did much more abound.

When there was no law, it was easier for men to kid themselves in the period between Adam and Moses. They might be tempted to think that though Adam failed, they would not have in the same circumstance. In the absence of law, they might concoct their own law and their own rationalizations when they broke it. All were locked up under sin when Adam fell, but they might not see the true depth of their sinfulness absent the law. And so law was given. It put man under even more sin. It made men more aware of their sinfulness because they then had a Divine standard to which to compare their actions.

Though this enumeration of rules bound man up in sin, it also allowed man a way of escape. For if the law could be kept by a new stand-in then we might be protected, even as they were protected in the absence of law. They were protected by their ignorance of God's requirements, but we are protected because our stand-in not only fulfilled the requirements but paid the debt for our failure to do so in His own Person. This is another way in which the free gift of God is greater than the offense. Let's take another look at verse fifteen:

But not as the offence, so also is the free gift. For if through the offence of one many be dead, much more the grace of God, and the gift by grace, which is by one man, Jesus Christ, hath abounded unto many.

Here Paul compares the spread of grace to the spread of death and says that grace was spread on different and better terms. If man was in perfection instead of just innocence before "the fall", then this makes no sense. Why did the grace of God abound "more" than the spread of death? They are on the surface quite symmetrical. Through the offense of one, death spread to the many. Through the obedience of one, grace abounded to the many. So why is the second better than the first?

The answer for the spread of grace being better is simple: Death spread to the many, but those many were already doing things which would have been counted as sin if only they had been given God's just law. They were only unaccountable because there was no law- sin was dead before Adam's choice brought sin to life. The grace abounds more because not only does it spread by God's gift rather than our own works, but it pays the penalty for sin. Whereas before sin came to life there was no penalty to pay but the *potential* for one to spring up was always there. The spread of sin unleashed the potential of sin that was already latent. It did not "make" the sin. The free gift took away the penalty for the sin- it removed the "potential energy" sin had to come to life.

It is the difference between living on a field of land mines which have never been activated and having someone detonate all the mines safely for you. Once the mines are activated, your situation is worse, but the potential for them to cause you trouble was always there, even before activation.

The problem of the land mines becoming activated is a problem, but the solution of someone safely detonating all of them for you is a blessing which is better than the original problem of the mines coming to "life". Not only is the "activation" threat gone, but the underlying thing that was activated is also rendered harmless. Sin has lost its power to ever keep us from entering into life, thanks to the finished work of Christ!

What does this say about the doctrine of Original Sin? **It doesn't change the bottom line**. Mankind, disconnected from God, is inherently prone to sin. It only changes the reason why this is so. It is not so because Adam was our forebear, it is so because connection to the Creator is the only way we can be righteous. We must abide in the vine.

Creation was designed to be disconnected from God yet retain the ability to re-connect with Him. Until that re-connection is made, we choose with a flawed moral compass. Only the absence of law in the beginning, not early man's moral perfection, kept sin out of the world as a live force. Even the best of our motives will be mixed, tainted with sin. Christ came to reconcile the creature to the Creator.

The Subjection of Creation to Futility

⤙❈⤚

To understand once and for all that creation did not start in a state of moral perfection let's look at the passage which lays out the situation in the most depth. That is the middle of the eighth chapter of the epistle to the Romans, from the New International Version:

I consider that our present sufferings are not worth comparing with the glory that will be revealed in us. For the creation waits in eager expectation for the children of God to be revealed. For the creation was subjected to frustration, [some translations say here futility or vanity] *not by its own choice, but by the will of the one who subjected it, in hope that the creation itself will be liberated from its bondage to decay and brought into the freedom and glory of the children of God. We know that the whole creation has been groaning as in the pains of childbirth right up to the present time. Not only so, but we ourselves, who have the firstfruits of the Spirit, groan inwardly as we wait eagerly for our adoption to sonship, the redemption of our bodies.*

There is no hint in any of these verses that the subjection of the creation to frustration was something that occurred after Adam's sin. There is no hint here that it means that the original condition of creation was one of sinless and deathless perfection. Based on the initial conditions of creation in the first two verses of Genesis chapter one, there is every reason to suppose that it was in a sorry state at the beginning. Nor is there any hint here that creation wants to get *back to some prior condition* which it once possessed. Nor does it say that creation is waiting for the "children of God" to get *back* to some previous condition. Instead, it says that it is waiting for

~ 221 ~

them to *be revealed*, as if they were something creation had not seen before. Verse twenty-two says that creation has been suffering the pains of child-birth "right up to the present time". In other words, from the beginning until now.

The text just doesn't teach that "the fall of Adam" produced the futility of the present creation. The subjection to futility was complete on the second day- when God produced a place where His perfect will was done at once, but the natural universe was left out of it! Adam was supposed to help humanity use our dominion as agents of God, to uplift this creation. God set things up so that we could take over His work as His agents, making this world a better place. The garden was meant to become the millennial kingdom. Adam's fall didn't send creation into its present state, but his fall meant that God's plan to make it better was temporarily set back.

I am fully convinced that many of the horrible and senseless tragedies we now face are a consequence of Adam's fall. But just in the sense that man never fixed the things God sent us here to fix, not in the sense that God put us in a creation that didn't need His further will put into it. We should have found a cure for childhood bone cancer thousands of years ago. We should have beaten our swords into plowshares thousands of years ago. Due to the fall of Adam, and our own lack of faith, we will have to wait longer for His Kingdom to Come, and His will to be done, on earth, as it is in Heaven.

The passage says that creation will be liberated from bondage and decay when we are. When we are revealed "in the redemption of our bodies" the whole creation will benefit. That's when creation gets a makeover. But Adam hadn't had that makeover. He was referred to with a term which has connotations of "mortal" (*enosh*) in Genesis chapter three just *before* the he took the forbidden fruit. In addition, he needed access to the tree of life to live forever, as if he hadn't chosen access to it yet. Adam did not have the "imperishable" state the Apostle Paul describes in First Corinthians 15:50-54, else he could not have died. We are not trying to get back to Adam's state. We are trying to get to where Adam was meant to go.

Verse twenty clearly says that "creation was subjected to frustration, not by its own choice". Creation did not make the choice to be subjected to frustration, which the verse later ties to "its bondage to decay". If Adam's choice had been what subjected creation to frustration and "its bondage to decay" then it would have been the choice of creation- at least the part of creation that was Adam. Instead, creation was subjected to its bondage to decay "by the will of the one who subjected it, in hope that the creation itself will be liberated from its bondage to decay". Adam's choice did not make creation that way, God made it that way. It was His choice. But He did not make it with the intent for it to stay that way.

The One who subjected creation to the bondage of decay was God. Creation does not desire to be in this condition, but God subjected it to this condition. Not permanently. It was subjected in the hope that "creation itself would be liberated from the bondage of decay and brought into the freedom and glory of the children of God". That is, it was God's hope that mankind would choose to connect with Him rather than remain disconnected. Once that happened, God would elevate creation to reflect the improved condition of Man.

Creation was subjected to frustration because God is waiting for mankind to make our choices. This creation is a "change zone" between two places where choices are permanent- Heaven and Hell. That's why things unwind. That's why we clean one day, and the next day things begin to get dirty again. We have to decide if we are really committed to keeping them clean or not. And those commitments we make form the basis for who we are.

It is common for children to think they are going to grow up to be an astronaut and a medical doctor and President and several other things. As we grow up though, we find our situation and our past choices combine with the limitations of the length of our lives to narrow our future choices. This is the purpose of the natural decay in our bodies. It forces us to choose who we will be with the limited amount of time to decide that we have. We cannot prevaricate indefinitely, and because time is limited, each choice restricts future choices.

It is the same thing with our lives. We must choose who we are, and we are compelled to keep choosing because there are steps forward and backward for all of us- those on the narrow path to Heaven and those on the broad highway to Hell. Some of us on the dark road can turn about. For them those "steps backward" towards the light can become their new way forward. Our choices in this world are not permanent until we reach the end. But then they are permanent. And only when they are permanent is it fitting for us to live in a world without the futility of decay.

In addition to the limitations of time which force us to choose, decay forces us to keep choosing. Decay is frustrating because we always must *fight* the unwinding of everything. Things never stay as we wish them. We must make a new choice every day to continue to hurl ourselves against the unwinding, not only to get things as we wish, but to keep them there. But that decay is the very thing which forces us to choose and re-choose what it is we wish to fight.

The wicked are frustrated that their wicked schemes are constantly unwinding and need to be propped up with more effort. The righteous are frustrated because that decay is always unwinding the effects of their good works and forcing them to work again. Decay forces us to a life of choices. Those choices in turn refine us and define us, culminating in the discovery of what sort of eternal and unchanging world suits us.

It would be a disaster for us to live in an eternal and unchanging world without decay until we decide what sort of eternal and unchanging world suits us. It would be torturous for a person whose standard was pride to be placed in an eternal world where the standard was humility. It would be hellish for a person whose standard was love of self to be placed in an eternal and unchanging world where the standard was love of others. Those fit for an eternal world free from sin are different than those fit for an eternal world free from faith.

Verses twenty-two and twenty-three tell us that not only do we groan for a universe without decay, but even creation itself does the same. This situation, where nothing lasts, is just wrong. It is OK to think that it is wrong, because it is wrong. It is not how things are "supposed" to be, but it is how things must be. It is how they must be for things to be right when God lifts the veil and remakes things as they are supposed to be. It would be unfitting to have a prevaricating and changeable mankind in an eternal and unchanging creation. That is why creation had to be subjected to futility. Creation is waiting on us to be ready for eternity.

It is very sad to see our loved ones, and even ourselves, suffer and be diminished by the ravages of time on our minds and bodies. If this life was all that there was, it would be a cruel thing imposed by a cruel creator. But this life is not all there is. This life is the place where we decide who we are before going to a place where none of that decay happens. In that sense even the decay, as terrible as it is, can be a gentle way to ease us out of this life and into the next. It is futile to grasp onto this present universe too tightly. It, and our existence within it, was always meant to be temporary. Decay reminds us of this.

Creation was subjected to futility. It was subjected to decay by God. This was not done as the result of Adam's sin- the text does not say that. That is more theology that is not in the Bible. God created the earth formless and void, lacking in the light of His Word. And that is how it would have stayed had God not put His Word to work, bringing increasing life and order to the present chaos and darkness with each intervention. At some point, without His intervention in the universe, it would once again slip into that state- a formless void full of darkness. But then He made a realm of light, beyond our evening shadows. Yet He left this realm in evenings and mornings, with a longing in our hearts that our mortal coil has no capacity to reach. *That* is futility.

God did not want the universe to be in this condition. It wasn't His real goal. It's just a temporary state of things He is putting us through in hope. It's the hope of getting to His real goal, which is living souls in an eternal home with Him.

When Was Adam?

⊹ ⇢⊱◉⊰⇠ ⊹

If Adam was not the first human being, but rather a figure of Christ, then the question of when Adam was formed becomes much less important. The scripture (Rom. 5:6) says that "at the right time, Christ died for the ungodly". Even so Adam would have lived "at the right time" for God's purposes of getting an errant mankind on the right track.

But when was Adam? I have a favorite idea, but I do not have **the answer**. Rather, as I will do with the location of the Garden of Eden, I will lay out the most reasonable possibilities which are consistent with the text and "let each be fully convinced in his own mind." In the Christ-centered model for Genesis we need have no fear about when Adam may have come, nor as you shall see later, when the flood of Noah might have come.

Some well-meaning old-earth creationists have suggested that the genealogies in early Genesis have significant gaps in them. That is, many patriarchs whose names were not recorded lived between the death of one patriarch and the mention of the next. This is an effort to find a view of the scriptural record which aligns with the record of nature regarding the existence of mankind. Therefore, it is suggested by some that these records have substantial gaps.

I find that idea unlikely, at least as it concerns gaps greater than the lifetimes of the patriarchs. The genealogies are constructed so as to track time as well as lineage. If they are riddled with gaps, then they are useless for their intended purpose. In fact, they would be worse than useless, because they would be misleading.

I don't have a problem with their being difficult to sort through, because they are very ancient records translated from a very different culture. We should expect that. But that is not the same thing as being misleading even when properly understood. At any rate, the truth of the matter is that Adam does not have to be placed back at the beginning of mankind. Once you know who Adam is, the age of the human race versus the scriptural record of the age of Adam becomes a non-issue.

Before we dive into the complications of calculating these ages from scripture, I want to make two points. One is that some readers whose minds have been conditioned by empirical assumptions will be tempted to recoil and dismiss the idea that the extremely long lifespans recorded particularly in Genesis chapter five could be literally accurate.

Ironically many of these same readers will come upon some article about science's power to extend the human life span to comparable figures and simply accept at face value that someday we will be able to accomplish the task. For example, Aubrey DeGrey has claimed, without drawing notable derision from mainstream science and media, that the first person who will live for 1,000 years has probably already been born.

Modern man has little trouble believing that *he* can extend human lifespans to around 1,000 years, but immediately dismisses the idea that God could have done so! We need to examine our hearts with our heads and understand that our faithlessness is not the rational position, but rather it is the depths of irrationality.

Further, by the view of Genesis described in these pages, the Bible does not make the claim that *all* ancient humans had extended lifespans. Rather only Adam and some of his near descendants *who lived in the presence of the Lord* (from which Cain had been exiled in Gen. 4:16) enjoyed such lifespans. The last half of Genesis four shows Cain's line up through seven generations while the line of Seth only goes one generation further.

In Genesis chapter forty-seven Jacob is brought before Pharaoh. Pharaoh asks him right away how old he was. This surely indicates that Pharaoh was impressed with his age. Jacob replied that he was 130 years old, and that his days were few in number compared to his forefathers. If everyone's near ancestors attained to such a number of years, then Jacob's age would not have been notable enough to be the first topic of conversation. Thus, the Bible implies that not all humans had extended lifespans.

Perhaps Adam possessed genetic and epigenetic gifts that we are only now beginning to understand how to reclaim. Perhaps his time in the very presence of the LORD God had a healing and life-giving effect on him which lasted several generations. How long would we live if Christ came to visit us every month and healed every infirmity, even the ones we didn't know we had? We shall see in scripture that patriarch life spans begin to decline rapidly once *Yahweh* changes His methods and quits interacting with them as much. But I get ahead of myself.

The second point I wish to make before describing this view of the genealogies is that those who claim they contain large generational gaps do have a point regarding the meaning of the word "begat." It is an interesting word. It can mean "became the father of", or it can mean "became an ancestor of." The idea of "Father" for this culture went back multiple generations. The Jews of Christ's sojourn thought of Abraham as their "father" (Mat. 3:9). The context in which "begat" is used determines its meaning.

The two great genealogical records in Genesis are in chapter five and in chapter eleven. Except for the beginning and ending generation in each, they have a similar format. Here is an example:

And Seth lived an hundred and five years, and begat Enos:
And Seth lived after he begat Enos eight hundred and seven years, and begat sons and daughters:
And all the days of Seth were nine hundred and twelve years: and he died.

The second genealogy has a similar format, except that the last line is omitted in most but not all texts. That is, the total lifespan of the years of the patriarch is not stated separately. It is necessary to add the number of years until the patriarch "begat" with the number of years the patriarch lived after begetting it to determine the total length of life of the patriarch. This is a trivial calculation.

I mentioned that there were well-known issues which make calculating dates difficult. Perhaps the most basic is **"Which text do we use?"**

There are two primary sources from which these numbers can be drawn-the Septuagint or the Masoretic Text. They do not agree, particularly on the chapter eleven genealogy. There is probably no place in which the two texts differ more than the numbers in the genealogies. The Septuagint, or LXX, is a Greek translation of a Hebrew text we no longer have and was compiled around 150 B.C. The Masoretic Text was compiled well after Christ in Hebrew by Rabbis, hostile to the Christian view of Jesus, using Hebrew texts which we no longer have.

Even though the Masoretic text is the basis for Catholic and Protestant bibles today, for the first thousand years of church history the Septuagint was routinely used as the "Old Testament" of Christians. The Septuagint is still the basis of the Old Testament for most Orthodox Churches. Because of this, appealing to the idea that "God wouldn't let us get this wrong so let's use the one in our bibles today" does not work here. Either the church got it wrong for the first 500-1,000 years or it has (except for Orthodox) gotten it wrong since then. There is plenty of evidence that the writers of the New Testament and the church fathers cited from the Septuagint, or from a lost Hebrew text which mostly agreed with it over the Masoretic text.

I will add that, when calculated in the manner of Bishop Ussher, the Masoretic text would have Shem and the Genesis eleven patriarchs as living contemporaries of Abraham. Yet none of them are explicitly mentioned as interacting with father Abraham. This is a hint that either the dates in the Masoretic text are wrong, the method of calculation by Ussher is wrong, or both. Perhaps in recognition of this problem, a later school of Jewish thought tried to say that Melchizedek was Shem. But they had mixed motives in their late assertion. It served to answer the Christian claims that Melchizedek was a Christophany. Concerning him I will have more to say later.

Indeed, it seems there was a whole school of Jewish literature in the early days of Christianity which was devoted to recalculating dates so as to rule out any possibility of Jesus being the Messiah. The Seder Olam is an example. There was a belief that Messiah would not come until a certain number of years had passed. So perhaps it became more convenient to the Jews to adopt the proto-Masoretic text even if it was only a minority variant in the first century and their predominant text prior to Christ was that on which the Septuagint was based. On the other hand, the Septuagint was compiled by a small group, behind closed doors, and there may have been some pressure to lengthen dates to make them more compatible with Greek/Egyptian history.

I think the joke is on them- the dates should mostly be calculated in a different manner than they and Ussher believed. I am going to give dates based on the majority readings of both texts, the Masoretic and the Septuagint, and let you decide.

Other problems we face when determining dates for Adam include the following:

What to do with the second Cainan? In the great majority of surviving Septuagint texts there is a "Cainan" listed as the son of Arphaxad in Genesis chapter eleven. This is in addition to the one in chapter five. The Masoretic texts lack this Cainan in chapter eleven, which means your Bible lacks it in Genesis chapter eleven. So, it should not be there, right? Well, in almost all early Greek texts of Luke the second Cainan is listed in the genealogy of Christ- Luke 3:36 in virtually every English Bible translation.

So then, did the Masoretic text skip a generation? I don't think so. After all the genealogy in First Chronicles chapter one also skips the second Cainan, no matter which text you are using. Some of the oldest references to the chronologies in the Septuagint hint that there wasn't a second Cainan in Genesis eleven, including those of Flavius Josephus and Julius Africanus. Dr. John Gill, a prominent 18th century Hebrew scholar and Baptist theologian, was convinced that the second Cainan began as a copyist error in an early copy of Luke. This mistake precipitated adding this generation into the Genealogies of Genesis in the Septuagint, which was the working "Old Testament" used by the early church. Dr. Gill believed this over two hundred years ago, and was a defender of biblical inerrancy, so you can see that this has been a dispute for a long time.

The oldest papyrus we have of Luke chapter three, called "P 75" in the Bodmer Library in Switzerland, is indistinct but so far as we can tell also lacks the second Cainan. The Greek used in the Septuagint lacks spaces and punctuation. Accidentally repeating part of a line in transcription would be an easy mistake to make. I agree with Dr. Gill. I think an early copy of Luke which was used to make many other copies had an extra "Cainan" added in by mistake. Early Christians compounded the problem by adding the extra Cainan into their copies of the Septuagint (in Genesis eleven but not First Chronicles). Because of this the texts of the Septuagint after 220 A.D. also contain the extra Canain. I won't be counting the second Cainan no matter which text I compute with, but you may see it differently. If you think it should be in there then add these numbers to my tables below- lifespan 460 years, begat sons at 130 years old.

The Different Ages Problem: even if you take the second Cainan out, calculating dates based on the Septuagint will give you older dates than those based on the Masoretic text because the lifespans and the age they begat are much higher (especially in the Genesis chapter 11 genealogy) in the Septuagint. There is ancient support for both so let's try both.

The Methuselah Problem is not much of a problem. If you are using the Masoretic Text, it is not a problem. In most Septuagint texts it seems that he lives 14 years after the flood if you calculate time from birth-to-birth. I do not calculate it that way, so it doesn't matter for my numbers. There are a few copies of the Septuagint which suggest that the age at which he fathered Lamech was late enough so that the remaining years of his life did not take him past the flood.

The Method of Calculation Problem: To calculate his dates, the famous Bishop Ussher added, for example, the 130 years of Adam until Seth was born with the 105 years of age at which Seth "begat" the subsequent line of Enosh. This seems like a reasonable possibility in the case of Adam to Seth because the previous text makes clear that Seth is Adam's direct son, and Enosh is the direct son of Seth, since it says just before the genealogy that Seth named Enosh. Bishop Ussher kept counting time from one age of "begetting" to the next. After all the plainest meaning of the Hebrew text would indicate that this is the correct procedure.

Even though it seems straightforward, such a method of calculation leads to some oddities like Shem as a contemporary of Abraham. But the real problem with the bishop's method is that in the two instances in the genealogies where we have enough information to cross-check his figures, both show that his method doesn't work. His figures "lose time" and show younger dates that those found from the more detailed information.

Let's look at the first example to see what I mean. There is an important exception to the pattern of the genealogies in Genesis 11:26-32. Things get a bit fuzzy because the text does not tell us in what year of Terah's life Abram (soon to be Abraham) was born. It only says that he lived seventy years and begat Abram, Nahor, and Har'an. The reader may find it odd that the age of the previous patriarchs at the birth of the succeeding patriarch is carefully documented throughout the chain until one gets to Terah and Abraham. From our perspective they would be the most important figures in the chain, yet Terah's age at the birth of Abram is not given.

Quite the opposite. Even though the text here says seventy years, we know from Acts that Abraham was not born until Terah was 130 (205-75 = 130). Acts 7:2-4 says that Abraham left for Canaan *after* his father's death, and according to Genesis 12:4 Abram was 75 years old when he left. It seems that seventy was just the age that Terah *started* having sons. The Jews calculate a date for the flood using the same method as Ussher. But because they do not take into account the information from the book of Acts, they come up with an even more recent date than Ussher. This is in large part because they consider that Terah fathered Abram at age seventy whereas Ussher knew it was at age 130 because of what was in Acts.

Noah provides another example. Gen. 5:32 just says that Noah was 500 years old and begat Shem, Ham, and Japheth. As with Terah, this is just the age he *started* having sons. Gen. 11:10 says Shem begat Arphaxad two years after the flood when he was 100- which means that Noah begat Shem when he was 502. We know that Ham was the youngest. The wording is unclear in Gen. 10:21 as to whether Shem or Japheth was born first, but if Noah really had his first son at 500 then Japheth was the eldest, and Shem came along two years later.

If we had not been given extra information about their ages at the flood, then applying Bishop Ussher's method of calculation would under-estimate how long ago Shem was born by two years- just as the Jewish calculations of the flood date underestimate it because they assume Abram was born when Terah was seventy. In each of these instances the date listed for begetting was *prior* to the date of birth of the actual person who took over the line of the genealogy. They were born later- two years in one case and sixty in the other.

What if this was typically the case? What if the practice when compiling a man's story was to do just what was done in the cases of Noah and Terah? That is, list the age that you *started* having sons and then list all your children? Suppose that when Noah and Terah were constructing genealogies, they had a collection of tablets from family history. All of them listed the age the ancestor *started* having sons and then all his children, just as Noah and Terah did. It seems the age at which a father *started* having children was counted as the age he "begat" all the descendants which followed him. Including sons born much later.

Noah and Terah were trying to construct a genealogy of just their own lines, not all the side branches. We may hypothesize that they listed the age the patriarch first begat a child, then picked the child that was their own ancestor out of the list of children. Then instead of including the other brothers and sisters, they merely noted that the patriarch "had other sons and daughters." The age of begetting did not necessarily apply to the next person in their genealogy, it was just the age that the first patriarch *began* to have descendants. The previous patriarch could have fathered his first son at age one-hundred and thirty, but the next patriarch listed was a son who was not born until his father was three-hundred and thirty!

If that was how the genealogies were constructed, then the methods that Ussher and the Rabbis have used can only find *minimum* dates. The years from age of "begat" would only be as great as the actual years when the next person in your family line was the first-born son. In every other case there would be more years than is shown because your ancestor was not the first son of their father. Even if they are right about the procedure, they are mistaken about what the numbers are saying. They are not factoring in the cultural oddity described in the narrative portions of how "begat" is used.

If this is a mistake, it is an understandable one, for if you just look at the verses from the genealogies in isolation, they appear to be giving the exact age that the first patriarch fathered the specific named son on the list. It is only when you consider the extra information given for Terah and Noah, along with the flexibility inherent in the Hebrew word "begat", that you can see how this is not necessarily the case.

It seems that the compilers of the genealogies did not care about making them useful to track time as Ussher computed it. Perhaps this was because they computed it another way. The problem of how to track time is something we never think about because we have had the B.C./A.D. system for many generations. For early human civilization there was no such system in place. They had to create one. They did so in an environment where at least some blessed men could live hundreds of years.

So perhaps at some point they used the *whole lifespans* of the patriarchs as a calendar. When one died, they used a *descendant* born around the same time as the next calendar-patriarch. This would explain why they didn't care about whether the age of begetting matched the exact year the next-named patriarch was born. Maybe they used *total lifespan* to track time, unless the surrounding text made it a point to say the next patriarch was a direct son. They combined the information on the list with the narrative from the same tablets because it was all family history. We err when we try to view them separately.

Is that needlessly complicated? Yes, but the genealogies were not started to track time. Any time-tracking function of these genealogies was a derived and secondary function of their main job- which was to track ancestry.

If a calendar-patriarch system grew from the genealogies, then in those cases where the text did not clarify that the next generation begotten was a direct son, it was instead referring to a *descendant* who was born about the time the previous patriarch died and who would then be used to track time. The year of begetting only indicated the year that a patriarch *started* having sons. The "generation" was in the sense of the whole life of the patriarch, not the time until they started to have children, even though that age was also listed.

An exception to this pattern would be found right at the beginning of the genealogy. In the case of Adam to Seth for example, the wording makes it clear that the counting is to be from the "birth" of the patriarch until the time the patriarch begat their son. But maybe that wording was not trying to define a rule for the other entries which lacked it, but rather trying to highlight that this generation was an *exception* to the rule used to track time in subsequent generations. That is, from lifetime to lifetime, not from birth to birth.

In Terah and Abraham's case this procedure would have presented an embarrassing difficulty. Indeed, as lifespans got shorter and fertility lower the system would grow less workable. When men lived long enough to see their sons to the fourth or fifth generation it was easy for them to have a descendant who was born the year of, or the year after, their death. A man with three sons whose descendants also had three sons would have eighty-one great-great grandsons. Someone would soon come around to fill the role of being the first born after the death of the calendar patriarch. For ancient people in their situation, it would have been a very sensible way for them to communicate with fellow clan members about when in the past specific things happened. For example, "in the days of Reu."

But Terah and Abraham were no longer in that situation. For one thing, Terah lost one of his sons so young that he was only able to produce one son of his own- Lot. Another of his sons, Abraham, had a wife who was barren during the life of Terah. The third son of Terah (Nahor) had sons, but he separated from his father. Nahor stayed behind in Ur and did not immigrate with the rest of the family to Har'an. The clan was small, and it was broken up due to the immigration of Terah.

I do not think it is a coincidence that after Abraham we don't see another great genealogy in the style of those found in chapters five and eleven. The conditions under which those genealogies were created ended when human lifespans went down, and the fertility of Abraham's line took a temporary dip. That specific form of genealogy stopped when the conditions necessary to sustain it – long life spans and high fertility, no longer existed. This was the calendar-patriarch system.

A possible exception is the short genealogy in Exodus chapter six. I won't do the math here but the bottom line is that a "long sojourn" view is only possible if the genealogy was done as a calendar-patriarch list. The only way to get to 430 years with so few generations is if each succeeding name on the list was born the year of the death of the prior patriarch. If you assume that, it comes out just right. I'm not sold on a long sojourn though.

In this system, unless the text explicitly indicates that the next generation is the "son" of the previous man named, they used the entire length of the life of the patriarch to track time. The age of the preceding patriarch when they "begat" the following patriarch is a record of the age at which that patriarch began having descendants (*including* the second patriarch), not the age of the first patriarch at the birth of the second. The age of the first patriarch at the birth of the second would be the age of their death, unless the text makes plain that the second patriarch was a direct son of the first.

We don't have the information that they did in sorting all this out, so we can't produce a single date for important events like the formation of Adam or the flood of Noah. We can only produce a range of dates which represent a reasonable minimum and maximum with the understanding that the truth may be somewhere in between.

The theoretical minimum would be the dates of Bishop Ussher. Even these dates would be further back in the past if we calculated them using the Septuagint figures. But I think I have shown here that it is extremely likely that even if he was correct about which text to use, his figures will be much too recent. That's because even if he was right about the rest, and they did not use a calendar-patriarch, the age of birth of the next patriarch would only be correct if they were the *first* son the previous patriarch had.

Is the figure for Adam to Seth the age Adam begat Seth or are we counting Cain and Abel? I think it is from Adam to Seth, but given what we saw with Terah and Noah we don't know. Was Enosh the first son of Seth? I think so, but we don't know. We don't know if anyone else on the list was the first son either. Given what we discussed here combined with the Old Testament penchant for favoring younger sons over older ones against cultural expectations, I am confident that many of them weren't first born.

Considering this, even if they didn't move to a calendar-patriarch system the true year of birth of the next name on the list could be much higher than the "begat" year. Noah started having sons at five hundred, so these dates could vary widely. The text could say someone begat at age one-hundred and thirty, but the next patriarch was a younger brother who was not born until this patriarch was three-hundred and thirty! That is more than doubling the distance in the past found from a strict application of Ussher's method. This is the "Use of Begat" variable.

Notice that setting the "Use of Begat" variable to its maximum possible-that each patriarch sired the succeeding son in the last year of his life – produces numbers like those produced by assuming they moved to what I call a calendar-patriarch system.

The calendar-patriarch method of calculating dates eliminates the "Use of Begat" variable for almost all the list because it doesn't calculate based on the age of begetting, except at the start and end of the genealogies. We have the information needed to calculate accurately for Abraham. The only thing we assume is that the age of Adam's begetting Seth is correct, and that Enosh was the first-born son of Seth, and perhaps that Noah was indeed the first-born of Lamech, or at least that he was not born long afterward. Even if one of these assumptions is wrong, all of them are un-likely to be. Just bear in mind that even though I am going to call the numbers I derive from this method the "theoretical maximum"; if any of these assumptions are incorrect then the real dates could be slightly older. Not by thousands of years, but some number.

Going back to the genealogy in Genesis chapter five, we use 130 years to count from Adam to Seth (230 in the LXX), because the text makes it clear that Seth was his son. The same can be said for Seth to Enosh, since the account says that Seth named him. But from that point onward we use the whole lifespan of the calendar-patriarch to measure the years.

One may count time in this manner until one gets to Lamech. The text indicates that Noah was not only begotten by Lamech, but was also named by him, and further that Lamech made a curious prediction about his son. Because the text does not follow the rule of the previous passages in for-mat, we revert here to the method of calculation used for Adam and Seth. Lamech begat Noah at 182 years of age (188 in most LXX) so we add that number of years to the total calculated to this point, bringing us to a total of 5,423 years from the formation of Adam until the birth of Noah.

If we then consider that Genesis 7:6 says that Noah was 600 years old at the time of the flood, we find that a space of time of 6,023 years would have occurred between the formation of Adam and the flood of Noah-6,229 years in the LLX. Notice in this method there is only a very meager time discrepancy in the two manuscripts. This is the total from the first of the two great genealogies. See the Appendix for more details on the calcu-lation of this number.

We then go to the second great genealogy in Genesis Chapter eleven to determine the space of time from the Great Flood to Abraham. This gene-alogy omits total life span in most manuscripts. This is a trivial calculation, but even if time was calculated in total years of life in the first genealogy, we should be open to the idea that at some point after the flood they switched to birth-to-birth dating. Still, as I have shown, this will still pro-duce a date which is too young. The real events would still be further back in than Ussher calculates, but not so far back as the dates produced by a calendar-patriarch view of things. Nevertheless, to calculate a theoretical maximum amount of time, let's use the same procedure we used for the chapter five genealogy....

In the chapter eleven genealogy we find that besides Arphaxad, there is one generation where the narrative portion makes it clear that the second name is a direct son of the first- Eber to Peleg. Interestingly, the Septuagint gives longer lifespans for all the patriarchs in chapter eleven than the Masoretic text does, except one: Eber lives fifty years longer in the Masoretic.

This generation feels different. That combined with the fact the narrative hints that Peleg was a direct son of Eber persuades me to use the "Age at Birth" number to calculate my maximum for the Eber-to-Peleg generation. This is thirty-four years in the Masoretic text and 134 in the Septuagint. So again my "theoretical maximum" could be further stretched by as much four hundred and thirty years. Or it could be increased by some lesser number if Joktan was the first born and Peleg came along much later. The text says the division of the land in 10:26 occurred in Peleg's days alone, not those of both brothers. This may be simply because Peleg was the next in this family line, or it may be something else. We can't be sure.

Verse ten says that Shem begat Arphaxad two years after the flood. If we then add the life of each patriarch up using the total span of years (except Eber for which we use the age he begat) just as we did in the previous genealogy, we find there are 1,763 years from the flood until the birth of Terah in the Masoretic text, and 2,277 years (omitting Cainan) in the LXX.

If we add 130, the true age of Terah at the birth of Abraham, to the previous totals from chapter eleven we come to a figure of 1,893 years by the Masoretic text or 2,407 by the LXX. This is a calculation of years from the flood to the birth of Abraham. Please see the Appendix for details.

Now the question becomes "how long ago was Abraham born?" Due to the end of the calendar-patriarch system I described, the numbers in the text of Genesis are much more straightforward counting from Terah back to Adam than they are counting from Abraham forward. Still, such calculations can be done.

To do so we must have a date for the Exodus. Dr. Bryant G. Wood has made a compelling case for an earlier date than that which many scholars have suggested. He gives a date of 1446 B.C. which is the same date First Kings 6:1 (Masoretic) gives when it says that the Temple of Solomon was completed 480 years after the Exodus. The LXX says 440 years, which would be around 1406 B.C. I'll use Wood's date, but hold to it loosely.

The biggest textual support against Wood's early date is a mention of the "city of Rameses" in Exodus and Numbers. That city was built later than 1446 B.C., but on the site of a previous complex. Dr. Wood demonstrated that it was common for scribes to update place names in later copies of the Torah. The "city of Rameses" was the name of a re-built royal complex from the remains of an earlier abandoned (due to the Exodus?) royal complex. The idea is that the site wasn't called "city of Rameses" when the children of Israel left from there. It was called something else, but since that name fell out of use immediately after they left, and the city was re-built later with a new name, the scribes used the new name. This allowed people of their day to know where the referenced place was located. So then if we start from an Exodus date of 1446 B.C., we can connect the Exodus to the entry of Abraham into the promised land.

This leads to the Last Variable, the amount of Time Spent in Captivity. There is some dispute whether the period of 430 years refers only to the time Israel was in Egypt, or whether the clock began with the promise to Abraham. In the latter view the mistreatment in a land not-his-own that his "seed" would endure began with Isaac- a figure of Christ who was the true Seed of Abraham. But if this trial refers only to the period in Egypt, then we must add in the period from Abraham receiving the promise to the time that the children of Israel entered Egypt- an extra 215 years. So, depending on your view, from the Exodus in 1446 B.C. we either need to count back 430 years or 430 + 215 years to get back to the date Abraham entered the promised land (at age 75).

I am not dogmatic on it, but right now I think that the shorter sojourn in Egypt is the correct view. Kohath the grandfather of Moses was among those who originally left with Jacob for Egypt (Gen. 46:11). He lived 133 years and Amram the father of Moses lived to 137. Moses was eighty years old at the Exodus. Thus, the stay could not have been 430 years long.

Galatians 3:16-18 supports the view that the 430 years included the time in both Egypt and Canaan. I conclude that Exodus 12:40 is rendered correctly in the Septuagint and that the Masoretic text in our present bibles omits the "and Canaan". Canaan was under Egyptian control during much of this period anyway. Abraham and his seed did not spend 430 years in Egypt, but in Canaan and Egypt together. I surmise that at the time the Masoretic Text was compiled, Canaan was occupied territory of Egypt and thus both places were considered "Egypt", so neither text is wrong. The question is whether Canaan was Egyptian territory at the time.

Therefore 1446 B.C. plus 430 years plus 75 years (his age of entry) equals 1951 B.C. as the birth of Abraham. If you disagree with my conclusion on the time in captivity, simply add 215 years to the figures below.

Abraham was then born around 3,970 years ago. From that starting point, here are the dates I derived using each text according to the methods described above, and the Ussher method.

Table of possible dates for key events:

Method	Date of Adam	Date of Flood
Ussher	4,004 B.C.	2,348 B.C.
Ussher using LXX	5,467 B.C.	3,211 B.C.
Mine using MT	9,867 B.C.	3,844 B.C.
Mine using LXX	10,587 B.C.	4,428 B.C.

Remember that if you think the children of Israel spent 430 years in Egypt then add 215 years to my dates.

Ussher did not compute dates from the LXX. For "Ussher's" dates from the "Septuagint" I used the numbers from Flavius Josephus as modified by

Ussher's correction on the age of Terah at Abraham's birth. Josephus used the same method of calculation as Bishop Ussher but used a Hebrew text which had numbers more in line with the LXX than the Masoretic text- except that it also omitted the second Cainan. On my numbers using the Septuagint I too omitted the second "Cainan". If you think the second "Cainan" should be included then add up to 460 years to my calculations.

I call my numbers a "theoretical maximum" to the dates while the Ussher numbers are a theoretical minimum. Even so, there were several places, previously noted, where my assumptions reduced the dates. It is possible that the real dates were somewhat but not a great deal older than my "theoretical maximum". This is because it is *my* maximum, based on the set of assumptions I laid out here, not an *absolute* theoretical maximum. The actual answer could be somewhere in the middle, particularly if the calendar-patriarch system was used for the Genesis chapter five genealogy, but a switch was made to track time from birth to birth at some point on the chapter eleven genealogy.

On the other hand, the older dates for "begetting" in the LXX could be from scribes who understood what I have explained here- that the genealogies could give only minimum dates. If they knew this, perhaps they added years in order to make a better estimate of actual dates. If that is so, perhaps those dates would not need adjusting, because they had *already* been adjusted. The LXX would then be the most accurate (unless the calendar-patriarch system was used). So Adam and the flood would then be more recent than I suppose- yet still older than the dates from the MT.

Here's an archeological nugget which favors my LXX text date for the flood: not that I am sold on the location as the landing place of the ark, but I note that in 1953 a German, Dr. Friedrich Bender, obtained a small bitumen-covered wood sample from a region on Mt. Judi in Turkey where it was said that pilgrims were taking wood left from the ark of Noah. His C-14 dating showed the wood to be just under 6,500 years old (so from a timber hewn ~ 4,500 B.C). *The Bible and Spade Journal* reprinted his findings in English in 2006.

Returning to Adam, the calendar-patriarch view, even if only applied to the chapter five genealogy, produces a date for Adam which makes a lot of sense considering what the Bible says about him. It puts the date and location of Adam just before the dawn of agriculture and the domestication of livestock around 9,000 B.C.

I do not think this is a coincidence. Humanity had lost its way, and instead of becoming protectors of the earth, it had become the most terrible of its predators. Man was a plunderer, not a nurturer as originally intended. We were far from the intent of God in Genesis chapter one when He had created them and granted them dominion.

In short, humanity had abused the dominion they had been given. Instead of becoming stewards of nature and what was in it, they became super-predators. In contrast, Adam was specifically made and trained "to tend the garden and to keep it" (Gen. 2:15). In Adam, as in Christ, God provided the pattern. He became the example which they could live by. Adam's clan were the pattern agriculturalists and pastoralists of mankind.

Although there may have been several early domestication events for our major livestock animals of today, most seemed to have happened near one another, as if copying an original example. The initial domestication of sheep, goats, pigs, and cattle all appear to have happened in the same time and region- the same region in which I place the Garden of Eden and right around my older date for Adam. The domestication of wheat and barley, along with grapes, can also be traced to this region and time frame. It is ground zero for human civilization.

I do not say that agriculture and animal husbandry were never tried earlier. I feel sure they were, since it was the God-desired orientation of man from the beginning. But the earlier attempts did not stick. Man had not pulled it off. He had backslidden into a less civilized manner of life.

Perhaps Adam, in terms of both time and place, was in the right spot to have introduced these things to mankind in a way which did stick. The human race had a Great Leap Forward which began about the time and the place which I am suggesting Adam lived. As we will see, it was not due to any innate superiority Adam had which permitted this, but rather Adam was given a very privileged position which permitted him to help propel humanity into civilization. It was what the LORD God did for him through their fellowship which permitted this progress. I am not dogmatic that Adam was the very first true farmer, but at the very least he was placed early in the first area where it began, and given aid in a way which allowed this manner of living to "take off".

If this is so, then how ironic indeed is the modernist or postmodernist man who looks on faith in God as mere superstition which more "civilized" people are beyond. I will make the case that without the personal intervention of *Yahweh-Elohim* in the garden, mankind might still be in an uncivilized state. Indeed, man has shown himself capable of behaving uncivilly despite the advantages of civilization, which in and of itself does not solve man's sin problem.

Adam and The Man

❧

I have gone to great pains to show how the first account, the account of the heavens and the earth, is describing things happening in high heaven as well as the natural universe. God is shaping creation in two realms. The creation of man in verse 1:27 is no exception. I have shown that this verse is most appropriately translated "So God created *the* man in His own image, in the image of God created He him...". And I have begun to make the case that *the* Man in heaven (who is in the image of God as man and the living image of God as the Son), is the pre-incarnate Christ. The echo of this on earth, the man Adam, is the reason verse 1:27 echoes, "in the image of God created He him." Things on earth are copies of things in heaven.

"The Man" in verse 1:27 is the second person of the Trinity, the Logos of God, fusing with humanity in the heavens. I will have more to say about this further on. The "him" in verse 1:27, the echo on earth, is Adam. Chapter two tells that story. Christ is the Man in heaven in 1:27. Adam is "the man" on earth in chapter two. You can almost look at early Genesis as a complicated math equation. You are trying to find a variable, and when you plug in the right variable and keep working the equation, the answer makes sense. I think you will see as we continue that if you assume what I have written above- stick it in as the variable so to speak- the accounts will make more sense than any other model.

~ 247 ~

I have previously mentioned how versatile the word *a'dam* is in the Hebrew. This versatility can lead to translation issues. Different versions of the Bible are not that consistent as to when they translate different forms of the word as "the man" as compared to when it is translated as "Adam" or just "man". Again, I am no Hebrew scholar, but in this case apparently it does not help to be one. The experts themselves have been of varied opinions. For example, the King James says in verse 2:7:

And the LORD God formed man of the dust of the ground, and breathed into his nostrils the breath of life; and man became a living soul.

In the Hebrew of this verse, "*ha-a-dam*" is used rather than "*a-dam*" in both instances where you see the word "man". In other passages this is translated "the man", or in some contexts "of man". The English Standard Version, for one, does translate it "the man" in both places. So, with the direct articles it should read, "And the LORD God formed *the* man of the dust of the ground, and *the* man became a living soul". This is a phrase which was also used (John 19:5) to describe the Second Adam, Christ Himself, when Pilate said, "Behold the Man".

Even though many translations personalize the account in chapters two and three, in the actual Hebrew it is not using "Adam" as a proper name. Rather, it is using the title "the man." From Genesis 2:7 to Genesis 5:2 is the "account of Adam". So why does Adam refer to himself as "the man" in chapter two? Later in the account, the term used does change to "Adam". When does this happen? Curiously, Adam does not become Adam until God's judgement is pronounced on him. Until then he is something else- such as "the man."

Why use "the man" to describe Adam in his own account? It may be that Seth or some other near descendant told his story, as was common for sons to do in the ancient near east. It may be that Adam simply wanted to put some distance between him and the flawed character in the account. But it also fits nicely with the idea that he had a title, and a function. He did not use his name because it was not only his story. There was "The

Man" above to consider, of whom he was only meant to be a figure and a shadow.

Even as the LORD God, who incarnated as Christ, was The Man in heaven, so Adam was The Man on earth. Adam was meant to be an image-bearer, one made in (and by, that is the story of chapter two) the Image. He was thus the vizier of the King in Heaven.

The word "vizier" has an interesting etymology. Most experts agree that it comes from an Arabic word which means "to bear a burden". Later they became high government officials, but in the beginning they were merely helpers or representatives. Adam was meant to be an intermediary whom God would use to lift mankind upward. He failed, as man on his own efforts must fail - and that was what God wanted us to learn thoroughly. It was a hard lesson and a dark mystery for the ancients, but we are blessed to peer back through the ages and see the end of the story. We see how God worked it all out despite our lack of faith. The heavenly ruler Himself had to incarnate and complete the work that man- even the most privi-leged- could not do for himself. Through the work of our Savior both the earthly intermediary and the heavenly ruler are now combined in the person of Christ.

In earlier editions of this book, I failed to distinguish the person of Adam from the person of Christ in his proper role of governing humanity. I don't believe that Adam was ever meant to rule other men. Indeed, he was not even assigned rulership over his own wife, drawn from his side, until the fall. The man Adam was always meant to be a helper, or intermediary who assisted the true King, God Above. In the creation account *all* men were given dominion over the land itself and the creatures in it, but no man, including Adam, was given dominion over other men. This fact is surely a basis for human liberty among those who believe.

Remember in Matthew 3:9 where Jesus admonishes his listeners not to rely on having Abraham for their father (ancestor)? He told them that God was able to make children to Abraham from the stones lying around them! In a like manner though men may have been around, God formed the man Adam from dust. In chapter two we get additional detail from the middle segment of verse 1:27- "in the image of God created he him". Chapter two zooms in on that fragment of the first account.

Again, this view of things is a better picture of the Incarnation than the currently prevailing view of Adam. Like Adam, Christ is fully human. Even so, like Adam Christ was not formed in the normal way. Adam was meant to be the image of God on Earth, as the true King was in heaven. Just as Christ came after mankind had gone its own way for ages, so had Adam come. Adam was supposed to be the start of a royal priesthood, a holy nation, to bring the realm of the King of Heaven to our realm. Christ has done this, as both God in heaven and as the human intermediary between God and man. First Peter 2:9 tells us that this is now the position and condition of believers everywhere, even if we fail to live up to it, or even recognize it.

Where the similarities end is on the God side of things, though the picture of a special relationship is taken as far as possible. One of them, Adam, had fellowship with the LORD God, the other was with God and was God (John chapter one). As quoted before, one was a living soul and the other a life-giving Spirit. In this contrast we see that man is unable to obtain righteousness on his own merits, even when God goes to extreme lengths to give the man every advantage. It is only when God Himself became the intermediary is eternal access to the Divine available.

Notice that it is said that the man was formed from the dust of the earth. Though in our heads we try to make that dust into clay, because wet earth is easier to form than dry, the actual word used emphasizes the dryness of the soil used to form The Man. Please consider my comments on the emergence of "the dry Land" on the third day of creation. Water represents God's judgements, which to the righteous are life-giving but to the wicked come as a raging sea of destruction.

That Adam was formed from the dry ground indicates that he was in a state of innocence. Not even the amount of judgement required to moisten and shape him with more detail was used. He was not shaped as the potter shapes the clay. He was loosely shaped, without the binding force of judgement. This describes a state of innocence.

What is man? This verse says that man is a soul. When connected to God, he is a living soul. And what is a living soul? A human soul is the result of the unification of a spirit and a body. The urges of the spirit and the desires of the flesh are mediated by the soul. It arises and develops from, their interactions. The soul becomes shaped as it mediates the harmony or disharmony of spirit and body.

Unlike the spirit, the soul is not necessarily immortal. Ecclesiastes 12:7 tells us that on physical death "the spirit returns to God who gave it." Woe to the soul which is not taken as well. At that point the unsaved soul is as close to God as it will ever be. From that point forward, it will have no more spirit pulling it towards heaven. It will still have whatever sinful appetites that it clung to in life. These are described in scripture (Mark 9:48 *et al*) as "their worm".

A worm is all appetite and no intellect. Without the spirit present as a countervailing force, the soul can move in only one direction- its ultimate total consumption by the appetites which it chose in life to love more than God. "The soul that sinneth, it shall die" (Eze. 18:20), but it won't be God who is doing the killing. Those souls will be consumed by their own sins.

Genesis 2:7 says that when God breathed into his nostrils the breath of life, Adam became a *living* soul. I have already shown how the breath of life is a reference to the Holy Spirit. I have already demonstrated how scripture uses the terms "living" and "dead" in a different and more absolute sense than we do in everyday usage. Again, "the soul that sinneth, it shall die", but Adam became a *living* soul in that he was connected to God via the Spirit. That is not said of the other humans created in Genesis chapter one, but it is said of Adam. Not because he was a different sort of being than they, but because of his connection to God. Adam became alive, in the natural and spiritual sense of the word.

Adam in the Garden

⌁⌁⌁

In chapter two, God gets a title or another name which reflects His nature. In chapter one He was *Elohim* – translated God (or gods). In chapter two the man's interactions are with *Yahweh Elohim* which in the King James *et al* is translated "The LORD God". Once sin is animated by the man's disobedience God is most often referred to as just *Yahweh* – often translated 'the LORD'.

I think it is a mistake to treat these different labels as if they meant the same thing. And by that I do not mean that the "Higher Critics" are right in their faithless conclusions. Rather, the Trinitarian nature of God and the precursor to the Incarnation are on display even in the very beginnings of scripture.

The LORD God (*Yahweh Elohim*) of chapter two and beyond seems much more anthropomorphic than the God (*Elohim*) of chapter one. He plants a garden and walks about in it. He fashions clothes. And He converses with men, even asking them questions as if the answer is unclear to Him. This is very unlike *Elohim* in chapter one who has no need of questions and does not converse so much as proclaim.

By now many of you have realized that I consider the Heavenly Man created in 1:27 (as the fusion of uncreated God and Created Humanity) to be The LORD God of Genesis two and the LORD beyond chapter two. Scripture says that "no man has seen God at any time" (John 1:18 *et al*) and yet many characters from the Bible saw the LORD. *Yahweh* appears to Mankind as the visible image/substance of the invisible God, which is just who "The Man" in Heaven is. When He incarnated in mortal flesh, we began to know Him as Jesus Christ.

This also explains why chapter one used "*Elohim*" for God and chapter two used "*Yahweh Elohim*". The second person of the Trinity did not fuse with humanity in heaven until the sixth day (the first triplet of 1:27, "God created (the) Man in His own image"). One should not think that "The LORD God" is absent from creation's account. He is there, but is He named by another name, reflecting what He was to creation: The (heavenly) Man from verse 1:27, who is God and Man joined. That is who He is to Creation. The second account uses the name for God as Adam saw Him- The LORD God (*Yahweh-Elohim*). Adam knew God by name, not just position.

The earthly Man was formed some place (verses 7-8). Then the LORD God planted a garden. And then the LORD God put the man in that garden. The text does not tell us where The Man was formed, nor does it tell us how much time he lingered there before God put him in the garden. My guess as to the location of his formation would be somewhere within the boundaries of Israel, but that is just my guess. Wherever it was, one view of the text is that the Garden of Eden was east of it, for it mentions in the text that the garden was planted "toward the east". The length of time it took before he was taken from where he was formed and put in the garden is unknown.

Notice in verses eight and nine that the LORD God did all the work to bring it about. It was the LORD God (the Heavenly Man, the pre-incarnate Christ) who planted the trees. It was He who made to grow every plant good for food. This is the Heavenly Man, the LORD God, who does all the work. This too points to the spiritual truth that Christ has done the work necessary for salvation and our good works can add nothing to it.

What is done in the garden is not "creating" plants and trees. Nor is it commanding the earth to bring forth those things. Nor does it mention every category of plant, as is mentioned in creation's account. Nor did He "make" the trees. Trees were already in existence. He simply "made them to grow" in the garden. This is not a creation account of either the heavens or of the earth. This is the account of The Man on Earth.

The Garden of Eden was the point at which The Land Above met The Land Below. The realms of Heaven and Earth intersected. We should not waste too much effort seeking its remains. The garden which the LORD God planted, including the Tree of Life, is no longer superimposed on both worlds. It is only in the land above.

This sad situation will not be eternal. Some of us will be conformed to His image and the way to the Tree of Life will then be passable for us as well as Adam. But in that day its fruit will not be restricted to the land above. Revelation chapter twenty-two informs us that in the age to come the Tree of Life will grow "on both sides of the river" which proceeds from the throne of God. That is to say, the "Tree of Life" will be in this realm and in the next. In a way this process has already begun- to the extent believers allow Christ to rule their hearts by the power of the Holy Spirit. But again, I get ahead of myself.

Though the Garden is gone, there was some place on this earth which was touched by Heaven. The Garden of Eden was not just a myth, or a symbol. Yes, it is a symbol, like so many of the things in scripture, but it was not *just* a symbol. It was a real place on earth that was a symbol of an even more real thing in eternity. It was an actual garden in an actual location, inhabited by an actual man named Adam.

The location is given in scripture, but its meaning is obscure to us. I do not claim any special revelation regarding its location, but I can tell you what I know to help you dispense with some of the more outlandish theories. Unless we are wrong about what "the mountains of Ararat" are, I favor a northern location, but the text is ambiguous.

The first problem is the ambiguity of Genesis 2:8 which says, "And the LORD God planted a garden eastward in Eden". Does this mean that the Garden of Eden was planted on the east of the "Land of Eden", or does it mean that both Eden and the garden were east of the location where the man was formed? The next ambiguous statement is in Genesis 2:10:

And a river went out of Eden to water the garden; and from thence it was parted, and became into four heads.

A second question relates to the phrase "from thence it was parted". Was "thence" referring to the land of Eden, or the Garden, or both because the garden was within the land? Let us start with the view that the text points to a garden which is within the land of Eden and that the "thence" is referring to a garden in the midst of the land.

So, we are looking for a place where a river is parted into four "heads". The word there is "*ra-sim*" and means "chief". So, it is not necessarily referring to four headwaters or sources, it is just saying that from Eden the river divided into four big rivers.

Of the four rivers listed in the following verses, the locations of two are well known. Their courses have varied somewhat through the centuries, fortunately mostly downriver from our area of interest. But even upriver their flow today has been altered greatly by man-made reservoirs and irrigation projects. These two rivers are the Tigris and the Euphrates. Today, if one counts the Eastern Euphrates as part of the whole system, they come within five miles of one another. This is near Lake Hazar and the Keban Reservoir in southwestern Turkey. The former is a major source of the Tigris River and the latter is stocked by the Eastern Euphrates.

Indeed, the small tributaries of those two standing bodies of water (Hazar and Keban) come very near to touching. It is not hard to imagine that they are fed from the same underground water table, or even that there was a day when some small part of the northern and more elevated river fed into the Tigris somewhere nearby. That is, from the Eastern Euphrates through the gorge, which is now the Keban Reservoir, and from there into the northern tributaries which now feed Lake Hazar.

Now I say "Eastern Euphrates" but from ancient times that river has had another name, the Aranias. The Aranias of old is in modern times called the Murat River. The Euphrates River proper is said to begin at the point where this river intersects with another river- the Karasu - also called the "Western Euphrates". The Karasu and the Murat rivers together are the headwaters of the actual Euphrates River.

Imagine if you will an "X", except that in the middle of the letter is a horizontal dash rather than a single point. The result would look something like ">-<". The lower right-hand corner of this figure could be said to represent the headwaters of the Tigris River. The upper right-hand corner, and the dash in the middle, could be said to represent the Murat, or Eastern Euphrates. The upper left-hand corner of the figure would then be the Karasu River. The lower left-hand corner, at the meeting of the Karasu and the Murat, would be the Euphrates proper.

The "dash" represents a stretch of the Murat just before it links up with the two others. This has nowadays mostly been made into the Keban Reservoir. It runs a length of almost forty miles. I believe that this stretch of ground, now underwater, is a prime candidate for the location of the Garden of Eden.

For my theory to be correct the Murat would have to be the "Gihon" and the Karasu would have to be the "Pison" rivers mentioned in the text. That produces some difficulty because it says of the Gihon that it flowed either through or around the "whole land of Cush."

Later in scripture where it speaks of Cush it is referring to the land of Ethiopia. Those later references are post flood and post scattering. Even the table of the nations is describing where some of these clans wound up *eventually-* after the scattering from the tower of Babel.

The "Cush" of Moses's day was not the "land of Cush" described in chapter two. It is much more likely that the first "land of Cush" was very near to the same region where Eden was, and where the ark landed. When Adam was driven out of the garden, the guard was placed at the east- indicating that he went east. When the descendants of Noah journeyed after the ark landed, they journeyed "from the east." They roughly went back the way Adam had come in.

Names like "Cush" or "Kish" were not uncommon in ancient Mesopotamia. There was a prominent city called Kish near the center of what is now Iraq. Up the river from it, near the Syrian-Turkish border, was a possibly even older settlement called Urkesh. An overlooked candidate for the Gihon is the old river which flowed around the land surrounding the ancient site of Kish. What is left of it is now the Hillah Branch of the Euphrates.

Perhaps many settlements were named after Cush. It is sort of like "York" in England. Many states have a "York" or a "New York" as a city or county name. We cannot even be certain that the land which Adam described was named after the same Cush who came so much later. Maybe it was instead the young Cush who was named after the land they left behind as the clan of Noah "journeyed from the east."

None of that rules out the idea that Ethiopia was also later named "Cush". What I am ruling out is that one of the four rivers of Eden flowed around, or even through, what we know as Ethiopia. That is not the Cush Adam is referring to. Ethiopia is a land which was possibly named after a son of Noah who was in turn named after an older land in the Near East. That older Cush is the land we should seek.

The land of Cush Adam is referring to is so familiar to him that he assumes that it needs no further description. This is not surprising if the Murat is the river which flows through it, for its source is the mountains near Lake Van, near to the famed two Mountains of Ararat. But I would not ignore the Hillah Branch of the Euphrates which ran through and around the prominent ancient city of "Kish", as a candidate for the Gihon.

The Euphrates was apparently even more familiar to the reader than the Gihon because no description of it at all beyond the name is given. Perhaps the account was first delivered to people who lived along the Euphrates, and therefore no clarification was needed as to which river it was.

Verse eleven says that the Pison River flows through or around the land of Havilah. There is not one, but two nations called "Havilah" to consider in the table of nations. One is from the line of Ham and the other of Shem.

It is very probable that the Semitic one further down the list of generations is in the Arabian Peninsula. The location of the Hamitic one is less certain.

Over the centuries, men have struggled to ascertain which of these two Havilahs the account of Adam refers to. I do not believe that either one necessarily corresponds to the one discussed here. After all, there are two Havilahs in the Table of Nations in Genesis chapter ten. Why can't there be a third many thousands of years before back in Genesis chapter two? At least in this case there is information given about the land. It says that there is gold, and onyx, and resin there. We have more to go on than place names.

Based on the resources that are said to be found there, the Karasu River fits the description of the Pison (or Pishon) quite nicely. The Erzincan-Copler mine is one of the five largest gold mines in Turkey today. It lies near to the course of the Karasu. There is also a significant supply of onyx in the region. The bdellium or resin is another matter. Most such resin today is produced by a plant native to Ethiopia. This can cause much consternation for those trying to equate the Cush of Genesis chapter two with Ethiopia. This important clue seems to point to Ethiopia being Havilah rather than Cush!

The resolution to this conundrum is that the resin referenced is not that which is made by the shrub most commonly producing it today, but rather either the *Pistacia terebinthus* or the closely related *P. lentiscus*. These species grow in the right place and are also used to make resin. Perhaps even that used in the Biblical "Balm of Gilead". So, we can place gold, onyx and resin in the lands around the Karasu River. That is enough to make it a good guess for the identity of the Pison/Pishon. If you think I am cheating by counting the Karasu as its own river rather than just the "Upper Euphrates" then consider the idea that the Pison was the sacred Munzer River, which has similar attributes and also flows into the Keban Reservior.

So that is my first of three proposed locations for the Garden of Eden. I will be the first to admit that it isn't much. This is a speculative subject and, fortunately, far from a salvation issue.

Now if the Garden of Eden was not in the center of the "X" perhaps it was somewhere along one of the four legs of the "X". That is, one of the rivers came out of Eden to water the garden and that river was divided into four chief rivers somewhere along its course.

It is the Euphrates River which is not described at all in the account in Genesis chapter two, as if it needed no introduction. Further there was much later a kingdom referred to in Isaiah 37:12 as the "House of Eden" which has been connected to a place known from certain ancient inscriptions as "*Bit 'Adini*"- the house of Eden. These artifacts were found near to the present Syrian-Turkish border on the Euphrates.

It is reasonable to suppose that the ancients knew about the area where Eden was, though it is unclear if the "House" of Eden was the same thing as the "land" of Eden. Perhaps they were immigrants from Eden who came down from the hills of the north and east and settled in that location. Still, if the garden was located on one of the legs of the "X" of rivers then the existence of the "Bit 'Adini" kingdom is another point which makes the Euphrates a reasonable guess. The area to the east of there did seem to be a hotbed for the domestication of both plants and animals, as well as strange religious sites like Gobekli Tepe. *Something* was going on in that area.

My final proposed location for the garden is the easternmost of the three. This would be the Murat River near to Lake Van. There, in the Bitlis Province of Turkey, is a valley with a volcano called Nemrut at the eastern end. It is dormant now but would have been active during my proposed life of Adam. Its geography is therefore very similar to that of the location which David Rohl proposes in the book of his that I mentioned a few chapters back.

Compared to my other possibilities, this one is closer to Rohl's proposed location for the "land of Nod" to which Cain went in exile. That is important because even if I do not think he is right about the location of Eden, I think he is right about the location of Nod. If this final choice is indeed the site of the Garden of Eden, then the Murat is the river which flowed through the garden, with the Euphrates, Karasu and Tigris (near the river cave tunnel south of Genc that the ancients thought was its major source) making three of the four chief rivers.

The fourth river would then be the Aras. The Aras River does not split off the Murat per se, but the same mountainous area feeds them both from opposite sides. Thus, the Aras would be the Gihon which runs through "the whole land of Cush".

Once it passed through the garden the Murat began splitting off into those rivers one after another. The list from Genesis chapter two is given in an order as if someone had a map and was listing them from the northwest corner and proceeding in a clockwise direction. And that is the last of my three hypotheses as to the location of the Garden of Eden. I shall now share with you another view, and this hypothesis comes from a professional in ancient near eastern history.

In his remarkable book David Rohl points to the almost over-looked discoveries of a man named Reginald A. Walker. In 1986 Walker had some of his work published, but only in the obscure English newsletter *Ancient and Medieval Book Club*. In this paper he outlined his discoveries about the location of the land of Nod and the Garden of Eden itself. A few years later he died, and his work was largely ignored until Rohl came along.

Rohl verified and deepened Walker's profound discoveries, as well as adding some more questionable narratives of his own. The land of Nod was located about thirty-five miles inland from the southwest corner of the Caspian Sea, in the Ardabil Basin. It turns out that some villages in the region still bear signs of the name "Nodqi"- a dwelling place of Nod. There were government records which indicated that the region was in times past called "Upper Nod" and "Lower Nod".

I have other evidence which points to this region being the home of Cain and his offspring. Some ancient human remains from this area contain a high proportion of the DNA of a mysterious group called "Basal Eurasians" or a similar group called simply "Deep". I will have more to say about this at the end of the book where I concentrate more on science than scripture.

Rohl and Walker place the Garden of Eden just east of Lake Urmia near the present-day city of Tabriz with Eden itself corresponding to the land of Armenia and eastern Turkey. His view is that the river which runs through the garden is itself a fifth river, the Adji Chay.

This river flows from Lake Urima through Rohl's garden location. So, imagine he also has an "X" for the four rivers, but coming from the right side of the center of the "X" is a line which represents yet another river - the one that flowed through the garden. The "thence" in Genesis 2:10 refers to the Land of Eden according to Rohl and the text is simply saying that these four great rivers flow from the same greater Armenian highlands. If you count the Murat as simply the first leg of the Euphrates rather than a river in its own right, that is true.

The hardest two rivers to identify are the Pishon and the Gihon. The Gihon River is said to flow through the land of Cush. Near Rohl's proposed location for the Garden the great mountain to the south of the Aras River still bears the name of Cush (Kusheh Dagh). Further, the Aras was formerly known as the Gaihun-Aras. So "Gaihun" corresponds to the Gihon. Note these two points also support my easternmost proposed location. Through geography and an even more intricate hypothesis of language transition Rohl also connects the Pishon to the Uizhun River which flows into the Caspian Sea.

I will be the first to admit this topic is rife with speculation and short on hard facts. It does not fit elegantly together as do the pieces used to construct a cosmology from scripture. The cosmology is important. The location of the Garden of Eden is a nice extra. There are some mysteries in these texts which may never be fully resolved.

The exact location of the Garden of Eden may be lost in the mists of time, but it was not a myth. It was not just a story. It was a real location and whoever wrote the account of Adam went to a lot of trouble to try to communicate to us what this location was. Given the antiquity of the information and how place names change over time, I am amazed we even have enough information to narrow it down as much as we have here.

Wherever it was, verse fifteen tells us that the LORD God put man in the Garden "to dress it and to keep it." He had a purpose, and he had a calling. Yet the Garden was not Adam's destiny, it was his training ground. The LORD God was training him to be His agent in exercising dominion over the earth and making it all into something like Eden. Like many training programs, or even social experiments, there were tests along the way. Adam had to choose whether he would have faith in self or faith in God. And that choice would manifest in the form of a single prohibition, found in Genesis 2:16-17:

And the LORD God commanded the man, saying, Of every tree of the garden thou mayest freely eat:

But of the tree of the knowledge of good and evil, thou shalt not eat of it: for in the day that thou eatest thereof thou shalt surely die.

Looking at things from the serpent's point of view, he was up against a very stacked deck in his efforts to entice Adam to fall. Adam was in paradise, living a fulfilled life, and in training to assume lordship over the earth. He had free rein to enjoy everything around him without guilt. And talk about interesting company- the LORD God Himself. Every need on Maslow's hierarchy was fulfilled in an earthly paradise- or at least it would be once Eve came into the picture. There was only one thing denied him- the ability to decide what was good and evil for himself. Instead, he was to trust The LORD God to define it for him.

There was no voting booth or button or lever by which to make this choice. Instead, the choice would be delivered by what Adam put into his own body. Christ told us that we cannot be saved unless we eat of His flesh and drink His blood. The choice of separation between God and Man was demonstrated by consumption, and the choice of reconciliation between God and Man is also demonstrated by consumption.

The Man Gets a Helper

⸱⸱⸱⸱⸱⸱⸱⸱⸱⸱⸱⸱⸱⸱⸱⸱

The second chapter of Genesis, verses 18-25, is another badly misunderstood passage of scripture. A face-value reading of it as a second creation account puts it at odds with the first account. For example, the most consistent translations describe animals as being made *after* the man but before the woman, which is contrary to the account in chapter one. In chapter one, being fruitful and multiplying was God's first command to humanity. In contrast, in chapter two the creation of the woman is almost an afterthought and does not even seem particularly tied to reproduction. Indeed, a superficial reading of the text of chapter two makes it sound like some animals were considered for the job of being the man's helper. Only when they were found inadequate was the woman then made for the man.

Some translations say that verse nineteen of chapter two should read that the LORD God "had formed" the animals from the ground. They are trying to look for wiggle room to reconcile the paradox of animals being formed before man in chapter one and after man in chapter two. The Christ-centered model has no need to wiggle here. The chapter two account is a smaller work within the larger account in chapter one, the purpose of which was to set in motion God's plan to redeem and reconcile that larger creation back to Himself. The animals from chapter one got created/made in some unspecified way and the much smaller set of animals made in chapter two were formed out of the ground.

One problem with claiming that the first words in verse nineteen should be "had formed," is that it's not at all different from the other verbs in the passage. The account uses waw-consecutive, in which every verb is continuing the story after the first use of *waw* at the beginning. And this is true for the verbs both before and after "waw-formed" in verse nineteen, like so:

18. "**waw**-said Yahweh God, not-is-good *qal*-become ha-man to-apart. *qal*-I-make him helper from-beside.

19. **waw**-formed Yahweh God from-ground, all-souls ha-field, **waw**-[accusative] all-bird ha-air. **waw**-he-brought to-ha-Adam *qal*-see thing-*qal*-he-calls them. **waw**-all that called-them, ha-Adam soul living, that name.

20. **waw**-gave ha-Adam names to-all ha-beasts, **waw**-to-birds ha-air, **waw**-to-all souls ha-ground - **waw**-to-Adam, not-*qal*-found helper from-beside."

Even if when viewed in isolation "had formed" is an allowable translation, it makes a hash of the flow of the narrative if translated like that here. Every "waw" is supposed to be a restart to a consecutive series of events.

Let us look at these verses in the NIV, one of the versions which use the "had formed" translation:

The Lord God said, "It is not good for the man to be alone. I will make a helper suitable for him."
Now the Lord God had formed out of the ground all the wild animals and all the birds in the sky. He brought them to the man to see what he would name them; and whatever the man called each living creature, that was its name. So the man gave names to all the livestock, the birds in the sky and all the wild animals. But for Adam[f] no suitable helper was found.

That's awkward in any language. It starts off with The LORD God saying He *will* make a helper suitable for Adam, then segues into Adam being presented with a stream of animals to name which ostensibly had *already* been formed, then at the end it says no suitable helper was found. If the presentation of the animals had nothing to do with the search for the helper that He says He "will make", then why even note that "no suitable helper was found" among the animals?

If God announces "I *will make* a suitable helper for Adam" then why is the next step showing Adam a stream of animals which had *previously* been formed? And why announce at the end that none of them were suitable as if they were candidates? If they had already been made, then why even say "I will make" before presenting the candidates?

Adam was clearly expecting a helper from this process of formation, that's why it says disappointingly "but for the man no suitable helper was found". He was expecting a helper because God had just told him that He was going to make him a helper.

The only reasonable conclusion is that the animals in the second account were formed *after* Adam. The LORD God said He would make a helper suitable for Adam, and then He started making animals. Adam was expecting to find his helper among them but was disappointed. It reads like the LORD God is pulling a joke on Adam.

In the traditional view of things, the account is puzzling but once you plug it into the true framework of early Genesis it makes complete sense. It makes sense in the cosmology of Moses, and Paul, and the rest. It's just that the church has not been teaching that cosmology. Chapter two is not another viewpoint of the creation of the world. The world had already been created and this is an account from the perspective of the man about The LORD God's dealings with him.

After all the days of God saying that things were good, a condition is discovered which The LORD God says is not good. The man's condition of being solitary in his work is not good. He has a good job to do, but it's not good that he is doing it alone. The LORD God declares that He will make a "helper" who is "suitable" for the man.

That word "suitable" or "meet" is interesting. It means "before" or "opposite of" in location. In some contexts, it can also mean a counterpart. The helper was to be complementary to the man, and not a copy of him. The "suitability" of the helper lay in the very fact that there were to be differences, and those differences would result in the new whole being greater than the sum of the parts.

Against that backdrop, God was to make the man a helper suitable for the job of exercising his dominion over the earth and the living creatures on it. Obviously, the beasts of the field could not be tame and domesticated when mankind himself was wild and undomesticated, but this man was different. God was molding him to be *homo sapiens domesticus*- the domestic man. Not a hunter-gatherer, but a civilization builder. In this account, domestic animals were fashioned for the domestic man.

When the LORD God formed from the ground the beasts of the field and the fowls (Genesis 2:19), it should be understood that these were not the first beasts and fowls to walk the earth. If the LORD God made, for example, a bovine and brought it to Adam, this should not be taken to mean that it was the first bovine. The first bovines had been created long before, back in chapter one, before man was created. Rather, Adam was given versions of these creatures which were more useful to him in accomplishing God's desire for the world than those which were then walking the earth.

We don't know the exact time Adam was formed. We have a range of dates. If it was toward the earliest part of the range, these could be the original domestic cattle, sheep, pigs and goats *et al.* If the later end of the range, men elsewhere had made some clumsy efforts at domestication, but Adam got his own better versions. Either way, the point is that God was doing the work for Him. He was doing *for* Adam what man was commissioned to do in Gen. 1:28. The whole garden is a "Grace Zone" as opposed to the "works zone" outside.

The "beasts of the field" and the "fowls" were supposed to get more and more domestic, more and more tame, as man exercised the dominion over the earth which God had given him. But instead of humans bringing members of the animal kingdom up into a higher state of civilization, mostly man had descended lower. The LORD God formed Adam in part to reverse this process. To help get back some of the time which had been lost, He provided versions of the creatures who were closer to the desired outcome in genetics and temperament. These creatures were "helpers" of a sort for Adam. They represented breeding stock which could help make up for the time humanity had lost in civilizing nature and themselves.

The animals formed in chapter two represent a much more limited set of animals than those created in Genesis chapter one. For one thing, there were no aquatic creatures mentioned, but even if we stick to terrestrial animals the language is much more limited. For example, on the sixth day three categories of animals are mentioned, the "beasts of the earth" (wild animals such as lions, bears, monkeys), the cattle, and "creeping things".

The word for "cattle" is Strong's Online Concordance word 929, *behemah*. It means large, dull-witted quadrupeds which commonly serve as livestock. The "creeping things" are small animals which move along the ground rapidly, such as lizards, hares, and the like. The fowls were created separately on day five of chapter one.

In contrast, in chapter two the types of animals formed are a category called "beasts of the field" and fowls. Obviously, the term "beast of the field" is a more limited category than "beast of the earth". The "earth" could be any sort of terrain. The field implies open ground, even pasture or cultivation. It even implies animals with a connection to humanity because the word for "ground" there is "adam'ah" from which the term for man is drawn. These were animals which were meant to be of help to someone who was an agriculturalist and engaged in animal husbandry. Only a very small proportion of the world's species fit that description.

What sort of animals fit the description "beasts of the field"? Notice that no creatures from the "cattle" category were specifically mentioned in verse nineteen, and yet Adam is naming creatures from that category in verse twenty. Ergo "cattle" must have been a subset of the category "beasts of the field." An important one too, for Adam mentions naming the cattle-like animals first, and then the fowls, and only then speaks of naming "every beast of the field". I take that to mean the rest of the "beasts of the field" were not in the critical cattle-like subcategory.

What sort of animals are "beasts of the field" ("beasts" here is "living creatures") yet not cattle like? We don't know for sure, but they fall into the category of "creeping things"- animals which move close to the ground or in short hops. We know this because in Genesis 6:7 *Yahweh* determines to destroy everything He had made. He then gives a list of those things. The list includes beasts (but using the same word for cattle or livestock, *behemah*), fowls, and "creeping things" (along with the descendants of Adam). Therefore, He made some "creeping things" as a subset of "beasts of the field" in chapter two. Perhaps not every kind of "creeping thing" in the world, but every kind suitable for the field. The category "Beasts of the Field" contains some *behemah* (cattle like) animals and some animals from the category "creeping things."

My guess is that those creatures in the wild, the fowls and the beasts of the field, had long ago lost much of the genetic and epigenetic potential to be domesticated. The new versions that the LORD God made for the man had that potential put back in. This will be an important point to remember when we discuss the great flood of Noah's day, and why it was so important for him to preserve the animals which were with him.

I also want to point out that the animals which were formed were formed out of "the ground" and not "the dust of the ground" as Adam was. You may recall in a previous chapter that the use of dry ground to form Adam, and in the emergence of "the dry ground" in chapter one, is significant. The LORD God used regular ground, with moisture, to mold them and shape them. If the text is different, it is because God is trying to say something different. The LORD God made Adam judgement free. Animals don't have the same moral accountability, so it did not matter.

All of this explains why this set of animals was formed. It was not because there were no animals on earth before this point. It was not, at least solely, about getting the man a wife so that he could start reproducing and filling the earth. That was being done by the other male and female humans created in chapter one.

The formation of these animals was about getting the man some help. And these versions of the animals may have been helpers in that they were genetically and epigenetically more disposed to domestication than was typical of their kind. I do not wish to go into detail in these pages, but so near as science can tell us the first and still most important farm animals which mankind has been able to domesticate can be traced to the region and era in which I locate Adam in these pages.

There are some caveats to this. For example, the pigs which formed the original domesticated stock in the near east had significant later contributions by wild varieties and other strains which were subsequently domesticated. Dogs were domesticated before other animals were, and likely before our date for Adam. Yet there is a separate domestication event for dogs which matches well with Genesis two, and Near Eastern dogs from this stock largely replaced those earlier domesticated strains.

In many cases of domestication scientists detect a genetic distance between wild and domesticated populations of the same animals which seems too large considering the time the animal has been known to be domesticated. It is as if populations of animals destined to later be domesticated were separating from their wilder kin for millennia before man even tried to tame them.

That explanation might make sense by chance once or twice, but it seems implausible for as often as it is being discovered. Another explanation which fits the same evidence is the account in Genesis chapter two as I am describing it here. The LORD God sped the process up by making new populations of some types of existing animals whose domestication potential was enhanced. Due to the enhancement, their genes look like they have been domesticated, or separated from their wild kin, for longer than they have been known to have been domesticated.

But to get into all of that in detail would be enough to require a separate book, and there are people out there more qualified than I am to write such a tome. I want to focus on the account here in Genesis. My point is just that the animals were helpful. They were not unrelated to the subject of getting the man some help for his mission. But they were not what the man had in mind when he heard the LORD God declare His intentions either.

So, the LORD God was not messing up. He was not churning out creatures trying to fulfill that need and "missing" on what He was trying to do. Rather all the creatures which He formed were able to help the man accomplish the Gen. 1:28 commission in some manner, but they were only opening acts. He was just warming up. The 'grand finale' was yet to come. Adam needed his natural counterpart or "other half".

Look at it from the man's perspective, which is how this account is written. The LORD God tells him that He is going to make the man this special helper. Then all he gets is one animal after another. He names one after the other. Who knows how long this went on. I get the idea that the LORD God was having more fun with the process than the man was. Adam was expecting a special helper, based on the LORD God's word, and as the day dragged on all he got was beasts and birds. His reaction simply highlights that beasts and birds already existed and were to some extent known to Adam. Thus the disappointed tone in verse twenty which says, "but for the man there was not found a help meet for him".

We do not think of the LORD, *Yahweh,* as having a sense of humor later in the scriptures. But those later accounts are after millennia of disappointment with the wretched condition of His handiwork. Here we see Him as He really is, when not burdened with the sorrow of our sinfulness. He does have a sense of humor. He is playing a day-long joke on the man. The man is expecting a woman for his "special helper" and The LORD God keeps making all these animals!

After the LORD God spent the day pulling the man's leg, he put the man to sleep and pulled a rib! The LORD God fashioned a suitable helper out of a rib (or perhaps "side chamber" is a more literal translation) taken from the man's own body. Just as with the animals made in this chapter, God did not make a new human female because there were no human females around to select. They were out there, but it would have ruined the point of what followed if the LORD God had just selected one of them instead of using the man's own flesh to form the woman.

Those who ask why, if other women were around, the LORD God did not just choose one of them to be Adam's wife, are not mindful of the main point of this book~ all of early Genesis points to Christ and cannot be understood apart from that perspective.

Instead of a "my fair lady" scenario where he gets a wild woman from the hills and civilizes her, he gets a wife from his own flesh. Thus, later in the story when Adam tries to blame the woman, and indirectly the LORD God Himself, for giving him the forbidden fruit, his excuse rings as hollow as it is. It would have been a different account if an outsider had been the one bringing him down. It was not an outsider. It was, as he said himself, "bone of my bone and flesh of my flesh."

Looking far ahead to the real point, salvation was destined to come through Adam's line, but Adam blew it. So instead, the true intermediary would be the Seed of the woman. This "loophole" was possible precisely because she came from Adam's flesh. God's intent that the line of Adam would produce the redeemer was still intact, but through the seed of the woman who came out of Adam, not the seed of the man.

The LORD God also took the woman from the man because He was creating a shadow or picture of Christ and the Church. In them He is trying to demonstrate for us what His intended natural order of things should be, both for us as people and as children of God. We are not to deny our differences but embrace the way that they complete us when we are properly united.

Because of the pattern the LORD God established with Adam and Eve, the woman comes from the man before the man comes from the woman. The church comes from God before God is manifested in the church. The human race did not emerge separate from God. It is not added to Him from outside. It was not something independent or underived from Him which He shall capture. Rather mankind was something which He set free in hopes some of us would choose to return to Him. It was something lost which is to be reconciled and reunited to Him. The man on earth must show in a small way what The Man in Heaven is doing in a large way. As it says in Second Corinthians chapter five:

Therefore if any man be in Christ, he is a new creature: old things are passed away; behold, all things are become new.
And all things are of God, who hath reconciled us to himself by Jesus Christ, and hath given to us the ministry of reconciliation;
To wit, that God was in Christ, reconciling the world unto himself, not imputing their trespasses unto them; and hath committed unto us the word of reconciliation.
Now then we are ambassadors for Christ, as though God did beseech you by us: we pray you in Christ's stead, be ye reconciled to God.
For he hath made him to be sin for us, who knew no sin; that we might be made the righteousness of God in him.

This pattern cannot be demonstrated by the man being joined to a woman who is not of himself. It would not be a picture of our reconciliation for the man to "become one flesh" with just any woman who wandered into the garden. But it was aptly demonstrated by the man's own flesh being used to form his suitable helper. What was of the man to begin with is reconciled to him again in the form of the woman. This is so with the man on earth in the form of the woman Eve, and it is so with The Man in Heaven in the form of the Church. Mike Winger has said that this is a picture of Christ in another way- the church sprang forth from the wound in His side!

The LORD God then universalizes what happened to the man and the woman and extends the pattern to the whole human race. What happened in that case was a rejoining, but in every case for all of mankind marriage is to be a joining. For the LORD God declares in verse twenty-four that "the two shall become one flesh." It is a joining together in every case, but a re-joining in the case of Adam and Eve, and Christ and the Church. The last part of Ephesians chapter five makes it clear that even this was a shadow pointing to Christ and the Church. But even if we do not rejoin, it is His intent that men and women be joined as one flesh when they become husband and wife. He wants us to connect, not collide.

The Fall of the Man and His Wife

***

Now the serpent was more subtil than any beast of the field which the LORD GOD had made. And he said unto the woman, Yea, hath God said, Ye shall not eat of every tree of the garden? – Genesis 3:1

In recent times it seems that mockers have more frequently made a show of their own ignorance by deriding Christians who believe "stories about talking snakes." There have doubtless been some Christians who have believed that the serpent was just a talking snake. After all, Christianity is the most prominent religion in human history. When billions of people hold to the same scriptures all sorts of ideas are bound to be had concerning what they mean. But what should matter here is not what some people think that the Bible says about the serpent, but what the Bible actually says about the serpent.

The book of Revelation has a lot to say which is very mysterious. But there are some things about which it is very specific. One of them is that "the serpent of Old" is the Devil, Satan. It says this in Revelation 12:5-12 and again in 20:2. Christ said so too in John 8:44. In addition, the Hebrew word for serpent which is used here (as opposed to the several other Hebrew words for serpent) is "*Na-chash.*" When this word is used as a verb it means "to practice divination" or to use an enchantment. The connection to serpent is through this use, the hiss of the snake being like the incantations of the diviner. But this 'hissing one' was also the hiss of an accuser.

This was not just a reptile who could somehow speak. The Bible is not saying that snakes are more cunning than other predatory animals. This was a divine being, doing what such beings do- divination. When it says it was "more crafty than any beast of the field" it is not implying that it was one of the beasts too. It was not among them; it was smarter than they were. Man's dominion over the beasts did not mean that man was smarter than the serpent. This was a whole different level of crafty compared to what Adam and Eve were used to.

When the LORD God pronounced the curse on the serpent it will be shown that what was being prophesied was not about snakes and people. It was and is about the triumph of Christ over Satan. The Bible says that the Bible uses metaphor. This is one of those places. Eve did get beguiled, but it was not by a mere snake.

We can only speculate as to the backstory from the hints given elsewhere in scripture. It is obvious that Satan, the serpent, wanted the man to fail. Maybe when God created The Man in heaven it became clear that one day men would rule angels, just as the New Testament teaches. Perhaps not every resident of heaven was sold on that prospect. Perhaps after thousands of years of observing the works of man, the idea of serving under such lowly creatures was an affront to their pride.

Satan means "accuser" or "adversary". *The* Satan is a divine being whose heavenly function seems to have been to give God an account of mankind's sins. That is not a job liable to produce a charitable view of the human race. After thousands of years of watching us degrade ourselves and one another, I can see where someone could go from reluctantly reporting on our miserable condition, to a self-righteous heart which took relish in telling God just what wretches His human children were.

It is easy to imagine a scenario where, embittered at the thought that a "wise and worthy" divine being such as he was destined to abide by human judges, Lucifer snapped. Like a cop or prosecutor who crosses the line from enforcing the law to entrapment, Satan did not stop at just reporting man's sins to God. If this particular man, the man, would not sin on his own, then Satan would coax him into it. The fall of man may also be the outward fall of Satan. It is where the unbelief in its heart was manifested as outward disobedience on the earth.

I shall not repeat all the theology which has been associated with this passage, for this volume is mostly about the cosmology of Genesis. Many of the theological errors about Genesis have root in the fact that the cosmology of Genesis is misunderstood. By correcting the cosmology, I hope that the errors in theology will more easily fall by the wayside even without going through them all. But I would mention this- that God did not say He would curse the ground because of Adam, He said that the ground was cursed because of him. The difference is that the latter allows for a scenario like the one laid out here- where Adam could have lifted the ground from its state of futility and brought the garden to the whole earth by living in faith. Instead, because of his failure, the ground would stay in its present condition for a long time- that was the curse, not nature changing.

Notice in verse six where it is written "she gave it to her husband; and he did eat" that the word used for "husband" is from the root word "*enosh*" and not the word "*adam.*" Enosh also means "man" but stresses the mortality of man. Its best translation is "mortal." She did not give the forbidden fruit to "the man", she gave it to "the mortal". Adam was mortal, even before he ate the forbidden fruit. Had he stayed in faithful fellowship with the LORD God without eating of either tree would he have grown old?

I think the answer is "yes", but he would not have died. God's hope for mankind in the earth was and is the Enoch scenario. It is said of Enoch (Genesis 5) that he "walked with God and was not, for God took him." In Hebrews 11:5 this event is referred to as a "translation". After a long time walking with the LORD God, one is changed from a frame suitable for a temporal world into a frame suitable for an eternal one. That, and not physical death, was God's desired goal for all of mankind. This smooth transition was interrupted by the fall.

First Corinthians 15:51-53, without calling it that, speaks of our translation, which for the great mass of us is deferred until the end of the age:

Behold, I show you a mystery: We shall not all sleep; but we shall all be changed in a moment, in the twinkling of an eye, at the last trumpet. For the trumpet shall sound, and the dead shall be raised incorruptible, and we shall be changed. For this corruptible must put on incorruption, and this mortal must put on immortality.

Notice that even after the fall, for example as with Cain and Abel and Enoch, the LORD God was in the habit of walking the earth with humans. After Genesis chapter five that changed, and such personal interactions tapered off dramatically. Look at it from the LORD God's perspective. You are the union of God and Man in heaven- the pre-incarnate Christ. The world is created so that it will produce men, and those among them with faith are then translated to join you in the Promised Land above.

But with the fall, the party you want to have is very slow to start. There is not a lot of human company up there for a long time. If you want human company, you must go to the earth below to get it. We see a lot of the LORD God personally interacting with humans on earth in those early days. Once Enoch is taken, and particularly after the flood, we see fewer such visits on the earth.

Let's return to the narrative in the third chapter of Genesis. One thing which stands out is how Eve took the fruit first, but Romans chapter five says that sin entered the world through Adam. This bolsters the idea that Adam was designated by God to be the Federal Intermediary or stand-in for humanity. When Adam fell, we all did, not because he was our physical ancestor, but because he was the designated intermediary for us all. If Eve had taken the fruit and Adam refused, Eve surely would have fallen but Adam need not have. For those outside the garden, their eyes were not opened to their sinful condition when Eve took the fruit, but when Adam took the fruit, for he was the stand-in, not her.

If any of the host outside the garden had taken the fruit, it would have been the death of them alone. But for Adam to take it meant sin and death for us all, just as the Atonement made by his descendant through Eve gives life to all. The symmetry is profound and is most exact when neither Adam nor Christ is the natural father of us all, but rather both were the God-appointed stand-in or representative of the race.

When the LORD God pronounces the curses for these acts of disobedience He says to the serpent (chapter three):

... upon thy belly shalt thou go, and dust shalt thou eat all the days of thy life: And I will put enmity between thee and the woman, and between thy seed and her seed; it shall bruise thy head, and thou shalt bruise his heel.

Yes, the curse is superficially written as if it might apply to a snake, but in context it can only be applied to the Devil. Even "literalists" admit that God uses figurative language here. So why not earlier? Breaking down the curses: On his belly he shall go: He will fall into a degraded state, as even humans who live a life of prideful sin sink further and further away from personal dignity and into a debauched condition. People in such a state tend to be touchy about any suspected affronts to their self-worth, even while they dissipate this worth by their own actions.

Dust shall thou eat: Immediately afterward the LORD God reminds Adam that he is dust. Without God's animating breath of life that is all we are. The serpent shall consume not dirt from the ground, but the essence of man himself (see First Peter 5:8). Our protection from this fate is to turn to the God who crowns us and dignifies us so that we do not return to a godless condition- fit only for the serpent's food.

It shall bruise thy head: In Galatians 3:16 the Apostle Paul made much of the fact that Genesis chapter fifteen used "seed" rather than "seeds" to say that Abraham's name would go on through Isaac. Paul said that the use of the singular meant that the seed was Christ, not all descendants of Abraham. Some Hebrew scholars may object that "seed" is a collective noun, but even that fits because the "body of Christ" is also a collective noun as used in scripture. It still boils down to some of Abraham's descendants will make the cut and others will not. Those in "the Seed" will.

While I am far from an expert in the nuance of collective versus singular shades of meaning in these Hebrew terms, it seems to me that the same argument can be made here. The textual case is even stronger here than in chapter fifteen that a single seed is being specified when speaking of the "seed of the woman". The seed is referred to as "it" rather than "they". Then the same seed is translated "his" as opposed to "its".

Christ is the seed of the woman being referred to here. The Seed of the Woman shall crush the head of the serpent, and it will be a decisive blow. The serpent shall only bruise the heel of the seed of the woman. The feet of the eternal body of Christ are those parts still on this earth. The saints which have passed on before us into the Heavenly realm are also a part of His body, but that part is out of the reach of the serpent. He can only bruise the heel of that part of the total body of Christ which is still touching this earth. Not even the whole foot, but just the hind part, or heel.

This is why in the Lord's Prayer we are instructed to ask God to deliver us from the evil one. On the cross, Christ crushed the head of the serpent, by ending the legal basis through which he could accuse and convict even those whose faith was in God.

That this meaning was intended is shown even by Adam's reaction to the LORD God's pronouncements. In Genesis 3:20 we read:

And Adam called his wife's name Eve; because she was the mother of all living.

At a superficial glance, this is a problematic verse. For one thing, her willingness to be deceived by the serpent had just helped get them both killed. It is strange to say at such a time that she was the "mother of all living." This has been misinterpreted to mean that Eve was the mother of all succeeding members of the human race. If that is what was meant, the view of Genesis 1:27 expounded in this work would be incorrect.

The paradox is resolved when it is understood that the LORD God revealed to them His plan to one day redeem mankind by making Himself born of a woman. Verse twenty isn't an out-of-the-blue statement about human origins. It should be taken in the context of the Seed mentioned in verse fifteen. He would, under much more demanding circumstances, live the sinless life which Adam was supposed to live, and thus redeem from the curse of eternal separation from God (death) all who had faith.

This is why Adam said that Eve was the "mother of all the living". It was not because she was the ancestor of every human on earth, but because she was the ancestor of The Seed. The Seed is He who would crush the serpent's head and restore whosoever will come to eternal life with God. The Seed is also the collective body of Christ- if our life "is hid with Christ in God" (Col. 3:3) then He is also "all the living."

The man had blown it badly. It would not be his seed which restored mankind, but that of his wife. The Father of the Divine aspect of The Man in Heaven is God the Father. But through His mother He is the seed of a woman, albeit a woman who was taken from the man and was one flesh with him. Ironically, The Man in Heaven became the "father" of the man on earth (begat the man) by forming him (Luke 3:38). So He is both the "father" of Adam and (via Eve) the "son" of Adam through Mary. Therefore, in Isaiah 9:6 He is named both "father" and "son".

The first thing that the LORD God does for the newly fallen couple is to make for them coats of skins to cover their nakedness, and thus their shame. This is a foreshadowing of the system of animal sacrifice later instituted to cover man's sins. It was meant to point out both the seriousness of sin and condition people to understand the true ultimate sacrifice of Christ on the Cross. Of course, some men put their faith in that religious system itself rather than what it was pointing to.

It was after covering their shame that the LORD God dealt with another, very serious, threat. The cosmology which God had set up, whereby man lives on earth and then either dies or is translated into the true life, was at risk. The fruit of the tree of life was meant for those who had faith in God. To eat of its fruit was to call for judgment, to make permanent the existing spiritual conditions. But to do so when man was his own determiner of "good and evil" was also to render judgment chaotic and meaningless.

I do not think that the consequence of eating the fruit of the Tree of Life would have been to make the earthly existence of man last forever, but rather to make true death impossible and true life linked to a cursed state. Perhaps the Man in Heaven would be forever linked to the rest of mankind, whether they loved Him or hated Him. The righteous would never get the peace they wanted free from the sin nature, nor would the wicked ever get the "peace" they wanted (being left to their sins undisturbed by the urging of God's spirit).

If Adam wanted to bring faith in man into the Kingdom of Heaven, then the eternal realm above would look like the world below. Sin and faith would stay mixed. The condition of Evenings and Mornings would never become a condition of eternal light. In taking of the fruit of the first tree, man had decided what the realm below would look like. Man would be "like God" deciding for himself what was good or evil. Taking the fruit of that tree would take things to the eternal realm. It could not be undone.

On this earth, the evil that men do to one another is often held in check by the thought that our lives are short. One day we may have to face judgment in the next life for what we do in this one. Evil is thereby restrained. Without this restraint, the rebellion and evil of men would be worse than it is. Thus, heaven would be made like earth and both would be made worse by making us all our own gods in both realms. God made a choice to remove the man's access to the garden, and the tree of life within it. By running the man off from the garden, the damage was limited to the temporal realm, where it could be cured.

The LORD God drove the man and his wife from the garden, and placed guards to its east to prevent the man's return. There are some misconceptions about the guarding of the way. Cherubim were placed there, and also what is translated as a "flaming sword which turned every way". I've seen artist's depictions of angels wielding iron swords with flames coming off the blade. There is nothing in the text which indicates that the Cherubim were using the "flaming sword" as a weapon. Instead, the text reads like whatever this was operated independently to discourage access.

Nor for that matter, does the text really say "flaming sword". Closer to the sense of the words is "sword of flame" in that flames were not coming from an implement, but rather the implement was composed of flame. Nor does the word often translated "sword" there necessarily refer to a sword. It often was in later usage, but it could be used to refer to any kind of cutting implement such as an ax, a mattock, or a sickle. Swords came along much later than my suspected date for Adam. Sickles have existed from the dawn of true agriculture. Like many farm tools, they can be used as weapons.

I say this in part because I have a pet theory about Genesis 3:24 and the "sword of flame". It is just a hypothesis, but it does connect some dots. The mysterious passage in Ezekiel chapter twenty-eight mentions the Garden of Eden, and then shortly after that the "Mountain of God" where a strange figure "walked among the fiery stones". Later the "Mountain of God" is in Israel, but this seems to be a previous "Mountain of God" associated with Eden. One that has characteristics of an active volcano.

All of my proposed locations for Eden have mountains around them. At least one has a volcano on the east end, which was active in Neolithic times. The curious reader may want to look up pictures of a "Strombolian" or "Vulcanian" eruption. These are characterized by giant curves or arcs of flame shooting out in all directions. It looks much more like a flashing sickle of flame turning in every direction than a steam locomotive looks like an "iron horse." And it would function in much the same way too- discouraging the man from trying to make his way back into the garden. Perhaps such an event was a part of the LORD God giving Adam an emphatic send-off.

The need for such precautions is long past. Though the man was one of us, as Christ was one of us, I suspect that he was also different from us. He was formed as one of us, but not formed like us. Perhaps there was something about him that allowed for passage between the realms. Regardless, the threat was not that *any* man would go into the garden and eat of the tree of life in a cursed state, nor that Adam *or* Eve would do so, but only that *the man* would do so (3:22). This is more evidence that Adam was a federal head or stand-in for humanity- a type of Christ. When his eyes were opened, so were the eyes of all men. Innocence was lost everywhere.

If Adam was somehow special in his access to the garden, then on the death of Adam there would have been no way left to guard and therefore no need for guards to remain. There yet remains a way and a gate, but it is no longer tied to an earthly location. Jesus described Himself as "the Way" and as "the Gate" (John 10:9) and through Him we will "go in and go out." For those of us who are born again, the passage back is once again open, in the person of Christ.

The Tree of Life is where the LORD God dwells. We will see that in the pre-flood days He stayed close to the descendants of Adam. But the ancient world, characterized by the LORD God walking among His people on a regular basis, was destroyed in the judgement of the flood. The text will show that after that He will not walk so intimately among His own, until the Advent. Though some trace of the Garden may remain buried in the earth, we should expect that when He withdrew the tree went with Him- it may even be but another manifestation of Himself.

That the guards were placed to the east of the garden indicates that this was the direction which Adam and Eve were driven. It does not seem they were driven very far. You may recall that the "Garden of Eden" was within the land of Eden. They left the garden, but stayed somewhat near the land, where The LORD continued to interact with them. For example, the next chapter says that Cain also went east when he fled "the presence of the LORD". Still, his family was able to keep up with him, as is shown by their reporting on the exploits of his immediate descendants. They stayed close to Eden, and Cain wound up in the land of Nod "on the east of Eden" (4:16), at least for a while.

Sometimes I think about *Yahweh* on the day after Adam and Eve had been driven from the Garden. This garden that He had built for the man, and planted with every good tree, must have been quiet, empty, and very lonely. All the time they had spent fellowshipping, all the joy of discovery He had seen in the man's face as he learned new things, all of it was gone now. I can see *Yahweh* walking alone in the garden which He had made for them, silent and brooding as the shadows of evening lengthened into darkness.

Adam's Line Takes Root

⊱⋅☙◉❧⋅⊰

In chapter four, Adam and Eve begin having children. They are not in the Garden anymore. The LORD God is not doing all the heavy lifting for them anymore, they must do it themselves. But He has not abandoned them. He still walks with them, and presumably protects them from the more established peoples around them.

Why do I say that there were other people around that the Lord was protecting them from? Because the text in chapter four indicates that this is the situation. When the Lord punishes Cain for murdering Abel, Cain's lament shows that anything outside of where his family lived was full of potentially hostile people:

Behold, thou hast driven me out this day from the face of the earth; and from thy face shall I be hid; and I shall be a fugitive and a vagabond in the earth; and it shall come to pass, that every one that findeth me shall slay me"

The word translated "earth" there is "*ha-ada-mah*". That is, the earth or ground from which Adam gained his name. Cain was complaining that he was being driven from the civilized territory of his family, where the LORD visited. He seemed to think that people from outside were dangerous. The word translated "fugitive" (נוּעַ "*nua*") doesn't mean that and is only rendered so here. There is no hint in that word that he is fleeing retribution from his family, just that he will be in an unstable situation.

As I asked previously, who was Cain so worried about? He talked as if the world was already full of people. People who he believed would not hesitate to waylay a lone outcast from his family group.

Those who think Cain was worried about other members of his own family killing him should explain why Cain only complained about being killed in response to the news that he was being driven *away* from the face of the "A-da-mah" where his family was. He did not think they were a threat when he was present with them. If there was a big empty world out there with only one family in it then there would have been plenty of room to hide. Cain's concern only makes sense if there are other humans who were outside the garden, as laid out in the Christ-centered model. The children of Adam were the "spoiled rich kids" of the earth. They blew their inheritance but were still protected by the presence of the LORD.

Even Cain was favored by the LORD. He puts a mark on Cain that somehow offered protection from these mysterious others. If there were no other humans in the world then marking Cain makes no sense. In a world with no Others, if you see a stranger in the woods, it's Cain, who the LORD told us not to kill! But it makes sense in a world of tribes to say "the one with this mark is not your typical outcast. He's Mine."

By this mark, the LORD puts the word out that if anyone kills Cain then they can expect sevenfold vengeance- i.e. seven of yours for one of Mine. Apparently, this was the language that the inhabitants of that day understood. Such harsh retribution makes no sense in the context of deterrence for his family killing him. Cain is being treated with relative favor here.

Cain is exiled to the "land of Nod" and finds a wife, apparently before the birth of Seth (Genesis 4:25). And not only does he find a wife, Cain winds up founding a city (Genesis 4:17), which he names after his own son. It seems that in spite of his fear of interacting with the barbarians outside of his group, and even his own and The LORD's view of his future prospects, Cain found a way to fit in with them quite well. It turned out that Cain the Murderer was their kind of guy.

Cain's near descendant Lamech kills "a man". Not "my cousin", not "Fred", but "a man." The text supports the view that the world was already at least sparsely inhabited during the life of Adam and Eve.

The rest of mankind may have had a long hunter-gatherer phase, but there was no "Stone Age" for Adam's ilk. Abel was a pastoral farmer. Cain- before he was driven out- was an agriculturalist. In verses 20-22 of chapter four we learn that one of the sons of Lamech introduced the lifestyle of the nomadic shepherd to the world. Another invents musical instruments. Another son, Tubal-Cain, was a "sharpener" or instructor of those whose work is metallurgy. The phrasing does not quite indicate that Tubal-Cain invented the concept of working in metals, but rather than he invented processes which greatly advanced this art.

On that last part, the verse specifies they worked with "bronze" and "iron". Do not be confused by the timing of the "Iron Age" coming later than the "Bronze Age". There is every reason to believe that the ancients knew about both early on, but so long as tin was available bronze was easier to work with. Iron was only an improvement on bronze after mankind learned how to carbonize it- forming steel.

The earliest objects made of metal that we have found so far have been dated as far back as eleven thousand years ago, but the big advances in working metals did not come along until much later. The "Bronze Age" proper did not begin until after the time I think these events from chapter four occurred. But the term "Bronze Age" does not refer to the age that bronze was invented so much as the age when the use of bronze became *widespread*. In part, according to Genesis, due to the discoveries and instructions of Tubal-Cain seven generations removed from Adam.

Superior metallurgy was powerful knowledge. One can understand why the early practitioners would be careful who they instructed in these arts. Perhaps it was practiced by a closeted guild restricted to the area of Adam's kin and their allies for many centuries. I suspect that many of these advances did not really filter out to the rest of humanity until much later. Possibly even after the Deluge.

The last two verses of this chapter are critical to understanding both the revealed cosmology of early Genesis and the material which is to follow:

And Adam knew his wife again; and she bare a son, and called his name Seth: For God, said she, hath appointed me another seed instead of Abel, whom Cain slew. And to Seth, to him also there was born a son; and he called his name Enos: then began men to call upon the name of the LORD.

The name Seth means "substitute" or "stand-in". The name makes sense in the context of Eve seeing him as a substitute for Abel, but it also makes sense prophetically. Of all the offspring of Adam and Eve, it is the line of Seth which leads to the Messiah, the true substitute or stand-in for all of us when it comes to payment for our sins.

In addition, in chapter five it says that in Seth Adam had a son "in his own image, after his own likeness." This is not said of any of his other children. Seth is like his father Adam. This phrasing is like that which God gave for His intent for man in 1:26. Seth is also said to be the "seed" of Eve. That is, he carries the promise that one day the serpent's head will be crushed by the seed of the woman.

God has His own version of evolution going on. He chooses some and rejects others. The scriptural term for that is a "remnant." Of all of Adam's sons, only the line of (1) Seth will be chosen to produce the line of Messiah. Of all of Seth's descendants, (2) only the line of Noah will be chosen. Of all of Noah's descendants, only the line of (3) Abraham will be chosen. Of Abraham's sons, (4) Isaac will be chosen over Ishmael and the rest. Of Isaac's sons, (5) Jacob will be chosen over Esau. Of Jacob's descendants, (6) David will be chosen. And the seventh and last to be chosen is The Seed Himself.

Further, Seth names his own son "Enosh". This is simply the word which means "mortal man" turned into a name. Just as his father's name meant "Man", so his son's name would be "man", but in a form reflecting their current situation. There is a parallel here, with Seth and The Heavenly Man. Both are referred to as "The Seed". Both make a son in their own image, and after their likeness. Both name their son after the human race itself.

But even though Seth picked a name for his son which applied to mankind generally, the Clan of Adam still held to their distinctive identity. Not that they saw themselves in their essence as something other than the rest of "*enosh*", but they saw their relationship with God as distinctive. This is indicated in that last verse. They were separated by their position relative to the LORD, not in their persons.

The last verse of chapter four has been badly translated, and most modern translations will account for that by noting that the verse can also be read that they "called themselves by the name of the LORD", or "in the name". The key to understanding some of the mysteries of chapter six lies in understanding that in the days of Enosh the clan of Adam began distinguishing themselves from the rest of humanity. And they did this in that they called themselves by the name of the LORD (*Yahweh*). The rest of humanity did not do so. They had the personal relationship with God, and called themselves by His name, as if they were His family. There were the LORD's people, and then there was everyone else. Has anything changed since?

Chapter five is mostly a genealogy and has been discussed as such. Enoch has already been discussed. He was the one who was taken up and translated to the Land Above without dying (perhaps a shadow of what was originally meant to occur and what will occur in the last generation). With this understanding we go directly to chapter six and the set-up for the great Deluge.

A Note about the Strange Number Pattern in Chapter Five

The genealogies in chapter five, with one exception, all end in a number divisible by five, or a number divisible by five plus seven (so two would be added to the last "five" in the age). This has been seized on by the usual suspects as evidence that the ages in the account are fictitious, at best inserted to make some vague spiritual point using numerology.

There is a better explanation- one which supports the Tablet Theory. I believe that the numbers from the table were originally written in a number system that had irregular-length years and regular five-year cycles. These cycles were further divided into a two-year and a three-year portion. If a man died in the first portion a new cycle, he was given credit for the unit which would later be counted as two years, if he made it past that, then he was given credit for the full unit, which would later be counted as five years. They were no longer using such a measure of time when Moses transcribed the tablets, so he converted the larger units to years.

The Vedic calendar had five-year cycles called "yugas" from 6,000 B.C. to 3,000 B.C. The "classic" Babylonian calendar had a longer cycle consisting of two and three-year periods indicating when to "add a month" of thirty days to keep their 354-day lunar-based calendar aligned to the seasons. But if I am right that was developed long after the genealogy was written. The Babylonian calendar used complicated cycles that had more three-year segments than two-year segments. Prior to that, local kings would add the months in a more ad hoc manner. For example, every two years they could add a "short" month of around twenty-two days, and every three years a "long month". The lengths of the added months could be adjusted as necessary on the next cycle to realign the calendars with the sky.

That would mean that years varied in length quite a bit, since some had a short month added, some a long month added, and some no month at all added. So, it makes perfect sense that years would not be used to measure long periods of time, but rather they used these five-year (2+3) cycles which were of more uniform length.

If a long-lived man died in the last three years of a cycle, his year of death was divisible by five, and the same if he died in the last three of the next. If he died in the two years between, year-of-death would end in 5+2. That's a two out of eight chance of ending in 5+2. If one compares the proportion of entries in chapter five where the years end with a seven added, it is very close to the predicted proportion (twenty-five percent) if my hypothesis is correct. The genealogy in chapter five is of great antiquity.

The Sons of God and the Nephilim

The opening passage of the sixth chapter of Genesis is one of the most mysterious passages in the bible. Please put aside any preconceptions you may have about what these verses are saying in order to evaluate this evidence fairly. I believe this is yet another passage of scripture where much of the church has just adopted the teachings of Second Temple Period and later Rabbis who opposed Christ instead of looking at the material through the lens of Christ. In other words, the church has had this completely wrong. Here are the first two verses:

And it came to pass, when men began to multiply on the face of the earth, and daughters were born unto them, That the sons of God saw the daughters of men that they were fair; and they took them wives of all which they chose.

There has been endless speculation about who "the sons of God" and the "Nephilim" mentioned just afterward were. To sort it out, let's start from the other end. Let's look at who the "men" and "the daughters of men" were in this passage. This is a question which has not adequately been considered before, because prior to this point the church has simply accepted the Jewish view of Adam. That is, he was the first man and the sole male founder of the human race.

Now that we know that he is *not* the sole father of the human race, but that his proper role is as a Christ-figure, it makes sense to re-examine the text. When we do, it turns out that verse one actually reads "when *ha-adam* began to multiply." The "ha" means "the" or in some cases "of", so this verse should not have been translated "when men began to multiply", but rather when "*the* men" began to multiply.

The traditional translators were used to thinking of Adam as the sole founder of humanity. If you do that, what the text really says, "the men", seem superfluous. Why say "*the* men"? In that line of thinking there were no other men around other than the clan of Adam, and so there would be no need for a definite article to refer to a particular group of men. Yet the article is there, and as we have seen there is a strong textual case to be made that there were already humans, *adam* the race, when Adam The Man who was formed to stand in for that race was placed inside the garden.

So, when Gen. 6:1 says "the men" it refers to a specific group of men-Adam's line who this account has been following. The people who, according to the last verse of chapter four, called themselves by the name of *Yahweh*. This is a verse which has in modern times been retranslated, in my view to a more correct form. The correct translation of last verse of chapter four gives us another vital clue. Rightly rendered, it says that in the days of Enosh the descendants of Adam began "calling themselves *by* the name of the LORD".

Why would they give themselves that moniker? One purpose could be a way to differentiate their tribe from those of other people groups. The rest of humanity did not have The LORD interacting with them on a regular basis. The Heavenly Man was still walking around on the earth. He was still guiding Adam's descendants in human form. He was still correcting them and still protecting them in person up until this point. Once you look for it in chapters two through five, it becomes obvious. Verse three in chapter six says it outright when He says "My Spirit shall not always strive with man". The word *strive* means "to contend with, to judge or administrate." More on that later.

The "daughters of Adam" in verse two of chapter six were the offspring of Adam. They called themselves by the name of the LORD. They were of the LORD's line because "the man" Adam was formed by the LORD God. The offspring of "the man" were the original "chosen people." They called themselves by the name of *Yahweh* to distinguish themselves from the other "sons of *Elohim*". That is, the other people groups in the earth.

The fifth chapter carefully traced their lineage from the Man on earth (and thus also his wife Eve). If Adam were indeed the sole male founder of humanity, there would be no point in tracing one's linage back to him, because *every* linage would end there. Yet scripture, Old Testament and New, traces the linage of the patriarchs and even Christ Himself back to Adam. Those texts were establishing that they were in the line of The Seed promised in Genesis 3:15 that would crush the serpent's head.

Ha-adam can fairly be translated "of men" in verse two. And if you were never shown the verses we discussed earlier, pointing to other members of the adamic race outside the garden, then you'd never think to look at the details of 6:1. And if you don't see that 6:1 is mistranslated and should say "when *the* men", a particular group of men, the line of Adam that the narrative is following, then you'd think that the "daughters of men" refers to *all* human women. You'd never think to wonder if it isn't saying "daughters of Adam". Therefore, you would reasonably conclude that "the sons of God" in the following verses must be something *other* than men.

There is nothing wrong with this reasoning. The reasoning is correct, but it is based on bad information. These verses are not necessarily talking about all human beings on earth, and therefore we must look closer to determine who the "sons of God" could be. After all, in Genesis 1:28 God gave the people outside the garden authority to exercise dominion over the earth. Maybe this is where those people come back into the story.

But aren't "the sons of God" divine spirit beings, whether good or evil, and not human? Well, not necessarily. Many theologians believe that both humans *and* divine beings can be considered "sons of God".

If that's the case then you have to find context to determine which is meant here. A lot of people think they have already done that work, but have only heard one side of the evidence, the side that basically tries to shoehorn spirit beings into every possible passage. The case that "the sons of God" should ordinarily be interpreted as "spirit beings" is more controversial than many might think.

Even if the sons of Adam did not view these other tribes as sons of the one true God, we should consider the context of the times. Ancient Near East rulers considered themselves descendants of the gods. So, it could be that they are referred to as such because that is how the chieftains of these tribes spoke of themselves. Not because they were Divine Spirit Beings, and not because they were worshippers of the One True God, but because that was what they were known as in the time and place that they lived. If so, the correct translation would be "when the sons of gods saw..." or "when the sons of the gods saw...".

The clearest reference to the "sons of God" as spirit beings is found in the book of Job. There it is clearly referring to something other than humans. The question with Job isn't whether these references are really to spirit beings, but whether these references really said "sons of God" in the original text, and even whether that phrase meant the same thing in Job versus the rest of the Pentateuch.

The Septuagint (LXX) is the Greek version of the Jewish scriptures. It was used as the first Old Testament of Christians for almost 1,000 years. It is *still* the Old Testament used by Eastern Orthodox Churches. In most of the west it was replaced by the Masoretic Text, which is now used for the translation of almost all English Bibles. But many New Testament quotes from the Old Testament sound more like the Septuagint than the Masoretic Text, which is understandable since the Septuagint was already around when the New Testament was written while the Masoretic text was completed much later, by Rabbis who had explicitly rejected Jesus as the Messiah.

What does this witness say of the matter of the "sons of God" in Job? The Septuagint in each instance says "Angels of God" where the Masoretic text says "Sons of God", yet the LXX keeps "Sons of God" in Genesis chapter six. It seems as if they wished to distinguish what was spoken of in Genesis chapter six from what was spoken of in Job. The Dead Sea Scrolls have some fragments of what is called the *Targum of Job*. It quotes Job chapter thirty-eight, which is the clearest witness in scripture that the "sons of God" are non-human Divine Spirit beings. But this document, though in Aramaic and not Greek, renders it like the Septuagint does, as *"Angels* of God." I would consider it controversial to even assert with confidence that the original text of Job said "sons of God".

Even if it did, it is quite possible that it meant something different than what was meant in Genesis by that term. The book of Job isn't just disputed in its translation on the verses which concern us here. It was part of a separate cultural stream than the books of Moses. Job wasn't in the camp of Israel. He was a man of the east. We don't know when it was written, but the oldest estimates put it around the time of Abraham, the more recent around the Babylonian Captivity.

Either way, if the Tablet Theory is correct, early Genesis was written long before the book of Job. At some point in Babylon, they developed traditions about "the sons of God" which did emphasize the divine being aspect. This does not mean that the Old Testament Patriarchs shared their worldview, because they were guided by a different Light. A book which was the story of "a man of the east" might affect eastern usages for terms, even if that was not the way the mainstream of Mosaic thought at the time would have used them!

It is said by critics that much of the Torah was influenced by ideas acquired during the Babylonian Captivity. I suspect the reverse was true- that a lot of knowledge was lost during that period. They kept the scriptures, but the understanding of them became hidden knowledge. The meaning of the term shifted. Instead of reflecting what the scriptures said about it, the term came to reflect the meaning which their captors ascribed to it. The verses in Job are disputed in translation. The first clear use we have of the phrase "son of God" to describe a divine being rather than a human is uttered not by a man of faith but by the Medio-Persian Ruler Darius in Daniel 3:25.

Moses was not shy about using the term for angels- *maloch*. It is used in the Pentateuch at least a dozen times. So is the term Cherubim. The guard of the way back to the Tree of Life was so identified in Genesis chapter three.

These terms were available to use for angelic or spirit beings, but they are not used in Genesis six. On the other hand, several scriptures describe men as sons of either the LORD or God. Exodus 4:22 says, "Israel is my son" for example.

When it comes to equating the sons of God to human beings, Hosea 1:10 uses similar, though not exactly the same, language in this famous verse:

Yet the number of the children of Israel shall be as the sand of the sea, which cannot be measured nor numbered; and it shall come to pass, that in the place where it was said unto them, Ye are not my people, there it shall be said unto them, Ye are the sons of the living God.

The term for "living God" there is "*El-hay*" which is the singular of *Elohim* combined with the word for living. Still, God's sons are shown to be humans, not angels.

But we don't even have to go that far from Genesis. Deuteronomy 14:1 says "*Ye are the children of the LORD your God.*" The word translated "children" there is the same as that translated "son" throughout the genealogies. They are told this in the context of a command not to participate in certain practices that other peoples engaged in. This is what I have been saying of the early descendants of Adam's clan. They called themselves "by the name of the LORD." Their *Elohim* was *Yahweh*. Other peoples didn't have the same personal relationship with God that they did. They didn't know Him by name. They may have even been worshippers of other so-called gods, or deified their ancestors. If so Genesis 6:4 should read "sons of the gods" (you can't tell in Hebrew if "*elohim*" there is singular or plural) and the writer was referring to them in the way that they described themselves.

Long after the flood, many Ancient Near East kings claimed descent from one of "the gods". *Yahweh* tells His people, so long as they live in faithful relationship to Him, they are *all* His children. It wasn't just their kings and priests that were descended from the "gods" as with the pagan peoples. God Himself was their king, and His intent was for the whole nation to become His sons and daughters. This is exactly what God does in the New

Testament. Believers are the Sons and Daughters of God. See Romans 8:14-16, Galatians 3:26 and 4:6, John 1:12, 2nd Cor. 6:18, et al.

Did God change His view on this question or was it always His intent? I submit to you it was always His intent. It was His intent to show this to the whole earth through His son Adam's (Luke 3:38) clan, but they re- jected their calling and had to be destroyed. It was what He was pointing to with Israel and the Law of Moses. And it is what is fulfilled by grace through faith in Christ.

If I am right about the Tablet Theory, these early, pre-flood chapters of Genesis speak from a time when the LORD God Himself walked among men on a regular basis. Perhaps they understood what was forgotten over time- that men were created as God's children and our rightful path is to become that which we are by His declaration- His sons and daughters.

The first two chapters of Hebrews shed light on these questions. I would recommend reading them both, because they make the case even more thoroughly, but verse five of chapter one is enough:

For unto which of the angels said he at any time, Thou art my Son, this day have I begotten thee? And again, I will be to him a Father, and he shall be to me a Son?

The passage compares the glory of Christ to the glory of angels, and of course Christ comes out on top. But the interesting thing is that the writer of Hebrews asks the rhetorical question "when did God ever say that the angels were His Son? "Never" is the answer that the writer expects. This lends even more weight to the idea that the "Sons of God" in Job should be correctly translated "Angels of God" and that *none* of the Old Testa- ment references to the "sons of God" refer to spirit beings except the dec- laration of the pagan king Nebuchadnezzar in Daniel.

Now you may say, "This verse is talking about the Messiah and not us", well it is talking about Him, but it is also talking about one of us because the verse is quoting Psalm 2:7. Its original fulfillment was in the context of King David, even though we know he was but a shadow of its true ful- fillment in Christ. In our re-birth, our new life is in Him (Gal.2:20). The new man in us, which is the part that is a son of God, is the part that shares His life. The second chapter of Hebrews extends this concept to us as well.

So, my point remains. There is a strong textual case that the books of Moses considered at least some men "sons of God" and that this was God's intent for men from the start. The textual evidence that spirit beings were considered "sons of God" by God and the Mosaic literary tradition may seem strong on the surface, but it fails close inspection. It was a concept grafted into the interpretation of the text by those who came later.

The Case Against the *Book of Enoch*

I don't wish to make an aside to write about the *Book of Enoch*, but I feel compelled to because so many Christians have been taught to take it seriously, even though it isn't canon in the Eastern or Western Church. It didn't even make the Apocrypha, though the Coptic Church uses it for some liturgies. Nor, with the possible exception of the first page, is there any good reason to assume that any of it really was the testimony of the biblical patriarch Enoch. The early versions show up about the 4ᵗʰ century B.C. Other sections were added to it over the next couple of centuries or so. This even though it claims to have been written by Enoch before the flood of Noah.

But didn't Peter and Jude refer *The Book of Enoch* repeatedly? I am going to make the case that they did not. Some bible teachers are just connecting the wrong dots. Most of it was due to the Apostles drawing from a common tradition about God's judgement on abhorrent spirit beings which the *Book of Enoch* also drew from. But you don't need the book itself to refer to the common tradition of which it also spoke. Consider this passage from the Gospel of Luke chapter eight (NIV).

When Jesus stepped ashore, he was met by a demon-possessed man from the town. For a long time this man had not worn clothes or lived in a house, but had lived in the tombs.

When he saw Jesus, he cried out and fell at his feet, shouting at the top of his voice, "What do you want with me, Jesus, Son of the Most High God? I beg you, don't torture me!"

For Jesus had commanded the impure spirit to come out of the man. Many times it had seized him, and though he was chained hand and foot and kept under guard, he had broken his chains and had been driven by the demon into solitary places.

Jesus asked him, "What is your name?"

"Legion," he replied, because many demons had gone into him.

And they begged Jesus repeatedly not to order them to go into the Abyss.

"The Abyss" is that same place where the Jews believed that evil spirits were held captive for the day of judgement, as is mentioned in Jude.

Notice that these demons weren't cohabiting with human women. They didn't exchange their spirit bodies for bodies of flesh and blood, they were only possessing a man of flesh and blood. Yet they still feared that Christ was going to command them to go to the same Abyss described in Enoch. Why? These demons possessed a man and forced him to commit acts of violence against other people (the parallel account in Matthew chapter eight mentions that no one could pass that way because of the violence).

If angels were sent to the Abyss around the time of the flood, murder fits the reason better than fornication with human women, because violence is the only specific *complaint* mentioned (Gen. 6:13) and seems to fit here too. Apparently, there are boundaries that evil spirits are not supposed to cross, under penalty of premature banishment to the Abyss. Inducing your host to murder seems to be crossing that boundary.

Christ was interested in saving the lost, not tormenting demons, so He didn't send them there. But this shows that premature confinement to the Abyss wasn't something that was a one-off before the flood and was never a factor again. It was the first thing that came to their minds. That's why I say that *The Book of Enoch* draws from a common tradition that the book of Luke also references. But this does not mean that the *Book of Enoch* really happened, just that it refers to a potential punishment that did.

It is sometimes claimed that First Peter 3:19 refers to events in Enoch where it says, *in which He also went and preached to the spirits now in prison, who once were disobedient, when the great patience of God was waiting in the days of Noah, during the building of the ark...*

But it says He was "preaching", something which is not relevant to demons. It has been suggested that after He victoriously won at the cross, He was basically "rubbing their noses in it". Yet in the account in Luke Jesus had no interest in tormenting the demons while He was on earth. Why would He be interested in doing so afterward? I have an alternate explanation for this verse later on in this volume which fits more with who Jesus really is.

Second Peter 2:4-7 is also associated with *Enoch,* because of the similarities in the descriptions of how spirits are bound. But again, this can be explained by appealing to a common tradition. After all, it doesn't say anything about what the sin of the angels was, and it certainly doesn't pin the blame for mankind's corruption on fallen angels. *Enoch* does so, and it is very human to say "The devil made me do it", but Genesis puts the blame on the men themselves. You cannot show that either of these verses from Peter are referring to the *Book of Enoch* without circular reasoning, assuming whatever it is you are trying to prove is already true.

Yet there is one place in the New Testament that does have a strong connection with *The Book of Enoch,* and that is the short epistle of Jude. These two verses in Jude are essentially a quote from verse nine of the first chapter of *Enoch:*

And Enoch also, the seventh from Adam, prophesied of these, saying, Behold, the Lord cometh with ten thousands of his saints,

To execute judgment upon all, and to convince all that are ungodly among them of all their ungodly deeds which they have ungodly committed, and of all their hard speeches which ungodly sinners have spoken against him.

Moses also spoke words similar to verse fourteen, in the context of bringing the law, in the first five verses of Deuteronomy chapter thirty-three. Was Moses aware of these words attributed to Enoch and used the same imagery? We don't know. But my own opinion is that the original prophecy cited in the first chapter of *Enoch* did come from an ancient tradition. If you read it, the first chapter doesn't sound anything like the rest of *The Book of Enoch*. It is like someone stuck one page of ancient prophecy as the preface of a story and then wrote a series of tall tales after it which are hardly connected to that original prophecy.

In other words, just because the original prophecy quoted by Jude was legitimate doesn't mean that the whole book was legitimate. Anyone could take a passage of scripture and use it as an introduction to an otherwise fictional story. *The Book of Mormon* for example, seems to me to do something similar.

But what about the earlier passage in Jude which many have claimed is *also* referring to Enoch? The strongest verse in the bible to support the idea that *The Book of Enoch* is a true account, and that the demons were imprisoned for cohabiting with human women is also found in Jude. I will cite the surrounding verses as well:

For there are certain men crept in unawares, who were before of old ordained to this condemnation, ungodly men, turning the grace of our God into lasciviousness, and denying the only Lord God, and our Lord Jesus Christ.

I will therefore put you in remembrance, though ye once knew this, how that the Lord, having saved the people out of the land of Egypt, afterward destroyed them that believed not.

And the angels which kept not their first estate, but left their own habitation, he hath reserved in everlasting chains under darkness unto the judgment of the great day.

Even as Sodom and Gomorrah, and the cities about them in like manner, giving themselves over to fornication, and going after strange flesh, are set forth for an example, suffering the vengeance of eternal fire.

Likewise also these filthy dreamers defile the flesh, despise dominion, and speak evil of dignities.

Yet Michael the archangel, when contending with the devil he disputed about the body of Moses, durst not bring against him a railing accusation, but said, The Lord rebuke thee.

But these speak evil of those things which they know not: but what they know naturally, as brute beasts, in those things they corrupt themselves.

One thing I get out of this passage is that perhaps Christians should not focus on demonology and railing against evil spirits. We don't understand their role in God's plan. Maybe we should focus on the work of Christ and what that means for how we should live! Of course, it is always more fun to go off on the bad guys and brag about our authority than it is to put to death the flesh in us, but that's not our calling.

Verse six and verse seven have often been construed to be taken together rather than as separate examples. Therefore, they are said to imply that the angels took human wives and produced the Nephilim per the *Book of Enoch*, just as Sodom and Gomorrah committed sexual sin.

The Greek in verse seven isn't as clear cut as advocates of this position would have you believe. The truth is that it is ambiguous as to whether it is saying that the angels participated "in a like manner" as Sodom and Gomorrah, or that *the cities around Sodom and Gomorrah* participated in a like manner. Going back to the Old Testament we see that the cities around them did indeed participate and were judged with them.

Further, verse eight seems to treat the three examples given in verses five, six, and seven separately. The third thing listed is "defiling the flesh" which was what happened in Sodom and Gomorrah. In the middle it says they "despise dominion" which is "authority". This is what the angels did when they "kept not their first estate" and "left their own habitation." The last thing mentioned in verse eight is "speaking evil of dignitaries" or "glories" which is likely to be a reference to the wicked children of Israel in Numbers chapter twenty-six. The result there was that the earth swallowed up those who strove against Moses and Aaron, the "glories" mentioned.

So, the fact that verse eight lists three separate complaints which match the three examples given in five, six, and seven in reverse order indicates that verses seven and eight are not the same offense. They are separate examples, and the ungodly men which had crept in, mentioned in verse four, did all of these things. They weren't going to escape the consequences for them any more than did the unbelieving Israelites, the angels who left behind their original dominions or jurisdiction, and those of Sodom, Gomorrah, and the surrounding cities.

We don't know exactly what is meant by the angels leaving their first estate and original habitation, but Jude isn't connecting it to sexual sin. That's what the example of Sodom and Gomorrah is for. Perhaps they grew to love a creation which had been subjected to futility, with its wildness in need of taming, its chaos and lingering disorder, more than the orderliness of the realm above. We don't know and can only guess.

Compare also the Archangel Michael's behavior in verse nine of Jude above with chapter nine of *The Book of Enoch*. There Michael, with three other angels, does bring what pretty much sounds like a "railing accusation" against the fallen angels. This is textual evidence that Jude was not quoting from *The Book of Enoch* in verse six.

In verse nine Jude describes the behavior of Michael in terms which are virtually the opposite of Michael's behavior in *The Book of Enoch*. Jude does describe something similar to what Enoch says happened to the angels in prison, but this does not mean that Jude was appealing to *The Book of Enoch*, rather He was appealing to a common tradition also found there.

I would further note that when Jude does appear to quote from *The Book of Enoch* in verses fourteen and fifteen, he identifies the quote as being from Enoch, saying "and also Enoch seventh from Adam...", as if it were the first time that he was introducing material from that source. Why even introduce "also Enoch, seventh from Adam" in verse thirteen if you have cited *The Book of Enoch* just a few verses previously? Between that and the incongruent reference to the Archangel Michael, I conclude that Jude is not referring to material which is found in *The Book of Enoch* until verse fourteen. And again, it is only from the first chapter- material which could stand alone as a legitimate prophecy that was lifted and put into the opening of an otherwise uninspired work.

The bottom line is that the church fathers rightly did not include *The Book of Enoch* in the canon of scripture. Paul, who advised that we "pay no attention to Jewish fables", doesn't cite any of it. Nor does his associate Luke. Peter makes allusions which refer to what seems to be a common tradition regarding the fate of devils, but we don't need the *Book of Enoch* for that. Luke chapter eight discusses evil spirits being confined to the abyss, and it isn't citing *Enoch*. It is the demons themselves mentioning it as something they fear will happen to them in the present. Nor does Jude offer the support for the Enoch narrative that many have imagined. A close look at the text shows the passage isn't connecting the sin of the angels to Sodom and Gomorrah, but it is a separate example of a separate sin.

****

I apologize for the diversion if this was not an area of interest to you, but it is important to a lot of people. Let's return to Genesis chapter six with the understanding that there were other humans around besides Adam's clan, and they were exercising God's commission to rule the earth.

The daughters of Adam's clan would have been a worthy catch for the chieftains of the area. If I am right about Adam, they had access to seed and stock of a superior variety and much practical knowledge of the domestic arts. I've mentioned that when it says in Genesis 6:4 that the sons of God saw that the daughters of men were "fair" the word there is *towb*. It is the same word which is translated "good" in Genesis chapter one. It really means "suitable". They were suitable wives for chieftains to have.

I thought that there could be some sign of strong females from a single genetic line in eastern Anatolia or the South Caucasus which helped give their houses great success back when civilization was young. I would like qualified scholars to investigate the connection more thoroughly, but a gentleman by the name of Marc-Olivier Rondu has written some papers which point to mtDNA H2a1 as fitting this signal. It is associated with the spread of certain cultures from India to the Atlantic. No wonder their off-spring were the "mighty men of old" and "men of renown".

It is well known that Indo-European myths from India to the Atlantic also have certain common elements and characters. For example, a hero or thunder-god battling a serpent or dragon, often with multiple heads. Entering the realm of the dead involves crossing a river, and it is guarded by some kind of canine. There is a god of metallurgy or craft in the pantheon. I do wonder if the reference to these mighty men of renown isn't a reference to the very men whose deeds formed the basis for some of the common legends in proto-Indo-European mythology?

And this brings us to the Nephilim. Here is what verse four says:

There were giants in the earth in those days; and also after that, when the sons of God came in unto the daughters of men, and they bare children to them, the same became mighty men which were of old, men of renown.

Surprisingly, at least to me, there is nothing in the English or Hebrew which indicates that the giants (Hebrew *Nephilim*) were the offspring of the sons of God and the daughters of Adam. It only says that they were in the land in those days. The children of the sons of God and the daughters of Adam were instead the "mighty men of old", the "men of renown". Because of the influence of the of *Book Enoch* and many Bible teachers today who take their cues from non-Christian rabbis, we read that verse and often make the assumption that the giants were the offspring. But it doesn't say they were the offspring. It just says that they were in the land during this time, and also afterwards.

In Mesopotamian legends these giants have a mixed image, but northwest of there, in the western realms of the same Indo-European legends I mentioned earlier, there is a curiosity which could shed light on this verse. The giants or titans were the old order, the ones who were there first. They were those that the gods overthrew. It was so with the Olympian gods and the Titans. It was so with the Norse gods and the Ice Giants. And in the Bible, the giants are also shown to be the original inhabitants of the land who are opposed to God's people. They are not depicted as sons and daughters of the protagonists, but as their early nemeses. They are to be dispossessed, just as in the case of the Olympians and the Titans.

I see this as more evidence of the extreme antiquity of these accounts. The giants were yet another people group, a disfavored one. The heroes of old, the result of the union of the daughters of Adam with the sons of God, overcame them in remote antiquity. And the children of Israel and their relatives overcame what was left of them later.

Notice that verse four says they were on the earth in those days, "and also afterward". This indicates that the flood of Noah did not completely eliminate the Nephilim. Later in the Old Testament (Numbers 13:33 *et al*) they are reported to still be walking the earth and very imposing in size. Hebrew spies reported that Nephilim were in the land, and not even the faithful spies challenged that aspect of their report. Nor did the hearers demand to know how the descendants of Anak (Nephilim), could still be around.

I find it likely that in the time of Moses the Israelites knew that the flood was not global. They understood that the "world" of the disrespectful sons of Adam, the people of *Yahweh*, was what was destroyed, not the whole globe. I will offer evidence on that subject later.

I reject the idea that when the spies saw large people, that they just assumed that they were Nephilim. There was a second race of huge people around and they had a separate name for them – Rapha. The most famous person of great stature in the Bible, Goliath, is not said to have been a Nephilim. They knew the linage of the "sons of Anak." They knew to distinguish Nephilim from other types of large humans. The Nephilim were worse, perhaps not because they were bigger, but rather more capable.

It is not necessary to invent any fanciful stories of angels breeding with human women to explain the Nephilim or the "sons of God". We can stick with the understanding that Christ gave us about angels in Matthew 22:30 and in Luke chapter twenty. The Greek in Luke 20:36 in particular distinguishes "the Sons of God" from angels, though many translations don't make that clear. But in both accounts, angels in heaven don't marry and when we are like them, we won't either.

What of fallen angels? Even if they somehow took new bodies of flesh, why would they honor human women with the commitment of marriage? That is, treat their women with more respect than many of us treat our girl-friends today?

Adam's Line Grows Most Wicked

The LORD still wanted to groom the line of Adam. It was a different world before the flood, one in which the LORD God walked among His people. For those people it would not have been shocking for Him to walk up to them and start talking. He continued to visit them and walk among them, offering His wisdom, help and guidance. Cain's complaint on hearing of his banishment was that he would be driven from the LORD's presence. Then there is the account of Enoch "walking with" Him for three hundred years before Enoch was taken up. This is also shown by the meaning of the word translated "strive" in Genesis 6:3 of which I will say more later.

In addition, for the recorded interactions with Abraham and Moses it often says words to the effect that He "appeared" or that unusual visitors were received. Such language is not used before the flood. The first five chapters read as if He were someone who could be expected to be around. The first instance of distance is after the flood when the LORD "came down" to see the tower of Babel. He was little seen then in the land below until Abraham, and even then, only on rare occasions.

This might be a good place to fulfill a promise to the reader. I had said early on in this volume that the normal limitations on the oral transmission of accounts did not apply until after the flood. The account from Adam could be accurately transmitted even if Adam had died thousands of years before true narrative writing was developed. I am not speaking of the extended life spans, although that would make the transmission of an oral account for a thousand years just a matter of repeating a story you heard from your grandfather. But they had something better than that. Until the flood, the LORD God lived among His people. He was there to keep the story straight from generation to generation. Only after the flood was there even a need to resort to written records, and writing was either available by then or would be relatively soon, depending on when the flood occurred.

 Maybe that personal approach worked when there were only a few of them around, but this chapter begins by saying that they had begun to multiply. How much can one being in human form accomplish operating this way when there are five hundred descendants of Adam to mentor? How about five thousand? The number could have been much higher.

In John 16:7 Jesus tells the disciples that it is better for them if He goes away. He knows, from experience if I am right about the text here, that He can do more by going to heaven than remaining on earth. Sending the Holy Spirit into our innermost being to renew us from the heart outward is better than remaining on this earth as a single individual trying to induce us to come to faith- or even to conform on the outside to a standard which we do not love in our hearts.

Imagine the frustration of the LORD going around to Adam's one thousand descendants who just wanted to misbehave. Imagine trying to admonish them to believe in Him rather than themselves regarding what right and wrong conduct looks like. He might have gone from the most popular guy in the land when He was handing out benefits to the most unpopular guy in the land when He was instructing them in righteousness. Shades of when a similar thing happened to Him during the incarnation.

The difference in the account of Cain from that of his near descendant Lamech (not the Lamech who was the father of Noah) illustrates what very quickly happened with the descendants of Adam, and still happens with us today. When confronted with his sin and punishment, Cain basically groveled and was in fear for his life. His appeal to the LORD drew a response- that the LORD would avenge sevenfold any who killed Cain. Lamech just a few generations later had a different response to a similar situation.

Lamech killed a young man for striking him (Gen. 4:23-24). He did not appeal to the LORD, nor ask the LORD for protection. Lamech was a prominent person whose offspring were very accomplished. He would be his own judge and enforce his judgments with the power of his own clan. After the killing Lamech declared that if he were killed vengeance was to be taken seventy-sevenfold. Lamech declared on his own authority that he was entitled to eleven times the retribution that the LORD allotted to his ancestor Cain. He told his wives that if someone retaliated by killing him, then his family was to wipe them out- 77 for 1!

When we think we are weak, we beg the Lord to intercede for us. When we think we are in a position of strength we grow arrogant and think we should be calling the shots ourselves. At the first, so desired was the LORD's favor that Cain murdered Abel in a fit of jealously over it. As the descendants of Adam grew in numbers and in power, He became more like the prophets who went around preaching to people who chafed at or avoided the message.

And the LORD said, My spirit shall not always strive with man, for that he also is flesh: yet his days shall be an hundred and twenty years.

The exact form in Hebrew for "man" here is "*ba-adam*", the only place in scripture this form is used. This is literally saying that His spirit will not always contend "with Adam". Does it mean "mankind" or does it mean "Adam" here? Well, in this case that is a distinction without a difference. His interactions with humanity are focused on the line of Adam, even if His point in doing so was to grow and spread the blessings of righteousness to all men. He was *contending* with the descendants of Adam.

From the perspective of this writer, humanity is at this point divided into those of Adam, who call themselves *Yahweh's* people, and the rest of our race. His quarrel is with His own special people here, but in declaring He will not strive with them forever it also means that he will not strive with any of mankind forever. He wanted to *start* with them in spreading His blessings to all of mankind. To give up on the line of Adam is to give up on all of humanity, as will be made clear in the chapters that follow.

I said that His quarrel is with His people and I think "quarrel" is a suitable term here. The root word translated "strive" in verse three means to "administer" or "judge". It implies that He was mediating their disputes. He was acting as their Lord on earth. But good government is not fit for, or appreciated by, bad people. He wanted people who would be like the Psalmist David (19:9), "*the judgements of the LORD are true and righteous altogether*". That is not what He experienced. Instead of rejoicing at His wisdom, they contended with Him.

Why were they contending? The Man is of Heavenly form. His body is not of corruptible flesh, but of the incorruptible sort which those who are Christ's will one day have according to the end of First Corinthians chapter fifteen. He had no sin nature and no ungodly impulses of the flesh. His soul was therefore free to conform to the Spirit. It was not shaped by the corruptible flesh.

Romans 8:6 says, "*the mind set on flesh is death, but the mind set on the Spirit is life and peace...*" The mind represents the soul there. He was spirit-led. The offspring of Adam were led (astray) by the desires of their corruptible flesh. His outward ministry for them did not change the fact that on the inside they were configured differently from Him. They were not operating from the same motives- He from Spirit, they from corruptible flesh.

In Genesis 6:3 He announced that He was not going to keep operating the way that He had been operating. He was not going to keep going around contending with the descendants of Adam to do good when the growing population of them increasingly wanted to do evil. They were not helping the rest of humanity, the other Sons of God, as He desired. In terms of having the heart of God they may have even been pulling the rest of humanity down. He was not setting a time limit for human life spans, as some suppose. The LORD decided that He would set a time limit on continuing His course of action. He would only operate like this for another one hundred and twenty years. From this time forward His people only had that much longer to straighten up.

I am not sure that He kept trying for the whole number of years. There is nothing in the text about the LORD having any interaction with humans from verse 6:6-8 until one week before the flood, a period of over one hundred years! All we see in the text after the time limit was given is complaints about how awful they were. It may be that He got too disgusted with the bunch of them- and perhaps they were as tired of Him as He was with them. It seems that shortly after giving His one-hundred-and-twenty-year time limit He realized that He would have to destroy them (verse 6-7). He would bring judgement on His own house, for judgment begins with the house of God (1st Peter 4:17).

Verse five says, and I am paraphrasing, that men spent all day just trying to come up with evil things to do. Again, this is an instance where it does not really matter if it is translated "of Adam" or "of man" (as in all of humanity) here. I have no doubt that those outside of Adam's line were as rotten as those who were of his line. Maybe they were not as bad regarding familiar contempt and irreverence, but if so, it was only because they lacked the privilege of access. All of mankind was rotten, but Adam's line was the one He was personally mentoring to help Him start fixing it. This was the group that He had constantly nurtured and had guided. But they were as rotten as they could be, and they did their dirty work with His name on it. It is likely that even the animals He had made as their helpers had been polluted and misshaped by their wickedness.

The children of *Yahweh* had no respect for Him even though He walked among them regularly. That lack of due reverence is the very meaning of "ungodly" when it says in Second Peter 2:5 that He "destroyed the world of the ungodly." It did not mean ungodly in the regular sense of moral failings that we all have. It was specifically that due reverence, even outward superficial respect, was not given to God. It was no wonder that He had had enough of it.

Now I want you to pay special attention to these next few verses. Do not read into them what you think they say, but what they actually say. Think about *Who* is going to wipe something out and exactly *what* He says He is going to wipe out:

And it repented the LORD that he had made man on the earth, and it grieved him at his heart. And the LORD said, I will destroy man whom I have created from the face of the earth; both man, and beast, and the creeping thing, and the fowls of the air; for it repenteth me that I have made them.

It does not say here that *Elohim* repented that He had made man on the earth. *Elohim* will be along in a few verses, but that is not the Who being discussed here. It says that 'The LORD (*Yahweh*) repented that *He* had made (the) man on the earth". In verse seven it says, "I will destroy (the) man whom I have created." The articles in parenthesis are mine in both cases, but the underlying form of the Hebrew in both places (*ha-adam* rather than *adam*) indicates that the articles should be there. It should be translated "*the* man" or "*the* men". If it referred to all men, it could have just said "adam" and left off the articles. Regardless of whether you want to include the articles indicating a *set* of men rather than mankind, in this verse *Yahweh* says He intends to destroy what *He* has made.

Once we understand that Genesis chapter one records everything being made and Genesis chapter two records the more limited set of things that *Yahweh* made more personally, we can see the context of *Yahweh's* remarks. When *Yahweh* talks about striking down what He has made it is not the same thing as wiping out all living things on the whole face of the earth. He is not going to go around and destroy everything *Elohim* made together as the Triune God in chapter one. He is talking about blotting out the results of His own efforts which are recorded in chapter two.

Do not let it throw you that it says "created" in verse seven like in chapter one instead of "formed" as in chapter two. The word "created" in that verse is from a form of the word "*bara*", but one which emphasizes shaping and molding rather than an ex-nihilo creation. In other words, its sense is like the word "formed" (*yatsar*) used in Genesis chapter two even though it has the same root as "*bara*". Both words imply shaping, but this form of "*bara*" is not as locked into a good result as is implied by the word *yatsar-* a picture of a potter fashioning clay.

Add it all up and the text is saying that *Yahweh* is disgruntled with the results of the man that He made. He wanted to destroy what He did, not what the whole Godhead did together. It was not an intention to destroy everyone on the planet. It was an intention to destroy the line of Adam which He had made and which had gone bad. They were filling the earth up with violence and spending every day thinking of new ways to do evil. He made them to make the earth a better place and instead they were making it even worse.

This was not a plan to destroy every dog, lion, gazelle, eagle, bear, rhino *etc.* that was on the planet. He was going to destroy the lines of the animals which He had made. Those were the ones which had been corrupted by His deviant mentees. He was going to destroy the ones He had originally made as helpers for the man way back in chapter two.

Some mockers have dared to judge *Yahweh* for bringing the flood. They rail against what they do not understand. This was the theme explored in Mary Shelley's famous novel. Dr. Frankenstein realized that he had to destroy the monster he had unleased on creation. No one faults Dr. Frankenstein for trying to destroy the monster he had made. That was considered an attempt to "make it right". People only fault him for making it in the first place, on the basis that he should not have tried to "play God." Clearly, that is a charge which cannot rightly be applied to *Yahweh*, who is God. It is terribly wrongheaded thinking which approves of Dr. Frankenstein's efforts to stop the monster he was responsible for making yet dares to judge the LORD Himself for doing the same.

It was even more personal than that. If He didn't know from the beginning, from the fall of Adam it must have been understood by Him that in order for this people to be redeemed from eternal corruption, the sinless Messiah had to die in place of Adam. He had to do what Adam failed to do while also paying the price for Adam's unbelief. In other words, unless

He died, they were all ultimately dead already. And there seemed no way to save them in faith anyway.

Things look bleak in verse seven. He has determined to destroy His own works, and at this point no intent is shown to save any of it. There is only one small caveat of hope in verse six, before *Yahweh* goes silent for about 120 years: "*But Noah found grace in the sight of the LORD.*"

Please hold that thought while we take an essential detour in the story to understand some background about the nature of the characters. The fact that *Yahweh* (the LORD) is sorry that He ever made the Man tells us something about Him. He is not all-knowing. He can be caught by surprise and things which He did not expect can happen which can cause Him to change His course of action. He is not like *Elohim*, translated "God", either in chapter one or here in the flood story. Yes, He is Divine, but He also seems to have some human limitations. Does that remind you of anyone?

I realize these are strange things for many to consider, but what I imply here, and will speak about at length in the next chapter, is not a novel view of God. It is what the apostles taught. Consider this quote from Church Father Justin Martyr in chapter sixty-three of his book *Apology*:

"*The Jews, accordingly, being throughout of opinion that it was the Father of the universe who spake to Moses, though He who spake to him was indeed the Son of God, who is called both Angel and Apostle, are justly charged, both by the Spirit of prophecy and by Christ Himself, with knowing neither the Father nor the Son. For they who affirm that the Son is the Father, are proved neither to have become acquainted with the Father, nor to know that the Father of the universe has a Son; who also, being the first-begotten Word of God, is even God. And of old He appeared in the shape of fire and in the likeness of an angel to Moses and to the other prophets; but now in the times of your reign, having, as we before said, become Man by a virgin, according to the counsel of the Father, for the salvation of those who believe on Him...*"

Yahweh, Elohim, and the LORD God

‑‑⇥‑⇒⊛⇐‑⇤‑

*Y*ahweh and *Elohim* don't seem quite together as we continue reading the flood account. It becomes apparent in this account that they are two persons. Here in chapters six and seven the LORD and God say slightly different things. This is even more apparent in the Hebrew than in most English translations. Think about how the terms used for God have shifted in the first six chapters. In chapter one God was "*Elohim*" (translated "God"). In chapter two he was "*Yahweh Elohim*" or "The LORD God." In chapter three both terms are used. Then it was just "*Yahweh*" (The LORD). Later in the scriptures, when men speak of God these terms seem to be used interchangeably. What gives here?

Now many scholarly people have tried to attack the veracity of the scriptures in early Genesis by claiming that texts which call the Almighty *Elohim* alone are from one source and those which call Him *Yahweh* are from another. They claim that early Genesis was cobbled together from sources which had different ideas about who God was.

The reason so many of these scholars don't understand anything about what they study is because they have no faith. They are reading the text looking for ways to "deconstruct" it. Instead, we should be trying to understand the motivations of the characters and the cosmology of their system, without the "premise of unbelief" which discounts the thought that God was present not only in the narratives but in their composition through the movement of the Holy Spirit. We should try to see it from the view of the writers of the accounts, including their belief that their *Elohim* was the one true God. Wisdom is more than looking for ways to pick holes in their stories. I am reading it with the premise that what the New Testament teaches about God the Father and God the Son is true, and that it can be detected from the very early parts of the book. That is how you see truth that cannot be seen from the critic's perch.

Their problem is not their lack of credentials, or their lack of wisdom. It's their lack of faith. They are not looking in the right place to find truth because they don't believe that it is there. This is a perfect example of why Christ said (Luke 10:21): *I thank thee, O Father, Lord of heaven and earth, that thou hast hid these things from the wise and prudent, and hast revealed them unto babes...*

There is a reason for these changes. The revealed cosmology is that the person we know as Jesus Christ was first made "in the likeness of men" not at the incarnation in Judea, but in some sense from the foundation of the world in Genesis 1:27. He is the "Heavenly Man" alluded to there and in First Corinthians 15:49. He is the Man made in the image of God, and if you have seen Him then you have seen the Father (John 14:9). His name here is *Yahweh*. *Yahweh* is Christ in different circumstances.

The concept of the Old Testament Theophany, or Christophany, is well-established. Many respected theologians accept that Christ appeared in anthropomorphic form at various points in the Old Testament. That is, many distinguished theologians have accepted the idea that there were pre-incarnation appearances of Christ. One explanation for this is that the Logos was hopping in and out of human form throughout the Old Testament. What I am suggesting instead is that the Logos took human form in the beginning, in Genesis 1:27, but not corruptible human form. Rather the Logos assumed the state that Christ currently has in Heaven. That is, incorruptible, the heavenly man at the right hand of God the Father (Acts 7:55-56; Romans 8:34; Hebrews 1:3, 1:13, 10:12 *et al*).

From the accounts of Christ after the resurrection, we know that He is still visible, that He still has a body which can consume food and take drink.

His body is no longer like our bodies because it is imperishable as we one day hope ours will be, but the disciples could see Him and touch Him. I propose that He is in the same state now that He was from Genesis 1:27 to the Incarnation. John 16:28 may speak to this:

I came forth from the Father, and am come into the world: again, I leave the world, and go to the Father.

The Greek word translated "again" not only means "again" but in terms of place it means to return, to go back to where one was. He is going back to where He was before Mary was with child by the Holy Spirit. Based on what the scriptures say about Him after the resurrection it seems that this was not a disembodied state. He was fused with man in the heavenlies in Genesis 1:27, and He was fused with man in this realm in the Incarnation. Whether this state is eternal or is ended when sin and death are finally defeated is another question, one I won't delve into here.

This is who *Yahweh* is in the flood account, the image of God in visible human form. When His people look at God, He is who they are supposed to see, The LORD God (*Yahweh-Elohim*). The oldest manuscripts of Jude 1:5 say "Jesus" instead of "the Lord". Therefore, many translations, like the ESV, say "Jesus" instead of "the Lord" there. That is, Jesus delivered them out of Egypt, and Jesus destroyed those who did not believe. That was not the Father Moses was dealing with, mostly that was Jesus! Jesus is *Yahweh*. Justin Martyr had it right in the quote I ended the last chapter with.

The things I am saying and will say about God here are not new. Not in their essence. Rather they are long-forgotten or near forgotten. I do not claim to have "discovered them", at best I have "rediscovered" them. And that only after being pointed in the right direction by (I believe) Divine unction. This has been a part of the Christian faith from the very beginning.

While I think the church has terribly misunderstood Genesis, by the Grace of God the foundational creeds of the Church are right. I am orthodox with respect to these creeds. The Athanasian Creed is the most intricate of the three great creeds of the early church. It is the one which goes into the most detail about the relationship between the three persons of the Godhead. Here is a part of what it says:

So the Father is God, the Son is God, and the Holy Spirit is God. And yet they are not three gods, but one God.

Likewise, the Father is Lord, the Son Lord, and the Holy Spirit Lord. And yet not three lords, but one Lord.

For as we are compelled by the Christian verity to acknowledge each Person by Himself to be both God and Lord, so we are also forbidden by the catholic religion to say that there are three gods or three lords.

The unity in their character, purpose, and love for one another takes precedence over their individual personalities regarding the manner in which they execute the offices which are intrinsically connected to their nature-Lord and God. This allows each of them to fulfill their offices without distinction of character or nature. Different offices, same nature.

If the Father were the Son, He would have fulfilled the office in the same manner as the Son. Were the Son the Father, He would have fulfilled the office in the exact manner as the Father. If either of them was the Spirit then they would have acted just as selflessly, with all attention directed to the others, as the Spirit has done. There is no difference in how they fulfill the office of God. Therefore, there are not three Gods, but one God expressed in three persons whose traits which pertain to that office are perfectly identical and each of whose natures are such that they are intrinsically connected to that office.

And because of this it can also be said that God loses none of his majesty, character, or function if a particular one of the three persons subordinates himself from the unity of persons which is God, nor is anything added to God in those things when and if that person should re-assume His place.

I do have a point of order here. When the creed uses "Lord" it means in the sense that Jesus Christ is Lord, not whatever translators meant later by substituting "LORD" in all capitals in place of the tetragrammaton now most frequently translated "*Yahweh*". That practice took root long after the creed was composed. That is a different use of the word even if I appeal to a similar principle to make sense of the text.

Now if you will think back to the chapter "Verse Twenty-Six: A Plan to Make Man in Image and Likeness" you might remember that I showed seven verses of scripture which demonstrated that the apostles taught that God cannot be seen. In order to make us into his image therefore he first made the Image of himself visible, that we who are visible might be conformed to that Image. This image we know as Christ, both God and Man, who was manifested in the heavens before the foundation of the world was complete (that is, before the work days of Genesis Chapter one concluded), and on earth in corruptible flesh at the proper time.

So, we have the Source, and we have the Image. And both are the One True God. Both have the same nature and share the same substance. Yet both have their own personality. In Exodus chapter three (v. 13-15), when Moses asked God what his name was, God replied with an obscure phrase which most often translates to "I AM who (or that) I AM". And then he said to tell them that "I AM" sent you. That is, a single "I AM" to represent the two. Moreover, he said that he was "*Yahweh Elohim*" and that this was His name for all generations. In the obscure machinations of ancient Hebrew, "*Yahweh*" is derived from the same word root as "I AM" or "to be."

The very name of *Yahweh* proclaims the self-existence and unchangeable character of both the Source and the Image, even if they serve different roles. The Source and the Image are not two gods, but One God. They are not two *Yahwehs*, but one *Yahweh* expressed in two persons, in Source and in Image. Hence the two "I AMs" of Exodus 3:14 are fully represented by and are converted to a single "I AM" at the end of the verse and in the name *Yahweh*. The two are one. It goes deeper than that, but lest I go too far astray from early Genesis the rest must wait for another book.

The mistake which many have made, and I confess to you that I have made in the past, is that the plurality of persons in *Yahweh* and *Elohim* does not mandate that one of these persons is always and only referred to as *Yahweh* and the other should always and only be called *Elohim*. Both are *Yahweh*, though one is the Image and one the Source, and both are *Elohim*, though one is the Image and one is the Source. Yet there are not two *Yahweh's*, but one. *Yahweh* is a family name. Nor are there two *Elohim's*, but there is one. As it says in the Law: *Yahweh* your *Elohim* is one *Yahweh*. The same principle discussed in the Athanasian Creed applies here as well.

The Image is a different person than the Source, but both are of the same substance. This explains passages like Zachariah 3:2 and 3:7 where the LORD (*Yahweh*) speaks in the name of the LORD. See also the second chapter of Zachariah where (vv. 8-11) the LORD says that He is sent by the LORD. It also explains passages like Hosea 1:7 where God speaks and says that He will save Judah by the Lord their God, as if some other person was also the Lord their God. Even earlier, in Genesis 19:4, two persons, both acting as *Yahweh*, seem involved in *Yahweh* raining down fire on the Sodomites. See also Jeremiah 11:21.

This gets very intricate and deserves a whole book, but the conclusion is that the two persons sometimes reference each other. Normally they are so completely on the same page that the one wholly speaks for the other, acts for the other, or is sent by the other. In such cases it is often not apparent that the Source and the Image are two persons.

Jesus alluded to the reason for this in passages like John 5:9 when he said, *Verily, verily, I say unto you, The Son can do nothing of himself, but what he seeth the Father do: for what things soever he doeth, these also doeth the Son likewise.* There would not be a difference from what the Father would do if He were Christ and what Christ was doing. Christ, as the Image, was only doing what he saw the Source doing. And in John 12:49 He said, *For I have not spoken of myself; but the Father which sent me, he gave me a commandment, what I should say, and what I should speak.* So, He was not speaking on his own initiative. He was acting as an Image for a Source who was beyond them.

Despite all of this, there is a difference in perspective between the two Persons, Image and Source. Prior to becoming the Image, the Logos is all-knowing. He had to understand what he would eventually have to do, yet He still chose to become The Man in Heaven.

Once he became The Man, did he still know his fate from the start? Or did he have to, like Christ in the flesh, *"learn obedience through the things which he suffered"* (Heb. 5:8)? What limitations might be inherent in the Logos incarnating, even in incorruptible form, I cannot say. All we can do is notice the limitations which he had when he incarnated in corruptible flesh and imagine that some of those limitations might be inherent to a member of the Godhead setting aside his original form to take the form of a visible and finite body.

For example, like *Yahweh* in early Genesis, Christ was not all-knowing. He learned things and as he did, he gained favor with God the Father (Luke 2:52). In Luke 8:45-48 he knew that he had healed someone, but he did not know who! He received information from the Father (John 12:49-50), but that is not the same as personal omniscience. Just the reverse, that He received information from the Father is proof that He was not omniscient. Indeed, some information was withheld even from Him (Mark 13:32).

Even though Christ and the Father shared the same nature, they no longer shared the same perspective, thus they had different ideas about what they hoped would happen- i.e. different wills (Luke 22:42). He is not omnipresent. He can go away (John 16:5) and even says that it is expedient for us that He does because that is necessary for us to receive the Holy Spirit (John 16:7). He may not be able to be everywhere at once, but the Holy Spirit can operate in all of us at once no matter where we are!

What we have in the Old Testament, per the "Two Powers" theology mentioned earlier in this work, are two persons who are *Yahweh-Elohim*, the Image and the Source. Yet because the Image has taken form, some characteristics of the Divine have been set aside. For example, the Source is invisible to men and the Image is not.

In the case of Christ, this resulted in the Father and the Son having separate wills and different hopes for the way that things would go. In the Garden of Gethsemane Christ prayed "if possible, let this cup pass from me, nevertheless not my will but thy will be done." Here we see that the Image does not believe that he has knowledge of all possibilities, and he has a will that is separate from that of the Source. But he also has faith so that he sets His own will aside and does the will of he who sent him.

At stress points what is true in the eternal realm can for a time appear unclear in the temporal realm. Just as the Garden of Gethsemane was a stress point for the temporal and eternal, so was the time from the expulsion from the Garden of Eden to the flood of Noah. The degeneration and destruction of Adam's line was very stressful and heart-wrenching for God. The way this plays out in the flood account is that the two persons of the Image and the Source have the widest gap between their words and actions of anywhere in the Torah. Not that it is a huge difference, but it becomes most apparent here in chapters six and seven that there are two divine personalities speaking.

The more anthropogenic of these two, who repents that he made the man, is the Image. In the flood account he is called *Yahweh*. The one who speaks as a voice but does not appear in person and who realizes all the consequences of the apostasy right away is the Source, *Elohim*. It is He who initiates the plan to preserve creation through a covenant with Noah. Later in scripture the stress point would be past and the two persons who are *Yahweh Elohim* behave in a more interchangeable manner. Thus, later they are labeled in a more interchangeable way.

The fall of the man in the garden reverberated all the way to heaven. It took time for the consequences of that act to begin to be reversed. The heavens and the earth were shaken, and when there is shaking going on even two people right in line with each other can appear to be out of alignment until reality re-asserts itself. I don't want to oversell it. It was not like the two were in conflict. It was just that one of them could see past the pain and the other could not yet. One was as the Father, and one was as the Son.

By the time of Moses this tear in the fabric of spiritual reality was fully restored. It becomes much harder to notice that there are two persons, an

Image and a Source. Each is *Yahweh*, but *Yahweh* is one. Each is *Elohim*, but *Elohim* is one. God's name is again revealed as *Yahweh Elohim* in Exodus (6:3). The Divine Symmetry is that the stresses appear when the Image had to destroy his people and when He had to be destroyed for them.

Yahweh before the flood is all about justice and thundering in His proclamations pertaining to righteousness. Eventually we see this uncompromising character *Yahweh*, so demanding of others, come full circle and reveal the rest of His nature. From the LORD who brought the flood, and who brought wrath on Israel when they sinned, to Christ. Christ did not demand sinless living from other people, but He demanded it from Himself on behalf of other people even though we are sinners. In His own person, on behalf of others, He met all the demands He had been putting on others.

Yahweh went from ruler of Heaven to suffering servant on Earth. He went from showing the justice in His nature to showing the mercy in His nature. He did this for love's sake. People who say that *Yahweh* is an unsympathetic character fail to understand that this is what God's justice looks like to the unrepentant sinner, but that Jesus Christ is the same person showing us just as accurate a picture of what He looks like to those who love Him.

Elohim Brings Destruction, But Also Preservation

◁─◈─▷

Verse twelve through the end of the sixth chapter speaks of interactions with *Elohim*, not *Yahweh*. Presumably, this is in the form of a voice or vision rather than a personal visit. There is no hint in the text of *Elohim* assuming the anthropogenic form as is the case with *Yahweh* in the flood account. The last we hear of *Yahweh* is in verse eleven, where it simply says that Noah found grace in His sight. There *Yahweh* concluded that He should destroy what *He* had made, and no plans are revealed at that point to save Noah, even though Noah is the exception to the wretched general condition of *Yahweh's* handiwork.

In verse eleven of chapter six (the beginning of the account of Shem, Ham, and Japheth) through the end of that chapter *Elohim* reveals to Noah what He is going to do, why it will be done, and what Noah should do to preserve his family. We should particularly look at verses thirteen and seventeen where *Elohim* lays out the consequences of the flood which He will bring.

And God said unto Noah, The end of all flesh is come before me; for the earth is filled with violence through them; and, behold, I will destroy them with the earth...

In verse thirteen the vernacular of what God is saying is "I am looking at the end of all flesh." That is what He is telling Noah. This looks like the end of His plan to reconcile creation with Himself. And He gives a reason why He is looking at the end of all flesh- it is because of the failure of the instrument by which He had declared creation would be reconciled. By this I mean through the work of mankind in general, and the line of Adam and Eve in particular.

When it says that the earth (or land) is filled with violence "through them" the word is "*mip-pe-ne-him*", a form of "*panim*" (Strong's 6440). The word picture there is "before their faces" or "before them" and it is usually translated that way.

God's complaint is that things are going corrupt right in front of them and the offspring of Adam are doing nothing about it. They may even be encouraging it. Instead of animals becoming more peaceful, perhaps they bred roosters to fight. Instead of condemning men of violence, they cheered them on as heroes. They were there to make things better, not worse!

Verse thirteen ends by saying "I will destroy them with the earth." But the Hebrew word used for "destroy" is not the same word which *Yahweh* used in 7:4 and 6:7 even though that word is also translated "destroy" in the King James Version (and many others). Hebrew has so few words compared to English I think it is very unfortunate that the translators used the same English word even though the Hebrew uses different words to describe what *Elohim* is saying versus what *Yahweh* is saying.

This weak translating gives the English reader the impression that both are saying the exact same thing while in truth there are important differences in what they are saying. If the text incorrectly conveys the impression that they are saying the very same thing then it obscures to the reader the possibility of a key understanding. This is that *Elohim* and *Yahweh* are different persons in the way that Christ and the Father are different persons (with the same nature). The text describes two characters working together, not one whose name changes back-and-forth throughout the account.

The word *Elohim* uses in verse 6:13 (and 6:17) is a variation of the word "*sha-chath*" (Strong's 7843). Yes, it can be and is fairly translated as "destroy", but the sense in which destruction comes is different than what *Yahweh* said He would do in 6:7 and 7:4. This word has connotations of going to ruin or spoiling or corrupting. When *Elohim* says, "I will destroy them with the earth" He is saying that they are bringing the earth to ruin, so He is going to use the earth to ruin them. He is going to use the earth to sever the ordained lifeline to heaven- the line of Adam.

And, behold, I, even I, do bring a flood of waters upon the earth, to destroy all flesh, wherein is the breath of life, from under heaven; and every thing that is in the earth shall die. But with thee will I establish my covenant...

Even at the end of verse seventeen, where *Elohim* says "everything in the earth shall die" the word for "die" which is used is "*yigwa*" or "*gava*" (Strongs' 1478). It comes from a root meaning "to exhale". The word is often translated "expire" or "perish" or even with the phrase "breathed their last".

The word here could have been "*muth*" (Strongs' 4191) which is the normal word for "die" in the Old Testament. That is the word *Yahweh* used to describe what was about to happen to His works, but that is not the word *Elohim* uses to describe what He is going to do. He uses "*yigwa*".

That "*muth*" and "*yigwa/gava*" have different meanings in Genesis is shown by Genesis 25:8. There both words are used in one phrase where it says that Abraham "gave up the ghost and died". "*Muth*" is translated "die" and "*yigwa/gava*" is translated "gave up the ghost". The word used for "gave up the ghost" in verse 25:8 is the word unfortunately translated "die" in 6:17 ("*yigwa/gava*").

These are two separate but related things. One inevitably leads to the other. That is why they are often lumped together, but the one thing is actually a *precursor* of the other, not the thing itself. In this case, separation from God, undoing the life God has put into us, leads to death. That is what *Elohim* is saying the flood would do to all of creation, save for the covenant He will make.

The plucking of a flower or the picking of a pear does not cause them to wither at once. They still have some life in them even though they are disconnected from the source of their life. Over time though, they will perish and ruin as a consequence of this separation. One of the uses for "*yigwa/gava*" means "perhaps go to ruin".

Therefore, *Elohim* did not say that the flood was going to cause all flesh on earth to die (as in "*muth*") in the flood. He said that because of the flood everything in the earth would perish ("*gava*" or "*yigwa*"). By destroying the line of Adam and Eve via Seth, that line ordained to produce The Seed which would crush the serpent's head, God would have caused all flesh to perish. The world would not have been redeemed. Things would have just gotten worse and worse until all was corrupted and ruined. This view of things understands the scriptures as Christians should see them, in that these accounts are meant to point to Christ.

Here is the contrast in verse seventeen and the start of eighteen: everything in the earth will die, "*but with thee I will establish my covenant.*" So, the earth is to be divided into two groups- one that is cut off from the deliverance which will be made available through The Seed of the line of Adam. Members of that group will perish. But there is another group, which shall be a part of a new covenant that God shall establish. Members of this group shall be preserved through the judgements of God.

So then, there is no more hope of redeeming it all, but neither would the whole earth be ruined. Life would be divided - into that which shall eternally perish and that which shall be preserved. This separation shall be between those in the covenant which He shall establish, and those who are not.

We shall see in a few chapters hence that God is speaking with a double meaning here. He is not speaking of one covenant, but of two. The word for "establish" means "against" as a location. For example, when I lean an object on something else it is "against" that something else. But it could be supporting it as well. It is sort of in the sense of "using to set up." God was going to use these circumstances to set up a new covenant. These events were to serve as pictures or shadows of a greater reality to come.

Now if we were to just look at this passage without an understanding of Christ and His redemption plan for the world, then we might think "this was a global flood which therefore had global consequences." But looking at it from a Christian perspective even a regional flood would have had global and eternal consequences- if the flooded region contained the descendants of Adam and Eve through Seth. In this passage, *Elohim* makes provision that the divinely appointed Way of Salvation is kept open.

****

A Note about "Gopher Wood"

God commands Noah to build the ark from "gopher wood". For ages men have wondered what that meant. The word appears nowhere else in the Bible. Nor is it a Hebrew word from anywhere else. Nor does it appear to be a word which was borrowed from languages which influenced Hebrew.

It has been noticed that the Hebrew letters which we pronounce like "g" and "k" look very similar. Those letters are called the "gimel" and the "kaf". It would be easy for a transcriber or translator to mix those two letters up, turning the actual Hebrew word for pitch, "*kopher*", into the unknown word "gopher".

What if the original text used "*kopher*" so that it would read "Make thee an ark of pitch(ed) wood..."? The mystery would be solved. There is no such thing as "gopher wood", rather it was "kopher wood" and was referring to the material used to waterproof and bind the wood together.

I am not suggesting a mistake in the text though. I think the LORD God directed Moses to change the letter when Moses was translating the tablets from which he compiled early Genesis. That the children of Israel did not catch the change is evidence that Genesis was compiled from tablets that were ancient even in their day. They didn't know what "gopher wood" was either, but they assumed that their ancestors did, just as we did!

The word "*kopher*" does not literally mean "pitch". Rather Strong's Concordance says it means "the price of a life, a ransom." A similar word, "*kaphar*", is the word translated "cover", as in "you shall *cover* it with pitch." It means, "to cover over, pacify, to make propitiation." So, the original literal meaning of the verse was to "make propitiation" with "the price of a life" for a ransom!

It gets better. The "kaf" letter which was taken out of "*kopher*" represents "palm" and stands for "crown" according to Hebrewtoday.com. In its form at the end of the word, it is said to represent a man bending down and humbling himself for his friends! A crown ("kaf") was given up by a man bending down and humbling Himself for His friends, and replaced with a "gimel" when turning "*kopher*" into "gopher".

The "kaf" was given up, but what of the letter that it was replaced with, the "gimel"? The same source says it is associated with the number three, and the similar sounding word "*gomel*" which Hebrewtoday.com describes thusly...

The shape of the Gimel also reminds of us something else. It looks like a man in motion. A nice lesson from the Jewish teachings actually pertains to this aspect of the Gimel. In Hebrew, the word "gomel," which begins with and sounds like the letter Gimel, means a "benefactor" or someone who gives to others. The letter after Gimel in the Hebrew alphabet is the letter Dalet, which is the first letter of the word "dal" meaning "weak." According to this teaching, the Gimel, the benefactor, is walking towards the Dalet who is weak.

I submit to you that even the supposed "mistakes" in the text are not mistakes. They were ordained by God to point to Christ and His work. Christ is the One who exchanged a crown to bend over and humble Himself for His friends, coming as a benefactor to we who are weak. What He gave us was propitiation for our sins with the price of a life when He spent three days in the ground!

Yahweh Comes Back into the Picture

The reverberations I spoke of two chapters ago do not in any way hinder the work of God or the knowledge of God. In fact, they can aid our understanding. Though both *"Yahweh"* and *"Elohim"* apply to both persons in scripture, in this account the former term is applied to the Image/Son and the latter to the Source/Father with great effect. It paints a vivid picture of the gospel and Christ's substitutionary work on the cross.

In chapter seven *Yahweh* is heard from again. The text does not mention Him doing or saying anything since 6:7-8 where he determined to destroy what he had made. The picture painted in this account is of someone getting discouraged in their work. His Father steps in and provides guidance to get them back on track. Notice that though it may have taken one hundred and twenty years to build the ark, *Yahweh* does not appear in the text again until the start of chapter seven- one week before the deluge begins.

Elohim is the one who initiated a plan which leaves open the path for at least some of the world to be redeemed- as many as are willing to enter the covenant which He will provide. When *Yahweh* steps back into the job He speaks as if He had been in charge all along. And He is in charge- of bringing wrath on those of His people who are bringing the earth to ruin with their wickedness and unbelief. And of giving instruction and deliverance to those who believe.

There is an echo of this in Exodus 32:9-14. *Yahweh* is ready to wipe out rebellious Israel and make a great nation of Moses instead. In that account it was Moses who talked The LORD out of destroying Israel. Something similar happened when they refused to enter the Promised Land. *Yahweh* consistently shows a human manner about Him which *Elohim* is beyond. Nevertheless, *Elohim* does things through *Yahweh* as an agent. In this case, *Elohim* says in 6:17 that He will "bring" a great flood, and *Yahweh* said in 7:4 that He will "cause" it to rain.

For yet seven days, and I will cause it to rain upon the earth forty days and forty nights; and every living substance that I have made will I destroy from off the face of the earth.

Note that *Yahweh* said that He was going to destroy every living thing that *He* had made. Prior to becoming the Man in Heaven, He was the Agent by which God made all things, but this refers to what He made *after* Genesis 1:27a. I have already demonstrated that chapter two is a much more limited set of animals than Genesis chapter one and we will see that the language for the animals in chapter six and seven supports the conclusion that the chapter two group was meant here. Also notice that living things in the water are not mentioned. He is only interested in cleansing the land from "every living substance" that He had made. This also indicates the chapter two list is meant and points to a regional flood. *Yahweh* isn't "un-making" the world back to what it was in Genesis 1:2, just to chapter two.

The word for "destroy" in verse 7:4 is from the same root word *Yahweh* used in verse 6:7. The word *Yahweh* used in both places is a form of the word *machah* (Strongs' 4229). Both forms of *machah* mean to "wipe out", "abolish" or "blot out". His intent was to make the earth just like it would be if He had never made the man or any of the beasts with him. After all, this account began by Him saying that He was sorry that He had ever made them. Obviously, the best way to undo His work in chapter two was to destroy only the region where they were located, not the entire planet.

Both terms are different from the word translated "destroy" which *Elohim* used in 6:13 and 6:17 because he was referring to the big picture. *Yahweh* was talking about blotting out just the line of Adam and the animals formed in the garden as helpers to the man. *Elohim* was referencing what that would mean for all the race *a'dam*, which is mankind. This regional flood would have had eternal and disastrous global consequences if the line of the Seed, the Redeemer of Mankind, had been ended.

There was going to be an exception though, and that exception was at *Elohim's* prompting. There would be a remnant that would not share the fate of the rest. One week before the flood, *Yahweh* began participating in the plan, giving His own instructions to Noah- a man who would follow them!

Commentators of the past have for a long time noticed that the instructions given by *Elohim* and *Yahweh* are different. This is made plain in the account. It is recorded in verse 7:5 that Noah did according to all that *Yahweh* commanded him to do, and in 6:22 and 7:16 that he did what *Elohim* commanded him to do.

Though the numbers of various types of animals Noah was told to take has been a topic of discussion, it is not the area I find of most interest. If someone tells me to take a pair of something to a place, and someone else tells me to take seven pairs of them to the same place, if I show up with seven pairs of them then I have done what both parties have asked me to do.

Of more interest is what sort of animals were and were not supposed to be on the ark. I have already shown that back in chapter two of Genesis there was a much more limited set of creatures made than was made in chapter one. Two categories were mentioned in chapter two. One was "beasts of the field" which we have seen includes "behemah", that is, livestock like cows, pigs, goats, and maybe camels, plus a minor quantity of small animals classified as "creeping things" (we infer there were some creeping things under the category "beasts of the field" because of Gen. 6:7). The other category was "fowls of the air."

The three categories of animals that *Elohim* tells Noah to load on the ark in Genesis 6:20 are therefore the same categories of animals which *Yahweh* made for Adam in chapter two. This was not every kind of animal on the planet. In other words, the command to take "two of all flesh" in verse nineteen must be taken in the context of the amplification of that instruction in verse twenty. The specific list in verse twenty limits the scope of the command which starts in verse nineteen.

If I told you, "bring me two of every kind of animal: two of all the livestock, two of every bird, and two of every animal of the field that scurries along the ground" then I would not expect you to bring me any elephants, gorillas, kangaroos, or polar bears. The additional instruction at the end modifies and limits the scope of the instruction given at the beginning. Yes, I said "every kind of animal" but I further explained what I meant by that-it was every kind of animal that fit the parameters I laid out in the following statement.

The three categories of animals that *Elohim* told Noah to take were livestock, birds, and "every creeping thing *ha-a'damah*", that is "*of* the ground." It is not the same as saying everything "that *creeps on* the ground" as Gen. 1:25 states. This group of "creeping things" is from Genesis 2:19 when *Yahweh* forms the "beasts of the field" for Adam out *of* the ground (*ha-a'damah*, Strong's 127). Noah was not instructed to load two of every creeping thing on earth but rather two of every member of this group which descended from those which *Yahweh* formed "from the ground" (*ha-a'damah*) in chapter two.

As for the "wild animals" category from 1:24, *they are not on God's list in chapter six*. This account limits the types of animals God wanted taken aboard the ark to the same categories of animals which *Yahweh* had formed in chapter two. It is reasonable to suppose that the animals aboard the ark were some descendants of that stock. Large predators were not a part of the list, though we might expect some dogs and small cats to have made the trip. Giraffes and elephants, though they are large quadruped herbivore herd animals, were not included. They were not livestock.

When *Yahweh* gives His instructions about what animals to take in verses 7:2-3 He describes an even narrower category of creatures. The word translated "beasts" in 7:2 is again "*behemah*" and is thus more properly translated "livestock". When He mentions the fowls, He specifies "fowls of the air", which leaves off emus and ostriches and perhaps even the broader category of waterfowl.

He does not even mention the category of "creeping things" in these verses. He seems ambivalent as to whether any of them make it onto the ark. Yes, He had earlier said that he was going to destroy the creeping things which he had made, but *Yahweh* makes no mention of loading them on the ark! *Elohim/Yahweh* don't act like it's a global flood.

To me this adds even more credence to the idea that when *Elohim* told Noah to include "creeping things", He was not referring to every type of "creeping thing" alive, but only those which descended from the group which *Yahweh* had formed "from the ground" in chapter two. If every creeping thing on earth had been included, it probably would have rated a mention from *Yahweh*, even if none of them were suitable for sacrifice.

There are hints (in 9:10) that they took more animal types than they were told to bring. They took animals from the "wild beast" category in Genesis chapter one even though they weren't on either list- *Elohim's* or *Yahweh's*. God didn't say to take them, the text just hints they took them. Maybe they didn't want to take any chances of blowing it. If in doubt, they loaded them up. I've gone back and forth on 7:14 but now favor the Amplified Bible translation, which does not say "wild animals" were loaded at God's command, but rather uses ha-hay-yah as a catch-all for "animals" and then lists the categories *behemah, remes,* and birds- leaving off wild animals.

But if taking creatures from this category was outside of God's specific instructions, if it was something the men did of their own initiative, then one cannot say that all animals in that category *globally* were taken. If the Tablet Theory is correct, verse fourteen was Shem, Ham, and Japheth reporting what they took according to their limited knowledge. The wild beasts of what is now Armenia perhaps. God knew the flood was not global in extent (just global in consequences if the line of Messiah was lost). That's why He didn't even say that they should bring anything from the "wild beast" category. It was about preserving the descendants of that limited set of creatures made in chapter two.

This was not an incredible number of animals. God was not trying to save every species or even genus on the globe from a planet-wide flood. There was no such flood coming, but rather a regional flood with eternal planet-wide consequences. *Elohim* is acting to preserve the works of *Yahweh*. The latter had determined to destroy His own handiwork, but that would have ruined God's plan of redemption.

The Adamic line, through the Seed of the Woman, via Seth the "Replacement", was destined to reconcile God's creation back to Him. If the line of Messiah had been blotted out, then the reconciliation would have been abrogated as well. Had that happened then creation could not have been redeemed. The story written out in heaven before the world began would have been shattered. The wisdom of God would have been confounded! Just as it says we cannot crucify Christ again, nor is there any other name in which salvation might be found, so it was that no other precaution or way had been ordained other than the one which was chosen by God. The end of the Adamic line would have meant the eternal separation, the corruption and the ruin, of all of creation whether man or beast.

This is why the question of whether the flood was local or global is the wrong way to look at it. If the descendants of Adam and Eve had been destroyed, particularly the line through Seth, then the line of Messiah would have perished. If that had happened, then any hope for creation to avoid ruin was also destroyed. A "local" flood could have "destroyed" the whole world, for the hope of the world would have perished in the flood were it not for Noah and his family.

The flood was local in its boundaries but global, nay universal, in its destruction. As we look at the scriptures in this chapter, we see how the words chosen for "destroy" and "die" used by *Elohim* and *Yahweh* reflect this difference. *Yahweh* was bringing physical death locally, and *Elohim* saw that this would bring the ruin of true death- spiritual death, globally.

Note also in 6:18 that *Elohim* proclaims that He will make a covenant with Noah. This is an agreement between God and man which is perpetual. A covenant is not just an agreement for a lifetime but applies to successors or descendants throughout all generations. Man will do something God directs and God for His part will give man blessings. In this case, Noah is faithful and keeps up his end of the bargain. God of course, always keeps His. The covenant of the Mosaic Law is also between God and man. It is *Elohim* who writes on the tablets. It is man who is to keep the law, and God for His part would then give life to man.

Notice the role of *Yahweh*, the God-Man, the Heavenly Man, in the covenants between God and men. His role is to 1) cause the judgement to fall on those who are not protected by the covenant and 2) help men to whom the covenant applies obtain the blessings of the covenant, doing what they cannot to see it through. In the case of Noah, *Yahweh* caused the rain to fall and bring judgement, but in 7:16 it is also written that The LORD (*Yahweh*) was the one who shut Noah and the rest in the ark. Perhaps the ark had a door which could be opened from the inside, but not closed and made watertight with pitch from the inside. The LORD stood in the gap.

There is a connection here to the new covenant. Christ will judge, and judgement will fall on those who are faithless, but at the same time He did what we could not, allowing us to obtain the blessings of being in right standing with God. He brings both judgement and deliverance.

It all fits together so beautifully that at some point it takes more faith to disbelieve than to believe. For example, the ancient texts could have said that the covenants were made with *Yahweh* instead of *Elohim*. That would have wrecked the pattern we see here. According to the cosmology which has been revealed, only *Yahweh* can stand in the gap between God and man. In Him, God can do for man as man the things required for man to keep the covenant of a just God.

****

As an end note to this chapter I want to comment on the issue of the pronunciation of the name of God. God's name consists of four Hebrew letters, and even centuries before Christ the Jewish people were reluctant to pronounce it out loud lest they take "the name of the LORD in vain." English translators took to inserting "the LORD" with capitals where they mean the four Hebrew letters which make up the name of God. These four letters are called the "tetragrammaton".

How should The NAME be pronounced (besides with great reverence)? My studies have convinced me that the four letters should each in turn be pronounced with their vowel sounds. Each of the consonants in the NAME has a vowel sound associated with it as well. I do not mean with the vowel *points* which were much later added to Hebrew. The Masorites deliberately gave the NAME alternate vowel points so that people reading aloud would not unintentionally say the NAME in vain.

This alteration of vowel points is the basis of the mistaken belief that the NAME is pronounced "Jehovah". Layered on top of that misdirection is the fact that the "J" sound did not exist in ancient Hebrew. Further, though the "v" and "w" may be interchangeable in the Hebrew it just so happens that the "w" is more helpful to English speakers in pronouncing the vowel sound that is important here.

Just one point of evidence in favor of this is that the great Jewish Historian Josephus described the Divine Name as consisting of "four vowels". He does this in Book Five of his *Wars of the Jews*, in chapter five and section seven of that book. As a Pharisee and a connected and educated Jew he was one of the insiders in position to know the true pronunciation, even if he was not allowed by his faith to use the true NAME in his writings. Though he did not use the NAME in that passage, he was always eager to please the Romans and gave them the key they needed to pronounce it.

This results in a four-syllable name for God. The first letter gives a vowel sound like "ee". The "ah" or "eh" sound is next. The third vowel, the sound used for "w", is more like the sound one would make on pronouncing the last syllable of the letter "W" in English. That is sort of an "oo" or "ou" sound. The last syllable can be understood as one of two vowel sounds, either "eh" or "ay". I now favor the *former*. Suffice to say that "*Yah-weh*", so long as we understand it is to be pronounced in four syllables, is a respectable representation of the NAME.

Shem, Ham, and Japheth Describe the Flood

***

In the six hundredth year of Noah's life, in the second month, the seventeenth day of the month, the same day were all the fountains of the great deep broken up, and the windows of heaven were opened. – Genesis 7:11

⟶⟫◈⟪⟵

As I have mentioned before, in scripture water is connected to God's judgement for both good and ill. Both water and judgement are necessary for life to continue and both are able to end the life which has been found unworthy. Much of the pain in the realm of Hades is that His life-bringing judgements will be absent! The verse above clearly connects water to negative judgement. Some scoffers have attempted to connect the verse to the ancient near eastern concept of a firmament in the sky.

While I have explained the firmament as referenced in the creation account and in Ezekiel, this isn't the same thing. The windows are not said to be in a "firmament", but in the sky. It's a different Hebrew word. No doubt they had a concept of an underground body of water, but such a body physically exists in the water table and in underground caverns such as those which feed the Tigris River. Noah's sons were simply using poetic language to describe a situation where water is flooding the land from above and below. The critics' attempts to drag this verse into the debate about the vagaries of Ancient Near Eastern Cosmology fall flat here.

In these pages I am going to make the case for a local, or at best regional, flood. This often raises two questions. One is "then why was Noah required to bring the animals with him? Couldn't he have gotten animals from elsewhere when he landed?" That one I believe I've answered. These were not just any animals. These were the descendants of the helpful stock which were fashioned for Adam in Genesis chapter two. They were "tweaked" versions of creatures which lived elsewhere. If they had perished there would be no easy replacement for them waiting in the next land.

The other question often asked is, if the destruction was not global, then why build an ark at all? If the flood was local, why didn't they just move?

Of course, Noah and his family would not even have had to move for God to bring judgement on the ungodly. God could have sent fire from heaven to consume the others. He could have sent a plague. Or the angel of death. God chose a flood because He was trying to paint a picture connected to the work He would do later in Christ.

God was trying to paint a picture of Christ delivering those of us who are in Him from divine punishment. We willingly pass through His judgement but are not destroyed due to the work of Christ. Those who are not in Him will later be destroyed by judgement. It was the same reason the LORD was upset with Moses for striking the rock a second time. God was trying to paint a picture where the Rock was struck only once, and after that, men are to cry out to the rock for water (God's life-sustaining judgements). Moses ruined the picture by striking the rock a second time. All these accounts were set up in a particular way to point to Christ. That's why it had to be done the way that it was. He told Noah "With you I will establish (set up) my covenant."

First Peter 3:22 tells us that baptism is the "antitype" of the flood. The flood was the type, and baptism represents the flood. That is, the people of God passing through the judgement of God. Noah was saved in the Ark. We are saved in Christ. Notice in First Corinthians 10:1-4 even the passing of the children of Israel through the Red Sea is counted as a baptism. A case could be made that passing over the Jordan River into the promised land is a third example. The Flood works *better* as a picture of baptism if they could have escaped it simply by travelling a thousand miles away. It is supposed to be a picture of us *choosing* to submit to God's judgement, in faith that because of His goodness God will preserve us through His judgement. A global flood leaves us no choice, and ruins the picture.

As a sidenote: If full immersion were a necessary component of baptism, then one would think that the scripture would clearly say so. What is essential is that God's children pass through waters (which represent God's judgement on unbelief and the unbelieving) in faith. That's the common element in the flood, the passing through the Red Sea, and the water baptisms in the NT. One might add the crossing of the Jordan River into the Promised Land to that list. Of course, many churches which also believe the gospel do not immerse in baptism, like the Lutherans. I personally prefer full immersion, but it is just that, my personal preference. It is not something commanded by scripture to make it a "real" baptism. For all we know, they stood in waist deep water and then a bowl of it was poured on their heads so all of us today have it wrong!

The flood comes. At this point in the text the perspective shifts. Remember that what we are reading is the account of Shem, Ham and Japheth. Until this point a lot of time has been spent relaying what *Elohim* and *Yahweh* have said about what is going to happen. They recorded the words of God describing things from God's view. As the flood overwhelms the land, there is a shift in perspective. Instead of God's view of what is happening, we get the narrator's view. That is, the view of Shem, and of Ham, and of Japheth.

In verse 7:19 the account says that the flood covered all the high hills that were under "the whole heaven." This is the sort of phrase which can fairly be translated "heavens" and is so translated in some versions. Therefore, some might seize upon 7:19 to say that this verse is the textual evidence which demonstrates that Genesis is describing a truly global flood. But this is Shem, Ham and Japheth describing the flood. The text is describing a situation where the flood seems worldwide to the limited perspective of the sons of Noah, but not necessarily from the perspective of God above.

When Elohim describes the flood's destruction of everything under heaven, He uses the term *shachath*. He will cause all under heaven to "*shachath*". As described before, that means "cause to ruin" or "bring to decay". "Perish" is how it is sometimes translated. That doesn't mean that the flood will cover it all, it means that it will all be brought to ruin by a flood that ends the line of Messiah. Everything under heaven will go to ruin. Not necessarily directly *in* the flood but *because* of it. But He has plans to preserve life through the flood by establishing a new covenant.

Yahweh, in describing what He will do in the flood, never uses the phrase "all under heaven" to describe the extent of the flood. Nor does He even say that all of the earth will be covered in the waters of the flood. Rather He says that what *He* has made (chapter two works) will be blotted off of the face of the earth. *Elohim*, the Father, uses global language but does not use terms suggesting instant death in a flood. *Yahweh*, the Son, uses terms suggesting instant death in the flood but does not use global language. He doesn't say that all the earth or everything under heaven will be covered by the flood. Only that everything He made will be blotted out.

I admit that I have a variant view of the text. The reason I have a variant view of the text isn't because "I don't take it literally". It is because I am reading it carefully! I don't assume that God is the narrator because the text says that this is the account of Shem, Ham, and Japheth. Therefore, I assume that when the narrator is making a statement it is coming from the perspective of what those three men saw, not what God sees. I don't assume that the translation of the original document from six thousand years ago has been translated into English so well that we never have to go back and look at the original language. I do assume that when God speaks His words are chosen very precisely.

If God had been the speaker in some of these chapter seven verses, then yes it would indicate that the flood was total and global. But verse 7:19 is not God's perspective of the flood. It is the record of Shem, Ham, and Japheth's perspective. God's view of it is back in 6:17 and His view does not use the language mandating that it was a flood of all land throughout the planet. It allows for a local flood which endangers all land throughout the planet because cutting off the line of Messiah dooms the entire earth to ruin. Everything "in the earth" will die, but all "in the covenant" will live.

To the sons of Noah, it seemed like all the land was under water. The text around this verse goes to great lengths to communicate the point that their world was destroyed. Since the First Epistle of Peter chapter three tells us that baptism is a figure of the flood, it makes sense that this would be so. Just as the sin in us is totally judged and put to death in the waters of baptism, even while the unbelieving world still lives, so it was in the flood that the world of God's chosen people was totally judged and put to death, even while the rest of the world lived on. More about that later.

If one translates verse 7:23 with the understanding that all men sprang only from Adam, then one would put it like we see in most bibles. That is, reading like the destruction was global. But what it says in Hebrew is that all was destroyed which was on the face of "*ha-adamah*" and that this included all "*me-adam*", or "from Adam".

In the same way, in verse twenty-one "*kol ha-adam*" is usually translated "all the men" but could just as well be translated "all of Adam". Even with the former translation, "all *the* men" instead of just "all men" hints that it refers to a specific group of men and not the entirety of our race. I'm not dogmatic here, but it seems to me that read in the light of what we have learned so far that it could be referring to the destruction of all the offspring of Adam in their own land.

Even if the current translations are correct, this was the report of the sons of Noah and what they saw. It wasn't an observation about what was happening in south Africa or Australia. "*Eretz*" should be rendered "land" here. It was what they observed happening in their world- the world of the irreverent ungodly, as Peter put it. That is, the world of those who had the LORD walking among them daily and yet still had no reverence for Him.

A local or regional flood dispenses with the argument that the stated size of the ark was too large for a sea-worthy wooden vessel. Ocean waves put stresses on ships and there is a limit to how big an ocean-going wooden ship can be without those stresses breaking the vessel up. I don't see any indication in the text that there were large waves, and in a local or regional flood there wouldn't have been.

There is yet another objection I have heard to the idea of a local or regional flood, and it also pertains to the question of what of Shem, Ham, and Japheth saw, or failed to see. Why did they report (7:20) after forty days the curious statement; "fifteen cubits upward did the waters prevail and the mountains were covered"? If the flood was local, why did they not report that "the tops of the mountains were seen" until about nine months later? In a local flood, especially one surrounded by highlands, distant mountains could have been visible for dozens of miles. Even if these verses are their report of the flood, and not God saying what the flood did, at first glance this part of their testimony seems inconsistent with a local flood. Particularly a highland one. But let's consider the verse more closely.

Is 7:20 saying that only fifteen cubits of water (about twenty-two feet) covered all the mountains in the world? Or is it saying that the tallest mountain was covered by a depth of fifteen cubits? How did they know how deep the highest mountains were covered? The verse isn't saying any of these things. The draft of their vessel was probably fifteen cubits. They had been drifting along and hadn't run aground, and that was the basis for their report. It isn't even based on visual scans of the horizon, or a survey of the Himalayan mountains. Their observation is based on the draft of their vessel, and that it hadn't bumped into any hills or mountains.

And that brings me to the issue of visibility. When most people today think of the Ark, they imagine a large wooden boat that has a row of windows on the top deck, and maybe some animals out on the top deck looking over the side. But a close examination of the text shows that this is not what the ark looked like. The "window" that Noah was told to put in the Ark (6:16) may have been constructed by leaving the last cubit of the roof of the ark unfinished so that light and air could get in. If it had a peaked roof, we might imagine the last foot-and-a-half of it left open. The other option is that the unfinished cubit was at the bottom along the roofline.

Either way, if this opening were not covered over, the rain waters of the flood would enter the ark and it would not save them. But it was covered over. Though it is not mentioned in the instructions for construction in chapter six, verse 8:13 speaks of them removing the "covering" or "cover" of the ark. The Hebrew word used to describe it indicates that it was made of animal skin. We might think of it as an awning. So, imagine an ark with an opening either in the center of the roof or around the edge of the roof-line. This opening is covered by an awning made of animal skin- my guess is lambskin because it would complete the picture of our being delivered from God's judgement through the blood of the Lamb.

That they were instructed to leave an opening, but not to make a cover, suggests an intriguing possibility. Verse 7:16 says that *Yahweh* "shut them in" the ark. What if The LORD made the cover, even as He made Adam and Eve garments of animal skin to cover their nakedness? Then He put it on as a part of the process of "shutting them in." If so, can you imagine the faith of Noah? Not only did he build an ark on dry land for all of those decades, but he left a big hole in the top! In faith, he followed the instructions exactly, even though the rains could get in through that opening! It made no sense! Then the LORD came.

Verse 8:13 indicates that they did not get an unobstructed view of the horizon until the cover was removed. Perhaps to keep the rain out the awning had to be placed far enough over the opening so that they could only see the waters immediately around the ark and not the horizon many miles away. If you have ever put up an awning, you know it's hard, and they would have had to work from the inside of the ship if they had removed it too early and needed to put it back on. You can understand why they would not want to take the cover off until they were very sure they didn't need the shelter of the ark.

Why would they have to release birds to see if there was dry land nearby if all they had to do was look out of their windows? The use of the birds to test for the presence of dry land nearby would have been unnecessary if they had an unobstructed view of the horizon. The window through which the birds were released is a different Hebrew word than that which has been translated "window" in chapter six. It seems to have stayed shut until it was used to release them, after the ark ran aground. Perhaps it was lower to the water and sealed with pitch from the outside just like the rest of the ark. Therefore, once they opened it the seal would have been broken and it would have been a potential source of leaks. All of this leads to the conclusion that they only had a very limited view of their surroundings.

This is the lens through which we should interpret the statement "the tops of the mountains were seen" in verse 8:5. It isn't saying that twenty miles distant they could see mountain tops via their great view of the horizon. It was saying that in the immediate area around their grounded ark they could observe by peeking under the awning that hilltops were just below the surface of the water. This would naturally cause them to wonder if there were not somewhat taller hills just outside their view which were already above the surface, and that's why they released the birds to check.

Further evidence for this understanding of the verse is that in 8:5 the Hebrew just says that the tops of the "hills" were seen. Earlier (7:19,20), when they wanted to say "mountains" the word for hills was modified with the Hebrew word for "high" in front of it. So, it wasn't even the tops of the "high hills" or mountains that was being seen in 8:5, just the tops of the regular hills. When they saw that the regular hills immediately surrounding their craft were close to breaching the surface, they sent birds out to test if there were higher hills nearby which had *already* breached the surface.

I say all that about the text to show that the observations of Shem, Ham and Japheth do not rule out a local or regional flood, even a highland one.

If the flood was not global, one might wonder just what was its extent? What constituted "the world" in the minds of Noah and his sons? I can only guess, and this is where I feel the least comfortable. Still, so long as it is understood that this is all I am doing I shall try to satisfy the natural curiosity of the reader as best as I am able.

The whole region we have been discussing here- the drainage basin of the Aras (Araxes) River, the Ardabil Basin, and near Lake Urmia, Lake Sevan, and Lake Van is a mountainous area. Yet I notice that this region, though elevated, is surrounded by mountains which are even more elevated. To the south, the Zagros Mountains run northeast along the Iranian border and then turn east-west into Turkey, just south of my proposed territory for Adam's descendants.

Were that area to the north of the Zagros to fill up with water then the mountains would hinder its drainage. The area to the north of this country would also be blocked where the eastern Pontic Mountains run along the coast of the Black Sea and into Georgia. The flow of water would be constrained both north and south.

It would also be largely blocked to the east, where the Armenian Highlands near Lake Sevan merge with the Albruz (or Elburz) mountains. These run along the very north of Iran on its western side. There would be some flow there where the Aras meets the Kura River, and I believe some trace of it might still be detected in the ground, but perhaps at not such a rate as to allow for a quick return of the waters as the Aras passes through a narrow gorge before joining the Kura. If instead the flood were just east of this area, where the Kura and Araxes rivers join, then this same gorge would serve to slow drainage upstream should the water rise high enough on the southeast side to reverse the flow.

If the flood went further to the west, it could drain through the channels of the Murat and the Karasu, but both of those rivers also pass through narrow canyons in much more elevated country as they approach what is now the Keban Reservoir. These canyons would serve as bottlenecks greatly limiting its flow into the Euphrates. They could not be counted on to quickly relieve flood pressure on the region. On the rest of the west, the Taurus Mountains turn north-south on their eastern end, which would also impede the drainage of a great flood.

The land near the Aras River and Ardabil Basins is a land full of mountains, but mountains which are surrounded by even higher mountain ranges or plateaus on almost every side. There are rivers to drain this vast region, but they are constricted by the nature of the ground through which they pass. For example, the Euphrates passes through steep and narrow gorges which would greatly limit the speed at which it could drain the waters of a vast flood, especially if choked by debris.

Imagine a very great bowl of stone whose bottom was filled with dirt. On the dirt are small stones which serve as mountains in our little world, though the highest mountains are represented by the sides of the bowl itself. As rain fell, the water would rise over the stones in the midst of the bowl while contained in the even higher stone of the bowl's sides. Not that there would be any escape from the very first day, for water would be coming off all the elevated areas in torrents.

After the smaller local mountains were covered any ark would be pushed to the center of the "bowl" while water was still pouring off the sides- which consisted of the even higher mountains beyond. Only much later, when the waters were draining away, would the current be reversed, and the ark then drawn to whatever cracks in the lip of the bowl allowed water to drain from it.

I do not mean to suggest by this that the great flood was restricted only to this area. Obviously, the Mesopotamians were "downhill" from this region, and could be expected to get at least a "glancing blow" from the flood. Their stories also tell of a great flood which wiped out civilization. Their versions speak of fewer days of rain, there is no mention of the "great fountains of the deep" breaking up, and the length of time which the earth was flooded was much less than that recorded in Genesis.

If the sons of Adam had expanded into parts of Mesopotamia, then a flood which wiped them out obviously would also have had to extend that far. There are many hints of connections between the rise of Mesopotamian civilization and people from the hills north of them, but I will leave that to the archaeologists to sort out.

We are told that the ark came to rest "on the mountains of Ararat." Even this is a bit ambiguous, though the general region is an area near the Turkish-Armenian and Iranian border. In this region there lies the greater and lesser Mount Ararat proper, two mountains in isolation. Across the valley from them there is a range of mountains which are also referred to as Ararat.

All of these are only a small subset of what the ancients considered the mountains of Ararat. There was in antiquity a kingdom called "Urartu" from which those mountains get their name. The "mountains of Ararat" could be any of the mountains in that old kingdom. It covered a much larger area than what we consider the present mountains of Ararat. When scripture says that the ark landed on "the mountains of Ararat" it could mean anywhere in that region.

Earlier in church history this was understood. It was mostly in modern times that the church began thinking that the ark of Noah landed on what we now call Mt. Ararat. The ancient church believed that the ark landed on a mountain called Judi, or sometimes Cudi. Muslims still say so, and I believe that they are partially right. Mount Judi is celebrated as the "place of descent" for the clan of Noah.

The mountain that they point to is near to the banks of the Tigris River in the Sirnak Province of Southeastern Turkey. This is near the point at which modern Syria, Iraq, and Turkey converge. This location would suggest the flood was south or west of there. But some evidence suggests to me that the flood was somewhat north and east of there. In addition, the text (Gen. 11:2) says "it came to pass" that after these events that they "journeyed from the east" and "found a plain in the land of Shinar."

The plains of Shinar would not be much of a journey from that location. Depending on where you were in the province, you could see them from there, and they would be more south than west. The plains begin only about fifteen miles away from the capital of Sirnak province, a city which goes by the same name.

On the other hand, this place makes good sense as a "place of descent" for Noah's clan when they came down (descended) from the mountains and "found a plain, in the land of Shinar." This may very well have been a "place of descent" and they may well have carried timbers from the ark with them for tent poles and other uses. It was just not where the ark landed. That was another place of descent, another "Mount Judi". Thus, we could have two "places of descent", one where they descended down the mountain or hill from the ark, and another where some time later the clan of Noah came out of the mountains and found the plain in the land of Shinar (Babylon/Iraq).

I would suggest that the actual landing place of the ark would be east of Mount Judi- perhaps a couple of hundred miles east, around the drainage basins of Lake Urmia and the Aras River Valley. There is no necessity for the hill or mountain they landed on to be the tallest landform in sight.

But I could be wrong about the location of the flood. Another possibility is that the basin of the Khabur River served as the flood area, with the Sinjar and associated southern mountains blocking drainage to the south. In such a flood scenario Mt. Judi could easily be the ark landing spot. The barriers to drainage from this basin would have had to have been more extensive pre-flood. This scenario would fit better if the location for Eden was the site I suggested just east of the Euphrates around the Syrian-Turkish border.

Regardless of where the ark landed, I greatly doubt we will discover it intact today. Josephus quotes Berosus as saying only "some part" of it remained even back then. The timbers which comprised the ark represented decades of work for Noah and his family. It is very difficult to hew timber with hand tools. Those first few years there may have been a serious lack of large trees around even if they were willing to do the work. But why do that work all over again when there was a giant ark's worth of ready-made lumber available?

It is my guess that the timbers from the ark were utilized by Noah and his immediate descendants. They may have taken some timbers with them on their journey, but it is likely that these have long since been taken bit by bit as talismans. This practice was mentioned in certain historical accounts, and the aforementioned modern account from Dr. Friedrich Bender.

The Aftermath of the Flood

⟿❦⟾

The main thing which singled out the Deluge from other floods is this: The previous order of things was gone. It destroyed the ancient world because *Yahweh* changed the way He related to mankind. Further, had those on the ark not been spared the works of *Yahweh* fashioned in the second chapter of Genesis would have been destroyed, both man and beast. And since it had been ordained by God that by those works salvation would come to the world, their loss would have meant that mankind would have been cut off from God forever. This would have resulted in the ultimate ruin of the whole world forever. This is what made the flood different from other great floods in the earth.

We will see that after Noah the LORD's interactions with humanity change. No longer does He walk among them on a regular basis. No longer does He attempt to administrate their daily affairs. Familiarity had bred contempt, and henceforth His default desire to dwell with His people would be restrained by the terrible experiences He had been through. He is a much more distant character after Noah, at least until Moses comes along. The flood destroyed the world of that time (2nd Peter 3:6), and so the world where God walked among His people was no more.

In chapter eight starting at the twentieth verse through the seventh verse of chapter nine, the text describes how both *Elohim* and *Yahweh* came to relax their standards for mankind. God spoke to Noah and told him to leave the ark, him and all the animals with him. After spending a year on the ark, what is the first thing you would do on exiting it? The first thing that Noah did on leaving the ark was to build an altar - an altar to the One who had shut them into the ark. An offering of one of every clean animal on the ark. This is more evidence that this was a limited set of animals.

Now *Yahweh* had not, so far as we know, told Noah to make Him an offering, but He had told Noah to bring *seven* pairs of every clean animal. Enough so that one could be sacrificed. Perhaps Noah actually took the hint. For ages the sons of men had disregarded His orders, His commands, and His admonitions. He had contended with them and been ignored by them for generations. At last He had found a man of faith, one who not only obeyed His commands, but even took the merest hint to fully honor the LORD.

So embittered had His relations with His chosen people become that *Yahweh* had determined to destroy them all. And not just them, but the animals He had made for them as well. There was but one family that was going to survive, and that plan was initiated by *Elohim*. So far as we can see in the text, *Yahweh* only participated in it on the last week before destruction fell. That is just how soured He was with them. Finally, He poured out His wrath on the wicked sons of Adam and swept them from off the face of the earth.

Imagine the scene when He initiates contact again for the first time with the last of them on the ark. He approaches the camp of the few survivors, ready to be disappointed. With a few noble exceptions like Enoch, *Yahweh* has known nothing but disappointment in thousands of years of trying to get them to do the right thing. Would they be afraid? Would they be angry at what they had to go through? Would they be sitting around imagining evil?

As He gets closer, the aroma of a sacrifice reaches His nostrils. Noah had done what *Yahweh* had hoped. *Yahweh* found a feast which Noah had prepared for Him. After all those centuries, the LORD had at last found a man of faith, a man who loved Him back. This man's descendants He would bless. This man's descendants would divide up the world.

Verse twenty-one of chapter eight makes it clear that the LORD was under no illusions as to the real nature of humanity. Even a people which had been pruned of all but their "finest" elements. He knew that they were not done disappointing Him, turning their backs on Him, and betraying Him. But in that one great act of respect, *Yahweh* found a reason to relax, and accept mankind for who they are.

They may not be righteous, but they can be loving. With God's help they can be faithful, which He had the power to make into righteousness. He determined in His heart that never again would He destroy them all with a flood. In verse 8:21 the LORD says "never again will I curse the ground". I now believe that this isn't a reference to how the ground was "cursed" by Adam's fall. For one thing, two different Hebrew words are used. The one in Adam's case literally means "a curse". But even there, God didn't say that he would put a curse on the ground, but rather that the ground was cursed because of Adam. That is, it would have to labor in its futility much longer and harder due to Adam's sin. It would linger in its current condition due to Adam's fall when it was meant to be elevated.

This word translated "curse" in chapter eight is a different word, and a broader one. It means to treat lightly or dismissively. Of course, a literal curse would be one way to do that, but this is in the context of the LORD accepting the human race for who we are, and not writing us off just because even the best of us are, well, ridiculously pathetic and sinful.

Even if He had not known from the first, from the time that Adam failed it must have occurred to the LORD that He would have to die in their place to truly redeem them. I have speculated that even Adam and Eve were told something of God's plan for the ultimate redemption of faithful humanity. It was "them or Him", and the last bunch was not the sort of folks He should want to die for. Neither are we, but in verse twenty-one He resigns Himself to our true nature. Does this seem something like personal growth? Let's hold that thought until later.

While the LORD pledged to never again destroy His people with a flood, the Devil has not, nor would a pledge from such an entity mean anything, for it loves lies. In Revelation 12:15 we see that the dragon spews a "flood of water" out of its mouth in order to carry off "the woman" who brought forth the man-child. This Woman is the mother of all who believe.

In the upside down "morality" of the dragon what is good is bad and what is bad is good. The Devil wants to sweep her away with his own judgments, represented by the flood of water from the dragon's mouth. It doesn't work because when God judges, He does so in accordance with the structure of the natural world which He created. The Devil's judgements are in opposition to the order of things in the natural world and so cannot be sustained. The earth itself acts against them.

In this day and age, we see this playing out before us. Spiritually blinded masses of people angrily demand that believers reject God's standards for human conduct. They insist that we change in favor of an ever-shifting "moral" code founded on nothing more substantial than the feelings and will of man himself. Such attacks will be intense, but this force of willfulness is opposed and absorbed by the construction of the natural world itself. Unlike *Yahweh's* flood of judgement, which did justly destroy His people when they erred, this satanically inspired flood of judgement will not prevail. The woman will be preserved through it because the natural order of things, the earth itself, is on her side.

It is not just *Yahweh* who takes a more relaxed view of human conduct after the flood. *Elohim* also makes allowances for man in light of these events. In the beginning of chapter nine He authorizes the eating of meat and acknowledges that their relationship with animals will be characterized by a fear of man. In Genesis chapter one He had only given plants to be used as food.

Is the authorization of man to eat meat a concession to the weakness of man, or was the original authorization of plants for food unnecessarily limiting? I don't know. Perhaps what is suitable for the unfallen man is different than what is suitable for fallen man- a condition which *Yahweh* comes to accept that we are in and that He is not going to change from the outside.

In Genesis nine *Elohim* authorizes meat to be eaten, with the proviso not to eat the blood with the meat. Lest our bloodletting of animals drive us into another frenzy of murder He then specifies that though we can kill and eat animals, we can't kill each other! He establishes the principle that human life is special when He says in verse five that when a human is killed, He will hold the killer accountable, be it man or beast!

What is His basis for declaring human life sacred? That Man was made in His image. One must take the verse (Genesis 9:6) which says that "God made man in His own image" in light of the larger picture of the cosmology of scripture. He did make "the Man" in His own image. In the Hebrew verse 9:6 says "*ha-adam*" rather than "*adam*", which is normally translated "the man" or "of man" rather than just "man". Therefore, the last part of 9:6 can, and in my view should be, translated "for in the image of God made He *the* man." But even if the whole human race is meant, the statement still only applies to the original condition of man, not his fallen condition, because the form of the word translated "made" indicates a past action. He made, past tense, the man in His own image.

This verse does not mean that men currently born into the world are in the image of God. Adolf Hitler was not in the image of God. Nor was Jack the Ripper. The elect in heaven are in His image, for this is where what *is* always reflects His will. It is what *can* happen on earth when God's intent is fulfilled in our lives. In Heaven His intent is already as good as fulfilled. In the view from there His people are already in the image of God, for He sees the future as present reality. Are we His image down here? Christ was. Us? Not so much.

When we are born in this world, we are not born in the "image" of God. All men are born in the likeness of God, but not the image. We have an earthly image. This is why it is written (John 3:7) "you must be born again." If you were born in the image of God the first time, you would not need to be born again a second time. When we are born again, we have a heavenly image, and through faith and the renewal of our minds by the Holy Spirit we become conformed to that new image which we have. Here are some scriptures which support this declaration, starting in Romans chapter eight:

For whom he did foreknow, he also did predestinate to be conformed to the image of his Son, that he might be the firstborn among many brethren.

And further in Colossians the third chapter...

Lie not one to another, seeing that ye have put off the old man with his deeds; And have put on the new man, which is renewed in knowledge after the image of him that created him:

And then from First Corinthians the fifteenth chapter:

The first man is of the earth, earthy: the second man is the Lord from heaven. As is the earthy, such are they also that are earthy: and is the heavenly, such are they also that are heavenly. And as we have borne the image of the earthy, we shall also bear the image of the heavenly.

And in Second Corinthians the third chapter:

But we all, with open face beholding as in a glass the glory of the Lord, are changed into the same image from glory to glory, even as by the Spirit of the Lord.

The prohibition against murder is based on God's original intent for man, and for the potential to once again be conformed to His image. It is not because mankind was in that state when God was speaking to Noah *et al*, or because we manifest that state today. Those of us who are believers are in a tension between the temporal and eternal realms. Those whose life is in Christ (Col. 3:3) do share that image. Though we are not conformed to it yet, we will be, for that is His goal and our destiny (Rom. 8:29).

God Establishes a Covenant with the Ark Riders

—◦◦◦◦◦—

In verses nine and ten of chapter nine God establishes a covenant that He will never again "cut off" all flesh with a flood. As with the rest of the scriptures concerning the flood, there are at least two opinions as to what it says about the extent of the flood. One view is that this was a global flood which destroyed every land on earth and all humans and all land animals except those which were on the ark. This is the position of Orthodox Judaism, and it was to the Jewish people that the word was delivered and by them it has been preserved.

But while they were given the word, the revelation of who Christ is has not, for the most part, been received by them. Because they do not understand what Christians know about the Second Man Christ, they also do not understand about the First Man Adam. They are basing their conclusions about Adam by seeing only the shadow, but we have the Substance which cast that shadow. The line of Adam was meant to bring the One who would redeem and rule the human race. It was not all of mankind.

Since they do not receive who Christ is, they do not understand who the Seed of the Woman is who has crushed the Serpent's head. They do not understand the true Sabbath. They do not understand the Third Day. They do not understand that *Yahweh* the Son is the Heavenly Man, the God-Man created in the "man" part to give God an image visible to lesser beings, and that *Yahweh* incarnated into corruptible flesh is Christ. Though they have received the model of forms and shadows, without Christ they do not understand, as Peter did, that the flood was a type of baptism (First Peter 3:20-22).

It is because they have not received any of these things that they cannot grasp the context in which the flood occurred or in which the Covenant of Noah was made. Unfortunately, the Christian church largely adopted the Jewish view of these scriptures. Even though they had the revelations necessary to put them in proper context, they did not make the connections. They accepted the flood account from the Jews pretty much as it was and did not seek out its real message. Even though the knowledge of Christ was received, they did not re-interpret the account in accordance with that knowledge. They did not retell it from a Christ-centered perspective.

When God was speaking to the Ark Riders, He was making the covenant with the survivors of the Adamic line fashioned by *Yahweh-Elohim* in Genesis chapter two. This was the people through whom He had destined that His creation would be reconciled to Him. But since God has already purposed to redeem humanity through them, cutting them off would have been tantamount to ending His plan to redeem humanity and the natural realm itself. The Devil would have gotten what it wanted- a humanity and a natural universe separated from God.

God's efforts to redeem humanity and the natural world have frequently come down to an individual person. First there was Adam, and when he failed then there was one more loophole by which the promise might be kept alive - Eve who was drawn from his flesh but of her own seed. That plan would still have perished if not for Noah and his sons.

After this the fulfillment of God's designs would pass through a single man yet again, Abraham, and then Isaac, and then Jacob. Then, in power though not in blood, it came down to Moses, and then David as a shadow of King Jesus. Lastly the success of the whole plan came down to a babe in a manger. From the cross onward, the Kingdom of Heaven on the earth was never again narrowed down to a single descendant of Adam and Eve. Instead, it grew to fill the earth and welcome in people from every tribe and tongue and nation. It may not be done growing to this day.

Next let's look at the covenant which God makes with the Ark Riders. When we look at the whole passage, we will see that God starts by making the covenant with those on the ark, but then extends that covenant to the whole earth. This should remind you of His covenant with Abraham, which was initially made with him and his descendants, and yet "*in thy seed all the nations of the earth shall be blessed*" (Genesis 22:18).

In other words, the same pattern is being shown here. A covenant which starts with Noah and those with him will be extended a few verses hence to the entire world. Just as we can enter the covenant of circumcision given to Abraham and become his grafted-in offspring, so we can participate in the covenant of Noah. In a like manner, we can participate in the covenant of the book of the law (Exodus 24:3-8) administered by Moses even though it was meant for the children of Israel. We can do this because Christ fulfilled the law and our life is now in Him.

In all these cases the pattern is the same. God makes a covenant with a small group but then extends it. The covenant begins with them but is extended to all who wish to enter in by faith. In the other covenants, there is a long gap between when the covenant begins with a select person or group and when it is extended to all men. But here, where the pattern of extension is first laid out, it is done so immediately. The covenant with Noah is explicitly extended to the whole earth just a few verses (13-17) after it is made with Noah.

Thus, the precedent was set here of the extending of a covenant. That way when the covenants of Abraham and Moses are extended to the whole world it could be recognized as a practice of God- even though there was a large gap in those cases between when they were given and when they were extended.

Let's look at what God says first about the covenant in Genesis chapter nine:

And God spake unto Noah, and to his sons with him, saying,

And I, behold, I establish my covenant with you, and with your seed after you;

And with every living creature that is with you, of the fowl, of the cattle, and of every beast of the earth with you; from all that go out of the ark, to every beast of the earth.

In verse nine God says that the covenant is established with Noah and His descendants. In verse ten God specifies that it applies to the animals with you, and "from all that go out of the ark". *Elohim* further specifies that He is talking about the animals that "go out of the ark." Why would it even be necessary to specify He was speaking to the animals "with you" and the animals "from the ark" if indeed all animal life on the entire planet had been destroyed by the flood?

If you had the last land animals on earth "with you" then describing them as "with you" is superfluous. "I am going to make a covenant with you and the animals" says the same thing, yet *Elohim* specifies twice that He is speaking to the animals "with you" and "those from the ark."

That word for "establish" in these verses means to "rise up" or raise- to set up. God had the plan for a covenant from the beginning, not merely this covenant, but *the* covenant of which this one is but a foreshadowing. He is going to cause to stand that which He had decided on, but which was till then lying down unused. The covenant with Noah will point to and establish the new covenant. If we look at that one rightly then we can see the new one.

It was the same in Genesis 17:19 when God said that He would establish His covenant with Isaac. Isaac went on to be used to paint a dramatic picture of God's sacrifice of His only especially-begotten Son. As we go through this narrative notice how the elements of this account "establish" the new covenant.

Please notice the next two verses of chapter nine:

And I will establish my covenant with you, neither shall all flesh be cut off any more by the waters of a flood; neither shall there any more be a flood to destroy the earth.

And God said, This is the token of the covenant which I make between me and you and every living creature that is with you, for perpetual generations:

When He said that He would never again "cut off" all flesh and "destroy" the earth with a flood, He is speaking to Noah's family and the animals with him in respect to the literal flooding, but He is also speaking to all of creation with respect to what the end of the Adamic line would have meant for creation. It would have meant that the means of reconciliation to God would have been severed.

One might think that God could have tried with another method or line but this story has already been written out in heaven. It has already been declared in heaven. Just like you cannot re-crucify Christ, there is no "plan B" if God's "plan A" fails. The details of how it works itself out may vary, but if God has declared that salvation was to come through Adam's line then that line either continues or salvation does not come.

Look in particular at the words used in verse eleven, where God makes His commitment: all flesh would not be "cut off" by the waters of a flood. The word for "cut off" is *yik-ka-retn* (from Strong's 3772). It means to "cut off" in the sense of being separated from something. When someone is promised that "they shall not lack a man" to stand before God this is the word that is used for the "lack a man" part. Examples include Second Chronicles 6:16, 7:18 *et al.*

This term does not mean to directly "exterminate" even though there is a term they could have used for that. There are many terms that could have been used that would better describe a slaughter or eradication. But a global slaughter or eradication is not what happened in the flood. Rather the flood threatened to cut off access to God's plan to reconcile creation to Himself. These words were chosen to point us to Christ. The promise was that we would not be "cut off" from the Father.

In the same way, the word for "destroy" at the end of verse eleven is once again a form of "*shachath*" (Strong's 7843) and has connotations of corrupting or going to ruin rather than being directly destroyed. The term used by *Yahweh* for what He would do to Adam's posterity was a different word which *does* indicate direct destruction ("blotting out"). God promised that the hope for creation to be reconciled to Him would not be removed by His judgements (which the flood waters represented).

In the next few verses, we see what I mentioned earlier- that God is not only making a covenant with the Ark Riders. He is extending that covenant and making it with the earth. It applies to every living creature. He is extending the same covenant with them as He makes with the Ark Riders:

I do set my bow in the cloud, and it shall be for a token of a covenant between me and the earth.

And it shall come to pass, when I bring a cloud over the earth, that the bow shall be seen in the cloud:

And I will remember my covenant, which is between me and you and every living creature of all flesh; and the waters shall no more become a flood to destroy all flesh.

And the bow shall be in the cloud; and I will look upon it, that I may remember the everlasting covenant between God and every living creature of all flesh that is upon the earth.

And God said unto Noah, This is the token of the covenant, which I have established between me and all flesh that is upon the earth.

The word for "destroy" in verse fifteen is again a form of "*shachath*", and once again refers to the consequences of cutting off the line of Messiah with waters. It has already been demonstrated that waters represent God's judgment. Those who complain that there have been many local floods since this time are missing the point. His promise is that His judgements will never again become a flood which will cut of the line of Messiah and thereby cause all flesh to perish (die apart from Him in a cursed state). He will always keep a lifeline, a way out. There will be a covenant of protection that humans will have access to, right up until the end of the age.

Rather, for those who love Him His judgements will be like life-giving rain, a cleansing sprinkle, or a river of Living Water which He places in our innermost being. There will be a way for His judgements to bring life rather than death. This is His promise.

The bow mentioned in these verses is presumed to be the rainbow, but it doesn't say that outright. The word used here is the word normally translated "bow" as in the weapon of an archer. The token of the covenant indicates that He has hung up His bow- meaning something very similar to our English phrase "hang up your guns". He is no longer at war with the human race, though we may be so wicked as to still be at war with Him. He gives His word that He will act going forward in just the way He acted with Noah- to find a way to deliver at least a remnant of creation.

His intentions are not new, and neither is the rainbow; what is new is that He declares it as a token of His good intentions toward creation. The rainbow in the sky is being designated as what we would call a "memory aid" - a reminder that He has "hung up His bow", His bow of war, as it applies to us. Not that God is forgetful, but *Yahweh* can and did afterward become exasperated with our rebellious, sinful, and ungrateful nature.

This extending of the covenant is a foreshadowing of the covenant which God makes with Israel when He gave the Law of Moses. That covenant would preserve life, but not in the way they thought, for they could not keep their end of it. But Christ did keep it, and as a result delivered not only those under the Mosaic Law, but all the world.

The covenant of righteousness under the Law was fulfilled in Christ and extended to all whose life is in Christ. In Noah's day, if you were in the ark, you were among the living; if you were not, you were among those who had been blotted out already or who would perish eventually. In our present day, either you are in Christ or you are among those who have been blotted out already, or those who will perish eventually. There is the living, in the covenant, and the non-living outside it. The covenant with Noah is pointing to the ultimate covenant and God is using the elements of Noah's covenant to point to that New Covenant.

What is baptism supposed to represent? Most evangelical churches, especially the ones who fully immerse, would say that it is identifying with the death, burial, and resurrection of our Lord Jesus Christ. Since I am obviously a big fan of Christ-centered teaching on scripture, that's the kind of view I could get behind and I do- at least as part of the picture. This view of baptism is pointed to in Romans chapter six verses one through four.

While that is true, that passage is not the *only* verse in scripture which speaks about what baptism represents. Jesus Himself was baptized in water before His death, burial, and resurrection. He wasn't doing it to identify with His future death, burial, and resurrection. He was doing it to identify with us. John was preaching "the baptism of repentance for the remission of sins" (Mark 1:4). But what is it about being washed in water which allows for sins to be forgiven?

Water in scripture has represented several things, but nothing more than judgement. Judgement can destroy but can also bring life. The Holy Spirit is a particular type of water, living water. That is, the Spirit produces God's judgments which bring life, as when the Spirit convicts us of sin which we then turn away from. In passing through the water of baptism we are submitting to God's just judgment and asking Him to send His life-giving Holy Spirit to convict us of whatever sin still clings to us and needs to be washed away by said water.

Without faith that God is just and His judgments right, baptism cannot produce salvation. It is not the act of passing through water which delivers, but what God does in us which can deliver, when conjoined with faith. Repenting of sinful works by itself does not make them less sinful. One who murders is still guilty of murder, even if he later repents. We dare not submit our lives to His just judgement without faith in Christ, that He has taken the wrath due us for love's sake. This is the only basis with which we can repent in confidence that we will be saved in the repenting. It is not enough to repent of dead works- as Judas did. That's not a saving faith.

Repentance must go together with faith in Christ and His completed work. Thus, any power in baptism is a work of God, not us.

First Peter 3:20 tells us that a few- eight persons- were saved from the flood by the ark. That is true in the context to which it applies. If one keeps reading the text says baptism is a figure like unto the flood. Once we understand what the archetype is, we can then see what scenario best fits the figure which points to that archetype. Let's read from First Peter:

For Christ also hath once suffered for sins, the just for the unjust, that he might bring us to God, being put to death in the flesh, but quickened by the Spirit:

By which also he went and preached unto the spirits in prison;

Which sometime were disobedient, when once the longsuffering of God waited in the days of Noah, while the ark was a preparing, wherein few, that is, eight souls were saved by water.

The like figure whereunto even baptism doth also now save us (not the putting away of the filth of the flesh, but the answer of a good conscience toward God,) by the resurrection of Jesus Christ:

The water of the flood points to baptism. It is not the water washing away the filth on us which saves us, but that we can undergo the judgements of a Holy God with a good conscience because our life is now in Christ. His judgements do wash away the filth in our lives, but we are not destroyed. We pass through the water which represents God's judgements and come out of the water in newness of life. When your church has a baptismal service, perhaps they too can say that "eight souls were saved through water." They don't mean that everyone else on earth suffered physical death. They mean those eight are truly alive.

Notice it says the eight in the ark were saved in the ark but through the water. That too is a little unclear because "through" can mean "passing through" or "by means of". Is it saying they were saved by means of the water, or by the ark through the water? The original King James is better here, because it says, "by water." It is saying that the water saved them who were in the ark. Though the translators have since tried to emphasize the "through" part while leaving out the sense of "through the means of" if you go look at the Greek and how the word translated "through" is used then it is clearly saying "through means of" or "by". They were saved by the water, in the ark.

If you have any doubt that the text of verse twenty is saying that they were saved "by" water, then simply keep reading to the next verse. The waters of the flood are considered a type of baptism, the waters of baptism being the archetype. Not that the water can save us in itself- without the protection of being in the ark it would have destroyed Noah, and without our protection of being in Christ the waters of God's judgement would also destroy us. In faith, we are giving God permission to judge our flesh so that the old man might be put to death, and the new man come in eternal life.

Recognizing that we are evil does not in itself save us. We need God to cleanse us of what is in us that is opposed to Him. That which is evil in us, we submit to God's judgement, in faith He will judge rightly. And of course, faith is a gift of God, not a work of man. All we can do without God is feel miserable about our sins. We cannot answer for them in ourselves, but as the verse above says, He is our answer.

What I have written above is a limited view of what baptism does. It is as far as one can take that passage without a proper view of early Genesis. Yet we know that baptism is not just about taking us as we are, but the beginning of that which is impure in us being washed away by the Holy Spirit. It is the typical start of sanctification. Yes, we are saved, but that which is impure in us dies. That in us which separates us from God is submitted to judgement and is put to death. We are saved to be new creatures, not just the old version of ourselves escaping God's wrath, but the beginning of being a New Creature in Christ.

This comparison does not work if just Noah and his family are the church and those destroyed are the unbelievers. The picture fails.

The picture which God painted with the flood, and baptism as the antitype of it, does not fit well with this misunderstanding. Baptism is not when unbelievers are submitted to judgement and are destroyed, but rather when what is sinful in God's people is subjected to judgement and destroyed. It is a purification of God's people, not those who are not His people. As it is written "judgement begins with the house of God." (1 Pet 4:17). The flood works better as a picture of baptism if the line of Adam does not represent all of humanity, but rather those who are supposed to be God's people. It is they who are "saved" by the flood putting to death that part of them which is ungodly and preserving that part which is in faith.

This also explains why, from the perspective of Shem, Ham, and Japheth, the destruction of the flood had to be seen as total. As an adherent of the tablet theory, I believe that the last part of chapter seven is describing what they saw in the flood. To them, the eradication was total. This is in contrast with scriptures before and afterward which indicate there were other people in the world, outside the clan of Adam, who survived the flood. But to them, the destruction was total.

In the same way, baptism is to be seen by the initiate as the total destruction and giving up of the sin nature- death to self. It is the Lord's people being purified in judgement, not those who are not His people. In practice the sin reappears, and the struggle continues, but ultimately the old man is dead and all that remains is in Christ, even as it seemed to the sons of Noah that all that remained was in the Ark.

By the way, this also answers the question of "why a flood". God told Noah "with thee I will establish (set up) my covenant" (Gen. 6:18). He was going to use these events to point to baptism so that no other means of wrath or of deliverance would do. Leaving the area wouldn't do. They had to pass through the judgement, not avoid it. Just like we stay and submit to the waters of baptism, not because they are global, and we cannot avoid them, but because we accept that they are just.

This is another reason why the flood had to be local or regional rather than world-wide. It fits the picture of baptism better if Noah could have avoided the judgement, but instead passed through it protected by God's grace. Verse twenty-one of First Peter tells us that the flood pointed to baptism. The covenant God made, to never "destroy" all flesh with a flood, was really about the covenant He would later make- the one which is associated with baptism. And that is not a washing which pertains to those who are not the LORD's people, but a washing which pertains to His people. Baptism does not destroy the unbelieving world, but the unbelief in us. It is a purification of that which is already His, not the destruction of those who are not His. Therefore, to fit the pattern, the deluge was also a purification of those who were already His, as the sons of Adam were meant to be.

Second Peter also references the flood in chapters two and three. This is to be expected because Peter was the apostle to the Jews (Gal. 2:8). The many references he makes to Jewish history clearly point to an audience which is expected to be immersed in that culture. He was writing to believers from a Jewish background, and his remarks should be interpreted in that context.

In chapter two he uses Jewish historical references to make the point that they should not follow false prophets as their ancestors did, but rather stay true to the revealed Christ. In chapter three he extends this warning to those who (though they knew what scripture said because of who they were) became scoffers who did not believe God would bring judgement. The flood is held out as evidence that He does balance the books and will again.

If one accepts the premise that the descendants of Adam were *Yahweh's* special handiwork amongst other people groups on the earth, then the picture of the flood being a judgement on the LORD's people fits the type of baptism much better than the Jewish view. Baptism is not God's judgement on unbelievers which causes them to perish. Rather, it is believers being preserved though God's judgement- not wholly preserved, for in it we recognize the justice of God's judgement on our sinful nature. There is a part of us we acknowledge should be put to death, but the faith part of us passes through the flood and is raised to newness of life in Christ.

This is yet another case of the church latching on to a Jewish view of early Genesis instead of re-interpreting it from a Christian perspective. The Christian perspective is that these events in Genesis were arranged to be a shadow and a picture of the reality which was to be revealed later in Christ. If we fail to understand that it is all pointing to Christ, then we fail to understand the context in which these events occur.

One's view of the flood should be connected to what is in the rest of scripture. It should be connected to what one believes that scripture says about, for example, whether one thinks that Adam was the first man in the sense of being the father of all mankind, or whether He was the first man in the sense in which Christ was the second man. And it should also be connected to what later scripture says of the deluge- that baptism is a reflection of the flood.

If you believe from prior chapters of Genesis that there were other people groups on earth, then it is understood that there were two realms which still exist side by side today- those who are the LORD's and those who are not. One's view of the covenant of Noah should also be connected to the scriptures which come later, specifically what First Peter says about baptism and the flood waters.

I find verse twenty in First Peter chapter three particularly intriguing because it mentions that Christ went and preached to the "spirits who were in prison" from the days when the Ark was being prepared. Why single out this particular group to give what amounts to a second chance? Maybe it was because He did not give them the same chance as was given other members of their clan the first time around. This is consistent with the idea that *Yahweh* had become so disgusted with His people that He basically quit pestering them for those last one hundred and twenty years. As Christ, who was tempted as we are but without sin, He learned just how hard it can be to be human.

Earlier (Gen. 6:6) the text said that the LORD was sorry that He ever made man (right after God noticed how evil they were in verse five). I had speculated by His absence from the account until a week before the flood that *Yahweh* had given up on them in embarrassment and disgust. One way to look at First Peter 3:20 is that Christ perhaps amends His earlier decision to quit contending with the sons of Adam while the ark was being constructed. To be more than fair, He went back and preached just to them- just to the ones He "quit on" in the generation before the flood.

Do not pretend that you would have done differently. I believe that whatever limitations resulted from taking the form of a Man, He must have known from the fall of Adam, if not before, that the only way to redeem the world was for Him to pay the price in His own Person. In such a situation, you would hope that they would at least have some faith in you, but that generation didn't.

If He knew that, then what was the purpose of His grooming them? He seemed very interested in for example, at least Israel having faith. My speculation: Many cultures have had human sacrifice. In some the sacrifice is dishonored, but in some they are highly honored. So, He would choose out a nation for Himself from the descendants of Noah, and groom them and be their God and protector. In return, it might be hoped that He would die as the honored King of the Nation doing what He must to save His people as they wept.

I say this for many reasons. For one, it would explain what He was doing in the guise of Melchizedek, King and Priest of Salem (later Jerusalem). Hebrews chapter seven gives a description of him which would fit *Yahweh* and no other. The Dead Sea Scrolls are not scripture, but I find it interesting that scroll 11Q13 says that Melchizedek is the God of Israel and he will atone for his own. It generally describes him as doing what Christianity says that Jesus did. Was *Yahweh* trying to set a pattern with Abraham about how He wished to be received upon incarnation?

Further, Deuteronomy 17:14-20 shows that provision is made in the Law of Moses for the people to set a king over them which He chooses but they set up. Yet Gideon says (Judges 8:3) that the LORD should rule over them. Later, in First Samuel 8:7 when they demand a king *Yahweh* tells Samuel that they have rejected *Him* from reigning over them. He wanted to be their King as was His right. If He had to live without sin yet die for the nation, then He might at least hope to prepare a nation which would honor His sacrifice. That sacrifice had to be made to redeem creation, but perhaps He hoped to avoid the shame (Hebrews 12:2).

We all know now that it did not go like that. The fickle mobs wanted a political savior, but not Him as King in their hearts. We didn't do anything to mitigate His suffering and about all we could do to make it worse. We did not meet Him halfway, or even a tenth of the way. He had to go all the way to save us while His own did everything imaginable to dishonor Him in collusion with the Gentiles.

Whatever He had hoped at this point, by the Prophets He knew better. He despised the shame (Hebrews 12:2) that He had to endure. The death was bad enough, but the hostility and contempt of those He was dying for, who butchered Him as if He were the lowest of sinners instead of the Great Lamb of God, was salt in those wounds.

After chapter nine the LORD is less to be found in the land below and more to be found in the land above. Before the flood, the text reads like the Sons of Adam could expect to see Him on a regular basis. After the flood, He will show up for an occasional visit with the patriarchs, but He is not found routinely walking among men, as He is shown doing prior to chapter six. I don't think it is a coincidence that the lifespans of the patriarchs begin to decrease dramatically after the flood. Less of the LORD in one's life means less life of every sort, for He is the Way, the Truth, and the Life.

The Table of Nations

There is more that could be said about the Table of Nations than I will say here. Perhaps that book is for another soul to write. My task is only to present the worldview, the cosmology, around these passages.

Prior to discussing the table of nations there is one verse upon which I should comment. In chapter nine, verse nineteen, the King James Version reads *"of these was the whole earth overspread."* This is speaking of the descendants of the three sons of Noah. The word "overspread" used at the end of the verse isn't a great translation. Some versions say that of these was the whole earth "populated." That is an even worse translation of the Hebrew word *na-pe-sah* (Strong's 5310 with a root of *naphats*). *Naphats* means "sunder, scatter, dash in pieces, or disperse."

Some versions do translate it "dispersed", which is at least within the allowable meaning of the root word. The word picture might refer to how the bits of something that has been shattered spread out over a large surface. Thus, it is saying that their descendants spread out over the whole earth. "Overspread" would be in that context. It does not mean populating or peopling in the sense that they constituted the whole of the human inhabitants. Just that they were all over the place.

There are other words which could have been used and were used to describe populating the land. The Hebrew word often translated "filling" (*maw-lay*, Strong's 5390) could have been used, as it is used so many other places to describe population growth (Gen 1:28, Exodus 1:7 et al). That this word, or any of the others, was not used here demonstrates that these verses are not describing a situation where Noah's family comprised 100% of the population on earth.

Rather I think the text indicates, both here and as we read on in Genesis, that the descendants of Noah dispersed- they spread out over the whole earth. An earth which had others in it. It seems they became the natural nobility of the surrounding peoples. They had all the advantages mentioned previously concerning the sons of Adam but were less likely to be so completely entangled in sin. Whereas the prior Adamic peoples may have been dominated by surrounding tribes, the descendants of Noah behaved more wisely.

As they lived their lives it would only be natural that they accumulated servants and hangers-on. Abraham, as a private citizen, was so powerful that the King of Gerar felt compelled to establish a peace treaty with him. Isaac grew even more powerful, so that the leaders of Gerar asked him to depart because his household was stronger than all of them put together! They were shunned, but not poor or powerless.

You may recall that Abraham was able to raise three hundred and eighteen fighting men on short notice, almost all from his own household. These were not his sons or his family. Rather that is just how many people attached themselves to him. These were not unmotivated slaves. These men enthusiastically identified with the house of Abraham. They defeated the armies of several city states! In the same way Esau gathered four hundred men with him for the showdown with Jacob.

If this was the drawing power of Abraham, and of Isaac, and even of Esau, imagine the force of attraction the nearer descendants of Noah had on the primitive peoples around them. By the time of Abraham, the knowledge of how to farm and the domestication of livestock were more widely disseminated. Not so in the day of these people. Can you imagine being a hunter-gatherer and coming into contact with people who had herds of "prey" animals willingly following along with them? People who, instead of foraging for berries, made all manner of fruits and vegetables rise out of the ground wherever they lived? For those who met the near descendants of Noah this must have seemed like an impartation of sacred knowledge which produced a better life.

Perhaps something like this had happened earlier in an even bigger way when the sons of Adam made contact with nearby peoples. The ancient inhabitants of Sumer said that they had been taught the arts of civilization "by the gods". Once you take Adam out of the "founder of humanity" role, he fits well with the figure "Adapa" son of the god Ea, (again, pronounced much like the shortened name of God in scripture, *Yah!*). Adapa was the first of the seven pre-flood Sumerian Demigod Sages called the Apkallu. A number of commonalities exist between the Seven Sages and Adam and his descendants. It is just one more example of how the Christ-centered model for Genesis explains so much.

But I digress. Let's get back to the Table of Nations. What I am suggesting is that most of those nations, established with a descendant of Noah at its head, were not necessarily wholly comprised of the direct descendants of Noah. They were largely composed of whatever people attached themselves to the heads of the extended households of the clans of Noah. These households in time became new nations.

The clans of Japheth mostly stayed to the north from the beginning as they journeyed "from the east." Notice verse five says the Japhethites divided "the isles of the Gentiles". Gentiles originally meant "foreigners"- folks previously outside of their circle. Surely this also indicates that there were other people around, and this clan of Noah wound up dividing their land. It seems that the clan of Japheth split from the other two clans and mostly did not settle Shinar. The "scattering" at Babel thus did not apply to them- they were already gone. Japheth stayed north and is associated with peoples across Turkey, between the Black and Caspian seas, and around the Aegean. The clans of Shem and Ham settled in the plain of Shinar.

It is interesting to note where those clans settled in Shinar. The clan of Cush, under Nimrod, held the center. A clue in the text indicates that the clans of Canaan were likely there with him, perhaps in a subsidiary role per Noah's curse (9:25).

It looks as though he assigned the clans of Shem the positions on his flanks. Asshur's clan went out of Shinar to found what became Assyria to the north. Elam (father of the Elamites) secured Nimrod's east. Arphaxad, father of the Chaldeans, took territory to his south, and Aram (father of the Arameans or Syrians) took that land to his west. It is as if the Semites were satellite states around the imperial center of Nimrod and the sons of Ham.

If Nimrod is associated with the Tower of Babel as tradition asserts, then the text implies that the first section of the chapter occurred before that time. He comes into the account in verse eight, so that section describes his beginnings. By verse eighteen it mentions what happened to the Canaanites "afterward", which I will connect to the Babel account. By verse twenty-five it says of Peleg "in his days was the earth divided." Whether this dividing is also a reference to Babel, or to the establishment of irrigation canals, then this fits well time-wise. We see that this chapter covers a long period of time, some before the events of Babel recorded in chapter eleven and some after it.

Verse eighteen says that "*afterward were the families of the Canaanites spread abroad*". But the word used for "spread" is just that Hebrew word which is translated as "scattered" in chapter eleven verses four, eight and nine. I therefore connect verse 10:18 to the following account of the Tower of Babel. In other words, what the men were afraid would happen (11:4,8,9) was that they would be scattered. This is just what the LORD did at Babel (11:8-9). He scattered them. The Canaanites got the worst of it, for they were "afterward spread (scattered) abroad."

Why did it single out the Canaanites? The clans of Japheth were already gone, and some of the clans of Shem were far enough away from the capital that they could endure it when the empire had a catastrophic event. It was those common folk closest to the imperial center which had to flee the greatest distance in the most disorganized manner when it suffered calamity. Many of those other clans had what could almost be described as a deliberate and orderly assigning of lands by comparison.

Regarding the assignment of lands, how does one describe such a process? An accurate description of this situation would be to say, as it does in the King James translation of verse 10:32, "by these were the nations divided." This is not to say that every person in all those nations was a direct descendant of the patriarch which formed that nation. Rather, the peoples were *divided up into nations* by them. These men became the founders of those nations in the sense that their households- those of their blood and otherwise- were forged into those nations.

At the end of this work, I will compose a brief anthropological epilogue. There I will focus on how the events described in early Genesis mesh with evidence from the natural universe with an emphasis on chapters nine through eleven.

The Tower of Babel

***

And the whole earth was of one language, and of one speech. And it came to pass, as they journeyed from the east, that they found a plain in the land of Shinar; and they dwelt there.

-Genesis 11:1&2

The original language in the verses above makes it unclear whether the clans of Noah journeyed *from* the east or if they moved east or were simply in the east relative to the narrator. Various translations reflect this ambiguity, but if we zoom out a bit the King James Version seems to have it right. The Septuagint says, "from the east" and the Jews who compiled it would have been most familiar with the nuances of the original Hebrew. Therefore, I read it that they came from the east and found a plain in the land of Shinar (which has long been identified with Mesopotamia).

That they had to journey to get Shinar tells us that those who believe the flood was regional *and* that Mesopotamia was ground zero for the flood can only have it half right. It is another hint that there was a more localized highland flood from which Mesopotamia took a glancing, though probably still enormous, blow. Vast amounts of sediments from the highlands likely wound up there, and this might be something to look for in finding evidence for the flood.

The Ark had landed on "the Mountains of Ararat". I have already mentioned that in antiquity "the Mountains of Ararat" were part of a large region corresponding to the ancient land of Urartu. This included what today is the region of Nakhichevan on the Iranian-Armenian border, and nearby is Lake Urmia. It is in the hills surrounding this area that I think the ark landed. If one begins there and journeys "from the east" and also south, one finds a plain "in the land of Shinar" -i.e. Mesopotamia.

In the Hebrew, the phrasing of the whole world being of one language is not the usual way to put it. It literally says everyone was of "one lip." Another word, which literally means "tongue", is the regular word for "language". I can speculate as to the reason for the alternate word use, but we just do not have enough to go on. Perhaps it means there was a common trade language even though different groups still spoke their own tongue as well. So, it was not everyone's native tongue, or the language in their heads, but they could all speak it with their lips as a *lingua franca*.

Greek once played this role for much of the world. Then Latin, and today English. Swahili plays a similar role in Africa. I would be cautious about claiming that the Bible teaches that there was only one language prior to the scattering at Babel for a couple of reasons. One of them is that the account does not even use the regular Hebrew word for language in verse one of this chapter.

An ancient Sumerian legend quotes a bit of an epic called "Enmerkar and the Lord of Aratta". Enmerkar was a King of Uruk, a very ancient Mesopotamian city ("Erech" in Genesis). According to David Rohl, he is the same figure as Nimrod in early Genesis. A section of this epic sounds very much like it is referring back to the events at Babel!

This legend is so old that scholars think that the knowledge of it was lost around 2,000 B.C. This baffles them, because it mentions things which could be understood to be a reference to a diffusion of languages as in the Babel account. The current scholarly consensus is that the Israelites picked up the story of the Tower of Babel during the Babylonian Captivity much later than 2,000 B.C. A more sensible view is that the Israelites always had the correct version of the story with them- their ancestors were from the same region and they preserved the same account from their perspective. Their descendants, the children of Israel, had the Genesis tablets.

In the epic Enmerkar is very keen on taking over the worship of the gods of other peoples and building them a new temple under his own control. There is a bit of a dispute as to exactly how the quoted epic should be translated. One way to translate it is that there is hope that the god Enki (called *Ea* by the Semitic Akkadians) is going to do the ambitious human kings and lords a favor and turn languages from many to one. The other way to translate it is that the gods have recently turned a single language into many, frustrating a human race that had conquered its environment and had no more fear of wild animals. Enmerkar then hopes that the god Enki would re-unite the tongues of men.

Regardless of which direction it went, the saga lists the lands which it considered "the universe" in which the alteration of tongues is at issue. The lands of Cubur, and Hamzi, Sumer, Akkad, and Martu are listed as the affected area. Some of these are obscure, but surely this indicates that the people of that time had a very parochial view of what constituted the "whole world".

This might inform us as to how to take the biblical text in chapter eleven, verse one where it says "*kal ha-eretz*" which is interpreted "the whole world" in the King James Version. The same phrase could be translated "all the land" or "the whole land". Rather than superimpose our global modern view of what this phrase means onto the text, maybe we should find out what their neighbors in time and space considered the "whole world" of their day to be and adjust our understanding of the text accordingly.

Who was Nimrod? Some favor Enmerkar, a Sumerian King who preceded Gilgamesh. I favor Etana the legendary Shepherd King of Kish (Cush?) who according to the Sumerian King's list "consolidated all the foreign lands". His reign, if he is an historical figure, was well before the time of Enmerkar. Some scholars place his reign after 2900 B.C. but that is only because there was a major flood in the region about that time, and Etana is considered by many to be the 13th king "after the flood" on the list.

That was hardly the only big flood in the region, just the first big one after narrative writing was common in Mesopotamia. The massive flood deposits at Ur excavated by Sir Leonard Woolley are sometimes said to be dated to around 3,500 B.C. But they had Late Ubaid period artifacts directly beneath them, which would indicate a date of about 4000 B.C. or maybe even older. This could be the "glancing blow" from the runoff of the highland flood I described earlier.

This age range fits well with my theory that the clans of Noah contributed to the period known as the "Uruk Expansion". Ultimately led by Etana who was the "first to be a mighty one". If so, what of the previous kings?

I doubt that Etana was even the thirteenth king because the name of the second king on the list (Kullassina-bel) means "all of them were Lord". It could indicate a period of oligarchy. The names afterward, until one gets to Etana, are Semitic names for animals and no names other than Etana's are attested to on any other list. Further, the period of the rule of "Kullassina-bel" (or "all of them were Lord") was said to be 960 years, which matches the longest reign of those ten names on the list prior to Etana. This isn't a Hebrew text. Those reigns were surely exaggerated or have been mistranslated, but regardless the two numbers are the same.

So, I think that many scholars are reading the list wrong. Those nine names were not sequential. There was a first ruler of Kish called "Jush-ur" or "Gusur". After that there was an oligarchy of men reigning concurrently. The reign of the longest-reigning member of the group (Kalibum) matches the total time of group rule (the time of "Kullassina-bel" when "all of them were Lord"). Then came Etana, (Nimrod if I am right) who according to the list "ascended into heaven and consolidated all the foreign lands." Nimrod was the first "to be a mighty man on the earth" after the flood, and so if Etana was historical, he would be the first to fit this description, not Enmerkar. In addition, Etana seems to be Semitic. He fits better as a descendant of Noah in a world where not everyone was.

But I get ahead of myself. Many readers may still be uncomfortable with the idea that others survived the flood. That there were other people in Shinar who were neighbors to the descendants of Noah and *not* solely his descendants, let us look at verse four of chapter eleven:

And they said, Go to, let us build us a city and a tower, whose top may reach unto heaven; and let us make us a name, lest we be scattered abroad upon the face of the whole earth.

Notice please that verse one says that the "whole earth" was of one language, but that they wanted to build a tower and "make a name for themselves" lest they be "scattered abroad" on the face of the "whole earth". So, they were not in the "whole earth" at that time, yet verse one said that the whole earth was speaking a common language! Who then was doing the speaking? Obviously, there were other people around.

The "whole earth" spoke the same language, but the families of Noah wanted to prevent themselves from being scattered abroad on the "whole earth." It seems to me then that the rest of the "whole earth" was inhabited by other people- people who spoke the same language. Nor does it make any sense to talk about the speech of "the whole earth" when your families are the only humans alive. This is another indication that the clans of Noah did not enter a barren uninhabited landscape when they found their plain in the land of Shinar. Maybe they had connections with those cultures from pre-flood times.

The fact that they wanted to "make a name" for themselves also shows that they were not the only people around. Why do you need to make a name for yourself if you are the only people in the world? Who else is there to impress? Why the concern about establishing the reputation of their family if it was the only family on earth? The text only makes sense if you see the descendants of Noah coming out of the mountains into existing human cultures- cultures which they had some previous knowledge of based on the lack of a language barrier. They wanted to stick together, and they wanted to be at the top of the heap rather than the bottom. And they had the means to do it.

Now I want to pause here and say a word about the tower. Many have suggested that the tower was a ziggurat. The date I am suggesting for these events, 3,100 B.C. to 3,000 B.C., is many years before the first true ziggurats which we know about. But the text does not say that they meant to build a ziggurat. It says they intended to build a tower. The same word is used numerous times in scripture, and it always means "tower." The precursors of ziggurats were huge single platforms/towers with temples on top, and those *were* in evidence around that time.

Many have tried to suggest that this ziggurat or that was the "basis for the legend" of the tower of Babel. These learned scholars seem to have a severe reading comprehension problem. The text does not even say they completed the tower or the city. They "left off" building the city and scattered. We should not expect to find the ruins of a finished city or the tower- for they were not completed in that time.

There is a caveat to the above. The most common ziggurat which is said to be the basis for the Tower of Babel is one built by Nebuchadnezzar II around the 6th century B.C. in Borsippa, which was a satellite city of Babel. But Nebuchadnezzar himself described what he did as *restoring* a temple which had been abandoned long before even his day! At the core of the ziggurat Nebuchadnezzar built were the ruins of a much older abandoned structure. This structure may have been on the site of the original Tower of Babel. Perhaps using some of the very same bricks whose baking was mentioned in Genesis chapter eleven. If this is so, there is one more ruler we must insert into the story.

There have been attempts to date this older structure, also called Ezida, Birs Nimrud, or the Temple of Nabu (son of Marduk). The archeologists involved found artifacts from the second millennium B.C. near this site and so proclaimed the structure to be from this period. Even this is not old enough to match my timeline. This structure is said to be the work of the famous King Hammurabi who built on this site around 1,740 B.C. Some sources claim he built a ziggurat with a temple there, but others that he *rebuilt* it. This ambiguity fits the idea of taking over incomplete ruins and making them into a complete edifice.

Under this hypothesis, the timeline would be like this; near 3,000 B.C. the original Tower of Babel is abandoned. Over one thousand years later Hammurabi decides to build a tower on the site of these ancient, and perhaps then-famous, ruins. He completes it as the temple of Marduk. His empire collapses after his death, and the temple falls into ruins. This is the temple site that the archeologists date to around 1,700 B.C. Over one thousand years later Nebuchadnezzar reconstitutes the Babylonian Empire. He wants to do what the greatest rulers of the original Babylonian empire did. So, he rebuilds the ancient ruins of Hammurabi, which were built on the incomplete ruins of the Tower of Babel. He then dedicates it to Nabu, the son of Marduk.

That is the most probable order of events as I see them. When the Jews of the Talmudic period said the ziggurat of Nebuchadnezzar was associated with the tower of Babel, they may have been right. It was built on the same site and was a "successor" of the original attempt to build a manmade tower to heaven. But modern scholars dismissed it as a tale because it came so late in history, from the period of the captivity.

Why professional archeologists of today have not connected these same dots and looked for evidence for an earlier structure on this site is puzzling. I can only say that for the last two hundred years a strange sort of modernism has overtaken the science of antiquities. The default position is to discount or even dismiss ancient writings, biblical and otherwise, unless and until they are confirmed with the spade.

This explains, for example, why it was up to a committed amateur, Frank Calvert, to discover the site of the ancient city of Troy simply by closely reading what Homer had written about its location! And if you will remember from our earlier chapter on the tablet theory, although professional archeologists were making the finds, it was up to their military attaché, P.J. Wiseman to connect them to the text of early Genesis. Unbelief seems to bring with it a sort of blindness of the mind.

There are other candidate sites for the tower as well. After all, the Hebrew word used for Babel refers to more than the city and its environs. It referred to the whole land or kingdom of Babylon. Other possible sites for the tower have been proposed, Kish, Eridu and Ur being foremost among them. We don't know for sure where it was, but it wasn't just a story concocted by the Jewish Priests during the Babylonian captivity. Rightly understood, the account ties well into history. I connect these events to the sudden end of the Uruk expansion around 3100 B.C. This is known to be a time when cities were abandoned and peoples in that region scattered.

But let's return to the account. The LORD went down to see what they were up to and did not like it a bit. When the LORD said in verse six that "nothing will be restrained from them", He was not concerned about their technological feats. I doubt the "tower" ever made it past two hundred feet tall. But the tower was an attempt to "reach heaven". They intended to put a temple atop it, as was done elsewhere. They wanted to start a religion of their own making. His concern was that they would supplant Him in favor of self-created religion. *This* was the lack of restraint He was concerned about, and frankly we still try to do this today.

Some traditions say that Nimrod wished to build a total empire; political, commercial, and religious. He is the prototype for all would-be totalitarian tyrants who dream of supplanting even God with their manmade state. The Beast and his Anti-Christ in the book of Revelation would be the archetype, but again I digress.

 The clan of Canaan was lightly esteemed in the existing order of things (9:25) and their character throughout scripture justified this appraisal. Who could Nimrod count on to help him cast off the faith of their fathers for a new religion in the service of the state? I believe that they were the core of the "toxic followers" which helped this toxic leader fuel his ambitions to rule humanity both body and soul. It is a pattern we have seen many times in the past and continues to this day. There is a longing for Messiah built into the human soul. Demagogues twist this God-given desire into something which exalts them as a worldly ruler. They try to put themselves in the place of Messiah in the hearts of the people.

It was true that this line, the line of Adam and Eve, was created for the very purpose of producing a Priest-King for the human race. Adam was not that One, but the line would still produce that king- Jesus Christ, the King of Kings, and the Lord of Lords. In Him there would be a Royal Priesthood and a Holy Nation (First Peter 2:9). But citizenship in this nation would not be determined by family lineage, but by faith in God. The gentiles would be grafted into the Kingdom of God (Romans 11).

In their desire to stick together and make a name for themselves, they were expressing a desire to do by their natural talents and gifts something that God wanted them to do by His Spirit. They wanted to be kings and priests in a religion and an empire of their own making. It is not that He did not want their descendants to rule the earth, but not like this and not their descendants only. Rather people from every tribe and tongue and nation would be included (Rev. 7:9-10). God had a plan to produce a collective Man, the Body of Christ, which was to include more than the physical descendants of Noah.

Moses was God's friend and chosen by Him to deliver Israel from oppression. Yet when (as a young man) he tried to do so in his own strength and in his own manner he failed completely. He was cast into exile and it was not until he was an old man that he got the call from God. It was a call to do in God's way the same thing that Moses had tried to do his own way many years before.

This is like the experience Moses had in Numbers chapter eleven. Prior to this (Exodus chapter seventeen), the LORD had commanded Moses to strike the rock at Horeb with his staff on the promise that if he did it would produce water for the thirsty and grumbling Israelites. In Numbers, once again the children of Israel were thirsty and grumbling. This time the LORD told Moses to speak to the rock and it would produce water. Moses instead again struck the rock with his staff. The LORD was angry with Moses and because of this act of disobedience it was decreed that he would never enter the Promised Land.

Why was the LORD so upset with Moses for what seems like a minor transgression? If the goal was to get the children of Israel water, then it worked. They got water, so why worry about the method? Well, if anybody should have known better it would have been Moses, that's one thing.

But the main thing is that the LORD was trying to form a picture pointing to Christ, and Moses ruined the picture. The Rock was Christ. Moses, representing Israel, in the first event struck the rock to get water, even as they struck Christ. The result was that Living Water (the Holy Spirit) was poured out. After that, Christ will come to those who call on Him. He will not be struck again, but men should rather appeal to Him and He will pour out the Holy Spirit. It was not just about getting the water. In his frustration, Moses messed up the shadow which pointed to the coming reality which cast that shadow.

So, this was not the way, nor the time, nor would these be the people, to fulfill God's plan for dominion over the earth. In verse three it says that they decided to use manmade "bricks for stone". Using manmade bricks for stone is symbolic of substituting human effort for God's design.

God has determined that His city will be built with stones, not bricks. In His city all His people are living stones (First Peter 2:5), with Christ as the Chief Cornerstone (Mat. 21:42). The Stone spoken of in Daniel 2:34 was cut without human hands. Man cannot accomplish God's will in his own way and strength. This is a lesson which even today has mostly gone unlearned and even when learned must often be relearned.

The sons of Adam wanted unity, but the LORD knew it would be best if they were scattered and mixed with the rest of mankind. God is trying to make a holy race, but not one centered on genetics. He did not need them to stay together and form a 'master race' or craft their own religion. He needed only one line to keep for Himself to produce a Messiah who was the heir of not just David, but Adam and Eve.

This line was preserved in the Israelites and even among them in the end only the tribe of Judah was required. Once Christ came however, it would be those who believe, Jew and Gentile alike, who would comprise this "Royal Priesthood" and "Holy Nation" (First Peter 2:9).

It is not ethnicity which defines this nation, but relationship to God. This nation is a family, not an ethnicity- and the members are adopted! The true people of God are of "one blood", but that blood is not the blood of

Adam, or the blood of Noah, or of Abraham, but the blood of Jesus! *In Him we live and move and have our being* (Acts 17:28).

When it says that their languages were "confounded" I find it to be an interesting choice of words. The root word in Hebrew there is "*balal*" (Strong's 1101). Its surface meaning is "anoint". The word picture is one of mixing oil into flour for a sacrifice. That is how it is used elsewhere- to describe mixing or mingling oil with wheat to make cakes. What this word does *not* indicate is that new languages were formed from the ether.

I think the heavenly agents speeded up a natural process. Here today in an America which has turned its back on God, I can't help but notice that our speech has also been "confounded". We are divided into groups who are more and more alien to one another. We can't talk to each other any- more as moral confusion leads to intellectual confusion and ultimately to confusion in all forms of human expression.

In mingling their speech, the effect was to scatter them and mingle them with the rest of mankind. Various clans of Semites and Hamites associated with those who spoke as they did. This spread the heritage and linage of Adam throughout the earth. In mixing Adam's line with the rest of the world the anointing of Adam's line was mixed in with them as well. Hence "*balal*" is the perfect word to use to describe what happened. One day it would be clear that the God of Noah's sons was the God of all the earth and that the people of all the earth are the people of Noah's God- if they choose it.

I want to emphasize that we should avoid attaching any spiritual signifi- cance to which people groups have more or less of Adam's ancestry. There is no difference in Christ between those who have the least share in Adam and those who have the most. Whatever separation or barrier there may have been from the dual lines of humanity has been broken down and made null in Christ. We are now one nation with equal access to God by faith. This is well attested to in a beautiful passage of scripture, Ephesians 2:11-19. I urge you to read that passage and marvel.

The Tower of Babel was not exactly "pointing" to something God would do in association with the coming of Christ and establishing the Kingdom of Heaven on earth. Rather at Pentecost in Acts chapter two the Holy Spirit undid what *Yahweh* did at Babel. At Babel, His chosen ones and those listening to them had their speech confused so that they could not understand one another. The intent was so that they would be scattered. At Pentecost, their speech was unconfused so that no matter what language the believers spoke, listeners from around the world heard each of them speaking in their own tongue. The gospel would thus be spread, not scattered.

Notice that what happened at Pentecost did not happen globally- but it had a global application. It happened to the believers, who were all together in one place, even as the rebellious descendants of Noah were in one place. At Pentecost, not everyone on the whole globe heard what the believers said, but people from around the world of the Roman Empire were there to hear it. This fits a lot better with a Tower of Babel model where the confusion of tongues was applied to descendants of Noah and those of the surrounding nations which were with them.

The people of God should no longer be consumed with establishing their own name, as they were at Babel. Instead, our proper task is to establish His name as King of Kings and Lord of Lords. The history books tell us that in the following centuries the gospel spread. The name of Christ spread, and His kingdom exceeded the greatness of the Roman Empire.

Though Rome founded the greatest and longest-lasting worldly Empire that humanity has ever known, it has long since been relegated to the pages of ancient history. Christ's Kingdom however, the Kingdom of Heaven above operating on earth, remains to this day.

Anthropological Epilogue

* * *

"There is something fascinating about science. One gets such wholesale returns of conjecture out of such a trifling investment of fact". – Mark Twain

I would like to end with some "science geek" stuff about human anthropology which speaks to what I have written. Though I do have a science background, please know that the science is not driving my theology. Indeed, while what this work says about creation and humanity is not in contradiction to what science knows, it is in contradiction to a few things which naturalism posing as science asserts. In its current state of degradation, that which is falsely called science holds Man to be nothing more than an ape with trousers, an accidental occurrence which evolved from lower life forms. Scripture, from the beginning, denies this.

Science is at present degraded in condition because it has become captured. Captured by the state operationally and captured by naturalism philosophically. Because it now relies so heavily on the former for funding, it tends to produce conclusions convenient to those in power.

Evolution- unguided evolution, not Divine Creation- is the scenario which gives the state moral permission to shape man without limits. Naturalistic evolution, not Divine Creation, is the scenario which gives the state moral permission to make human rights an ever-changing grant from itself to its subjects rather than a gift to every individual from their Creator- and therefore something to which even the mighty state should acquiesce. It is not surprising that a "science" establishment captured by an aggressively secular state will assert, dogmatically, that man evolved from lower forms and that by naturalistic means only.

Regarding the capture of science philosophically, naturalism is the philosophical position that the physical universe is all that there is and that all phenomena are the result of time, chance, energy, and matter colliding and re-colliding. This is what we see in postmodern science (which I consider a self-contradictory term). No room for consideration of anything we might now view as "supernatural" is permitted- not just in constituting experiments but even when one's "scientist" hat is off. It is a philosophical position which says that, if necessary, even the most unlikely naturalistic explanation must be accepted. And that no matter what the evidence might suggest, that even the most likely supernatural explanation must not be considered.

I feel that I should clarify the above because I don't want to be misunderstood. *Methodological* naturalism in conducting scientific experiments is understandable. That is, we can appreciate that the scientific method is a useful *tool* which is limited to testing for natural causes. It is designed to look for the laws of nature, not the Lawgiver who is beyond those laws. The scientific method is designed to discover truth about the natural universe, but it couldn't see God if God were standing right in front of it. The best it can say is "we have no verifiable naturalistic explanation for this, but we will keep looking."

That being the case, one should not be surprised that there is no "scientific proof for God" because, by definition, science cannot test for supernatural causes. It can only affirm or rule out natural ones. But the idea that "nature is all that there is" and that science is the only valid way to discover truth has become so ingrained in the thinking of many that they still demand "scientific" proof for God's supernatural action. One might as well demand supernatural proof that nature is all that there is! Such irrational demands seal the pseudo-seeker off from access to the truth of God, and I am convinced that this is what many of them want anyway. The appeal to science here is a ruse, a deliberate barrier erected from their heart to hide themselves from truth which they do not wish to see.

A man or woman should be bigger than the tools that they wield. That they use the scientific method to discover things about the natural universe should not compel them to believe "the natural universe is all that there is." They ought to be able to put down their tool, look beyond what it can show them and say, "It seems to me that this evidence points to God" even if the evidence is not strictly scientific. Not all truth is amenable to discovery via the scientific method.

The rejection of historical-legal evidence in favor of considering only "scientific" (testable, repeatable) evidence is a prime indicator of a mind which fails to rise beyond the tools which it uses. I have noticed of late a tendency by some to discount historical-legal evidence for God as "anecdotal" as if it were no more than a fifth-hand story without any other facts to support it. People cannot do that on other questions and decisions in their life, for one could hardly function in society by doing so. We rely on anecdotal evidence on a regular basis to make our decisions, and further we understand that for the person who observed it, the evidence was not anecdotal but empirical.

I would add that lumping together all testimonial evidence under the dismissive term "anecdotal" is dishonest. The account of George Washington chopping down the cherry tree is merely anecdotal. The accounts describing how he crossed the Delaware River to fight the Hessians are anecdotal *and* historical. The consequences of the testified-to action have reverberated through history and provide support that the "anecdote" is true.

Pretending that all "anecdotal" evidence should be ranked with the least-trustworthy type from the category is dishonest. The attempt to demean history and consider only evidence from a god who will do lab tricks for them on demand is something I consider to be a contemptible evasion. But it is one which the Creator allows men to get away with for the entirety of their lives on this earth should they so choose it.

All that said, the scientific method does have something to say about evaluating religious claims regarding the natural universe. It may not be able to detect supernatural causes, but it can evaluate claims of natural effects. For example, some have claimed that the universe is only six thousand years old, or that there was a global flood in historical times. Such claims can be tested scientifically with a reasonable degree of certainty. Nature can signal us when we have gotten what scripture says about the natural universe very wrong. This can induce us to take another look at the text and see if we haven't missed something.

So, I think science could have some role in either confirming or undermining some of the theological claims in this book. But because of the captured state of science, I will probably not live long enough to see the anthropological implications of what follows in this chapter tested in a vigorous scientific manner. Those implications are apt to produce questions which present science, attenuated in scope by government and philosophical shackles, is not permitted to ask.

That is a pity. If I am right about what I am saying, it should have effects which are measurable in the world. That is, it may to some extent be tested scientifically, if science were not captured operationally by the state and philosophically by naturalism.

The current scientific view of mankind is that around 200,000 or even more years ago, certain hominins split off from other hominins and became *Homo sapiens*. I know that young earth creationists will consider this date absurdly ancient, but even this age was uncomfortably recent for evolutionists of a prior generation. For a long time, they sought evidence for a "regional model" of human origins whereby the various races of mankind sort of "evolved in place" around the globe over a much longer period. The genetic evidence for a true regional model simply was not there, and so the focus became finding an "Out of Africa" model for human origins that was as far back in the past as possible.

The genetic story of man as told by most of today's scientists says that humanity split into two categories early on- certain African groups which included today's San (once known pejoratively as Bushmen) and Pygmies, along with a few rare West African populations on the one part, and everyone else in Africa on the other. Another event which occurred was that some small subset of that "everyone else" found its way out of Africa and became the human inhabitants of the rest of the globe.

Note that I am using the term "human" here to refer only to our species, *Homo sapiens*. I still treat the two terms as synonyms, as was originally the case. Once fossils of other hominins were discovered, the naturalist side started calling them all "human" or "a type of human". This decision was not based on science but on philosophy.

Since nature is all there is, they reasoned that there was nothing special about our kind. Therefore, they bestowed the "human" label on most of the big-brained, tool-making hominids. In contrast to this, the ancients had a category of things like us, interested in us, and yet not us. For the Greeks they were called satyrs. In other cultures, they had other names. This category has been diminished. I see the move to diminish it as a philosophical, not a scientific, decision. One based on naturalist assumptions that there is nothing special, certainly not Divine, about man.

I am of the view that these hominins from 100,000+ years ago, even those classified as "archaic homo sapiens", were very different creatures than you or I. If we met one, I doubt we'd have much to say to one another, if in fact they were capable of speech. I'm tempted to let them have the term "human" and start using "Adamics" to refer to our ancestors as a distinct population apart from even Archaic Homo Sapiens.

During all but the last perhaps thirty or forty thousand years the total effective population size of humanity over the entire globe has been estimated to have been absurdly small- from two to ten thousand persons. Note that an actual population can be a lot larger than a "effective population" size if we are talking about a genetically similar group, but it would still be a very small number compared to the human population in historical times.

So then, the current state of anthropological genetic research is basically saying that our race spent *at least* the first three-quarters of its entire history near the edge of extinction. It further claims that the San/Pygmy/ selected West African group of humans bounced around Africa with the other Africans for 60,000 years without significant admixture with them until more recent times (I will deal with possible admixture with other hominins shortly).

Does either claim sound likely to you? If one is broad-minded enough to consider that the hand of God intervened on this earth in the creation of Man, then other possibilities present themselves which explain the same facts. For example, if the initial human population was created more recently with some genetic diversity from the start, then this would affect the calculations when considering the age of humanity. They would "look" older genetically than they were because they did not start as clones of one another. They started with more diversity. Perhaps we didn't spend 200,000 years on the edge of extinction- those hominins who did fell off.

This could be so whether the broader human race created in chapter one was created *de novo* in the manner of Adam, or if God took some set of existing creatures and by a Divine Act made them into something more and different than what they were. Though Genesis chapter two is explicit about the formation of Adam, chapter one does not give us enough detail about the creation of the host of humanity to know just how it was done. The one thing it makes clear is that it was God's doing and not the work of nature.

Ironically this turns on their head arguments against a recent Adam and Eve based on the amount of human genetic diversity being too great to come from a single couple. Humanity didn't come from a single couple. "Humanity" is older than six thousand years, but it can still be younger than indicated by tests of genetic diversity which assume all humans came from a single couple or small genetically homogeneous group. If we started as a more diverse group rather than a single couple, then the "Most Recent Common Ancestor" dates are meaningless. They are estimates of the date of an event which never occurred.

The trouble is that this is going to be very difficult to find because scientists tend to arrange the assumptions in their data to match what they think they know. They may assume a certain ancient population size, or mutation rate, because it gives them answers which "fit" their model. Still, if one asked the right questions, one could expect anomalies in the data to present themselves.

We might, for example, expect to find that the most ancient samples of human DNA are more differentiated than present theory would predict because not all the genetic differences were the result of mutations over time. Some of the differences were simply present in the initial set of humans. Unless one automatically rejects supernatural explanations as non-parsimonious, this could even be a more parsimonious (if not strictly scientific) explanation for the genetic differences we see than present theory.

For example, there appears to be no more genetic distance between a Kenyan and an Englishman than there is between that same Kenyan and a Pygmy living in a forest nearby. How to explain this? The current answer is that there were populations of humans wandering around Africa for 60,000 years basically without admixture with each other until more recently. My hypothesis is that they were created with some amount of diversity to begin with. What we see as a divergence of various human groups might be a situation where they were somewhat diverse to begin with.

So scarce and murky is the evidence for the origin of humanity, and so subject to assumptions and interpretations is that evidence, that we may never have a conclusive answer about those events. In that sense what I am suggesting (and the presently most accepted hypothesis for that matter) are not strictly testable to a high degree of confidence. I have no scriptural evidence that the first people were genetically diverse anyway and Acts chapter seventeen hints that they were somewhat similar. Still, not nearly so similar as we might expect in a scenario where humanity sprang from a single couple in which the female was in effect "cloned" from the male!

There is another issue I should address before I move on to discuss Adam. That is the possibility that in the early days of humanity our species mixed in a small way with some of the "others" that shared the earth with them at that time. For example, there is a claim that all Eurasians have some Neanderthal ancestry. My own DNA test showed a rather typical 1.5%. A subset of East Asians also show some genetic legacy attributed to a Neanderthal-like population called "Denisovans".

The "Out of Africa" theory for humanity that I described earlier therefore has a caveat. It is that when those early humans came out of Africa, they found other hominins already there and there was a limited amount of introgression of their genes into the Out of Africa group. Now if this is so (and I will discuss that subject shortly) one might at first glance consider that the matter is settled. One might think that these other hominins *must* be human since to some extent they could successfully produce viable offspring with our ancestors.

If one thinks about it a little more though, it is easy to see that this is not necessarily the case. Lions and tigers are very different kinds of big cats, with social and behavioral impulses which are even more varied than their physical differences. No one would say that they are the same. Yet they can produce offspring that are viable although with reduced fertility. As can lions and leopards which are even more different. It is as though nature reluctantly lets the mixture through and then slowly goes to work rectifying the mistake via fertility issues.

In the same way, the evidence suggests that any hominin hybrids had fertility issues and that nature has been at work slowly purging many if not most of the foreign genes from our kind. For example, the Y-chromosome, inherited from fathers to sons, shows a dearth of such hybrid genes. This indicates that if such admixture happened, the male offspring of such unions had fertility issues, just as is the case with lion-tiger crosses. Further mtDNA, inherited from mothers, also lacks a contribution from Neanderthals or Denisovans. Plus, the overall amount of Neanderthal-like DNA in modern people is less than that found in populations tens of thousands of years old. Again, it is as if nature is purging a mistake. That's not a ringing endorsement of the idea that they were the same as us.

As I have mentioned, it seems that "science" journalism is pushing the idea that Neanderthals were very much like us based on the flimsiest of evidence. For example, some cave art discovered in the Maltravieso and La Pasiega caves in Spain was recently dated to be over 60,000 years old by D.

L. Hoffman *et al.* Since *Homo sapiens* wasn't thought to be in Spain that long ago, many scientists rushed to the conclusion that the art was produced by Neanderthals. But dating cave art is very difficult. The great majority of it hasn't even been dated. Further, other tests for dating came up with much younger ages for the cave art. It is also suspicious that Neanderthals were around for the next 20,000 years or so and there is no subsequent evidence of their producing such art.

But it gets worse. Some of the art in the caves is of a shadow-handprint. This is where someone puts their hand on a rock and blows paint from a reed all around it, leaving the shape of their hand as a shadow surrounded by paint. Not only is this a typical pattern of cave art unquestionably produced by *Homo sapiens* twenty thousand years later, but the handprints look like those of modern humans. Neanderthals have huge distal phalanxes (the bones on the fingertips), basically double or triple the size of ours. The bones that form palms are thick in Neanderthals but greatly reduced in length- they had very short palms. The fingertips in this cave art show no hint of enlarged distal phalanxes, and no reduced palm length, indicating that they were produced by *Homo sapiens*.

If all that wasn't enough to show how modern "science" is willing to torture the evidence to advance the idea that Neanderthals were very much like us, there is more. One of the caves has a very complex piece of art in it that looks like something called a "Spanish Tectiform". That is one of the same thirty-two symbols that *Homo sapiens* used in their cave art for 30,000 years! It is outrageous to think that any serious scientist would press the claim that Neanderthals from 66,000 years ago painted a form which was then adopted by humans who came along 20,000 years later while subsequent Neanderthals never made anything remotely like it. They have either misdated the cave art, which is easy to do, or *Homo sapiens* came to Spain earlier than they think.

Despite all that, the "science" media keeps proclaiming this as evidence that "Neanderthals made art". In truth, there was a "big bang" in human art around 36,000-46,000 years ago. The earlier examples of things held up as "art" are things like simple crosshatch patterns. Outside of perhaps

Blombos cave, "art" before 46,000 years ago pales in comparison to that produced after that time. And it doesn't really "evolve" much after that either. As I mentioned before, humans used the same thirty-two cave-art symbols for over 30,000 years! When Pablo Picasso emerged from seeing the cave art in Lascaux, he is said to have exclaimed "We have learned nothing in twelve thousand years!"

Humans are artists by nature. Not so other hominins. And remember I say this as someone who believes that the true difference that makes us human is not the ability to produce art, though art may be an outward manifestation of the true difference. The difference is spiritual. We were created to connect with one another and our Maker- we were designed to fellowship deeply. And yes, we were designed to worship. We were made "religious" and we were made for love's sake.

The genetic evidence is much harder to parse, but if there is an agenda biasing the issue of hominins and art it is reasonable to think there are other explanations for the genetic evidence as well. I question the claims of large-scale or even moderate-scale hominin introgression. I think an honest look at the evidence will show that there is no case to be made that living humans have genes from introgression from other members of the genus *Homo*.

The April 8th, 2019 edition of *Human Biology* published a study from two University of Tel Aviv professors; Prof. Ran Barkai and Meidad Kislev. The study demonstrated that two large ancient mammals which were cold-adapted had similar genetic mutations. The same genes were mutated in the same way, but this wasn't because they intermixed. The mammals were Neanderthals and Woolly Mammoths. The reason they had similar genetic mutations was because they lived in the same environment and had similar adaptations. Similar environment was driving similar adaptations, not interbreeding. I don't see why that should not go double for Neanderthals and the *Homo sapiens* who shared environments with them.

Viruses and other pathogens also drive adaptive evolution. That is, maybe some genetic regions are the same because both populations, *Homo sapiens* in Eurasia and Neanderthals, were exposed to the same immune system threats. Populations in Africa were driven a different direction by a different set of environmental threats. That's not even counting horizontal gene transfer which can occur in viral infections. The humans in Eurasia were exposed to the same pathogens as the Neanderthals in Eurasia, while the Africans were exposed to different ones.

A Cambridge Zoology professor named William Amos has another idea which indicates all or almost all the alleged Neanderthal introgression is an illusion. According to his 2017 paper the small group of humans which left Africa in the Out of Africa model were closely related to each other, and thus had very similar genes. During reproduction genes which are very similar tend to have a much lower mutation rate than genes which are heterozygous.

In other words, the increased diversity of the African population caused them to mutate faster, *away* from a small percentage of Neanderthal-like genes which were also shared by some early humans from the start. It wasn't that the Eurasians got genes that were more Neanderthal-like due to admixing, it was that the African population got *less* Neanderthal-like over time because their greater genetic diversity produced a higher number of mutations. They diverged further away from Neanderthals than Eurasians did.

This idea could have implications for the current consensus that Africans have more genetic diversity because humankind was in Africa a very long time before some of us left. Maybe they were more diverse from the start and that initial difference produced more mutations and more diversity, creating a genetic appearance of age.

Of course, all these folks assume that humans evolved from a common ancestor with chimpanzees. The tests that claim Neanderthal (and Denisovan) introgression are based on a statistical analysis. They look for gene alleles which are the same in chimps and sub-Saharan Africans but different in the same way in Neanderthals and *Homo sapiens* in Eurasia. Then they *assume* the reason for this was admixture.

Professor Amos points out that genes which mutate more often tend to "back-mutate" more often too. He thinks that the pattern they are testing for is better explained by Neanderthals and some early humans sharing the same mutations from the start, but that these were lost in the African population which reverted to a signature more like that of the alleged "ancestral" chimp allele.

I don't agree with all the evolutionary assumptions, but I do agree that many of the genes we supposedly inherited from Neanderthals are less fit than the versions shared by Chimps, sub-Saharan Africans, and some Eurasians. But I don't think that we got these less-fit versions from interbreeding. Eurasians started with a small population with low genetic variation and such populations are bad at getting rid of slightly worse versions of genes. They don't "purge" less-fit types as well. The larger and more diverse population in sub-Saharan Africa could have purged less-fit genes better. The few examples of helpful "Neanderthal" alleles typically involve the immune system. But if a version of a gene is very helpful against disease, then one doesn't need introgression to explain how it spread- natural selection will do.

In short, I agree with Dr. Amos. While there may have been some interbreeding, it left no meaningful genetic legacy in humanity. I say this as someone who doesn't see it as a theological problem even if they did. Any hybrids would presumably "choose" which direction they would go, humanity or not, and their descendants would follow whichever course they went. But I explain this because it is wielded like a sword against creationists from time to time and because it is a good example of how "what everyone now knows is true" is not necessarily true at all. And it may one day be exposed as false, if men like Professor Amos are not shouted down or dismissed by a mob in the name of "scientific consensus".

Maybe this sort of backlash is why another anthropologist with another controversial idea will not even use his real name to talk about it. Someone with the *nom de guerre* "Dienekes Pontikos" has suggested a hyper-introgression scenario, just the opposite of what Amos is suggesting. In his scenario a population he calls "Afrasians" represent a group of humans which started somewhere between east Africa and India around 55,000 years ago. This group included what the mainstream view calls the "Out of Africa" humans which expanded into all of Eurasia, according to most getting a limited genetic contribution from hominins such as Neanderthals and Denisovans along the way.

But Dienekes says that before it got that limited contribution it back-migrated into most of Africa too, where it met another population which he dubs "Paleoafricans". Paleoafricans represent a group which is older and more archaic than the Afrasian group, or a splinter of the Afrasian group which interbred with a more archaic hominin population. Modern Sub-Saharan Africans in his hypothesis are a combination of Afrasians and Paleoafricans. East Africans would be almost all Afrasian, while most of Sub-Sahara Africa is a mixture. San, Pygmies, and certain rare West African groups would be more Paleoafrican. The reason those latter groups look so much older than the Afrasians may be, in his view, because they have a significant contribution from hominins which were a separate population of an as-yet unknown type which was even closer to us genetically than Neanderthals.

It is a controversial idea. And it means that what we think of as greater human diversity in Africans is really the result of greater admixture (on the order of 8-10%) with something not quite like the rest of us but also not so different than us. Perhaps some of these "Archaic Homo sapiens" fossils we occasionally find would represent this unknown population.

Dienekes can point to some evidence for his (or her) scenario. Y-Haplogroup "E" is the most common in sub-Saharan Africa, but there is a case to be made that it originally came from Eurasia and went into Africa. There is also evidence to suggest that there was an earlier human population in Eurasia. In other words, *Homo sapiens* didn't first leave Africa 60,000 years ago. Perhaps they were already outside Africa- either because another group (besides the main "OOA" group) left Africa earlier or because there were some *Homo sapiens* outside Africa from the start which did not survive. Occasionally in some isolated populations in New Guinea scientists detect an odd genetic signal which could be a trace of this earlier group which otherwise went extinct or was absorbed by the OOA group.

The Hofmeyr skull from South Africa bolsters some aspects of Dienekies' speculations, though it could also be interpreted in other ways. The skull has been dated to around 36,000 years old. It is more rugged and robust than most human skulls today but still said to be within the modern range. The inhabitants of the region today are the Khoisan, who are also among the most genetically diverse and supposedly ancient human group. One might think then that the skull would look much like theirs. It doesn't. Instead, it looks very much like the skulls found in Europe from the same period. This indicates there was a single global human population around that time, which later diversified into our current assortment of human types.

Even though there are ancient finds classified as "*Homo Sapiens*" there are still subtle changes in brain shape that make them different from us. Our globular brain shape is a pretty modern occurrence. Not only did Neanderthals not have it, a lot of the older finds labeled "Archaic Homo sapiens" didn't have it either.

Dr. William Amos and Dienekes say the exact opposite thing on admixture among *Sapiens* and other hominins. Amos seems to me to have the stronger argument on that issue. I suspect that the same methods he uses to debunk Neanderthal introgression in Eurasians could also be applied to show that the so-called "Paleoafrican" signal is just an artifact of long-isolated human populations. But Dienekes has other strong points. Y-Haplogroup "E" could well be a migration into Africa instead of something which started there. There could have been a single Afro-Eurasian population of humans around 36,000 years ago. Perhaps mankind did not really start in Africa but instead mostly survived there. Dr. Amos could still be right about the lower diversity creating false signals of admixture.

False signals abound. I have been throwing out the mainstream numbers for these dates, but these are not facts. They are calculations based on assumptions which they hope are correct. They don't know if the mutation rates they are using to calculate the times to "most recent common ancestor" (MRCA) really apply well to the ancient populations that they study. That is a value that could drive dating in either direction, but another variable- so-called "back mutations"- would only drive dating in one direction. That would be to make these times to MRCA look older than they really are. And looking at these studies, I don't see where anyone except Amos is adequately factoring that in. This is especially true regarding Y-haplogroup and mtDNA MRCA dating.

Indeed, an intriguing study from Andrew G. Clark *et al* published in *Molecular Biology and Evolution, Volume 38, Issue 3, March 2021, Pages 1000–1005,* entitled *Mutation Rate Variability across Human Y-Chromosome Haplogroups* strongly implies we have much of our timescale wrong. They found that Y-haplogroups don't mutate at the same rate. The groups we deem older have higher mutation rates than those we deem younger. And since the number of mutations is the basis that was used to determine their age, this would mean that the "oldest" groups aren't really that much older than the younger ones, they just look it because they mutate faster. They didn't test the supposedly oldest "A" groups, but who knows what we will find when we do? Maybe they will discover, as I suspect, that the "A" groups aren't really their own thing, but simply represent rare deletion events from something like a "BT" founder where what was deleted included the marker for Y-haplogroup "B".

The conclusion of all of this is that it is OK if we don't know exactly how all of this happened, because, contrary to the façade they put in place, the naturalists don't know either. There are a tremendous number of things that they claim to "know" about human origins that probably aren't true. There are many "facts" they rely on which are not really facts. As we continue looking into these mysteries, I advise scientists who are believers not to neglect to look for the hand of God in human origins. If not as scientists, at least as people.

Before I move on to the dawn of historical times, the existence of near-human hominids is sure to draw a demand from naturalists for answers from the believer. Though they are far from having sure answers on so many questions, they may demand of us to know what God's point was in even having all these hominids. Especially ones that were close enough to mix their blood with us, even if it left no lasting genetic legacy- if such was really the case. We cannot know this for sure, because scripture doesn't say why. We can only speculate, as *they* so often do, and hold only loosely to whatever ideas we might have.

That said, it does occur to me that in the Christ-centered model the second person of the Trinity, the Logos who was the Godhead's Agent in ordering all of creation, changes form just before the creation of mankind. He assumes the form of the Heavenly Man. And in this change of form some aspects of his being change (but not His nature or substance- the qualities of His character). Things such as omnipresence, and even omniscience, may have been temporarily set aside. We discussed that at length earlier for reasons having to do with theology. So, without giving up His Divine character, He became Man in heaven, and then created man on earth.

But if this were the case, wouldn't it be reasonable to think that He, the Logos, would want to make a template close to what He had in mind before His translation? Say that you knew you were about to voluntarily and temporarily enter a state in which your ability and knowledge were restricted. And this right before you did a final, critical, engineering job. Wouldn't you want to set things up so that most of the task was complete and templates as close as possible to what you had in mind were available?

Perhaps He arranged things so that most of the physical, though not the spiritual, work was done in advance. It is not really a question which needs to be answered, but this model has a better answer for it than any other model of creation which I have seen. And it centers on what was happening to Christ. He lowered Himself to assume our form, for our sakes- though not as He would later in the Incarnation.

Let me move on then to Adam, a man for which some trace might be found in the natural world. When I suggest that Adam and his tribe introduced or re-introduced lost knowledge into the world, I am making a claim which can be tested against the evidence. We can compare these claims to when and where things such as farming, writing, domestication of plants and animals, pastoral shepherding, and metallurgical advances appeared or accelerated in the world. We can compare the places and times for which those things arose to that which I propose for Adam and Noah.

We can interpret evidence from historical finds and compare it to biblical claims. Our earliest dates for Adam put him in position to have been the impetus for the "Pre-pottery Neolithic A", and dates for Adam near the middle of the range could make him the epicenter of "Pre-pottery Neo-lithic B". Though called "Pre-pottery" they didn't lack pots, they ground beautiful and durable ones from stone. The timing of advances in metallurgy and the development nomadic pastoralism are other claims in the text which can be evaluated.

Another example, the ruins of Gobekli Tepe *et al*, appear to me to be an attempt to retell the story of "the man" in the Garden of Eden. The "stage" on which this is played out was constructed multiple times. It consisted of a long narrow entrance into a circle walled off from the rest of the world by stone- just as some suggested sites for the garden are walled off from the rest of the world by mountains. The Hebrew word for "garden" in Genesis chapter two has connotations of being an enclosed garden- as in one that is fenced or walled off. This fits with what we see at Gobekli Tepe.

The circle is ringed by stone pillars each of which have a rectangular block on top of them. Elaborate figures of birds and animals are carved into the rocks. At the center of each "stage" are two pillars, also topped with rectangles, which are larger than those which surround the edifice.

If those pillars represent trees, it is not hard to see that this is an effort to make a stage from which to tell the story of the Garden of Eden and the fall of Adam. The two large pillars in the center of each stage would represent the Tree of Life and the Tree of the Knowledge of Good and Evil which scripture says were "in the middle of the garden". They may have also been personified as beings- choosing to trust in God or in Man himself.

The long narrow passageways to the stage might represent that the Garden was accessed through a narrow mountain pass, or even a portal, or connection between this world and the next. The animals carved on the pillars represent those which *Yahweh* had the man name before springing his true helper, Eve, upon him. That so many versions of this were built could indicate that at some point they closed off access deliberately, just as access to the garden was cut off. They then built another structure to re-enact the story for the next generation.

The oldest of the temples is estimated by many to have been constructed around eleven thousand years ago. While this is within the early range of our proposed early date for Adam, I am intrigued by the work of Dr. Dimitrios S. Dendrinos. He makes a strong case that the methodology used to determine this date is flawed, and that the ceremonial megaliths at Gobekli Tepe are thousands of years younger than the ages claimed in sensationalist headlines. If so, this would put these structures more in the middle of our range of dates for Adam.

Terrible things happened at that site. I am not saying that the builders understood the true religion. But they went to a lot of trouble to build it, as if something had happened to them and it was important for them to understand what it was and why it happened. After the fall of the man, humanity lost its innocence. After that the Holy Spirit pricked the conscience of men to say, "this is sin." This didn't make them better, but it made them more aware of their lack of goodness.

Indeed, I have phrased it that they used the site to "re-tell the story", but they may have even been trying to "re-do" the story, with a better ending. If they were just telling the story, why bury the stage and build a new one? But if they were trying to redo the story then it makes sense that when they found one attempt didn't work that they would scrap the whole platform and try again. They might be even more inclined to start over with a new stage if the stand-in for Adam was sacrificed at the end of the performance to appease God and get Him to reverse their condition.

Perhaps this was some mangling of the original prophecy of the Seed in Genesis 3:15. Suppose Adam tried to share the good news that one day a stand-in from Eve would die to take away the consequences of what he had done, and the locals took that to mean that they should make it happen themselves with a seed of their choosing? No wonder Cain was worried! No wonder they left Eden in the opposite direction!

Conversely, these sites could represent the efforts of the men under the Genesis chapter one system to make sense of things. A degraded form of religion. The appearance of Adam's family and the LORD in their area could have brought about a rival of sorts, and in response they buried the temples which they had raised up in their former ignorance. Some of this depends on when Adam appeared and the true date of these structures.

There is one last hypothesis I would like to suggest by way of showing that the events of early Genesis could have left material traces in our world. Acts of history often cannot be confirmed by the scientific method, but we can look for evidence to support what can be confirmed with science so long as it is not artificially constrained by naturalism. This has to do with the exciting and fairly new field of anthropological genetics. If Adam and Eve were formed separately from the rest of humanity, then perhaps they had a genetic signature which was anomalous in some way. This signature could be detectable in the DNA of humans, past and present.

There are at least two candidate groups for such a genetic signature. One has been given the moniker "Basal Eurasians" by anthropologist Iosif Lazaridis. This is a "ghost population" which is not found in pure form, but is often found genetically mixed with other groups, such as the "Early European Farmers" who came from Anatolia (modern day Turkey). Genetic traces from Basal Eurasians are also found in early northern Iranian farming populations, and early farmers in the Levant.

Basal Eurasian can be described as a population which was "African like" but not sub-Saharan African. Genetically, it looks like the first group of humans to leave Africa had one small group which stayed off to themselves for tens of thousands of years. Meanwhile East Asians were splitting off from West Eurasians. Basal Eurasians are not any more closely related to any Eurasian group than they are the next, and they are also intermediate between all of them and the African genes from which Eurasians are said to have come.

What I have written about Basal Eurasian also applies to another genetic signal which Lazaridis has named "Deep". "Deep" looks even more basal than Basal Eurasian. As of this writing, "Deep" may be an even better candidate for a genetic signature for Adam than Basal Eurasian, though the two have much in common and may be hard to tease apart. A recent find from Dzudzuana Cave detected a Basal Eurasian signature from 26,000 years ago. If this is correct then that is too long ago to be a candidate for Adam's signature under our model, meaning that the "Deep" signature would be the best candidate.

These genetic profiles seem to show up weakly but fairly early (still less than 12,000 years ago) in some members of a group called the Natufians. These were the first known group to live a sedentary lifestyle due to the naturally plentiful region in which they lived. This was in what is now Israel which presently has a much harsher climate. They were not true agriculturalists, but their harvesting of abundant natural wild grains produced a similar way of living. If sedentary living had produced any genetic changes favorable to civilizing man, then *Yahweh* may have used those genes in forming Adam.

The Basal Eurasian/"Deep" genetics which show up *earliest* in Dzudzuana Cave and some Natufian remains in Israel show up *strongest* and most completely thousands of years later just east of our proposed locations for Eden. So, for example the finds from Dzudzuana might have 28% Basal Eurasian (and no "Deep") and the rest from hunter-gatherers. But a find from Northeast Iran was over 60% Basal Eurasian or "Deep" and had the highest "Deep" signature of any find in the Near East. You must go far into Africa to find a signature with as strong a signal.

The signal from Basal and "Deep" is from a mystery population that "looked" SSA in some of their genes but is in the wrong place and time for that to be the source and doesn't "fit" for other subtle genetic reasons. In other words, groups which came "Out of Africa" and stayed to themselves, or in the case of Adam, was formed *de novo* much later.

Another odd thing about them is that, unlike all other Eurasians, Basal Eurasian and "Deep" genes seem to have no genetic signature attributed to sub-humans such as Neanderthal man. As we discussed, Eurasians and North Africans seem to have some Neanderthal-like genes, even if they are not in fact from Neanderthals but rather an artifact of a failure to purge certain mutations. But to the degree that they are Basal Eurasian or "Deep" they don't have that signal. It is as if somehow these two groups missed all of that. Indeed, they did not admix with anyone for all those tens of thousands of years until they show up on a zone centered in Armenia and from there mixed with the three previously mentioned and widely disparate groups that were the world's first true farmers.

So, we have two genetic profiles that have a lot in common, which pop up in the same region and both are heavily associated with the emergence of farming. A possible scenario is that God made Adam with a genetic profile suitable for a domestic lifestyle and placed him in the region where at least some of his neighbors had a similar profile.

The "Deep" and Basal Eurasian populations have the right genetic profile for a "redo" for humanity. They are heavily associated with the first farming cultures and for that matter with many cultural advances. Today the people group which has the highest percentage of "Basal Eurasian" genes is the Ashkenazi Jews! Berbers from North Africa, Druze and Christians from Lebanon, and Kurds also seem to have a significant portion. I think the same will be found of "Deep" but as of now I am not sure those tests have been done.

Southern Europeans also have a fair proportion of this ancestry. Northern Europeans tend to have much less. Europeans get their genes from three sources 1) the hunter-gatherers which were native to the region, 2) Early European farmers (which were admixed with Basal Eurasian/"Deep") who came in waves starting perhaps seven or eight thousand years ago, and 3) Pastoral farmers from the Russian Steppe which had a much smaller proportion of Basal Eurasian / "Deep" and entered the rest of Europe in large numbers only 4,000 or so years ago.

Europeans have genes from these three groups, but in different proportions. The Greeks and Italians, having the most "Early European Farmer" ancestry, would be higher in Basal Eurasian and "Deep" genes as compared to Germans, English, and Scandinavians, but still less than those other non-European groups I previously mentioned.

The idea is that as the "sons of Elohim" mentioned in Genesis chapter six found wives in the daughters of Adam, the genes and practices of the children of Adam spread. If the offspring of these unions were "men of renown" we might expect that genetic signature to be selected for and experience rapid growth. We would be looking at an early expansion of these genes characterized by the male Y-chromosome offspring being no different than that of the original groups, but the other genes showing differences. The mtDNA and the autosomal genetic signature of the ruling class of these people would reflect the contribution of "Deep" and/or Basal Eurasian from the female side but not the male side.

After the descendants of Noah come out of the hills, they become men of renown- the kind of men who form nations around them. That is, the kind of men who can be expected to father a lot of children. So, I would expect to see another pulse of "Deep"/ Basal Eurasian. This time the rapid spread of these genes would come from both fathers and mothers, but predominantly from fathers.

To verify the hypothesis, we should look for evidence in the appropriate places and times for a ruling class with a male genetic component different from the common folk, and an enriched Basal / "Deep" component in this ruling group. These would be clues to look for, and measurements of living populations alone would not provide them. So kneaded into the whole of mankind are these genes that by now one would be hard pressed to name any population of significant size which did not at least possess a trace of them.

The group from which the Early European farmers came had a lot of Y-haplogroup G2. Cultures which held a lot of this haplogroup spread farming and civilization from Anatolia westward starting around nine thousand years ago. I suggest that these people were either among the "Sons of

Elohim" to which the daughters of Adam were married off, or the group into which Cain married. Their relations with Adam's descendants gave them the knowledge which accelerated civilization.

Another lobe of civilization spread north of this territory. This was the mobile pastoralist culture dominated by Y-haplogroup "R1". They eventually swept into both Central Europe and South Asia. I think this is another candidate group to be among the "Sons of *Elohim*" who took daughters from Adam's tribe. Their ancient heroes, which seem to have commonalities in the myths of peoples from India to Norway, could be connected to the "mighty men of renown" in Genesis chapter six.

While that group made a name for itself in the north, there was another pulse of civilization-building in the Bronze Age which radiated out from Mesopotamia. Y-haplogroup "J" males played an important but not dominant role in this event. I correlate this to the spread of the sons of Noah as described in Genesis chapter ten (the Table of Nations). Their households became the cores of new nations.

It may be that the hypotheses which I have advanced in this chapter are someday confirmed, or negated, or we may find results which are inconclusive. If the former it is a bonus, but I want to emphasize that I am advancing these ideas more to show how one might think in terms of connecting the narratives in Genesis to events in the natural world. I am non-dogmatic on the issue of whether these are the specific ideas which will do it. In fact, while I expect the theology in this book to still be relevant in one hundred years, it is hard for science questions to last ten!

The conclusion of things is this: Let no reasonable person close their mind to the possibility that what has been handed down to us over the ages is true even if for ages we did not understand it. Perhaps truth was waiting patiently to be shown as true in days such as these. Days where faith is tested and when mankind most needs to receive it.

Thank You from the Author

I hope that you have enjoyed reading this book as much as I enjoyed writing it. If I am known for writing anything, it is about government and political philosophy, not theology. The two books I have written on political philosophy are "easy reading" compared to this book. They are:

Localism, a Philosophy of Government and...

Localism Defended, the Narrow Path Between Anarchy and the Central State

Journey on the Outside, My Life as an Activist is an autobiography which, once I reach my mid-thirties, focuses on my political adventures, but is very much intertwined with my faith-walk throughout.

I invite you to read these books as well. Though political theory is not as important or seminal as theology, and I am not claiming any Divine insight there, I poured my heart and mind into them.

I have also written a couple of fiction e-books, just fun-reading novellas. They are *John Henry: Race Against the Robot* in which the folk hero is alive in our time and a champion race car driver. He is about to retire when a giant tech company announces they have developed a driverless car that can beat any man alive. My other e-book is set in World War One, *Thorns of the Rose*. It is sort of historical fiction in that it weaves a fictional story around people and events from history. In addition, I edited a little gift-book for my friend Dan Johnson, *Senior Graduation*.

At any rate, thank you for your time and effort reading this work. I did not have a dedication but really any book such as this ought to be dedicated to those who love the truth enough to read it.

Kind regards,

Mark

Appendix

Chapter Five calculation of time, Calendar-Patriarch method

Generation	Masoretic	Septuagint	Method
Adam to Seth	130	230	to 'begat'
Seth to Enosh	105	205	to 'begat'
Enosh to Cainan	905	905	Life Span
Keenan to Mahalalel	910	910	Life Span
Mahalalel to Jared	895	895	Life Span
Jared to Enoch	962	962	Life Span
Enoch to Methuselah	365	365	Life Span
Methuselah to Lamech	969	969	Life Span
Lamech to Noah	182	188	to 'begat'
Noah to Flood	600	600	Stated in text
Total Years: Adam-Flood	6023	6229	

Chapter Eleven Genealogy (second 'Cainan' omitted)

Flood - birth of Arphaxad	2	2	
Arphaxad to Salah	438	535	Life Span
Salah to Eber	433	460	Life Span
Eber to Peleg	34	134	to 'begat'
Peleg to Reu	239	339	Life Span
Reu to Serug	239	339	Life Span
Serug to Nahor	230	330	Life Span
Nahor to Terah	148	208	Life Span
Terah to Abraham	130	130	From Acts
Total Years: Flood to Abraham	1893	2477	

Acknowledgments

I would like to thank some of the people whose help and support were essential for this work to attain its present form and fitness. Without them, it would not be the same book.

First, I acknowledge the support of my wife Melissa, who encouraged me in this endeavor even though it meant dedicating much of my free time over the course of three years to authoring and honing a work which, let's face it, is not expected to find a mass audience or generate serious income. There was no grant, foundation, or institution behind us. I have a secular vocation, so it was of no service to my career. She did it because she loves me, and loves the same God I do, not for hope of profit. I should add that her grasp of church history and the evolution of certain strains of theology is superior to my own, and the wisdom and knowledge she provided was also quite useful in improving this book.

I would also like to thank Robert Hawes, an author whose editing skills and helpful suggestions were indispensable. Some of you who have read early editions of this book can testify as to how far it has come on that score, and Robert deserves much of the credit there.

I would also like to acknowledge the contributions of the late Dr. Sue Dykes, a paleoanthropologist from South Africa who was lost to us too soon. My correspondence with her was essential in improving the "Anthropological Epilogue".

Index